T0051706

American Survivors

American Survivors is a fresh and moving historical account of US survivors of the Hiroshima and Nagasaki atomic bombings, breaking new ground not only in the study of World War II but also in the public understanding of nuclear weaponry. A truly trans-Pacific history, *American Survivors* challenges the dualistic distinction between Americans-as-victors and Japanese-as-victims often assumed by scholars of the nuclear war. Using more than 130 oral histories of Japanese American and Korean American survivors, their family members, community activists, and physicians – most of which appear here for the first time – Naoko Wake reveals a cross-national history of war, illness, immigration, gender, family, and community from intimately personal perspectives. *American Survivors* brings to light the history of Hiroshima and Nagasaki that connects, as much as separates, people across time and national boundaries.

Naoko Wake is Associate Professor of History at Michigan State University. A historian of gender, sexuality, and illness in the Pacific region, she has authored *Private Practices: Harry Stack Sullivan, the Science of Homosexuality, and American Liberalism* and coauthored with Shinpei Takeda *Hiroshima/Nagasaki Beyond the Ocean*. She was born and raised in Japan.

AMERICAN SURVIVORS

Trans-Pacific Memories of
HIROSHIMA & NAGASAKI

NAOKO WAKE

CAMBRIDGE
UNIVERSITY PRESS

ShaftesburyRoad,CambridgeCBEA,UnitedKingdom

One Liberty Plaza, 20th Floor, New York, NY 10006, USA

477 Williamstown Road, Port Melbourne, VIC 3207, Australia

314–321, 3rd Floor, Plot 3, Splendor Forum, Jasola District Centre, New Delhi – 110025, India

103 Penang Road, #05–06/07, VisioncrestCommercial,Singapore 238467

Cambridge University Press&Assessment isa department of the University of Cambridge.

WesharetheUniversitysmissiontocontributetosocietythroughthepursuitof education,learningandresearchatthehighestinternationallevelsofexcellence.

www.cambridge.org
Information on this title: www.cambridge.org/9781108835275
DOI: 10.1017/9781108892094

© Naoko Wake 2021

This publication is in copyright. Subject to statutory exception and to the provisions of relevant collective licensing agreements, no reproduction of any part may take place without the written permission of Cambridge University Press&Assessment.

First published 2021
Reprinted 2021
Paperback edition first published 2023

A catalogue record for this publication is available from the British Library.

ISBN 978-1-108-83527-5 Hardback
ISBN 978-1-108-79990-4 Paperback

CambridgeUniversityPress&Assessmenthasnoresponsibilityforthepersistence oraccuracyofURLsforexternalorthird-partyinternetwebsitesreferredtointhis publicationanddoesnotguaranteethatanycontentonsuchwebsitesis,orwill remain,accurateorappropriate.

To all survivors with whom I spoke,
to all others with whom I did not.

CONTENTS

FIGURES

ABBREVIATIONS

In the text

AAP	Asian Americans for Peace
ABCC	Atomic Bomb Casualty Commission
AEC	Atomic Energy Commission
ALC	Asian Law Caucus
CABS	Committee of Atomic Bomb Survivors in the United States of America
FOH	Friends of Hibakusha
HPMA	Hiroshima-ken Ishikai (Hiroshima Prefectural Medical Association)
JACL	Japanese American Citizens League
JPHA	Nihon Kōshūeisei Kyōkai (Japan Public Health Association)
JUST	Japanese United in Search of Truth
MHW	Kōseishō (Ministry of Health and Welfare)
NAABSA	North American A-Bomb Survivors' Association
NCWA	National Church Women's Association
Oak Ridge	Oak Ridge National Laboratory
RERF	Radiation Effects Research Foundation
Shimin no Kai	Kankoku no Genbaku Higaisha o Kyūensuru Shimin no Kai (Citizens' Group to Assist Korean Survivors)

In the notes

AS	*Asahi shinbun*
Bill files	Series 1 Bill Files 1970–2004, Senate Health and Human Services Committee Records 1973–1974, LB118: 1–14, California State Archives, Sacramento
CABSN	*Committee of Atomic Bomb Survivors in the United States of America Newsletters*, Tokie Akihara Papers, Alameda, California
Chuman papers	Frank F. Chuman Papers, Japanese American Research Project Collection, Charles E. Young Research Library, University of California, Los Angeles
CS	*Chūgoku shinbun*
Dymally papers	Mervyn Dymally Papers, Kennedy Memorial Library, California State University, Los Angeles
FOHC	Friends of Hibakusha Collection of Oral Histories of US Survivors, Regional Oral History Office, The Bancroft Library, University of California, Berkeley
GT	*Getting Together*
HE	*Hayaku engo o!* (Support, Now!)
"Health hearing"	"Hearing on: Health Problems of Atomic Bomb Survivors, May 4, 1974," Bill files
HM	*Hokubei Mainichi*
Ichioka papers	Yuji Ichioka Papers, Charles E. Young Research Library, University of California, Los Angeles
JACLH collection	Japanese American Citizens League History Collection, Japanese American National Library, San Francisco, California
KM	*Kashu Mainichi*
Louie collection	Steve Louie Asian American Movement Collection, Charles E. Young Research Library, University of California, Los Angeles
MS	*Mainichi shinbun*
NBT	*Nichi Bei Times*
NE	*National Enquirer*

NWC	Naoko Wake Collection of Oral Histories of US Survivors, Families, and Supporters, in possession of the author, East Lansing, Michigan
NYT	New York Times
Payments hearing	Payments to Individuals Suffering from Effects of Atomic Bomb Explosions: Hearing before the Subcommittee on Administrative Law and Governmental Relations of the Committee on the Judiciary, House of Representatives, 95th Congress, Second Session on HR 8440, Serial No. 43, Washington, DC, Government Printing Office, 1978
PC	Pacific Citizen
PCr	The Paper Crane, Jennifer Miller Papers, Berkeley, California
RAR	Resthaven Auxiliary Records, University of Southern California Special Collections, Los Angeles
Roybal papers	Edward R. Roybal Papers, Chicano Studies Research Center, University of California, Los Angeles
RS	Rafu Shimpo
STC	Shinpei Takeda Collection of Oral Histories of North and South American Survivors, G. Robert Vincent Voice Library, Michigan State University, East Lansing
Yoneda papers	Karl G. Yoneda Papers, Charles E. Young Research Library, University of California, Los Angeles
ZBZAH	Zai Burajiru, Zai Amerika Hibakusha Saiban o Shiensuru Kai, Zai Burajiru, zai Amerika hibakusha saiban shien nyūsu [News in support of court cases regarding hibakusha in Brazil and America], Hiroshima

NOTES ON THE TEXT

East Asian names, terms, and oral history edits

Throughout this book, I follow the East Asian practice of listing the family name first followed by the given name when I cite names of people of East Asian ancestry currently living in East Asia. For people of East Asian background currently living in North America, I list the given name first followed by the family name. I romanize Japanese and Korean terms following the Japanese Romanization System or the McCune–Reischauer Romanization System, respectively, unless individuals expressed an explicit wish to have their names spelled in ways that do not match either system. In quotations from historical sources, I use the romanization used by the original authors. All translations between English and Japanese are mine unless otherwise noted.

I quote from the oral histories with minimum edits and deletions. I omit "uh," "um," and "you know" etc., and I indicate any other omission by an ellipsis. I do not change the original utterances to make them grammatically flawless because I wish to convey their force and creativity. In a limited number of cases where I judge the original utterances compromise our comprehension – for instance, when an interviewee said that people "laugh at me from the back" and her likely intended meaning was that people "laugh at me behind my back" – I amend the quote to reflect their likely intended meanings. I do not indicate these edits by *sic* for ease of reading.

ACKNOWLEDGMENTS

I am moved by the countless hours that US survivors have lent me. They could have easily said no, but they did not. I am grateful for how they have come into my life. No page of this book would have been written without their desire to tell and be heard. I think of this desire an awesome force of history.

I am thankful to those who not only talked to me, but also made sure that I had someone else to talk to. They were my informants, but they also brought much more to this book. I am deeply indebted to the kindness of Jack Motoo Dairiki, Jun Dairiki, Geri Handa, Izumi Hirano, Toshiko Hishinuma (pseudonym), Fumiko Imai, Kazue Kawasaki, Masako Kawasaki, Toshiro Kubota (pseudonym), Sachiko Matsumoto, Jennifer Miller (pseudonym), Ōba Yasushi, Kyohei Sakata (pseudonym), Junji Sarashina, Toyonaga Keizaburō, and Kathy Yamaguchi (pseudonym). I cherish times and places I spent with each and every *hibakusha*, their families, their supporters. And the food we shared.

I am fortunate to be in the Department of History at Michigan State University. Two chairs who have supported my research and writing – Walter Hawthorne and Lisa Fine – are as good as any historian could hope for. I thank my friends Rich Bellon, Liam Brockey, Emily Conroy-Krutz, Kirsten Fermaglich, Sean Forner, Karrin Hanshew, Charles Keith, Leslie Moch, Ed Murphy, Ethan Segal, Lewis Siegelbaum, Mickey Stamm, Ronen Steinberg, Helen Zoe Veit, and Mark Waddell. You are all incredible persons, and it feels great to record your names here. I am indebted to key support given by Nwando Achebe, Pero G. Dagbovie, Emine Evered, Laura Fair, Susan Sleeper-Smith, Tom Summerhill, and John Waller. I am grateful, too, to my colleagues in Lyman Briggs College, where the History, Philosophy, and Sociology of Science program is housed. Special thanks to Bob Bell, Robyn Bluhm, Marisa Brandt, Kendra Cheruvelil, Kevin Elliott, Michele H. Jackson, Aaron McCright, Daniel Menchik, Elizabeth H. Simmons, Jerry Urquhart, Sean Valles, and Ak Zeleke for their collegiality.

I cannot thank enough my friends at the Asian Pacific American Studies Program at Michigan State for their guidance, support, and care. Andrea Louie, Terese Guinsatao Monberg, Anna Pegler-Gordon, and Sitara Thobani, you probably do not know how much you mean to me. You do. My friends who call themselves APIDA/A Women Warriors – Maggie Chen-Hernandez, Jonglim Han, Sharon Chia Claros – you distracted me from writing this book, then helped me write it, too. The same appreciation goes to Kate Firestone, Ian Gallardo, Brian Hercliff-Proffer, Jeffrey Tsang, as well as my "teammates" in the Coalition of Racial and Ethnic Minorities – Eunice Foster, Kevin Leonard, Emily Sorroche, Stratton Lee III, Danielle Flores Lopez, and Melissa Martinez. It is incredible that we meet as much as we do while we have this other job that is our actual job.

Beyond Michigan State, I am grateful to Judy Tzu-Chun Wu and Lisa Yoneyama for their thoughtful reading of this book for Cambridge. Though in different ways, they each deeply engaged with my work, and very generously. Joonhong Ahn, Eiichiro Azuma, Janet Brodie, Kate Brown, Elyssa Faison, Peter Galison, Andrea Geiger, Laura Hein, Lane Ryo Hirabayashi, Jane Hong, Tom Ikeda, Robert A. Jacobs, Michael Jin, Mire Koikari, James Kyung-Jin Lee, M. Susan Lindee, Richard Minear, Brian Niiya, Gary Y. Okihiro, Leslie J. Reagan, Greg Robinson, Andrew Rotter, Takahashi Hiroko, Shinpei Takeda, Akiko Takenaka, Tsuchiya Yuka, Tsujimoto Masashi, Cathy J. Schlund-Vials, Ji-Yeon Yuh, and Ran Zwigenberg read or heard parts of this book at different stages, and taught me things I had not thought about before. I also thank Ellen Wu for helping me find a way into this project early on. Two editors at Cambridge who shepherded this book – Debbie Gershenowitz and Cecelia Cancellaro – were delightful to work with: Debbie stood firmly by the project that became this book; Cecelia read the manuscript closely and perceptively, while challenging me to think of the book broadly. The generous support from the Association of Asian Studies, the Huntington

Library, and the Nagasaki National Peace Memorial Hall for Atomic Bomb Victims was essential for my research, as were funds from the Center for Gender in Global Context, the Asian Studies Center, the International Studies and Programs, and the Office of Vice President for Research and Graduate Studies, all at Michigan State.

My father Wake Hirotsugu passed away before he had a chance to hold this book in his hands. He would have been delighted to do so. My mother Wake Shigemi and my sister Taniguchi Yumiko have continued to support me with love, something that I have come to appreciate more keenly than before. I am grateful to my brother-in-law Taniguchi Hiroshi, and my nephews, Kenta and Tetsu, for their joyful presence. No one can measure how much Steve Stowe has given to this book. I asked, and he always said, "Okay." At every turn, we wondered together. I know how fortunate I am to be with you.

INTRODUCTION

There are no right words to recount the nuclear holocaust. I feel this after reading thousands of words uttered by survivors of the 1945 atomic bombings of Hiroshima and Nagasaki and those who have thought much about them. "There is no one who can tell what happened at the hypocenter," wrote artists Maruki Iri and Maruki Toshi.[1] Survivors said they did not know what happened, and that they thought they were dreaming when they saw ghost-like figures staggering in the cities' flattened landscapes. With their clothes torn and flesh burnt, these women and men were indistinguishable from each other. How do I, a historian born long after 1945, reach out to someone else's nightmare? For years, most survivors remained silent about their experiences because of pain, fear, anger, or resignation. When they finally began to speak, it seemed impossible to talk about the bomb without altering memories or having them manipulated. What happened was mass, indiscriminate, and senseless death, yet those who listened wanted to distinguish it as worthy. After three quarters of a century, we still grapple with aspects of Hiroshima and Nagasaki that point to a breathtaking disregard for individual lives and human differences. Women and men, children and adults. Civilians and soldiers with varying relationships to the Japanese empire's mechanisms. All of the Japanese, Koreans, and Americans who perished in these cities.

That the nuclear weapons did not discriminate has raised questions about their morality, generating a large, rich body of work. This book about Japanese American and Korean American survivors of Hiroshima and Nagasaki – US-born US citizens of Japanese ancestry who were in Japan in 1945, in addition to Japanese and Korean people who came to America after the war and became US citizens at some point[2] – belongs to and builds on this genealogy. But my inquiry also diverges from it. This book is not about the morality of the US decision to drop the bomb at the end of World War II, although the subject and its closely related cousins – whether the use of nuclear weapons was legal, politically and militarily necessary, justifiable – continue to fascinate many, including myself. These concerns involve the time leading up to August 1945 and shortly thereafter, and they often revolve around tightly knit circles of politicians, military leaders, and scientists in decision-making positions.[3] Although these individuals made the bomb possible in the most immediate sense, they are not paramount to the history of US survivors or in their remembering of the nuclear destruction. For the same reason, this book is not about political constructions or cultural representations of the bomb's meanings, which took shape on both national and international scales in the Pacific region after the war. Though they provide important background for the history I explore and thus will be taken up as such, these political and cultural productions are more often counterpoints against which US survivors' history has formed rather than its encompassing contexts.[4] Individual remembering always varies and is never a perfect collective memory. For US survivors who have not belonged to the mainstream politics or cultures surrounding the bomb in Korea, Japan, or America, the tension between personal and public memories has been particularly pronounced.

The history of US *hibakusha* is a counter-memory of the bomb – a memory both marginal and resistant to the national remembering in America, Japan, and Korea – and, as such, their stories reveal with a certain clarity the indiscriminate way of nuclear weaponry and its historical consequences.[5] If, indeed, it is "not the centre that determines the periphery, but the periphery that ... determines the center,"[6] US survivors' history is a periphery that threatens to disassemble established meanings of the bomb that have not taken notice of it. When told that the bomb was necessary for America to win the war, US *hibakusha* wondered why they, American citizens, had to be attacked. When told that the Japanese government offered free medical treatment of radiation illness among the Japanese, US survivors wondered why their illness did not count. Either way, their experiences refute the assumption that the nuclear weapons were used singularly against enemy nationals. Too, their experiences call into question the notion that the bombs used in 1945 were slight in magnitude. As nuclear weaponry specialists tell it, hydrogen bombs developed after the war were many times more destructive than those used in Hiroshima and Nagasaki. True as this may be, one troubling consequence of the focus on scientific progress is the endless postponement of a nuclear holocaust into the future.[7] To be sure, a nuclear destruction may be unique in that it "signifies the simultaneous destruction of ... whole families, generations, and societies," hence it "reduc[es] survivors to *barbarism*."[8] This may be what separates a nuclear holocaust from other forms of killing; it is a global phenomenon by definition. And yet, because of the belief that its effects in 1945 were relatively contained, the use of nuclear weapons in Hiroshima and Nagasaki has been seen as less indiscriminate than a nuclear catastrophe that may happen in the future. This belief also has allowed us to consider the first and so far only nuclear attacks and their lasting aftermaths mostly in terms of a single nation or in a comparative perspective that assumes relatively clear-cut national boundaries. Frequently, more capacious, cross-national aspects of the bomb have been pushed aside.

US survivors are no less survivors of a nuclear holocaust just because they are not survivors of the worst nuclear holocaust we can imagine. They were affected by it regardless of who they are, sharply illuminating nuclear warfare's uncontainable effects from its inception in 1945. Because of their comparatively small number (compared to Japanese or Korean survivors) and their unexpected belonging to America, US *hibakusha* and their remembering about the bomb have been severely under-recognized in the scholarship and by the public alike. Particularly in America, where survivors of any nationality have not occupied as prominent a place as scientists, political and military leaders, and cultural critics in the research and writing about the bomb, US survivors have gone virtually unrecognized. The ideology of American justice that shaped the aim of the "Good War," punctuated by the dropping of the bomb and followed by the opening of the nuclear umbrella over America's Pacific allies during the Cold War, is still persistent in the twenty-first century.[9] Consequently, US *hibakusha*'s experiences, raising doubts about the justness of both wars, have occupied little place in national remembering of the bomb. This neglect does a disservice to the richness of their history and of what can be learned from it.

There were an estimated 20,000 American citizens of Japanese ancestry in Japan when the war started between the

United States and Japan in December 1941.[10] Many of them were children of the first generation, or *Issei*, immigrants who, after living in America for years, came to Japan before the outbreak of the war for reasons ranging from education (of their children) and care (of their aging parents), to retirement (their own). Many of these children – second generation, or *Nisei*, Americans – came to Japan for the first time, unaccompanied by their parents. They came to obtain a few years of education in their relatives' care in Japan while their parents continued to work and raise their families in America. On the US West Coast, where most of the Japanese and Japanese Americans resided, restrictive immigration and naturalization policies were made worse by racist, segregationist practices in housing, work, and education. Sending their children to a school in Japan was a necessity for many of those who cared about their offspring's future.

Of the 20,000 Japanese Americans in Japan in 1941, an estimated 3,000–4,000 were in Hiroshima, a prefecture sending the largest number of Japanese immigrants to Hawai'i and the US mainland since the late nineteenth century. The number of Japanese Americans who were in Nagasaki is unknown, although it was likely smaller than its counterpart in Hiroshima. Of the Japanese Americans located in either of these prefectures, an unknown number were affected by the atomic bomb. Soon after the war's end, the majority of those who survived went back to the United States, their home country across the Pacific. Because they did not come together until 1971 as a group called the Committee of Atomic Bomb Survivors in the United States of America (CABS), their number in the earlier decades is difficult to appraise.[11] As of 2007, the total number of Japanese American *hibakusha* residing in the United States was slightly less than 1,000.[12] Of these, US-born US citizens likely made up about half. The other half of the 1,000 living in the United States were Japanese citizens who migrated to America in the 1950s and 1960s and became US citizens at some point. In my estimate, one half of these "new" immigrants, about 250–300, had siblings, relatives, or acquaintances who were US citizens and were in America during the war.[13] In other words, these "new" immigrants were in fact part of the "old" flow of people going back and forth across the Pacific from the late nineteenth century onward. Taking advantage of "old" connections, these "new" immigrants came to America for jobs, education, or marriage.

The remaining 250 or so individuals came to America after the war without any prewar family connection to the country. Most of these survivors were Japanese or Koreans who had married Americans in Japan and followed them to the United States in the 1950s and 1960s. Japan was under the Allied Powers' occupation until 1952. Together with the Korean War (1950–1953), the occupation became a major ground for the formation of the anti-communist Cold War alliance on the East Asian front, increasing opportunities for Americans in US institutions, military or otherwise, to meet and, in some cases, marry Japanese or Korean nationals in Japan. An unknown, yet likely very small, number in this group of about 250 survivors were Koreans who came from the Republic of Korea (South Korea)[14] to America when the peninsula country was under the massive influence of the US military. By the early 1950s, about 23,000 of an estimated 30,000 Korean survivors had returned from Japan to South Korea, leaving about 7,000 of their cohort in Japan.[15] Then, some of these returnees decided to cross the sea again, this time the Pacific Ocean toward the United States. As is well known, American military bases remained a fixture in South Korea after the end of the Korean War. International liaisons occurred here, too, with some resulting in Korean nationals who were survivors following their American spouses to the United States. Because of the international, racial, and gender dynamism of the era, the majority of *hibakusha* who came to America either from Japan or South Korea were women, often referred to as "military brides."[16]

To understand the experiences of "military brides," it is crucial to note that in the racially integrated US army of the Cold War era, Japanese American and Korean American soldiers for the first time served side-by-side with other Americans stationed in a range of locations in Japan and Korea throughout the 1950s and 1960s. For some of the men, military service offered an opportunity to find a future wife, a rare chance to do so for Asian Americans in the pre-*Loving* v. *Virginia* (1967) era when interracial marriages between white and nonwhite persons were prohibited in many US states. Marriages between Asian and non-Asian minorities were not illegal but deemed socially undesirable. Before the passage of the Hart–Celler Act (1965), the number of Asian immigrants permitted into the United States remained low, hovering at around 100 per country per year. Marrying Japanese or Korean nationals while in service, and bringing them back to America, became one of the more legally feasible and socially acceptable options for Asian

Americans to build a family.[17] In particular, Japanese American soldiers' quest for spouses was often facilitated by their extended families and friends living in Japan. Again, because Hiroshima had long-standing ties to America through immigration, the courtship often resulted in a marriage between an American man and a Japanese woman who was a survivor. In not a few cases, both a soldier-husband born in America and a civilian-wife born in Japan were survivors, which seems a historical impossibility at first, but was a rather common occurrence made possible by family connections to Hiroshima as a city of immigrants. Simply put, people crossed national borders more frequently than we ordinarily imagine when we think about the bomb. In Nagasaki, too, international liaisons through marriages occurred, though in a number smaller than Hiroshima. Many of the US survivors joined CABS at some point after it was established in the early 1970s. A handful of Korean *hibakusha* who had migrated to America either from Japan or South Korea also came to the organization. Thus, since the beginning, CABS has been open to all US survivors regardless of their national origins.

The history of Asian American survivors traces wars and conflicts that significantly marked the twentieth-century history of the Pacific region. Indeed, as these survivors tell, their experiences of the bomb were intertwined with Japan's colonial rule of Korea, the Asia–Pacific War, and the Korean War. After they returned or came to the United States, their lives in changing Asian American communities continued to be shaped by the Cold War, particularly its heated manifestation in Vietnam. These survivors' history, then, compels us to consider the history of the bomb – and by extension, the morality of the nuclear holocaust – in a longer stretch of time than is usually assumed. Their history tells us that the legitimacy of nuclear weaponry may be considered not only through the immediate circumstances of their use in 1945 but also through lived experiences of those who were affected by the bomb throughout the twentieth century. Moreover, what we learn from their history is not simply the bomb's longer context dotted by wars; in fact, I write against a scholarly convention that makes it easy to collapse a history of minorities into a series of militarily significant incidents. Instead, the counter-memory of the bomb stays at the forefront of my analysis. Despite their small number, US *hibakusha*'s remembering broadly brings to light the twentieth-century history of trans-Pacific immigration through the lens of destruction, loss,

and illness unique to the nuclear attacks. It is not only that US survivors' history allows us to critically examine the bomb's history without privileging a majority's experiences, as do histories of other minority populations affected by irradiation such as the Marshallese or the Navajo.[18] US survivors' history also urges us to consider the historical and moral meanings of nuclear destruction in the modern world where people move, connect, and become attached across national boundaries. It is in this sense that US *hibakusha*'s history conveys their hope of transcending the nearly unspeakable horrors as well as capturing their remembered desolation. To be sure, the coming and going of immigrants led to family separations and, ultimately, to the devastation of the bomb. US survivors' status as immigrants and racial minorities made it difficult for them to talk about the suffering caused by their own government's actions. As the mainstream view of Asians in America shifted from "aliens ineligible for citizenship" to the "model minority" through the Cold War, they nonetheless remained "perpetual foreigners" who did not belong.[19] In this climate, US *hibakusha* found it necessary to not only heal, but also hide, their radiation illness. This explains, in large part, why it took US survivors until the early 1970s to come together as a self-support group.

And yet, their continuing movement across the ocean has also allowed them to use their trans-Pacific ties to define important aspects of who they are. As they grappled with radiation illness, for example, US survivors sought official recognition, medical care, and financial assistance from both the American and the Japanese governments. As they collaborated with other Asian Americans who supported their appeals to the US government, American survivors formed alliances with Korean, Japanese, and Brazilian survivors to make pleas to the Japanese government. In so doing, US *hibakusha* also joined hands with Japanese supporters of non-Japanese survivors overseas. US survivors certainly defined the lack of recognition as a failure of a nation state, an occurrence unique to a national polity. Simultaneously, however, they also insisted that the problem was cross-national, a failure on the part of all nations to see the universality of survivorhood. Their rights, US survivors claimed, were civil and human rights at once. Their cross-nationality that pieced together the uniqueness and universality of their experiences, I argue, shows the "strengths of weak ties" in the history of immigration in the Pacific region, to use a classic sociological term.[20] US *hibakusha*'s trans-Pacific ties are "weak" in that they have relied on small-scale, grassroots relations that have not been practiced on a daily basis. For some, their experiences of the bomb have not been central to their identity. And yet, when needs and concerns commonly shared by US survivors arose, they have used their cross-national affinity and affiliation – which are "strong" because of their multiplicity and their ability to relate more interconnectedly – more than did nonimmigrant survivors. These resources unique to immigrants rose to meet the disquieting universality of the nuclear holocaust, even when their prospects were uncertain, their results less than complete. Their history as immigrants pushed them to seek an understanding of nuclear weaponry through not only divisions but also unity.

US *hibakusha*'s history takes shape where the histories of the bomb and of Asian immigration to America intersect, thus they serve as this study's two pillars. As I weave together these histories, a few important focal points emerge. The history of Japanese Americans called *Kibei*, those who were born in the United States, received education in Japan, and returned to America, is one of my study's foci. Many US survivors fell into this group, so my exploration of their social and cultural histories in the early chapters illuminates an understudied aspect of the Asian American experience. Particularly, my focus on their layered national belonging throughout the critical years of the Asia–Pacific, Korean, and Vietnam wars adds to the literature that has largely revolved around autobiographical and biographical accounts of Kibei.[21] Too, the Asian American civil rights movement of the 1960s and 1970s and, by extension, the memory of wartime Japanese American incarceration that served as one of the movement's driving forces, will become this book's foci in select chapters. These well-known events in Asian American history spurred by racism had a close relationship to US survivors' efforts to obtain access to medical treatment for radiation illness in the United States, something not discussed in either Asian American history or the history of the bomb. Likewise, the rise and fall of antinuclear activism in both Japan and America from the 1950s to the 1980s will be discussed in contrast to US survivors' history that has been colored by silence, invisibility, and neglect. US *hibakusha*'s participation in public rallies for antinuclear causes was almost nonexistent before 1970. When some began to participate in the antinuclear movement in the 1970s, their participation was propelled by the Third World awareness that, indeed, a nuclear holocaust might happen again at the expense of people of color. Even so, US survivors' Asian American background was rarely mentioned in mainstream political and cultural discourses throughout these decades, further pushing aside the relevance of the histories of race, immigration, and cross-nationality as a way to understand the bomb.

Korean *hibakusha* in South Korea and Japan, too, will be discussed insofar as their histories have interacted meaningfully with their American counterparts. Until the end of the 1970s, the Japanese government did not begin to recognize Korean survivors living in Korea, severely limiting their access to the medical care and monetary allowances that had been made available to Japanese survivors by the Japanese government. After the decolonization of Korea in 1945, Koreans were not Japanese anymore, allowing the Japanese government to use their Korean nationality as a cover for a tenacious belief about their racial inferiority. As will be shown, both Japan and America had a long history of linking nationalism and racism to enhance state power, continuing discriminatory practices before, during, and after the Asia–Pacific War. Korean *hibakusha*'s demand to finally end these discriminations has inspired US survivors, who also have sought recognition of non-Japanese survivors by the Japanese government. By defining the bomb as a consequence of the "crimes against humanity" committed by the Japanese government during the Asia–Pacific War, Korean survivors brought a fresh force to US *hibakusha*'s activism which, if implicitly, had challenged the perception that the bomb was a "necessary military action" conducted by the US government. In my exploration of these issues, it becomes evident that US survivors' history cannot be told without considering racism and nationalism across the Pacific. Scholars have argued that the US decision to drop the bomb was not principally driven but certainly facilitated by racism, a consensus I value.[22] American nationalism and its legacy of colonialism that shaped the nuclear policy in the Pacific region throughout the Cold War, too, has been a frequent subject of scholarly inquiry.[23] But if we consider the bomb's history by including what has been pushed into the periphery, and over a long span of time as I do here, both racism and nationalism reemerge with fresh import. Who has been speaking on US survivors' behalf? Specifically, what were the racial and national compositions of the groups that came to support Asian American survivors? Who has been the chief source of the support – a governmental entity or grassroots organizations? Questions multiply: Who has had the authority to define radiation illness, and to determine what scientific research is to be conducted or what medical treatment is to be offered? Which country has taken a responsibility for recognizing, treating, and paying for Asian American survivors? How has this apportionment of responsibility revealed racial and national orders in the Pacific region, and how have they enabled the nuclear proliferation after the war? Answers to these questions are unequivocally shaped by racism and nationalism in Japan, America, and Korea.

The moment when the bomb exploded over Hiroshima or Nagasaki, it affected everyone regardless of age, race, gender, nationality, culture, and individual reasons for being there. Radiation illness and its lasting effects, too, have been indiscriminate. This dual indiscrimination – not only at the moment of detonation but also in the decades that followed – has separated survivors of the nuclear holocaust from survivors of other mass destructions sociopolitically and medically, most notably in Japan. Simultaneously, this paired indiscrimination has brought *hibakusha* together across many boundaries. Survivors from Japan, Korea, and America have shown a remarkable ability to collaborate, despite their small number, meager resources, and often hostile sociopolitical environment. Equally important as this history of indiscrimination, all sorts of discriminations and distinctions shaped survivors' experiences during the time leading up to the explosion and continuing from that moment on. In the hours and days following the detonation, Japanese Americans used their cultural resources as Americans to find, help, and heal each other. The clothes they wore, the food they ate, and the medicine they used distinctively marked their remembering of the bomb. Korean and Korean American *hibakusha* recalled how they were not given emergency food or care because of their Korean background. The human ability to discriminate in the face of indiscriminate destruction became part of their experiences of illness and injury for many years to come. In this light, it is not surprising that perceived national, cultural, and racial differences among the people of Korea, Japan, and America have exercised influence throughout the bomb's history extending to this day.

Gender, too, has played critical roles, frequently determining ones, in how survivors have formed their identity as sufferers of an indiscriminate destruction and claimed their responses to it as a crucial part of the bomb's history. US *hibakusha* expressed their gender variously – sometimes by attuning to common notions of femininity and masculinity, other times by blurring the line defining the dualism. Gender sustained US survivors' remembering as an adaptable but steady source of their cross-national identity. In 1945, it was largely women who offered care at ground zero in Hiroshima and Nagasaki. Although in no way formally organized or institutionalized, and thus rarely featured by the scholarship of the bomb, the care women devised, relying on their knowledge of folk medicine, became a lasting part of what US survivors remember about the nuclear destruction. It was also long remembered that it was often women who cooked meals from what little was left behind, sometimes using their familiarity with American ways of preparing food. Men, in contrast, were remembered as either child-beneficiaries of the care adult-women imparted, or courageous, manly adult-rescuers who removed rubble or rescued the injured. These men's memories, too, became important factors defining the course of US *hibakusha*'s history, particularly in the 1950s and 1960s when times of sharing their memories were still few and far between.

A considerable majority of US survivors – an estimated two-thirds – are women, and so it is fair to say that US *hibakusha*'s memory, identity, and activism have been shaped significantly by women.[24] Not only did women outnumber men, women have also contributed immeasurably to US survivors' efforts since the early 1970s to be recognized by federal and state governments, civic organizations, and medical associations on both shores of the Pacific. This is not to suggest that men did not take part in US survivors' efforts to obtain official recognition or to remember the bomb; they did, as passionately as women. Yet clearly, male survivors have been crucially supported or even directed by female leaders. Some women considered themselves to be facilitators rather than organizers, deferring decision-making processes to men who occupied official leadership positions in their group. But other women took up leadership roles and became public faces of US *hibakusha* by making the decision to go beyond accepted gender norms in Asia and Asian America. Many men in turn assumed shared leadership, working side-by-side with women and embracing what may be seen as "feminine" attributes as their own: that they are sufferers needing help. These are important, if under-acknowledged, factors that have made US survivors' "weak" ties across the Pacific "strong." They adapted their gender roles so as to keep together their trans-Pacific ties both within their communities and across national borders. To forge a universal survivorhood that fully recognizes layered national belonging, an ability to transform gender relations proved essential. Rigid gender roles could not assist US survivors' efforts to define their demands in terms of both civil and human rights.

Japanese women have been typically featured as either "innocent" victims or "maternal" and "caring" grassroots peace activists in the national remembering of Hiroshima and Nagasaki. Japanese men, in contrast, have been featured as prominent leaders of the socialist- or communist-led antinuclear organizations. Men also have been seen as scientists studying radiation illness in prestigious institutions.[25] To a significant degree, such gender division has also shaped our understanding of the histories of the bomb, antinuclear activism, and the peace movement in the United States.[26] In Asian American history, too, gender has been richly applied to scholarly analyses. For instance, histories have shown how different generations of Asian women in America have contributed to the making of immigrant community, race consciousness, and gender identity, often with a focus on the rise of Asian American feminism in the late 1960s and early 1970s that undercut their obedient image. Men in the community had been seen traditionally as quiet, effeminate, or devious by mainstream white America, images that they attempted to counter by playing explicitly masculine, patriotic roles (i.e. in the military) and by displaying their ability to fit in socially and politically in the postwar decades.[27] My inquiry into US *hibakusha*'s history adds to these explorations by delineating unique ways in which they, as at once immigrants, racial minorities, and *hibakusha*, grappled with the confines and entitlements of gender. Their layered identity pushed them to transcend gender norms, and this in turn has aided them in their continuing crossnational effort for better recognition of their history. By showing how women and men have creatively yet divergently made weak ties strong, I offer new perspectives on the role of gender in both the bomb's history and the history of immigration. Gender shaped key expressions by US survivors of who they were; perhaps with the exception of their childhood before 1945, gender always found a way into nearly every remembered aspect of their experiences related to race and nationality. I am uncertain if the same can be said about US *hibakusha*'s race or nationality in relationship to their gender. It is not a matter of these categories' relative import; rather, it is about gender's elasticity with regard to other categories of identity. Gender in US survivors' remembering covered and connected breaks caused by racism or nationalism, making stories more coherent to both tellers and listeners. Gender, in other words, made historical continuity more tangible in histories heavy with conflicts. In this light, I use gender throughout my analysis as one of the most potent constants that shaped the counter-memory of the bomb.

Much of my inquiry into US *hibakusha*'s history relies on oral history interviews that I and a handful of others have conducted with US survivors, their family members, community supporters, and physicians in Japan and America. Given the peripheral place their voices have occupied in the histories of both nuclear weaponry and immigration, it was imperative that I create many of these oral histories anew. My interactions with my interviewees have shaped not only the content of my study but also how I write, so a few words about them are essential. I conducted my first four interviews with US *hibakusha* and their supporters in San Francisco in 2010. I was introduced to my interviewees by Geri Handa, a member of a San Francisco-based support group for US survivors called Friends of Hibakusha (FOH). She then became my interviewee the following summer, in 2011, when I also had a chance to meet US survivors while they were attending a medical checkup at St. Mary's Medical Center in San Francisco. This medical checkup has been conducted biannually by Japanese physicians who specialize in radiation illness for US *hibakusha* in San Francisco and Los Angeles since 1977 (and several years later in Seattle and Honolulu, too), one of the notable fruits of CABS' trans-Pacific activism.

The checkups have offered rare opportunities for US survivors to see each other and be surrounded by others like themselves. There are many examinations that they must complete on a single day, so they stay in an exam gown even while they wait for the next exam in the hallway where they chat and exchange stories. This is where I introduced myself to survivors by going around the corridor surrounding a rectangular courtyard, and many of them subsequently became my informants (see Figure 0.1). Between 2012 and 2017, I continued to go back to *hibakusha*, relying on ones I knew to introduce me to others. Because there was no list of US survivors they were able to share with me (due to privacy concerns), the snowball approach was the only method available. US survivors' connections brought me to the East Bay, Sacramento, Los Angeles, San Jose, Honolulu, Hiroshima, Nagasaki, Columbus (Ohio), East Lansing (Michigan), and finally Osaka where the total number of my interviews reached eighty-six. I use them together with two additional sets of oral history collections: eighteen interviews conducted by members of FOH between 1976 and 1996, and

Figure 0.1 US survivors during the seventh biannual medical checkup conducted by Hiroshima physicians at St. Vincent Medical Center in Los Angeles. Masako Kawasaki papers, June 18, 1989.

twenty-eight interviews conducted by documentary filmmaker Shinpei Takeda from 2005 to 2010.[28]

There was a wide variety of *hibakusha* among my informants, although one obvious bias shaping my inquiry is that I relied on interviews with those who were willing to talk to me. Among these, though, there were survivors from urban and rural areas, as well as poor, working-class, middle-class, and affluent survivors. There were many more women than men, reflecting their gender-skewed demography. Similarly, the number of survivors from Hiroshima was much larger than the number of those hailing from Nagasaki. Historically, Hiroshima among Japanese prefectures was the largest source of trans-Pacific immigrants, so it is to be expected that Hiroshima *hibakusha* outnumber their Nagasaki counterparts in the United States. There were those who had been US citizens at the time of the bombing as well as those who had been Japanese citizens, including people who originally had come from Korea. Although they were only a few among my informants, this is to be expected because of the small number of Korean Americans among US survivors generally. My interviewees were mostly US citizens, but a handful were US permanent residents with Japanese citizenship. Some had taken leadership roles in US *hibakusha*'s trans-Pacific activism through CABS or other US groups, while others had had only minimal involvement in collective action.

Most of my US informants had not been interviewed before, although several had given interviews or speeches. This was different from the interviews that I conducted in Hiroshima and Nagasaki where most of my interviewees were clearly more experienced. Some of my US informants told me that they had never talked to their children or spouses about their experiences, which made me begin to think of their stories as a counter-memory of the bomb. I was deeply struck by the fact that people twice my age, whom I was meeting for the first time, were telling me their stories for the first time. As I heard more, I also began to notice a range of meanings found in both speech and silence. When more seasoned interviewees went silent, I wondered if it was because they could not align my question to a prepared answer. After responding to my question briefly, these interviewees often began to say something that they clearly had said before. In less experienced interviewees' silence, by contrast, I felt a more immediate presence of emotions – sadness, anger, and bewilderment. They had not touched on these feelings in the presence of a stranger, which seemed to add to the emotional intensity.

When anyone spoke about the silence that had surrounded their experiences, I was fascinated by the nearly borderless coexistence of silence and speech. They were not opposites – speech can fall flat, while silence can be eloquent. Indeed, US *hibakusha* talked about their silence in the past in varying ways: resentfully, confoundedly, matter-of-factly, fondly, or proudly. My analysis of the hiding and healing effects of silence, most extensively discussed in Chapter 3, originates in these observations. I also note that, when asked why they agreed to be interviewed by me, US survivors' answers ranged from "because I had time" to "because I wanted to do something to make a nuclear-free world." I assume that people declined to be interviewed for various reasons as well. In one case, an informant who agreed to be interviewed with the condition that I use a pseudonym explained how she was afraid of hurting others by making her personal recollections public. But it is unreasonable to imagine that all of those who declined to be interviewed did so for this reason. A range of meanings contained in silence and speech that I encountered at this stage of oral history-taking became a guide for my writing about the richness of things spoken and unspoken about the past.

Just as I started to think of US survivors' remembering as a counter-memory of the bomb through my interactions with them, I was encouraged by their testimonies to explore US *hibakusha*'s connections across the Pacific. Early in my work, I came across a few striking examples of cross-nationality at ground zero, where Japanese Americans relied on their American characteristics to find each other amid the chaos. May Yamaoka's memory of her sister in her "American slip," a Western-style undergarment made in the United States, is one such story that I discuss in Chapter 2. Tae Alison Okuno's story about the body of her cousin, distinguishable from other corpses by the "American underwear with a distinctive stripe pattern on it," is another.[29] Because of these early examples, I began to ask questions that prompted US survivors to talk about their experiences as Americans or Koreans in Japan, and as Asians in America. Clearly, these questions were not what they had expected me to ask. Not a few informants started to talk about "that day" in August 1945 early in the interview, without any prompting from me. My mode was to begin an interview by asking about their childhood, proceeding more or less chronologically. But in the first moments of many interviews, I often found myself already hearing stories of what they had been doing at the time of the explosion, how they had been injured, how they had (not) been able to find their families.

These are things they wanted to tell and expected me to be curious about. These stories also might have been easier to recollect because my informants had heard someone else tell a similar story. Public memories of the bomb, especially those that circulate in Japan, have recognizable plots, vocabularies, even characters. Many US survivors were familiar with these prototypes by the time they were interviewed. When I went back to my questions about their life history, showing that I wanted to know about that, too, most US *hibakusha* began to talk animatedly about their cross-national experiences. Some were ostracized in wartime Japan because they were Americans. Others had a hard time regaining their English after returning to America. Korean survivors who returned to South Korea after the war were made to feel ashamed of their radiation illness because it was a sign of their residence in, and thus their possible loyalty to, wartime Japan. These are things that they remembered well but did not think to tell until asked. Thus, the way my interviewees responded to my inquiry, as well as the way their stories shaped my questions, became a basis of my understanding and my argument. US survivors' counter-memory of the bomb, which has been muted and marginalized, is a trans-Pacific history. There was an established path to recall the bomb as part of the war's history; to tell it cross-nationally was to wander into uncharted territory.

There are other ways in which US *hibakusha*'s remembering and my understanding of it were shaped by the process of doing oral history. Here, I point to one outstanding example of memory co-construction, one relating to language. I conducted interviews in Japanese, English, or both, depending on interviewees' preference. I am a native speaker of Japanese, and I speak fluent and accented English. Virtually everyone was curious about how I came to be this person who speaks this way. Some tried to "locate" me by asking when I had come to the United States. *Were you in high school? College? And you teach American history in Michigan?* A few offered what sounded like an expression of comradeship: *It was hard at first, wasn't it?!* Clearly, I had stirred up something from their youth or, perhaps, memories of their parents' or grandparents' generations. They thought of me as another immigrant whose "adjustment" to American society must be measured. I was also struck by how many informants requested to be interviewed in Japanese, or spoke at least partially in Japanese, although they are clearly fluent in English, possibly more so than in Japanese. Many had not spoken Japanese for a long time. Japanese struck them as a better language than English to tell their wartime experiences. Some took obvious delight in uttering certain Japanese words. *Wow, I remember those words!* Others struggled with vocabulary, and they found it funny when they saw that sometimes I could not call up the right word, either. They did not think of me as an insider, but neither did they think that I was a total outsider. Despite our many differences, one thing that brought us together was that we had been in this fuzzy, in-between space before. If the nightmare of Hiroshima and Nagasaki separated us, the feeling of belonging to this ambiguous space of language, culture, and memory drew us close.

I believe this shared experience facilitated my informants' remembering of their cross-national experiences, which in turn has helped me refine my thinking and define a few key terms in this study. I use "cross-national" and "trans-Pacific" nearly interchangeably, although the former focuses more on a *process* of crossing national boundaries than the latter, which refers to a *phenomenon* that occurs in a particular geographical space. When I say "trans-Pacific activism," it means an activism that extends across the Pacific Ocean. When I say "cross-national activism," in contrast, I mean an activism made from the processes of crossing national and cultural boundaries. "Cross-national" indicates the tenaciousness of nation states and their persistent hold on people. As such, "cross-national" differs from "transnational," which suggests convergence, fluidity, and ease.[30] Something "cross-national" involves a process that is less smooth than the term "transnational" implies. US survivors have crossed national boundaries multiple times, but they have not done so effortlessly. In fact, the process of boundary crossing has provoked a strong sense of attachment to one country among US survivors even as they crossed over to another country and felt attached to it, too. As I see it, "cross-national" conveys US *hibakusha*'s subjectivity better than "transnational," an observation rooted in the fact that their history is told largely by oral histories of ordinary people who lived in the era of heightened hostility in the Pacific region. Equally important, the "trans-Pacific" coming and going of people has been frequently charged with "cross-national" meanings in the history I examine, so these terms echo each other and are in no way mutually exclusive. For instance, *Trans-Pacific* in this book's title describes a phenomenon that contains cross-national experiences.

I use the term *justice* in part because I want to highlight notions of justice specific to nations, as in American justice or Japanese justice, specific also to the historical contexts I discuss. The notion of American justice in the late-twentieth-century United States, for instance, included seeing the bomb as a necessary and just military action, while critiquing Japanese American incarceration during the Pacific War as an unjust infringement on civil rights. By the same token, the contemporaneous notion of Japanese justice in Japan underpinned the recognition of Japanese *hibakusha* in Japan as exceptional sufferers of the war who deserve a special compensation by the state. These nation-specific defin-itions of justice often aimed to protect civil rights and align them with national interests. Although US survivors certainly tried to attain either American or Japanese justice – their pursuit of racial justice in the United States, for instance, significantly shaped US *hibakusha* activism in the 1970s – their larger goal was to attain a cross-national justice applicable to people crossing national boundaries. The cross-national justice pursued by US *hibakusha* did not depend on their belonging to a nation state; instead, they believed they deserved rights to life, safety, and health because they are humans. When they claimed that their human rights were curtailed, then, it was necessary for more than one state to respond. And this response required a suspension of national interests, a cross-nationally corroborated redefinition of them, or both.[31]

Remembering is an important process that has shaped US survivors' history. Unlike "memory," which brings to mind a stable entity, "remembering" is an ongoing act that has changed in the past and will likely change in the future. "Remembering" can take a number of different forms and generate a range of meanings depending on when, where, and with whom a person remembers. I use "remembering" more frequently than "memory" in order to emphasize this transient nature of a person's memory. The process of remembering illuminates the tension between silence and speech, and its close cousin, cultural visibility and invisibility. As I will show, these tensions are key to understanding US *hibakusha*'s experiences as part of Asian American history, which has been marked by Asian Americans' perceived silence, invisibility, and foreignness. I consider oral history a record of remembering that has a significant relationship to a person's *identity*, another term I use. A person's identity can take shape in the process of remembering, although this does not necessarily mean that this identity is central to the person's sense of self or that it remains distinct at all times. A person has more than one identity, and an identity can become more or less pronounced depending on contexts. Thus, when I say "identity as a survivor," I do not suggest that a person being a survivor singularly or most importantly defines the person. Rather, the term recognizes that the person's identity as a survivor exists as one of many, and that it has produced and has been produced by historically appreciable currents of thoughts, emotions, and actions as survivors, either individually or collectively.

I refer to the nuclear attacks on Hiroshima and Nagasaki as *the nuclear holocaust* for distinct reasons. Initially, I took only a minor mental note when a few US survivors referred to the bomb as "the holocaust." Later, as my oral history-taking deepened, I came to think of the term as the most encompassing description of what they remembered. Not only the blast that took lives instantaneously, but also the radiation that continued to afflict survivors for years, pointed to a landscape that is ravaged, flat, and poisoned visibly and invisibly. Humans did not seem to be part of this landscape, yet the bomb that created it was wholly man-made. Its effect was thoroughly indiscriminate, a contradiction for a weapon and a war meant to destroy enemies only. Moreover, it made sense for US *hibakusha* to use "the holocaust" because they came to a collective identity as survivors in the late 1960s and early 1970s, when the term was most frequently used in the United States to describe a nuclear catastrophe that might strike Americans anytime in the future.[32] For Americans who had been bombed, it was not difficult to see that their experiences, too, constituted a holocaust – an American holocaust. The word "holocaust," especially the capitalized "Holocaust," came to be closely or exclusively associated with Adolf Hitler's Judeocide only after the late 1970s.[33] I follow US survivors' history and its relationship to the word "holocaust" by using it as they did. To always couple the term with "nuclear," as in the "nuclear holocaust," is an attempt to not obscure the gravity of the mass-murder of Jewish people. I do not compare Hiroshima and Nagasaki to Nazi extermination camps because I believe these incidences are strikingly different at least on one crucial score. The nuclear explosion was instantaneous, aloof, and indiscriminate; after the bomb detonated, there was nothing within human ability that contained or changed the weapon's encompassing effect. In contrast, a considerable part of the Holocaust's horror lies in methodical, arbitrary, and intimate discriminations practiced repeatedly by many perpetrators for a long time, for which human ability reached new highs during World War II.[34]

I organize the following six chapters chronologically, and the heart of each is the remembering of the bomb derived from the oral histories. Chapter 1 concerns the pattern of migration in the Pacific region and US *hibakusha*'s memories of childhood in the 1930s, both of which connected Korea, Japan, and America between the turn of the century and the outbreak of the war. By exploring the wartime separation of families, the heightened scrutiny of people of Japanese or Korean heritage on both shores of the Pacific because of their presumed "disloyalty," and their persistent sense of layered belonging even as this sense began to be questioned, this chapter reveals US survivors' continuing attachment to America or Korea even as their affinity to Japan grew. In exploring how race became entangled with nationality for American and Korean residents in Japan, though in strikingly different ways, I make use of the contrast between visibility and invisibility of their cultures throughout. By exploring how Hiroshima and Nagasaki nurtured many cross-cultural exchanges, I argue that these cities were indeed cities of immigrants – an important, if heretofore nearly forgotten, aspect of the bomb's history. Chapter 2 examines US survivors' layered sense of belonging as it played out at Hiroshima's and Nagasaki's ground zero in August 1945. I argue that their cross-nationality persisted as their culture, particularly with regard to clothes, medicines, and food, became the essential means of survival and care in the nuclear destruction's immediate aftermath. Although not as numerous as Japanese Americans, Korean Americans, too, recalled complex ways in which their cross-national attachment had shaped their experiences of the nuclear holocaust. In the harsh landscape that emerged after the explosion, both uniqueness and universality of experiences among *hibakusha* became salient. For instance, the bomb universally altered gender roles, making survivors look otherworldly; this drastic change, in turn, made it an urgent necessity for them to reclaim uniqueness for their gender. Altogether, US survivors' experiences are explored here as a cross-cultural history of the nuclear holocaust, recalled both in speech and silence, which became the foundation of American survivors' memory, identity, and activism after the war.

Chapters 3 and 4 continue to tell a cultural history of the nuclear destruction by examining how Japanese American *hibakusha* reconnected with their families in the United States during the decade and a half after the war, frequently through families and friends who came to Japan as part of the US occupation forces, the Atomic Bomb Casualty Commission (ABCC), or the US Army at war in Korea. While Chapter 3 focuses on US survivors' experiences as Americans in Japan, Chapter 4 examines their history after they came or returned to the United States and became Asians in America who grappled with the Cold War society of the Korean War era. A few cases of Korean American survivors who returned to Korea and then came to America, as well as Japanese survivors who migrated to the United States and became Americans around this time, fill out the picture. Because of the small number of Korean American *hibakusha*, I use oral histories of Korean survivors who stayed in Japan or returned to Korea in this era as well. Their experiences were not in every instance the same as Korean Americans'; but Korean survivors' remembering informatively suggests ways in which race, nationality, and gender shaped experiences of Korean American survivors especially before they crossed the Pacific. In Japanese society still reeling from the war, many US survivors grappled with the difficult task of (re)gaining US citizenship amid the shifting citizenship requirements by the United States. Once in America, US *hibakusha*'s citizenship continued to be scrutinized because of problematic assumptions made by the mainstream society about their race and national origins. By exploring these challenging times, I show how both Japanese American and Korean American survivors' silence about their experiences became an unspoken, yet powerful, norm, particularly for female Asian Americans in the Cold War culture that unfolded in Japan, Korea, and America in the 1940s and 1950s. For this purpose, in Chapter 3, I delineate the process of hiding and healing that *hibakusha* devised in order to counter many forms of the prejudice against them. In Chapter 4, I continue to explore this process by linking it to the shifting image of Asian Americans – from "aliens ineligible for citizenship" to the "model minority" – who continued to be seen as foreign regardless.

Chapters 5 and 6 discuss the rise of US survivors' cross-national memory, identity, and activism from the 1960s to the 1980s, which brought together survivors of different national backgrounds amid the Asian American civil rights movement. Working with younger non-survivors in Asian American communities, older *hibakusha*, women in particular, broke their silence and helped create a collective identity as survivors. Chapter 5 shows how this making of an identity occurred in tandem with the rise of an Asian American critique of Japanese American incarceration camps during World War II, the Vietnam War perceived as America's aggression against Asia, and the growing imminence of a nuclear war in the future. Both male and female survivors crossed gender, as well as racial, boundaries by relentlessly showing their suffering. Chapter 6 continues to explore the emergence of their identity as survivors through the lens of health, illness, and medicine. Radiation illness – physical and psychosocial – continued to concern US *hibakusha* greatly. Moreover, women were frequently primary caretakers of their households in Asia and Asian America, urging female survivors to consider illness from both patients' and caretakers' perspectives. I show how this dual challenge became a driving force for US survivors to form trans-Pacific coalitions with Japanese and Korean *hibakusha*, and with their grassroots supporters in both Japan and America. Simultaneously, I argue, US survivors in this era failed to gain a recognition comparable to that gained by former inmates of *Nikkei* concentration camps, showing the persistence of the military necessity argument surrounding the bomb. The Epilogue is about the decline of US *hibakusha*'s civil rights activism by the mid-1980s in the

United States, and the increased trans-Pacific collaboration among American, Korean, Japanese, and (to a lesser degree) Brazilian survivors toward the turn of the twenty-first century. Unlike the earlier civil rights activism that sought legislative means of recognition by the US government, the more recent activism aimed to obtain access to monetary allowances from the Japanese government based on a claim of human rights underpinned by Japan's highest court's proclamation of humanitarianism. Here, I highlight not only the changing coalition among survivors in the Pacific region for *hibakusha* causes, but also the still limited significance given to the histories of cross-nationality, immigrants, and their remembering in our understanding of the bomb.

US survivors may not tell us the right way to describe the nuclear holocaust. But their history shows how nation states' failure to grasp the injury and injustice that the nuclear holocaust has inflicted on their peoples continues to shape its moral meanings. US *hibakusha*'s history did not end after 1945; it continues to this day, urging us to confront many unending questions.

1 CITIES OF IMMIGRANTS

We are familiar with a map of Hiroshima or Nagasaki that cries "nuclear." With circles imposed on either city's layout, growing in size to indicate an increasing distance from the hypocenter, the map immediately brings to mind death, destruction, and an uncanny spread of radiation.[1] We have seen close-up images of the nuclear attacks, too. Whether humans, animals, or buildings, the targets of the nuclear weapons compel us to decode meanings – scientific, political, historical, or moral – that must be hidden somewhere. In the face of the destruction that we now know to be nuclear, we sense ultimacy. Nuclear "annihilation" rings true, as these images suggest an end devoid of new beginnings. Time stops. Everything is wiped out.

I want to look at the map and think about the sound and smell that filled the cities' streets before the bomb. In my endeavor, I am following many others who have sought to understand what lay beneath the mushroom cloud. A view from below, we might say, juxtaposed against a bird's-eye view from above. But my purpose here is not to reiterate this juxtaposition, which has come to embody the tension between Japanese and American understandings of the bomb after 1945.[2] Rather, I want to show how these seemingly oppositional understandings in fact had been converging in Hiroshima and Nagasaki before 1945, by exploring them as cities of immigrants. Certainly, a number of Koreans had been in these cities, some for decades. Contrary to the image of Japan and America separated by the vast Pacific, people traveled across the ocean until late 1941. Even after the war's outbreak temporarily halted the flow of people, histories of cross-national connections did not disappear. Indeed, they stayed strong, perhaps even more so because the war threatened to weaken them. And yet, because of the tension between the US focus on how the nation reached the decision to use the bombs and the Japanese focus underscoring how the weapons caused mass casualties on the ground, the history of the "strength of weak ties" has been pushed aside.

If we turn our eyes from the history of weapons and casualties to the history of the cities and their residents, the strength of cross-national ties becomes evident. For instance, we see a number of contrasts between Koreans and Americans in Japan during the war. Koreans in Japan proper had been forced or compelled to come to Japan, a status that distinguished them from Americans in wartime Japan.³ Unlike Koreans who were expected to remedy Japan's labor shortage at little to no cost to the empire, most Americans in Japan came of their own will or because of their family circumstances, some enjoying a relatively well-to-do status. Koreans were much more likely than Americans to belong to the lowest socioeconomic class. In contrast to their American counterparts, most Korean residences were confined to the least desirable neighborhoods, making their second-class citizenship plainly visible. Americans and Koreans, then, longed for a day of returning home from sharply different positions. But they also shared similarities. They both were outsiders in the cities of immigrants, who sometimes were made to feel as if they must hide their cross-nationality and their assumed loyalty to their homelands. Especially after the Pacific War began, many Americans stopped speaking English; they also refrained from showing any sign of difference, be it the way they ate, dressed, or acted. Koreans who had an option of hiding their Korean heritage – those who were fluent in Japanese – did so, too, to steer clear of discrimination. At the same time, they continued to express their belonging to Korea subtly but surely. The wartime propaganda, military-style training, and total mobilization furthered a broad indoctrination of imperial ideologies in all, including Koreans and Americans. Many remembered, often with irony, how they had felt passionately dedicated to Japanese victory. Most of them children, they absorbed Japanese culture as they grew up. But they also recalled how their sense of belonging to their home countries persisted. Oftentimes, these feelings were expressed in the most mundane ways of daily lives: the language they spoke, the clothes they wore, the food they ate, all sorts of daily habits, which continued to link Americans and Koreans to their people, their places across the ocean.

One origin of this layered sense of belonging is found in the communities of immigrants that had long predated the war. These communities, American or Korean, had not been fully integrated into those of the Japanese. But they existed side-by-side, becoming familiar sites for the cities' residents. Americans and Koreans had put down their cultural roots in Japan, and their Japanese neighbors, classmates, teachers, and coworkers had noticed them. Americans' and Koreans' layered sense of belonging, fostered by the cities of immigrants, counters the history of the bomb shaped by conflicting national interests. As this chapter illuminates, converging senses of national belonging, too, shaped the history. This chapter also shows how these communities' relationships with the Japanese changed over time, as well as how these relationships continued to vary widely both before and after 1941. Japanese Americans in Japan expressed their belonging to the United States relatively freely before the war. After 1941, these expressions became more muted, although this did not mean that Nikkei shed their belonging to America altogether. Koreans in Japan, by contrast, continued to negotiate their cross-nationality both visibly and invisibly throughout the 1930s and 1940s. Their linguistic similarity to and ethnonational difference from the Japanese created tensions over how they expressed their belonging to Korea. With wartime demands for national loyalty hanging heavily over their heads, immigrants' cross-national ties faced unprecedented impediments. As strong as it was, a layered sense of belonging felt by Koreans and Americans in Japan came into serious conflict with nations that assumed clear boundaries between peoples.

It is crucial to note that Koreans and Americans in Hiroshima and Nagasaki included a number of people whose profiles do not easily fit into those of the most salient casualties of the empire, racism, war, and nuclear weaponry. In the scholarship about the bomb, Koreans who were kidnapped in 1944 in their home villages in Korea, forced to work at a coal mine or steel mill in Japan, suffered the bomb in Nagasaki in 1945, and returned to Korea in 1946, were clearly victimized.[4] Koreans who were born in Hiroshima or Nagasaki and went to a Japanese military school were affected by the bomb, too, but their victimhood has not generated a comparable sympathy, attention, or scholarship. The same disparity has persisted until recently in the scholarship about

Nikkei during wartime. About 120,000 Nikkei who were sent to the ten concentration camps in the United States and lost their rights, belongings, and opportunities have been one of the most important subjects of Japanese American history. Clearly, these Americans were victims of the war, national hysteria, and racism.[5] But the same has not been said about Japanese Americans in Japan who endured the bomb. Similar to Koreans who attended Japanese schools, spoke fluent Japanese, and liked Japanese food, these Nikkei have appeared too "Japanese" and seemed to possess a sense of national belonging too dubiously layered.[6] Though in different ways, both groups found themselves on the peripheries of the nation states. Too often, these groups are left out of the history that features competing national interests, as well as people whose lives were crushed by them, as the chief players of change and continuity.

But these American and Korean people's experiences as immigrants are not exceptions to history. As their remembering shows, their histories would not have existed if there were no nation states attempting to expand their sovereignty from the late nineteenth century onward. To be sure, people moved across national borders because their leadership wished to use them as tools of internal and external expansion. The Japanese political establishment since the late nineteenth century saw immigration as a way to amplify the nation's geopolitical influence internationally;[7] the United States considered cheap laborers from China, then Japan, to be essential for building the country's agricultural business and industrial infrastructure.[8] The history of forced migration from the Korean Peninsula to Japan proper has been one of the most keenly discussed subjects of historical inquiry into the Asia–Pacific War.[9] Equally important, people also moved and settled as a means to provide for family and community, a means that they marshaled inventively from within the confines of empire. As will be shown, Nikkei discovered how they were not racialized in Japan as they had been in America. Koreans in wartime Japan made their Japanese language ability visible and their Korean cultural heritage invisible, so as to counter racism; they did so without losing either. Their decisions as immigrants often contradicted the imperial projects, showing the limit of nations' ability to wholly regulate individual, familial, and communal ingenuity.[10] Immigrants' decisions were not independent of national and international conflicts; because of this, their histories elucidate contradictions inherent in national interests. These interests, defined by imaginary, clear-cut boundaries between peoples, did not jibe with composite feelings of belonging that peoples were capable of possessing. US survivors' cross-national histories should not continue to surprise us; they are part of what led to, and ensued, the nuclear holocaust of 1945.

Americans in Hiroshima and Nagasaki before 1941: Cross-National Ways of Immigrants

Japanese American communities in Hiroshima and Nagasaki had their historical roots in the late nineteenth century. Hiroshima is one of the Japanese prefectures with a long history of sending its residents to Hawai'i and the US mainland. Beginning in 1885, about 600 Hiroshimans went to Hawai'i to complete a three-year labor contract, which they were allowed to extend if they desired. By the mid-1890s, the total number of overseas migrants from the prefecture exceeded 11,000, making Hiroshima the most prolific source of out-migration in Japan.[11] Nagasaki prefecture sent its first recorded migrants to a foreign land in 1899, and within ten years or so, the largest portion of the migrants' flow shifted from Hawai'i to the US mainland. At the same time, more migrants began to settle in their destinations permanently or semi-permanently, in effect becoming immigrants of the host societies.[12] People left Hiroshima or Nagasaki for reasons ranging from economic hardship, to entrepreneurship, to draft evasion. There are some indications that, particularly in Hiroshima, the number of tenant farmers rose sharply in the late nineteenth century, prompting many to pursue employment opportunities overseas. The decreased land ownership spurred the rise of public and private programs that assisted overseas migration, offering information about destinations, preparing visas and contracts, and loaning money for outbound travels. They generated a chain of immigrants, inspired by their friends and families who successfully had established themselves across the ocean.[13] For Japanese expansionists, the frontier of settler colonialism was increasingly comprised of these immigrants from a rural, economically disadvantaged, and uneducated class, although whether they met Japanese political, economic, and intellectual leaders' expectations – that these immigrants embody an image of the "superior" Japanese race – remained unclear.[14] For American capitalists on the West Coast and Hawai'i, these overseas immigrants supplied a crucial labor force for the booming economy, especially after the Chinese Exclusion Act stemmed the influx of Chinese workers in 1882. By the end of the first decade of the twentieth century, the accumulated numbers of immigrants originating from the prefectures reached 56,000 for Hiroshima and 6,800 for Nagasaki. Among the total of about 230,000 Japanese people who had gone overseas by then, the 56,000 from Hiroshima prefecture constituted nearly 25 percent, followed by Yamaguchi, Kumamoto, and Fukuoka, which made up about 9–14 percent each. Nagasaki's 6,800 made up about 3 percent, a smaller, yet still significant, proportion.[15] Throughout the 1920s and 1930s, Hiroshimans continued to constitute the largest group of Nikkei both in Hawai'i and the US mainland. The population exceeded 200,000 by 1940.[16]

These changes – from sojourners to immigrants, at farther destinations – did not dampen peoples' back-and-forth travels across the Pacific (see Figure 1.1). Families kept in touch, often through their offspring. Given the prohibitive cost of trans-Pacific travels, immigrants

Figure 1.1 Yuriko Furubayashi's family on board the *M. Sasama-maru* when they were "going back and forth" between Japan and the United States. The quote is from the author's interview with Yuriko Furuyabashi, June 21, 2013, and the photo is from the Yuriko Furubayashi papers, circa 1938.

carefully chose times to cross the ocean. Parents' aging, illness, or death were among the main reasons for travel.[17] Sometimes, these occasions prompted them to return to Japan permanently for the combined purpose of caring for the sick, inheriting family property, and settling in retirement. Equally important, many immigrants sent their children back to the old country for a few years of education, in order to ensure that youngsters acquired cultural knowledge about and personal familiarity with Japan. The increasingly discriminatory treatment of Japanese American children at US schools in the first decades of the twentieth century also contributed to a decision to embark on a prolonged family separation. Ties to the old country, immigrants hoped, would prove a resource for those growing up in the inhospitable host society.[18] This led to the presence of a number of younger, *Nisei* (second generation) and *Sansei* (third generation) Japanese Americans, as well as older, *Issei* (first generation) returnees who were Japanese, in the cities of Hiroshima and Nagasaki by 1941. Their citizenship status differed mostly because US law prohibited the naturalization of Japanese-born persons. Considered "unassimilable," they were not eligible for citizenship no matter how long they had resided in the United States. In contrast, Hiroshimans tended to describe all of the Issei, Nisei, and Sansei in Japan as "people who came back from America" regardless of their citizenship status.[19] This was an acknowledgement of immigrants as people who belonged to both countries. They could come "back" to Japan after thirty years of living in America; those who had never been to Japan, too, could be "back" in the country because of their family connection. And yet, they were also marked as different, even if they had been born in Japan. Their Japanese could sound different; their dress, too, could stand out as not typically Japanese. Their diet might differ, or even the way they smelled.

US survivors' oral histories reveal how a layered sense of belonging importantly shaped what they remember about prewar Japan. Looking back on being a newcomer in Hiroshima in the late 1930s, Kiyoshi Mike Nakagawa thought how the "funniest thing was food." Born in Lodi, California, in 1931, he had been accustomed to both American- and Japanese-style meals because they were served regularly at home. After his parents brought him to Japan in 1938, though, he realized that hamburgers and pancakes were out of reach. He recalled how badly he had missed them in Hiroshima; "I went out and looked at the sunset ... I thought about the smell of butter that

I used to smell on Sundays [in Lodi]. I looked up, only to see *daikon* radish hanging there to dry. I felt lonely." The roundness of the setting sun reminded him of buttery American pancakes, highlighting that his Japanese surroundings offered no such thing.[20] A memory of missing American food was first to come back, too, for George Kazuto Saiki, born in 1932 in the Moʻiliʻili neighborhood in Honolulu, Hawaiʻi. His favorite food was pastries that he used to buy at a local bakery near the Ala Moana Beach. After his parents took him to Hiroshima in 1939, there were no more of these goodies. He had to rely on Diamond crackers, made in Hawaiʻi, and chocolate kisses, both of which his mother had brought with the family to Japan. Saiki explained: "[In Moʻiliʻili] we used to eat those crackers with peanut butter and jelly … it was guava jelly. [In Hiroshima,] I made a cup of cocoa [from chocolate kisses] and dipped broken pieces of crackers in it. They made my breakfast." The supplies ran out in a year and half. "That's when the war started," recalled Saiki.[21] Neither Nakagawa nor Saiki disliked Japanese meals; they were used to them because their mothers had regularly served them. But when American food disappeared from the table, they missed it. Their cross-nationality was not about choosing between conflicting options; rather, it was about feeling a layered sense of belonging.

Partly because of the young age of these soon-to-be US *hibakusha*, simple things that made up their daily lives comprised a significant part of their remembering about the years leading up to the war. Too, there were holidays like the Fourth of July, Thanksgiving, and Christmas, which used to come with special meals but were no longer observed.[22] Before a severe wartime food shortage struck, though, some Japanese Americans in Japan were able to afford not only typical Japanese food such as dried-and-pickled *daikon*, but also things that made them feel connected to back home. Junji Sarashina was fortunate enough to enjoy meat, cookies, and ice cream bought at the "American store" in his neighborhood in Hiroshima.[23] Tae Alison Okuno recalled how her uncle once bought her an American-style apple pie in a downtown district of Hiroshima called Shintenchi or "The New World." The uncle who made the purchase was a Japanese military police officer, who nonetheless was persuaded by his niece who insisted: "We ate those in America!"[24] Kazuko Aoki's family regularly bought Carnation milk and Challenge butter from a shop in Hiroshima that sold imported goods. The shop's owner believed that the family owned some sort of fancy business, or else they would not be buying these expensive food materials regularly.[25] Izumi Hirano and Kazue Suyeishi (both of whom later became leaders of US *hibakusha*'s activism) recalled how their parents enjoyed a cup of coffee in the morning. Suyeishi in particular remembered how her parents had asked their family friends back in Pasadena to send unroasted, green coffee beans. Her parents kept them in a big can, stored in a small shed in their backyard. When the war neared, they asked returnees (traveling from the United States to Japan) to bring coffee with them. The carefully accumulated stock made it possible for the family to maintain its coffee-drinking habit almost through the war.[26]

These US survivors' remembering makes it clear that they did not let go of their American habits simply because they were in Japan. They were not shy about their ways either, insisting, as did Okuno with her uncle, that they had their preferences. They stood by their love of coffee even though green tea was the favored drink for most Japanese people. Some Nikkei in Japan before the war were indeed relatively well-to-do, a fruit of their success as immigrants in the United States.[27] They might have stood out because of their American diet or demeanor, but they were not entirely unfamiliar to people in Hiroshima and Nagasaki, either. Indeed, there were stores where Japanese Americans could go to buy steaks, even districts whose names reflected the city's history of sending immigrants overseas. Although the number of Japanese Americans in Nagasaki was smaller than its Hiroshima counterpart, hotels, shops, and restaurants that catered to immigrants from the West had been well established. One of the largest port cities in Japan that had opened its gate to Portugal and the Netherlands in the mid-sixteenth century, Nagasaki by the mid-nineteenth century set aside a designated residential district for its largely British and American population. In the early twentieth century, the district and its surrounding areas celebrated Christmas as an entire community; their residents enjoyed Western recreational activities such as bowling and bicycling.

Food materials from the West, and their smells, were not unfamiliar to the city's residents. Indeed, one of the first Western-style cakes to become popular in Japan, called *kasutera*, was invented in Nagasaki, becoming the city's well-known specialty by the mid-nineteenth century.[28] These histories of cultural exchanges that shaped the cities' landscapes likely made it easier for Nikkei to take root. Although Japanese Americans' coffee consumption declined at the height of the war, its smell came back quickly after the war ended. This was particularly evident in Niho, a neighborhood in the southern district of Hiroshima, which was home to a large number of returnees from Hawai'i. They began to drink coffee again when they reconnected with their friends and families after the war. The unmistakable smell gave the neighborhood the nickname: "The Coffee-Flavored Town of Niho." Evidently, this nickname was used by both Japanese Americans and the city's Japanese residents.[29]

For Nisei and Sansei children who had not been to Japan before, many things outside of the Coffee-Flavored Town, the New World, or American Village looked or sounded unfamiliar.[30] Katie Yanagawa, born in 1937 in Eatonville, Washington, who come to Hiroshima for the first time in June 1941, was perplexed by the sound she heard every day at her new home: "*karang-karong, karang-karong.*" As it turned out, it was the sound of *geta*, wooden sandals that Japanese people wore, and it was made by her neighbors "walking on the pavement" wearing their most ordinary footwear. Yanagawa explained her surprise by comparing these Japanese-style sandals to Western-style shoes: "I had no idea … because I wasn't used to it, having a noise like that, because in the United States you wear shoes and you hardly hear the shoes noise at all."[31] Kenji Takahashi, who was born in Hawai'i in 1926 and came to Hiroshima in 1931, was taken by surprise, too, in his case by *tatami* mats inside Japanese homes. "In Hawai'i they don't have *tatami* floors," he explained. Asked if it was difficult to become accustomed to it, he responded: "It must be so. That's what my mother always told me." In the family story, then, he became a child who found *tatami* difficult. Similar to Yanagawa, Takahashi explained how his struggle had been expected: "We were not accustomed to Japanese ways." Then, he said, amused: "We acted like dumb American kids the first year or two years," suggesting his recognition of how, in typically Japanese settings, Americans might not have seemed adept.[32] But soon they learned.

The most frequently mentioned difference between Japanese and American ways was not about floors or footwear. It was a toilet stool, or lack thereof. Born in Redondo Beach, California, in 1927 and coming to Japan in 1939, Hayami Fukino felt fortunate that at least she did not have to use a Japanese-style toilet at home. The reason for the good fortune was that her father, who had come to Japan before her, had "made it [the toilet] American style already." "So we didn't have to squat. He [her father] was a real handyman," said Fukino, with no small dose of appreciation.[33] George Kazuto Saiki was not as lucky. "There was no toilet that flushed" in Japan, "so the bathroom stank." Although he did not complain, his older siblings did not comply without a protest: "Dad, let's go back to Hawai'i!" they pleaded.[34] So it was that Japanese bathrooms smelled unclean, but Americans had a way to make things feel clean. Kazuko Aoki, a Japanese-born American survivor, recalled how Japanese friends of her American-born older sister Yoneko used to notice the way Yoneko smelled like an American. This was because of the baby powder that her mother put on her daughter after her bath. Because nobody else used the powder, it stood out. Although Aoki's sister seemed to feel a little embarrassed, the lightheartedness in Aoki's oral history indicated that the powder-story was something she recalled fondly. Her mother in Japan did not refrain from puffing her daughter with the American powder. For the daughter named after the country of her birth (Yoneko means "child of America"), this seemed only appropriate. For the other daughter, named after Japan (Kazuko, Aoki's first name, means "child of Japan"), it became part of a cherished family history, connecting Kazuko to America even before she went to the country for the first time after the war.[35]

Japanese Americans looked like Japanese but were not, and their differences were not missed by their Japanese acquaintances. Mitsuko Okimoto, a US survivor born in Japan in 1931 and thus a Japanese citizen at the time of the bombing (though she later became a leader in US survivors' activism), recalled "an extremely rich girl" who attended her school in Hiroshima. The girl had "come back from America," and her family kept turkeys in their yard, which Okimoto regarded as "American-style" as the girl herself.[36] James Jeong, a Korean American survivor born in Japan in 1925, remembered Japanese Americans mostly as his father's good customers. "His business was to trade precious stones, and so he frequented these wealthy people who came back from America to buy their rings," recalled Jeong.[37] In contrast, Kazue Kawasaki, also born in Japan and eleven years old in 1941, remembered the striking novelty of American things with less monetary value. Her neighbor across the street was an old woman, whose grandchild named Miyo came to visit her from Hawai'i. Kawasaki was fascinated by how "Miyo-chan" ("chan" is a Japanese diminutive) slept in "Western-style clothes," pajamas that looked entirely different from Kawasaki's *yukata* sleepwear. Too, Kawasaki recalled how Miyo-chan had decorated small boxes of sugar, gifts from Hawai'i for her Hiroshima relatives: "I was watching how she put ribbons on the boxes ... she pulled these ribbons, and sure enough, they curled up, *kuru-kuru*! I thought, Ah! Yes, she pulled the ends of these ribbons with her scissors, to make them curl up. I don't even remember her face, but I remember playing with Miyo-chan well."[38] Hawai'i left an impression on Kawasaki as sweet as her friend's gift. Instead of seeing the pajamas or the sugar as signs of wealth, Kawasaki followed the contours of the objects with her eyes wide open.

As we will see in Chapter 2, clothes were one of the visible signs of difference that helped US *hibakusha* to find each other after the bomb's explosion. Similar to food, what a person wore became a sign of composite belongings, a clue for survivors to identify loved ones at ground zero. Around the same time that Kawasaki was impressed by her Hawaiian friend's pajamas, in the mid-1930s, Izumi Hirano noticed how his father dressed differently than others in Japan. At the time, his father was raising chickens on his farm, taking advantage of husbanding skills that he had acquired in Hawai'i. He stuck not only to the occupation, but also to the clothing; an American-style overall made of denim, an outfit not worn by Japanese farmers.[39] Despite his ordinary line of work, his dress made him seem a bit extraordinary. Pak Namjoo, a Japan-born Korean survivor, remembered "Natt-chan of Shinagawa," her childhood friend in Hiroshima. She was a returnee from Hawai'i living in the Shinagawa district of Hiroshima, and her clothes were "*akanukete iru*" and "*haikara*," complimentary terms meaning "put together" and "modern," respectively.[40] Natt-chan was different enough to stand out because of her outfits, but also a friend dear enough for Pak to call her by her nickname. If the outfits of Hirano's father and Pak's friend were publicly noticed, other signs of difference were recognized more privately. Hirano's family, for instance, used Western-style bath towels at home. Although they were not likely to be seen or commented on by others, Hirano's remembering uncovers a reason why these household items were noteworthy: his family did *not* use Japanese-style towels, called *tenugui*, thin cloths with no suppleness.[41] Because everyone else was using *tenugui*, his towels looked and felt special. Even if these differences were on public display, however, Japanese Americans before 1941 did not try to hide them. Neither Kawasaki's friend nor Hirano's father thought of dressing in a more Japanese way, showing how "people who came back from America" openly wore what they were accustomed to. Moreover, the younger Hirano's remembering reveals how an observation about an everyday item could spur a reflection about cultural contingency. For Japanese Americans in Japan in the 1930s, there were moments to notice, times to contemplate. Seeing differences did not push people to exclude; rather, the act of seeing created ripples of thoughts and emotions that gently washed cultural borders. Although Okimoto's remembering about the "rich girl" and Jeong's statement about "those wealthy people" sound mildly critical of Americans' material abundance, many others revealed an easy coexistence of different national belongings in the cities, neighborhoods, and homes. Differences were there, but little effort was made to hide them.

In the immigrant cities, residents from different national backgrounds mingled, forging a culture of familiarity with divergence. Nurtured over many decades, this culture runs counter to the notion that the bomb brought a prompt destruction to an enemy. Imagined as targeting a single nation or people, the weapon in fact exploded upon a diversity of cultures created by the cities of immigrants. Part of this culture of divergence might have been shaped by the relatively privileged socioeconomic status that some Japanese Americans held in Japan. But many Japanese Americans were not particularly wealthy, making them more like everyone else. Nobuko Fujioka, a Japanese-born American survivor, recalled how some returnees seemed rich while others did not. She also remembered that some of her friends told her that the Nisei were "returnees from America," and that was it. Fujioka herself seemed to hold no particular sentiment about them.[42] Nisei were not all that foreign, although they might have been just different enough to be commented on. Seiko Fujimoto, another Japanese-born American survivor who was a Japanese citizen in the 1930s, even thought "America prefecture" was where all these Japanese Americans came from.[43] It was somewhere afar, but too familiar to be a foreign country. Alfred Kaneo Dote's remembering also accentuated the cultural proximity between Japan and America felt by Nikkei before the war. He recalled how, when he was growing up in Sacramento, California, he used to go to a picnic organized by the Hiroshima Kenjinkai, or the Association for Hiroshimans, an event made possible by the large number of people from Hiroshima residing in the California town. When he came to Hiroshima in 1936 as an eight-year-old, he found that there were many "people who came back from America" in his neighborhood, including the very people who used to come to the picnics in Sacramento. Surrounded by familiar faces, Dote experienced little difficulty in adjusting to life in Japan.[44]

One thing that emerges from the familiarity is that most Japanese Americans in the 1930s were not worried about being ostracized. Social ostracism was not entirely absent (as will be shown in the next section), but it was a rarity rather than a rule. Hiroshima and Nagasaki embraced both Americans' cultural belongings and Japanese people's familiarity with them. Nikkei's layered belonging was visible, with an expectation that it would be noticed but not rejected. For most Koreans in the cities, the relationship between their assumed Koreanness and the Japanese acceptance (or rejection) of it differed considerably from the Nikkei scenario. Accordingly, their layered belonging took on different kinds of visibility and invisibility in the cities' landscape. Before we make this comparison between Koreans and Americans fully, it is useful to look at how Japanese Americans experienced their schooling in America and Japan differently. Their national, cultural, and racial characteristics were interpreted by their peers, parents, and teachers in strikingly different ways across the Pacific. Perhaps more than streets and neighborhoods, schools were where most American survivors met shifting definitions of who they were and what their cross-nationality meant.

At School: Nikkei Students, Teachers, and Parents

As a public space, the classroom was a site where both cultural conflicts and conciliations arose. Japanese American *hibakusha*'s remembering of their schooling on both sides of the Pacific brings to a sharp focus how they negotiated their race, citizenship, and layered sense of belonging. Many recalled that their schooling in the United States had been diverse in two ways. First, many went to public school on weekdays and Japanese school on Sundays. Some Japanese schools held classes on late weekday afternoons too, so Nisei or Sansei pupils went there after they were let out of public school. The language of instruction in the former was English, Japanese in the latter. While the primary purpose of Japanese schools was language education, they also served as a kind of nursery for working families. Many of them were housed in Buddhist or Christian churches, a safe community space where Japanese American children could stay together while away from their parents.[45] Some children did not mind their time at Japanese schools, while others did not like going to an extra school. Secondly, the American public schools that they attended were racially and ethno-nationally diverse. Junji Sarashina's school in Lahaina in Hawai'i, for instance, consisted of "Japanese, Portuguese, and Caucasian" students. Although the "Portuguese" were white, US survivors remembered them as a separate group because they, too, were children of immigrants. "Whenever they baked bread," said Sarashina, "they used a stone oven, which was outside. They used log wood, and you can smell the aroma one mile away." Although Sarashina did not remember his classmates' faces, he did remember the sweet flavor of the bread more than half a century later. Together with "a lot of Japanese [American] students" like himself, memories like this led Sarashina to say that his school was "all mixed," and harmoniously so.[46] Francis Mitsuo Tomosawa, also from Hawai'i, recalled a somewhat different, yet equally diverse, student population at his school. Japanese Americans, Chinese Americans, Hawaiian Americans, and Caucasians made it "cosmopolitan." Although he befriended other Japanese Americans the most, he also had some friends from other racial or national backgrounds.[47] Similar to Sarashina, Tomosawa suggested a limited amount of interracial interactions that occurred in a relatively non-hostile setting for Nikkei. Racial distinctions were made, but they did not necessarily culminate in racial animosity directed to or by Japanese Americans as far as Japanese Americans were concerned.[48]

Japanese Americans on the US mainland, too, remembered racially or nationally diverse student populations, but many found themselves in a distinctively minority status both numerically and socially. Haakai Nagano, of Orange Cove, California, remembered: "There were very few Japanese Americans, so most of the children attending [my] school were all *hakujin* [Caucasians]." They were "Armenians, Syrians, and maybe even Croatians," Nagano recalled, "but they were all that race," that is, white.[49] Compared to Tomosawa who enjoyed "cosmopolitan" friendships, then, Nagano found the racial line difficult to cross. Children of immigrants from non-Japanese backgrounds were demarcated by race instead of being seen as fellow newcomers. Hayami Fukino, when she was growing up in California in the 1930s, attended a mostly Japanese American school in a neighborhood where Nikkei families clustered. The era's housing segregation, as well as the immigrant families' desire to stay close, had created a fair number of Nikkei-heavy neighborhoods across the state. But their large number did not mean that Japanese Americans were socially dominant. As Fukino remembered, "there was few *hakujins*, but we didn't get along, well, not get along, but did not talk to them too much." Unsurprisingly, a reason for this lack of interaction was racial segregation: "I remember one swimming pool that said 'No Japanese,'" recalled Fukino. Racism found a way into a family conversation. When Fukino's father learned that the first commercial flight would fly from Japan to America, his response was: "Oh, he's going to get a ticket," meaning that even an inanimate object could be segregated by race. Although her *hakujin* school teachers were "OK" and did not overtly discriminate, Fukino did not accept their attitude at face value. She said: "You know, you remember those things [about an airplane and a pool]," which brought to the surface how Nikkei were treated differently.[50] The lesson was that there was more than meets the eye.

Racism seemed no longer a problem after Japanese American children came to Japan. This did not mean, however, that diversity in their schooling ceased to exist. In fact, both dual-schooling and diversity in race and nationality continued to shape Nikkei experiences in Hiroshima and Nagasaki, if more mutedly. The main difference between Japanese and Japanese American children was nationality. This was in contrast to their relationship to children of Korean origin, which, as we will see, was marked by assumed differences in race in addition to nationality. Natsumi Aida, for instance, recalled how there was "a range of students" at her school in Hiroshima: "There were some from Canada, others from Hawai'i," in addition to those from the US mainland.[51] Fumiko Imai, born in Brazil and coming to Japan in 1933 as a three-year-old, remembered how her mother stood out when she came to Imai's school for a parent day. "She was wearing a suit and a pair of high heels," a sign of her family's foreignness and high standard of living in the eyes of her Japanese schoolmates. In Imai's remembering, her family's perceived affluence was the reason why her house was targeted by a thief a few times.[52] As was the case with some others, a nationality could translate into a socioeconomic class. Japanese Americans' distinctiveness could alienate, but it could also facilitate. For instance, Aida's remembering shows how her foreignness was a reason for her to become a target of teasing and, at the same time, a way for her to get out of it. In her oral history, Aida recalled how her classmate smeared *sumi*, a kind of ink used for Japanese calligraphy, on her back on her first day at a Hiroshima school. Although it is not clear if this act was directed at Aida because she was an American or because she was a newcomer, she felt that the incident highlighted her foreignness: unlike Japanese students, she did not know how to do calligraphy. She felt anxious, and the *sumi* incident only heightened the sentiment. But her foreignness also pushed back the bullying, thanks to cookies that her mother baked. These treats were the reason why her teachers, and eventually her classmates, grew to like her: "When they came over to my house, they enjoyed these cookies. My mother was good at baking them ... although she did not have enough ingredients [in Japan], she managed to bake cookies and cakes, etc."[53] Depending on circumstances, then, Nikkei students played their foreignness in divergent ways. This was distinct from the classroom that Japanese American students experienced in the United States, especially on the mainland, in which day-to-day interactions between different national groups were infrequent. Even less frequent in America was an opportunity for Nikkei children to test their difference to their advantage. In Japan, such opportunities seemed to spring up.

Indeed, Nikkei students were keenly aware of the meanings of both the differences and similarities that they embodied for their peers, something that remained true throughout wartime. To be sure, their remembering suggests that they experienced their cross-nationality – they looked like Japanese because of the racial sameness, but they also were dissimilar because of their national and cultural backgrounds – in more flexible ways before 1941 than after. This is not surprising, given the sharp rise of hostility against the United States among the Japanese after the war's beginning. Still, it is important to note Hiroshima and Nagasaki as places that reared a layered sense of belonging in strikingly open-ended ways through the 1930s and, in some cases, beyond 1941. In a way different than schools in America, schools in Hiroshima and Nagasaki continued to accommodate a range of cross-national interactions among their pupils, especially those who were deemed to belong to the same race. This was not only because of the treats like cookies that some Nikkei families were able to offer. According to George Kazuto Saiki, about half of the student population at his school was Japanese Americans.[54] Kenji Takahashi recalled a more modest number of Nikkei students in Hiroshima: "I could say, in my middle school about 20 percent of what you call the Nisei could speak English ... This was a private school they put us into, so maybe our school was not

20 percent, maybe 10 percent, but at other private schools, maybe 20 to 25 percent of the Nisei were attending."[55] Although these numbers may not be precise, it is striking that most Japanese American survivors remembered that there were others like themselves. Saiki also recalled that not only students but also one of his teachers was Nikkei – "Teacher Shiraishi" from Los Angeles. The teacher took Saiki under his wing, helping him study and making sure that he applied to an appropriate high school. Beside his kindness, the Aloha shirt that Shiraishi wore stayed in Saiki's remembering as a mark of their shared cultural belonging.[56] Jack Motoo Dairiki's uncle was an English teacher at Dairiki's school in Hiroshima. Trained in England, his uncle's British accent caused a family disagreement. "When the uncle said 'This is a dog' in his British accent," recalled Dairiki, "I would say 'It's not right! It's a *dog*!' in an American accent." Regardless of the discord, the fact that his family member was an English-speaking teacher greatly helped Dairiki's adjustment to Japan.[57] No others in Dairiki's class could speak as fluently in English, not to mention tell the difference between UK and US accents. Some, like May Yamaoka, felt proud to be one of the students fluent in English. As she recalled, one of her teachers, trained at the University of Hawai'i, asked her to pronounce the word "one," to serve as a model for others. Although Yamaoka thought "it's funny" and "felt embarrassed" by the request, the recognition helped her to feel accepted.[58]

The presence of other Nikkei, along with teachers and students from places such as Britain, Canada, and Brazil, was part of the cities' long history of immigration. Immigrants' sheer number, as well as city residents' familiarity with "people who came back from America," made a relatively agreeable coexistence of differences possible. The absence of an assumed racial difference between Japanese and Japanese Americans, too, facilitated their interactions, although their national, cultural, and linguistic differences were abundantly visible. Instead of seeing the lack of racism as a given, however, Japanese American children experienced it as refreshing. The reason for this was that racism shaped many aspects of their families' lives before coming to Japan. As discussed earlier, most Japanese Americans decided to return or send their children to Japan for family reasons. Often, these reasons were shaped by larger inequalities in America. Some Issei and Nisei parents worried about the future of their offspring in the United States, as hostility rose between America and Japan in the early decades of the twentieth century. Beyond daily signs of racial discrimination in public spaces, there were legal restrictions that made Issei realize that there might be no future for Nisei and Sansei in America. In 1906, the San Francisco Board of Education established a policy of racial segregation of Asian students, reversed only after the Gentlemen's Agreement was adopted in 1907 to curtail Japanese migration to the United States. In 1913, California passed the Alien Land Law that prohibited "aliens ineligible for citizenship" from buying land or leasing it for more than three years. Both Chinese and Japanese immigrants fell into this category. After the National Origins Quota Act passed the Congress in 1924, all "aliens ineligible for citizenship" again became a target, this time of a law that prohibited Asians from migrating to America. The only exception to this rule was immigrants from the Philippines, then a US colony.[59] These restrictions found a way into US survivors' remembering. Kenji Takahashi, born in Hawai'i in 1921 and arriving in Japan in 1931, explained the reasons for his family's return to Japan as caring for sick relatives and attending to family affairs. Then, he added another reason: "Because at that time Japanese Americans didn't get too good an education in this country. Also they couldn't get good jobs here so parents sent them to [places like] Hiroshima." If Nisei and Sansei were fluent in Japanese, they might be better off building lives in Japan. Takahashi's reasons for returning to Japan were family-driven, but they were also shaped by racism that extended across the Pacific.[60]

Because of their perception that racism prompted their departure from America, many US survivors found solace in the relative lack of discrimination that they found in schools in Hiroshima and Nagasaki. It was not complete acceptance; teasing could, and did, happen. But US *hibakusha* remembered their schooling in the 1930s fondly. Unlike American teachers who were "OK" or "good" in the classroom, Japanese teachers were frequently described as "kind" or "very nice."[61] This warmer recognition likely originated from the fact that Japanese teachers' attitude toward American students was not structured by racism or nationalism. Compared to the United States where both the federal and state governments implemented discriminatory policies against Nikkei, the Japanese government in the 1920s and 1930s did not enact specific policies concerning Issei, Nisei, and Sansei residing in the country. Japan determined citizenship as *jus sanguinis*, while America did so as *jus soli*, so all Nisei and Sansei were entitled to dual citizenship. Because Issei were not allowed US citizenship under US law, they by necessity maintained Japanese citizenship and family registry. This, in turn, helped the registration of Nisei and Sansei as Japanese citizens; all they had to do was register their names in their parents' or grandparents' existing family record, and file at a local bureau. They were not marked as American citizens, although their places of birth made it possible to infer if someone looked into the document. Until the early 1940s, however, the Japanese Ministry of Foreign Affairs and Legal Affairs Bureau did not check their records systematically. The underlying assumption was that the only foreigners were Westerners who held no connection to Japan either *jus sanguinis* or *jus soli*.[62] Surely, the absence of legal discrimination was not a panacea. By describing Japanese teachers appreciatively, American students showed they did not take acceptance for granted. It was an eye-opening moment when they found that they were not ostracized, although they spoke, acted, or ate differently. Something that seemed unchangeable changed right in front of their eyes; the line between universality and uniqueness became blurred, creating a space for cultural contingency. As we will see in Chapter 2, this kind of revelation – that uniqueness and universality conflict *and* converge – occurred at Hiroshima's and Nagasaki's ground zero, too. That US survivors trace similar experiences in their childhood suggests how they see the bomb as part of the history of immigration, not the other way around. In US *hibakusha*'s remembering, people's history of creating ties across borders was larger than the nuclear weaponry that ignored it.

Acceptance by Japanese teachers made American students' struggle with language somewhat easier. Language was one of the most visible signs of Nikkei's foreignness, something that distinguished Americans from Koreans in wartime Japan. And yet, language came up in both of their rememberings as an essential element of their cross-national experiences, revealing its power to connect as much as separate.[63] More fluent in English than in Japanese, many Nikkei children tried to learn, relearn, or unlearn these languages with varying degrees of success. Their efforts added layers to their sense of belonging. Most students not fluent in Japanese resorted to dual-schooling: they learned Japanese from their families after school. Unlike the dual-schooling in America, their learning in Japan was solely in Japanese. Junji Sarashina remembered how this dual-schooling took place out of necessity:

> When I first went to ... grade school, second grade or so, of course, I speak, my English is stronger than my Japanese. So some of the kids said there is a damn nut coming around to school. And it really upset me. ... So I went back to my mom, and said, gosh, they called me *baka*, dumb nut! ... So my mother said, alright ... you got to learn Japanese grammar. So I started to study, she taught me Japanese grammar from the second grade on.[64]

Although Sarashina acknowledged the initial difficulty of fitting in, he recalled that it was only for "the first year." His teachers "were very kind to [him], tremendously nice and kind." Indeed, thanks to these teachers' help and his learning at home, Sarashina was chosen to give a send-off speech for a graduating class three years later.[65]

For others, though, negotiating languages proved more difficult. Like Sarashina, Izumi Hirano acquired fluency in Japanese by speaking the language at home, a more solo process than the communal schooling he had experienced in Hawai'i. He described the effect of his dual-schooling in Japan: "When I went back to Japan, I spoke Pigeon English and odd Japanese. Then I acquired Hiroshima dialect." Because his only teachers were his family members, their dialect became part of Hirano's Japanese. Looking back on this, Hirano sounded slightly regretful that he had never learned standard Japanese.[66] In a sense, though, this kind of home-schooling in Japan might have been more practical than the language education offered in America. Nikkei children born to Hiroshiman parents could learn a non-Hiroshima dialect at a Sunday school in the United States, as did George Kazuto Saiki, which would later cause them problems in Hiroshima. Taught in Kumamoto dialect in America, Saiki spoke Japanese at schools in Hiroshima, but of course with a Kumamoto accent. Saiki had to learn how to say "mother" and "father" in the Hiroshima dialect, to avoid being laughed at.[67] Fusae Kurihara, too, remembered her struggle: "I was only five, so I think we used Japanese at home when I was in the United States. But even so, my mother's younger sister, who took care of me in Japan ... was saying she couldn't understand what I was saying. So I think I kind of mixed up Japanese and English."[68] One's speaking could split right in the middle. Others continued to rely on English as they never became fluent in Japanese. Asako Gaudette's friends fell into this group. As she recalled, they found it particularly difficult to pronounce English words that had been phonetically translated into Japanese. They could not say *kānēshon*; instead, they said "carnation."[69] Thus, dual-schooling in either America or Japan was hardly a solution for all. For those who struggled to fit in linguistically, the beginning of the Pacific War would shine a harsh light on their cross-nationality. For those who acquired Japanese but lost fluency in English, returning home after the war would pose an extraordinary challenge. For many others who fell in between, neither language felt right, contributing to their silence about their experiences as US survivors. Similar to other cultural products such as food and clothes, language embodied different shades of cultural affinity, leading Nikkei to respond to the war and the bomb in various ways.

And yet, it was still the 1930s. Japanese American remembering indicates that there was room for students with a range of linguistic ability and cultural familiarity to find their way. The process of adapting to Japan was not without obstacles, but the promise was that American children would be accepted if they could learn some Japanese ways, too. This did not mean that they had to shed their American habits, though. In contrast to US schooling colored by racial and national distinctions, Japanese schooling allowed American children to hold onto their habits. In a larger sense, this difference suggests the persistence of race in definitions of nationality. When people believed that they belonged to the same race, their difference in nationality did not greatly undercut the possibility of connection, sameness, and equality. When people believed that they belonged to difference races, their difference in nationality became an excuse for enacting racist policies and practices.[70] Equally important, race as people understood it was not based on biologically determined differences such as skin, hair, and eye color. The experiences of Korean and Korean American survivors in Hiroshima and Nagasaki in the 1930s elucidate this point.

Koreans in Japan: Visible Community, Invisible Belonging

After Japan's annexation of Korea in 1910, Koreans began to migrate in considerable numbers to Japanese industrial cities such as Nagasaki, Fukuoka, Osaka, and Hiroshima. Easy access from Shimonoseki, the Japanese port city nearest the southern Korean port of Busan, made these cities reasonable destinations. The Korean migration was driven by Japanese colonial policies. Soon after the annexation, the Governor-General of Korea initiated a major land survey, aiming to claim any unregistered land as imperial property. Because registering land ownership had not been a universal practice in Korea, many Korean landowners lost their properties. Once claimed by the imperial government, crops from these confiscated farms were shipped to Japan to supplant their food supply, leaving Korean sharecroppers in chronic malnutrition and, in the last years of the war, starvation. Poverty, as well as the lack of educational and occupational opportunities, became prevalent particularly in rural areas, driving many to emerging industrial centers in Korea.[71] Some sought jobs in the Japanese metropole, mostly in coal and steel mines, mills and factories, and construction companies.[72] The flow of migration became considerably larger after the Japanese Imperial Diet passed the National Mobilization Law in 1938, then again in 1942 and 1944 when the Japanese government began the forced migration of Koreans to Japan proper with the purpose of supplementing the wartime empire's labor force and military, respectively. Before 1938, the number of Koreans in Japan proper was just under 800,000. By 1945, their number exceeded 2,000,000, of which about 50,000 and 20,000 were in the cities of Hiroshima and Nagasaki, respectively. This rapid growth of the Korean population was more pronounced in Nagasaki. In Hiroshima, where a considerable number already existed prior to the forced mobilization, Korean communities in 1945 included not only recent migrants but also a substantial number of those who had been born or raised in the city. The history of Koreans who were forcefully mobilized by the Japanese empire after the Pacific War started in 1941, then were victimized by the bomb in 1945, has been central to the scholarship about Korean survivors. Those who had been in Japan for a longer time, in contrast, have been much less studied, suggesting a still-limited attention given to cross-nationality in our historical inquiry.[73]

Koreans in Japan raised mostly or entirely in Hiroshima or Nagasaki developed a layered sense of belonging, and showed a strong attachment to Korean heritage and Japanese culture. Throughout the 1930s they learned both the Korean and Japanese languages, which stood in contrast to Japanese Americans' education in Japan, which focused solely on Japanese. The proximity between the Korean Peninsula and the Japanese archipelago made it possible for Koreans to keep close ties to home. Many traveled back and forth frequently, helping to keep their mother tongue largely intact.[74] During the 1910s and 1920s, most Koreans in Japan were Korean monolinguals, using limited Japanese only when necessary. By the mid-1930s, however, second generation Koreans in Japan reached 20–30 percent of the population, raising concerns about their unfamiliarity with Korea.[75] Raising their children in Japan, most Korean parents approached language education with a determination similar to that of Japanese Americans in the United States. The education usually started at home, helping children to be familiar with the parents' mother tongue. Parents also hoped to prepare their children, who lived their daily lives under the Japanese rule, for future days under Korean sovereignty.[76] Yi Jougkeun, born in Japan in 1928 and still residing there at the time of our oral history in 2013, remembered how his parents made it mandatory that he spoke Korean when conversing with family members:

> My father always said to me that, although it is okay to speak Japanese in public, you must speak Korean at home. I did not think of myself as Korean, I thought I was Japanese. So I did not understand why I would want to speak Korean. . . . I just overheard my parents and began to understand a word here, a word there.[77]

Despite Yi's seeming lack of enthusiasm, the vocabulary that he had acquired in his childhood helped him communicate with his relatives when he visited them in the newly independent Korea after the war. His relatives did not think that Yi's Korean sounded authentic, but at least it made their cross-cultural interactions possible.[78] Such connection and continuity through spoken words, which pieced together the present and the future, were maintained by a strong commitment to language education among first generation Koreans in Japan.

Here, it is noteworthy that maintaining Korean language skills was an important means of political and cultural resistance in Korea especially after 1938, when the Governor-General of Korea began to enforce the use of Japanese as an official language of instruction at all Korean schools. In 1939, the Japanese forced Koreans to change their names to Japanese ones, further heightening a sense of urgency among Koreans that they must protect their heritage. Consequently, the number of Koreans fluent in Japanese remained limited in the peninsula even during the final years of the war, making it difficult for the Japanese Imperial Army to recruit Korean soldiers who understood military orders in Japanese.[79] In Japan proper, however, the relationship between Korean people and language differed. As long-term residents of Japan, in many cases since the 1910s and 1920s, they were more likely to be fluent in Japanese. For second generation Koreans in Japan such as Yi, Japanese was their mother tongue, and their exposure to the Korean language was limited. Unlike Korean people in Korea, their schooling in the compulsory education system had been always in Japanese. It is also notable that, unlike Nikkei in America in the early decades of the twentieth century, Koreans in Japan did not open a large number of Korean language schools that children could attend after school.[80] One such school, called Eneigakuin, opened in the mid-1920s in the Kichijima-chō district in Hiroshima, and at its peak the school attracted more than forty students. And yet, the school's finances remained dependent on parental donations, never becoming large or stable enough to collect tuition. Many Korean children worked to help their family income, making it difficult for them to attend school regularly. Moreover, Japanese police officers made frequent visits beginning in the early 1930s, damaging desks and blackboards.[81] But the reason for the relative absence of language schools went beyond financial difficulty and police harassment. Following the annexation, the Japanese government implemented inconsistent, even contradictory, policies of assimilation. After the mid-1920s, the Japanese government generally preferred Koreans to be assimilated, not only culturally but also legally to a degree. After universal male suffrage was introduced in Japan in 1925, Korean male residents of Japan received the right to vote if they had been registered on a family record with a Japanese address more than a year. Japanese schools, including some elite military schools, opened their doors to registered Korean residents, creating a pipeline for upward mobility.[82]

These policies of assimilation offered some impetus for Koreans in Japan to become fluent in Japanese. Many also felt that hiding their Korean language skills would lead to better opportunities. As we will see, these factors shaped an intricate relationship between visibility and invisibility for Koreans. Unlike Nikkei in Japan who experimented and expressed their foreignness publicly, Koreans in Japan had reasons to keep theirs private. These reasons were particularly relevant to those raised in Japan and adept in Japanese such as Yi. This did not mean, however, that younger Koreans in Japan were uninterested in learning about their Korean heritage. In fact, their desire to understand Korean culture appeared to intensify during the 1930s when discrimination against Koreans heightened. In their day-to-day interactions with the Japanese, Koreans were often belittled, seen as physically smaller and weaker, mentally impoverished, and racially inferior. Similar to contemporary racism against African Americans in the United States, Koreans in Japan were deemed dirty, loud and coarse in their speech. Outside elite military or political careers, their employment opportunities were limited. Among those employed, the average income hovered at around 40–50 percent of Japanese workers.[83] This kind of treatment fueled many Koreans' aspiration to return to an independent Korea at some point in the future, which necessitated that they learn the Korean language.

Indeed, evidence suggests that, despite the absence of language schools, Koreans in Japan during the 1930s taught their children and grandchildren Korean beyond the home; education also occurred in their community, to keep alive the possibility of returning home. Such efforts became critical not only because racism intensified but also because Koreans in Japan became multigenerational and different cultural belongings began to converge. Matsumoto Kisō, a survivor born in Korea who came to Japan in 1932, recalled days in the early 1940s:

> My mother and father's Japanese was weak, so they spoke in Korean. My wife came to Japan when she was eight, and her Korean was a little better than mine. So these three talked in Korean. I just listened to them. Also, in my neighborhood, there were ten, twenty tenement houses, barracks, occupied by Koreans. They were of all sorts ... and back then, they spoke everything in Korean.[84]

Matsumoto's remembering reveals a dual process of learning Korean. First, he would hear it at home; then in his neighborhood, too, though he did not necessarily speak it. This composite education arose because different language skills coexisted in families and communities. As second generation Koreans grew in number, Japanese became their main language of communication; at the same time, as more immigrants from the peninsula arrived in the late 1930s because of the war mobilization, the number of Korean monolinguals increased, too. In this context, teaching Korean by using it in families and communities became of a piece with Koreans' desire to stay connected to their home. The desire was felt not only by adults; it was also passed on to children. For instance, the significance of young Matsumoto's ability to understand Korean became evident when he discussed his father's occupational history: "My father was a ward mayor when he was in Korea ... so he was called *kujang, kujang* [in Korean] ... even after he came to Japan."[85] For Matsumoto, whose Japanese was stronger than his Korean, learning Korean was an act of learning his family history that stretched back to the home he had not seen. In this way, language connected the past to the present.

Equally important, Koreans' sense of national belonging was fostered largely within families and communities visibly separated from Japanese neighborhoods. Before, during, and after the war, Koreans rarely lived in physical proximity to the Japanese. Their belonging to Korea was plainly visible within the Korean districts.[86] Even when they stepped out of the boundaries, their foreignness was difficult to erase. Unlike some Japanese Americans whose speech signaled their foreignness, long-term Korean residents of Japan, especially those raised in the country, did not face a language barrier. Instead, blunt talk of the "Korean race," as many Japanese politicians, military leaders, and police officers of the time referred to them, demarcated their foreignness.[87] This mixture of sameness (in language) and difference (in residence and race imposed by the Japanese) offered a ground for Koreans in Japan to negotiate visibility and invisibility in their expressions of cross-nationality in a way strikingly different from Nikkei. Americans often expressed their layered sense of belonging in public, without being criticized for making it visible; Koreans, on the other hand, felt compelled to keep their cross-nationality in private, for fear of being punished by visibly expressing it. The experience of Pak Namjoo, a Korean *hibakusha* born in 1932 in Japan, suggests how Koreans in Japan maintained Korean belonging amid Japanese assimilation policies by balancing visibility and invisibility in private and public spheres. Her father came to Japan in 1929, followed by her mother the next year. Like Matsumoto, Pak lived in the Fukushima-chō in the Nishi district of Hiroshima, an area predominantly populated by Koreans. Also like Matsumoto, Pak emphasized a family history that she could be proud of. Pak's father was able to read and write, despite the fact that he worked as a janitor in Japan.

Her father also encouraged Pak to study hard to become fluent in Japanese, in part to strengthen her pride in being Korean:

> My father always told me to study hard, so as not to fall behind
> the Japanese. If I fell behind, I would not be able to go to an
> upper-level school; I would also be looked down upon.[88]

At first glance, a Korean student studying hard at a Japanese school seems precisely what the assimilation policies aimed to accomplish. And yet, Pak's experience was more complicated. Seeing that she excelled academically, a handful of Japanese classmates made fun of her by calling her *Chōsen*, meaning "Korean." To counter, Pak mobilized her academic excellence. She responded: "You dumb nuts! Before you poke fun at me, be smart enough to be a class president!" Using her intellectual superiority over the boys, none of whom were a class president, Pak pushed back against the belittlement of her cross-nationality, suggesting how Koreans in Japan used their adoption of Japaneseness outside their community to resist Japanese racism and nationalism.[89] She did not defend her Korean heritage by speaking in Korean in public; rather, she did so by mobilizing her excellence in Japanese. Inside their families and neighborhoods – in more private spheres – they protected their Korean heritage more visibly, so as to keep ties to their history as immigrants. This sharply differed from how Japanese Americans expressed their cross-nationality. Although they could also be taunted by Japanese bullies as "dumb nuts," as was Junji Sarashina, Nikkei experienced much less tension between their cross-nationality's visibility and invisibility. Their belonging to America flew between public and private spaces in Japan freely in a way not available to Koreans.

Koreans in Hiroshima and Nagasaki were no less determined to protect Korean culture beyond language as part of their cross-nationality than their Japanese American counterparts, although here again, their visibility and invisibility were carefully negotiated. In particular, food offered an opening for finding a place for cross-nationality for Koreans amid the Japanese. Korean and Korean American survivors almost universally remembered the smell of *kimchee*, which stood out at school. Because it was customary for school children to bring lunch from home, lunch boxes became something of a cultural showcase for those whose diet was not typically Japanese. Unlike Americans who proudly introduced their Japanese classmates to homemade cookies, Koreans paid the price for being different. Yi Jougkeun recalled:

> My mother cooked all meals, and she made *kimchee*, too. You
> know *kimchee*, which smells very garlicky. So [my classmates]

told me that Koreans smelled bad ... that they were dirty and smelly.... I remember that I took lunch to my school, which had a lunch box warmer [for winter]. It was heated from below by fire ... so we could eat a warm lunch. But my lunch had *kimchee* in it, and so it started to smell. I was told to take it out of the warmer.[90]

Yi's garlic became a sign of his foreignness, prompting his lunch box's removal from the warmer. Nonetheless, asked what his favorite food had been, his answer was *"miso tchigae,"* fermented soybean paste soup flavored with red chili and garlic.[91] To love Korea's cuisine was to be resilient in Japan. Pak's remembering conveyed a similar sentiment. Having *kimchee* in her lunch box regularly, she decided to eat her lunch at home instead of eating with her classmates.[92] Although this was hard for this strong-willed girl unafraid of talking back to bullying boys, her choice was eased by two circumstances that contained a measure of acceptance of her belonging to Korea. First, her teachers did not prohibit *kimchee* or stop her from leaving the school for lunch. Second, Pak's mother did not offer to do away with *kimchee*. Pak continued to enjoy the condiment thanks to these subtle accommodations.

Pak's remembering, then, illuminates a moment when the cross-nationality of Koreans in Japan found something akin to a balance between visibility and invisibility. Although the residential segregation was strict, it did not foreclose meaningful encounters between Korean and Japanese peoples. School was the prime site of these encounters, which allowed immigrants to forge a sense of layered belonging to Japan and Korea. The process did not culminate in either resistance or collaboration; instead, it highlighted the cultural contingency of both. These encounters took place outside classrooms, too. Pak, for one, remembered fondly the multinational neighborhood in which her family had lived. Unlike the often tense school environment, she recalled how Fukushima-chō residents were all "kind and gentle." Although they included some Japanese, none called her *Chōsen* derogatorily or treated her differently. She speculated if this was because the area was reserved for relatively well-to-do Korean families.[93] But these affirmative memories were not strictly class specific. Matsumoto Kisō, who lived in a less desirable neighborhood in the Yojima district of Kako-chō near the Hiroshima city jail, felt fine about eating *kimchee*, not only because his family affirmed it but also because it was a specialty appreciated by some Japanese, too. Initially, Matsumoto's remembering suggested that he liked *kimchee* simply because his family members liked it:

> The elders liked garlic. They would eat well if a dish had garlic in it. . . . There are people who don't eat garlic because it smells. But the value of garlic is in that smell. . . . If there is no smell, then you don't feel that you are eating garlic.[94]

Matsumoto's belief in garlic's goodness was further confirmed when a Japanese customer, a famous actress, came to his father's grocery store. She said that she was ill, and looking for garlic that would help her recovery.[95] The impact of her visit is evident in Matsumoto's still-fresh memory that, surprisingly, a Japanese recognized the value of Korean things, something that seemed to shift his relationship to the Japanese momentarily a step away from the airless hierarchy that colonial policies demanded. These encounters did not erase the fact of colonialism; instead, they opened a possibility for both Korean and Japanese peoples to make sense of it in their everyday encounters. Matsumoto, then, may be seen as using the visit by the Japanese actress to push back against the belittlement of *kimchee* by the Japanese. Not only his Korean family but also his Japanese customer found it nutritious. Confident in this knowledge, as Pak was in her Japanese, Matsumoto claimed an alternative way of smelling it. The strong, presumably undesirable aroma of garlic as Japanese students and teachers perceived it, did not exist in the Korean neighborhoods. The flavor was everywhere, and it was simply good for you. If you did not smell this way, you were missing the point.

This strong community attachment existed side-by-side with Koreans' familiarity with Japanese food. John Hong, a Korean American *hibakusha* born in Shanghai in 1926 who came to Japan in 1940, remembered all sorts of Japanese dishes that he had enjoyed. Similar to many Koreans who came to Japan before 1938, Hong's reason for coming was to find educational and occupational opportunities. The son of a successful businessman and a woman descended from an aristocratic family, Hong was fortunate enough to stay well-fed as a student in Nagasaki throughout the wartime. He could study "without worrying about making ends meet," and his meal options were wide:

I ate a lot of fish, but not so much meat. Vegetables were abundant, and a lot of breads, too. I remember eating *an-pan*, *mochi*, and *zenzai*. Also, I had *chanpon* frequently – it was served with pork. It was so delicious! I have it every time I visit Nagasaki. As a matter of fact, I go there every time when there is a school reunion. They let me know. We are all graduates of 1945.[96]

In Hong's remembering, Japanese dishes, particularly *chanpon*, Chinese-inflected noodles for which Nagasaki is famous, connected his past and present. All the dishes he recalled were Japanese and referred to in Japanese. This is partly because he was alone in Japan in his school years, away from his parents in Shanghai. In fact, Hong lived in a dormitory of the commercial high school that he attended in Nagasaki, so he usually ate with his classmates. This communal eating of Japanese food continued even after Hong moved to the Hiroshima Army Weapons School, an elite military institution. As he recalled, he wanted to show that, although a Korean, he was patriotic enough to train himself as one of Japan's future leaders. It was a declaration of the difference *and* the sameness between Korean and Japanese students. Thus, subsequently being invited to school reunions has meant something special for him. Not only his classmates, he recalled, but also "most of [his] friends were Japanese." His first love, too, was a Japanese, a sister of his *chikuba no tomo*, or boyhood chum. Unlike Hong, who left for Hiroshima, she stayed in Nagasaki, where she encountered the bomb just three days after he did in Hiroshima.[97]

Japanese food and friends are bound up in Hong's remembering, bringing back the times they spent together in the same breath as the days when the bombs changed everything. The war that devastated Korea comprised Hong's youth, which may be revisited only by calling up his belonging to Japan. The bombs threw the countries together by indiscriminatingly destroying both peoples. In this composite of remembering, Japanese discrimination against Koreans accented colonial dissonance. Instances of discrimination were woven into those of nondiscrimination, yet the former protruded in one's remembering like a piece of puzzle that never fit. In Nagasaki, Hong's teachers praised him for his academic excellence, which made him susceptible to bullying. He fought back, and the teacher who called him into his office afterward eventually let him go "because he could see that he [Hong] had a legitimate reason to fight back." Hong remembered another teacher in Nagasaki, Mr. Suzuki, who taught *jūdō*, as particularly "good." In Hiroshima, too, his section commander "treated [him] kindly" although he knew that Hong was from Korea. Even as Hong expressed gratitude for such teachers, he vividly remembered the discriminatory acts of his classmates. They were jealous of Hong's success; he should have known his place better, they seemed to say. Once, they beat him so badly that Hong could not go to school for a week. "Good" teachers did not intervene.[98] These daily realities, which unfolded at the schools training the future leaders of the empire, revealed how colonialism was failing its own expectations.

James Jeong, too, recalled a case of colonial dissonance. Although he was frustrated by limited educational opportunities available for Koreans, he also discovered how they could be widened by carefully crafting his interactions with Japanese authorities:

> After graduating from an elementary school, I went to a teacher training school. It was commonly assumed that Koreans in Japan could not attend a regular middle school. To apply for a teacher's school, I only had to submit a record of residence called *koseki shōhon*. My family record, *koseki tōhon* [that would have shown Jeong's Korean lineage], was not necessary. I had my Japanese name "Okada" on my record of residence, so no one noticed that I was a Korean. You could stay out of trouble if you stayed away from government offices.[99]

Jeong adeptly made his belonging to Korea invisible by taking advantage of Japan's assimilation policies. The Japanese government in 1939 began to demand that Koreans register their Japanese names and addresses on *koseki shōhon*, so as to promote Koreans' assimilation into Japanese people, policy, and culture.[100] On the other hand, if a student's Korean origin became known, some Japanese schools would not accept them. But this act of exclusion was not consistently exercised. As Jeong recalled, teachers' schools did not intentionally exclude based on race or national origin, nor did the commercial school to which he soon transferred, by asking for *koseki shōhon* only. Around the time he transferred, Jeong's Korean relatives came to Japan, necessitating that he teach them Japanese. Frequently speaking in Korean, Jeong assumed that his teachers and classmates noticed that he was a Korean. Nobody brought it up, however, suggesting that they acted as if visible signs of Jeong's cross-nationality were invisible at least in public. In a way similar to how Pak's teachers quietly allowed her to eat *kimchee*, Jeong's teachers left him alone, without bringing his foreignness to anyone's attention. Jeong felt that at both schools he was treated well, especially by his teachers.[101] Koreans' foreignness and, by extension, their cross-nationality was either visible or invisible in Japan, according to official limits set by the Japanese empire. In their daily lives, however, the line between visibility and invisibility shifted, opening up a space for immigrants to persist in ways that might defy colonial policies.

And yet, Korean students perceived Japanese teachers as merely "good," rarely giving a warmer praise of being "kind."[102] Just as most Japanese Americans assessed their teachers in the United States as "good" but not as "kind" as their Japanese counterparts, Korean students cautiously assessed their encounters with authority. No matter how good teachers might be, they were part of the system that could crush students' opportunities. As Koreans learned of the need to assess either the visibility or invisibility of their cross-nationality, both in their private and public lives, they found little opening for changing the larger structure of inequality. Many days, they could keep it at arm's length. Other days, they were caught by surprise by how precipitous discrimination could be. Although Yi Jougkeun spoke Japanese and went by a Japanese name, he recalled how his foreignness could suddenly be revealed:

> Japanese children were dressed neatly but we were poor and could not dress well. Perhaps this was why some adults could tell at a glance, in a second, that we were Koreans. When I went to my girlfriend's house in the countryside to meet her parents, I was stunned; her mother told her, "He may be Korean."[103]

Yi was unprepared for this, and he wondered if the comment was made because of his clothes or his face. He asked his girlfriend: "Do I have a Korean face?" to which she responded: "Maybe so." Although Yi laughed as he recalled this incident decades later, the sway of the sudden intrusion was palpable.[104] Be it face or dress, what seemed invisible could become suddenly visible.

Equally important, Koreans' fear of visibility was intertwined with a pride that prompted assertions of histories as Korean immigrants. To be sure, they wondered if they were indistinguishable from the Japanese. But they also actively sought to be distinguished as Koreans by the way they ate and spoke, dressing and acting in ways that they believed would advance Koreans' standing in Japan. For instance, after the 1925 law granting Koreans in Japan the right to vote, and especially after voting in Korean letters, *Han'gŭl*, became permissible in 1930, Korean residents began to head to the ballot box in large numbers. In 1932, for instance, *Nagoya shinbun* (Nagoya newspaper) reported: "Korean voters in white clothes have become such a common scene at a polling place."[105] Here, "white clothes" referred to *chŏgori*, plain shirt-like clothes typically worn by Koreans. That they went to polling stations in this distinctively Korean outfit meant that their act of political participation was of a piece with their assertion of cultural belonging.[106] Not only in Osaka, where the number of enfranchised Koreans reached 12,000 in the early 1930s, but also in Hiroshima, Yamaguchi, and Kyoto, where the number remained in the thousands, Korean communities began to enlist candidates of their own. In some cases, Korean candidates made their way into national elections. Some candidates were endorsed by Japanese supporters of assimilation policies, raising questions among some Korean voters about whether they represented Korean interests. Other candidates, however, were Koreans who occupied leadership positions in their communities, such as managers and overseers employed by construction companies. In their campaigns, they often addressed issues of immediate concern for Koreans, including wages, working conditions, and housing.[107]

As the 1930s came to an end and the Pacific theatre of the war opened, Hiroshima and Nagasaki continued to be where not only American but also Korean children negotiated their layered sense of belonging. Simultaneously, their schools, homes, and communities began to unravel. When the total mobilization started, the communities of immigrants and their histories, too, had to be mobilized. Their cross-nationality was questioned in a whole new light.

Navigating Race, Nationality, and Belonging during the War

Japanese Americans continued to arrive in Japan after 1941. Their number was smaller than before, their reasons different than their precursors'. Their coming to Japan was a thorny, lengthy process. Nobody shows this better than Minoru Sumida, who was eight years old when his entire family was forcefully transferred from Honolulu to Yokohama shortly after Pearl Harbor. He explained the ordeal:

> In the evening of the day when "Japs" came [to Pearl Harbor], we were imprisoned. . . . The way it seemed to a child was that we were treated as slaves. They had guns pointed at us. . . . We did not eat dinner that night. We were confined in the Japanese Embassy.[108]

This was only the beginning. The Sumidas had become hostages, to be exchanged with American hostages taken by the Japanese. Throughout the process, the Sumidas were fed well to ensure that they would be exchangeable. But they were completely deprived of light. After boarding a ship in Honolulu, Minoru Sumida did not see the sun rise until he arrived in Los Angeles. The next leg of the trip was on a train, which transported the Sumidas and a dozen other hostages to a prison in Arizona. After a few weeks of confinement, the Sumidas were transferred again, this time to New York. From there, they boarded a ship again, to be taken to Brazil, where the exchange finally occurred. To avoid the active war zones in the Pacific, the hostages then had to go all the way to the Indian Ocean before reaching their destination. By the time he arrived at Yokohama via Singapore, it was already July 1942. His schooling was further delayed because Japanese schools did not start until the following April.[109] Throughout, Sumida's birthright as a Hawaiian-born US citizen did not come up.

Another group of Japanese Americans who came to Japan after 1941 consisted of those who renounced their US citizenship after they were sent to the Nikkei concentration camps in early 1942. More than 2,200 Nikkei, mostly Issei with immediate family ties to Japan, requested repatriation to Japan by the year's end. After the Loyalty Questionnaire was conducted by the War Department and the War Relocation Authority (WRA) in 1943, the number of Nisei who requested expatriation to Japan rose to more than 9,000. Two of the most problematic questions in the questionnaire, questions 27 and 28, asked Nikkei inmates if they were willing to serve in combat duty for the US army, and if they would swear an unqualified allegiance to America and foreswear any allegiance to Japan. The questions provoked fear and confusion. Issei had been long excluded from the right to naturalization as "aliens ineligible for citizenship," so they were concerned that they might become stateless if they renounced their Japanese citizenship.

Nisei, too, feared family separation that might be triggered by renouncing their parents' country of citizenship.[110] By 1944, the number of requests for expatriation or repatriation reached nearly 20,000. Of these, about 4,300 were to be deported to Japan.[111] And of these, 368 individuals were deported before August 1945 under the oversight of the WRA and the Department of State. Given the large number of Japanese in America who hailed from Hiroshima and Nagasaki, an estimated quarter to one-third of the 368, about 100, were in either one of the prefectures by 1945.[112]

These deportees' trips to Japan were as onerous as the hostages'. Julie Kumi Fukuda, for example, recalled her lengthy travels from 1942 to 1944, during which her Issei husband had answered both loyalty questions with a consequential "no":

> I had never been out of California before, until I went to Montana [where I got married in 1942. Then I went to] Manzanar. We went to Arizona to another camp. ... That was Gila. From Gila we went to Poston Camp, an Arizona camp. From there ... by train we went clear across the United States to New York. They picked us up by bus, took us out to the boat, and just like that we sailed. On the *Gripsholm*. It's a Swedish liner, motorship *Gripsholm*. ... From there we went to South America, to Rio de Janeiro. ... And so we went, we would see Java and Sumatra in the distance as we sailed.[113]

The rest of the trip included a stop at Singapore, another at Manila, where her family (which by then included a newborn son) stayed for six months. Her husband worked as an interpreter there, but soon was drafted into the Japanese army. On board a military ship, the Fukudas stopped by Taiwan and, finally, they arrived at Hiroshima in the spring of 1944.

Although she was welcomed by her in-laws who, because of their family connection to the United States, "had like half of it [their house] an American-style," she was not treated in the same way as Japanese Americans were in the 1930s. She noticed, for instance, she was assigned the toughest work:

> We farmed every day. Also I got to get up at five o'clock and would have our *misoshiru* ... and go on, we'd go out and farm, and – oh, and heating the manure, you know. Oh, it was good

thing I was a farmer's daughter. I don't know how I could have survived that. And my sister-in-law's mother and father had an antique shop in Hiroshima city, so they were happy that I was there, because I could farm and their daughter was brought up to be an *ojō-san* [a pampered daughter], so she stayed home and mother-in-law and I worked.[114]

Similar to Nikkei who arrived earlier, Fukuda struggled with unfamiliar things such as *tatami* and *misoshiru* (miso soup). But her remembering did not center on cross-cultural encounters; instead, she mostly remembered work. No longer was there time to reflect on cultural differences.

Japanese Americans' cross-nationality began to affect them in new ways. Setsuko Kohara, born in 1930 in San Fernando, California, came to Japan in 1940. She recalled how she did not want to wear colorful outfits after the war began. The point was to downplay her belonging to America. "I wanted my clothes to be just like everyone else's," said Kohara. In fact, this was a repeat of what her teacher had told her students, so as to make sure that Kohara would not be bullied at school. "My teacher kindly talked to my classmates," recalled Kohara, to say that she was "the same as everyone." After this lecture, "nobody said anything" about Kohara.[115] Although this seemed like a happy ending, the story also conveys how, before being lectured, Japanese students *did* say something about Kohara. This was not an isolated incident. As seen earlier, when May Yamaoka, born in 1929 in Lodi, came to Japan in 1938, her Hawaiian-trained teacher asked her to pronounce English words. But after 1941, such affirmation of cross-nationality ceased to exist. Before, although she was sure that "there were times when they [her classmates] used to laugh at me behind my back," she did not "remember too well about being picked on." Now, with Japan at war against America, her classmates "really started saying *teki, teki*," a Japanese term for "enemy"[116] (see Figure 1.2).

Some of the harassment was based on an idea that Nikkei were untrustworthy, suggesting how they became a target of national hysteria and cultural suspicion on both sides of the Pacific. George Kazuto Saiki, who described his school population as half-Nikkei, remembered frequent fights that erupted between American and Japanese students. The Japanese side taunted their American peers as "Yankees" and "spies."[117] Their nationality made them American, while their race made them look like perfectly disguised spies. This undue characterization, which

Figure 1.2 Jack Motoo Dairiki in the top-left corner of a photo taken at his school in Hiroshima when he was a newcomer. Dairiki felt that he stood out because of his American "plaid jacket" in the sea of Japanese black school uniforms. Jack Motoo Dairiki papers, 1942.

resembled the hostility against Nikkei that culminated in their mass incarceration in the United States in 1942, shaped Tim Nakamoto's remembering about Japan, too. Born in Fresno, California, in 1930 and arriving in Japan as an eleven-year-old just months before Pearl Harbor, Nakamoto experienced extreme difficulty at school. Seeing him struggle with Japanese, his classmates taunted: "Here's a freak guy; he looks like us but can't speak Japanese." They decided that his nickname should be "Merican," a derogatory term for Americans. "Merican," though, was not the only name assigned. Because Nakamoto helped at his uncle's business of making dried-and-pickled *daikon* in Kure, Hiroshima, his "hands were yellow all the time from the ... dye" used for coloring. This prompted his classmates to call him "Yellow Hand," which was not "very complimentary." As Nakamoto summarized, he was both "Yellow Hand and Merican" throughout the war. The irony of this dual-naming is that his uncle catered his *daikon* to the Japanese Navy. The condiment was a luxury, and sailors could enjoy only four slices per day.[118] Nakamoto's yellow hand, then, could be seen as a sign of his loyalty to the Japanese empire. But for his classmates, his nationality was a good enough reason to interpret everything as objectionable.

The layered sense of belonging, once met by gentle curiosity and acceptance in Hiroshima and Nagasaki, became reasons for Nikkei to change or hide their ways. Looking Japanese while being American was not safe or intriguing anymore. Masako Kawasaki, a US survivor born in Japan in 1937, realized how "people who came back from America" stopped speaking in English after 1941. Married to a Sansei born in Watsonville, California, who had narrowly escaped the incarceration by leaving America early in 1941, Kawasaki also learned how Nikkei in Japan at that time were frequently checked on by the military police.[119] Because their belonging to America had been so visible, it was easy for Japanese authorities to come after Nikkei. The older siblings of Saiki were not fluent in Japanese, so they simply began to speak less in public. But their effort to hide their American traits had only limited success. They were seen as possible spies, as monthly visits by the military police made clear shortly after December 1941. The police's primary interest was a short-wave radio, but they also aimed to intimidate. As Saiki recalled, his house "had *tatami* mats on the floor, but they [the police] came in with their shoes on, so as to show their contempt for us."[120] The norm was to take your shoes off when entering a house. Once an unfamiliar Japanese artifact, *tatami* had become this Nikkei family's belonging; it felt close enough for Americans to feel humiliated if not treated in a properly Japanese way.

Although Japanese Americans felt a big change of tide, this did not mean that their belonging to America disappeared. What seemed like weak ties showed their persistence, often at unexpected places. Francis Mitsuo Tomosawa, whom we discussed earlier, was a teenager during the war. One day, he was riding a bicycle that his older brother had brought from Hawai'i. It was a hot day, so Tomosawa was shirtless, wearing only a pair of short pants. When he passed by the police station, he was instantly in trouble. "The police chief came out. He was infuriated because I was wearing shorts and riding an American bicycle. ... He slapped me." Although Tomosawa described the episode as a result of his "child-like carelessness," such persistence of culture could be seen as making a quiet claim of one's national belonging.[121] Tadachi Kohara, too, offered a case in point. A Nisei born in 1930, Kohara as a young boy loved motorbikes. Having taken one with him to Japan, he would not give up his hobby of tinkering with them. This drew the attention of the Japanese police, but Kohara managed not to be caught. He recalled: "The policemen were on a bicycle [that was slower than my motorbike]. They frequently came to my house and made a fuss about my bike, but they really wanted to catch me when I was on it. They could easily tell which one [was mine] on the street because my bike was red."[122] Red was a girl-color in Japan, so a boy on the street on a red motorbike definitely stood out. He had to be an American. Nonetheless, the police could not catch him because he was faster. For a time, Kohara turned Japan's war-business into a cat-and-mouse game.

This kind of resilience was rooted in the persistence of Nikkei communities, familiar sites in the cities of Hiroshima and Nagasaki. In contrast to Japanese Americans on the US West Coast, Nikkei in wartime Japan did not experience a mass uprooting of their belonging to America. It was Nikkei's resourceful use of cross-nationality, as well as the lack of state-sanctioned incarceration, that aided their persistence. Some became streetwise as did Kohara; others learned to find loopholes to protect their rights. Toshiaki Yamashita, born in 1928 near Long Beach, California, was asked to submit proof of his Japanese citizenship when he entered a junior high school. Because of the visibility of Nikkei culture before 1941, his American citizenship by birth had been well known. His Japanese citizenship, in contrast, was not as visible. Although it could be established by his blood and documented by his family record koseki tōhon, it was a matter of private choice, not something publicly exhibited. As discussed earlier, a person's nationality based on family lineage was shown on koseki tōhon, while nationality associated with residency was indicated on koseki shōhon. This was the reason why some Koreans in Japan, such as James Jeong, could exercise a degree of civil rights using koseki shōhon. In Yamashita's case, it was koseki tōhon that was on his side. He submitted this document that showed him alongside his parents, Japanese born in Japan. Instantly, it proved Yamashita's Japanese citizenship, erasing the question about the other – American – belonging. Meanwhile, the documentation of his US citizenship on his US birth certificate remained intact by staying invisible in Japan. Yamashita kept his dual citizenship through the war.[123]

As Yamashita's experience shows, extended families of Japanese Americans played crucial roles in protecting Nikkei from wartime persecution. Compared to the earlier years, ties that connected families cross-nationally became more discreet. Still, there were times when Japanese and Japanese Americans claimed their connections outspokenly. When Kazuko Aoki's father, one of the "people who came back from America" in the late 1920s, became highly critical of Japan, his neighbors rushed to protect him. Knowing America firsthand, Aoki's father fiercely questioned the wisdom of Japan's decision to fight America. "No doubt, Japan will lose," he insisted, during a town hall meeting attended by, among others, the police chief. The chief, along with organizers of the meeting, worried that their neighbor's outspokenness might attract unwanted attention from the military police.[124] Despite everything, they were long-time friends of the Aokis. Izumi Hirano's experience, too, showed the persistence of cross-nationality in Hiroshima. He recalled how, one day at his school, all students from the US mainland and Hawai'i were given an excuse to miss a class. Instead of attending school, they were to go to a lecture given by a Nisei. The lecture was about how there was no reason to be ashamed about being from the United States. "You would not be able to win the war without knowing the enemy," the Nisei man insisted. Thus, "you must feel proud of yourself. Some of you could speak English, and you must think about how to take advantage of it." This overzealous propaganda spurred a strong objection by Issei parents who feared disintegration of the Nikkei community. They cautioned their Nisei children against following the lesson, and students who expressed Japanese patriotism that day came back the following day mute. Only a few pursued a military career at Hirano's school. That Nikkei could speak English did not mean that they were ready to use it to help Japan beat America. In Nikkei's assessment, such use of English would be incompatible with their cross-nationality and Hiroshima's and Nagasaki's histories as cities of immigrants.[125]

Aoki's and Hirano's rememberings illuminate how Nikkei maintained their cross-nationality through the war variously, even as they felt compelled to side with either Japan or America. Many were torn between the two. US treatment of their families and friends across the ocean added a burden to their cross-nationality. The moment the war started, Toshiro Kubota's father began to worry about his friends back in America. "He understood America's segregation, because he had been in the United States," explained the younger Kubota.[126] Although many Nikkei in Japan did not know that their families in America were incarcerated in the camps – the lack of communication made family correspondence impossible – those who did felt it impossible to side with either one of the countries. Born in 1917 in Loomis, California, Yasuko Ogawa had been in Japan since 1921. Partly because she was relatively old by 1941, she recalled the tension provoked by the camp better than most. She heard about the camp from her nephew, who was deported to Japan because he had "refused to serve in the [US] military." (Most likely, this meant that he answered "no" to the 27th question on the loyalty questionnaire, then applied for expatriation. Answering "no" to the question did not warrant deportation.) He told her that her siblings had been imprisoned, and that there were "rumors that they [Nikkei] were tortured in the camps." Since she could not communicate with her brothers and sisters, Ogawa had no way of confirming the rumor and continued to worry about their safety. To further complicate matters, her husband served the Japanese Imperial Army, while her father continued to express his outrage over Japan's "mistake to wage war against such a large, rich country."[127] As her families became split across the ocean, her cross-nationality found little room to breathe.

For many younger Nikkei, the beginning of the war meant the end of the money, clothes, and food that their parents in America had been sending them. Often, this created a resentment among their Japanese guardians. As food shortages worsened in Japan, bitterness intensified. Born in America and immediately sent to Japan in 1930, Miyoko Igarashi's loneliness heightened whenever she thought of her parents back home in the United States. In Japan, she lived with her relatives who constantly reminded her that she was not one of them. Her grandparents were "strict," and her aunt's face turned "stern" when talking to Igarashi. "My parents went [back] to America, abandoning their child. 'Abandon' might sound too blameful, but that's what I thought," said Igarashi.[128] Although Nikkei in Japan might have escaped incarceration, their layered sense of belonging became increasingly stifled in Japan. Children left without parents in effect became stateless. The distinction between cross-nationality and statelessness became ever more slight. As the space for visible expressions of cross-nationality narrowed, it transformed into an invisible statelessness.

Tim Nakamoto, born the same year as Yamamoto and nick-named "Yellow Hand" and "Merican" since 1941, thought that he had nonetheless become a Japanese patriot. Apparently, the wartime propaganda had an effect. But when the US bombing of Japan started, his cross-nationality came back powerfully. Initially, Nakamoto sounded like he was simply recalling an air raid by B-29s:

> Toward the tail end [of the war] there were several large vessels ... anchored ... in ... Kure Bay. And my uncle had a house on a hillside that overlooked the whole bay, so it was just like watching the San Francisco Forty-Niners playing football, you know.... That's where the planes would circle just over my uncle's house, you know, z-zuhh [makes flying noise]. You could see the pilot's face. And three of them just went straight down into that battleship and dropped bombs. The next thing you see are big clouds. When it cleared, just the mast was sticking up. To me that was the most exciting thing that I have ever witnessed in my life.[129]

The interviewer, surprised by Nakamoto's observation that the Kure bombing "was more than the atomic bomb on Hiroshima," asked "which side were you rooting for?" Nakamoto's response revealed a sense of dispossession:

> You know, when people ask me that, it's hard to figure, really, which side I was on. Maybe I wasn't, I don't know. Maybe I was at a point where I didn't care which side, really, because nobody cared for me.[130]

Without a family or community that claimed him on either side of the Pacific, there was nothing for him to feel attached to. This was one way in which cross-nationality shaped Nikkei experiences before they were affected by the bomb.

The number of Koreans who came to Japan after 1941 far exceeded that of Nikkei, prompting an expansion of the cities' Korean communities. For one thing, the expansion meant the influx of Koreans into the existing residential areas designated for Koreans. As James Jeong's remembering has already shown, older immigrants assisted newcomers, helping them to learn language and find employment.[131] Kwak Chae-young, who migrated from Korea to work at a pharmaceutical company in Hiroshima in 1944 because of his former neighbor's enthusiastic recruitment, recalled how women in the old Korean district had frequently fed him. Their kindness made him conclude that the neighborhood was a home away from home.[132] A much larger number of post-1941 migrants, however, found residence outside of the old Korean communities. In 1939, mining and construction industries in Japan began to aggressively recruit Korean laborers. By 1942, the Japanese government reorganized the recruitment system to make it more efficient. The Japanese method of "recruitment" became saturated by blatant deception, intimidation, and coercion, bringing an estimated 1.1 million laborers to Japan proper by 1945. A similar escalation of forced migration occurred in the military. From 1939, a considerable number of Korean laborers were in fact enlisted into the Imperial Amy and Navy, serving as military porters. In 1944, the Japanese government began to conscript Koreans, despite a concern that they were unwilling to join the Japanese military or incapable of understanding Japanese. The desperate shortage of soldiers in the final years of the war pushed Japanese leaders to shed the concern, placing nearly 150,000 Koreans on the war's front. Most laborers, porters, and soldiers were given living quarters apart from the older Korean communities, mostly shacks and bunkhouses hurriedly built near their workplaces. Thus, many, if not most, Korean people in Hiroshima and Nagasaki lived within the city limits where factories and construction sites clustered. The residential areas for Koreans who had come to the cities in the 1920s and 1930s, too, were within the cities' densely populated areas, though their communities had more urban facilities such as restaurants, grocery shops, and clothing stores. Regardless, both of the areas lived in by Koreans were to be most severely affected by the bomb because of their proximity to the hypocenter.[133]

Korean immigrants who came to Japan after the late 1930s were paid (if at all) far less than the Japanese, and they were assigned to the most dangerous work. Safer, less arduous tasks were taken on by Japanese laborers. Korean workers' situations were comparable only to those of American prisoners of war. Kim Tong-il, a Korean *hibakusha* in Korea who had come to the Fukahori shipyard in Nagasaki in 1944, remembered how American prisoners-of-war had been brought to the shipyard along with Korean laborers. Although "Koreans worked alongside with Koreans only" as a rule, American POWs joined a task when "it was the toughest kind." In Kim's assessment, this was because Japanese overseers were afraid of "killing" Koreans by overworking them. By letting Koreans share danger with Americans, the Japanese reduced the chance of losing the Korean workforce.[134]

These encounters between Americans and Koreans were not limited to factories. Francis Mitsuo Tomosawa, for instance, recalled a troubling encounter with Korean students at school. Born in Japan and fluent in Japanese, these Korean students' hostile attitude – they "verbally abused" Tomosawa – at first surprised this Hawaiian boy. Tomosawa had anticipated that he might be teased by Japanese students, but not by Koreans. One day, their bullying seemed ready to escalate into physical violence. A group of Korean students awaited Tomosawa by the school's gate, planning to "knock and kick him down hard." Thanks to his friend who told Tomosawa of their plan, he escaped the grim prospect. Tomosawa went to his teacher, who came out with him and scolded away the Korean students. By considering this incident side-by-side with the bullying of Koreans by the Japanese in the 1930s, it becomes clear that, by the early 1940s, racial and national tensions in the immigrant cities ran unprecedentedly high. The more the Japanese empire attempted to assimilate immigrants by the use of force, the less plausible assimilation became. Discord erupted everywhere, and colonial dissonances became a daily occurrence. Tomosawa observed: Korean students "learned to discriminate because the Japanese government discriminated against them. . . . Because they had been bullied by Japanese kids, they wanted to discriminate against American children."[135] The discord was not conducive for Nikkei children to "take advantage of" their cross-nationality so as to benefit the Japanese empire.

The increasingly aggressive assimilationist treatment of Koreans rendered their hope for liberation all the more urgent. Kim Tong-il took hope in the words of his coworker, who sounded certain that Korea would be freed soon. The man was a newcomer from Chungch'ŏngdo province in Korea, offering Kim much-needed stories of hope from home. Still, Koreans in Japan did not simply sever their belonging to Japan.[136] Kwak Chae-young, for one, received sushi and *mochi* from his Japanese coworkers at the pharmaceutical company, in addition to the meals given by the women in the old Korean neighborhoods. "Kind people were kind," recalled Kwak. "Because of the [Japanese] government's policy, they [my coworkers] thought, we [Koreans] had been taken from a foreign country to work in Japan. . . . Some of my female workers felt sorry for me" and brought him food.

The memory of kindness remained vivid after Kwak went back to Korea after 1945.[137] Pak Namjoo, too, felt torn by her cross-nationality, perhaps more so than Kwak because she stayed in Japan after the war. Her story about her younger brother dying of tuberculosis toward the end of the war involved two contrasting interactions with the Japanese:

> There was nothing we could do for him, so we were waiting for him to die. At that time, we were not allowed to fully light our room.... We were supposed to cover the ceiling light with a black cover [so that American bombers would not locate Japanese houses].... Our light must have been too bright. My parents were watching their son die, and we were crying. Then, they came in, without taking their shoes off. They kicked my father, yelling: "You Korean spy!"[138]

"They" were members of a wartime neighborhood group called *kei-bōdan*, whose responsibilities included ensuring that houses were unlit after dark.

Hearing the noise, another one of Pak's neighbors came to her house:

> Mr. Kiyozaki Masayuki, who used to be the chief of the *kei-bōdan*, came and yelled at them: "This family is facing an emergency, their son is dying. You cannot do what you are doing to them." So they left, without saying a word. [Mr. Kiyozaki] then asked us: "Please forgive them ... it is a time of emergency for them, too."[139]

If Mr. Kiyozaki, also Japanese, had not intervened, "I would have felt resentful and I would have been hurt," said Pak. Nonetheless, the incident became unforgettable. Pak chose to stress how she escaped resentment rather than the resentment itself.[140] For a Korean who was born in Japan and stayed in Japan after the war, a story of resentment could be harder to share than a memory of overcoming it. Equally important, all existing oral histories of Korean and Korean American survivors are conducted by Japanese interviewers. No known collection of Korean remembering recorded by Korean persons is publicly available today, likely limiting the range of cross-nationality that interviewees might express.[141] Perhaps for this reason, too, most Korean *hibakusha*'s remembering joins resentment with attachment, pushing them toward both Japanese and Korean peoples.

Koreans who went to America after the war, too, showed a persistent capacity for cross-nationality. John Hong, as before, felt comradeship with his classmates at the Hiroshima military school. On August 6, 1945, they were getting ready for a trip to Osaka, scheduled to take place later that day. They had completed school, and were to receive graduate training at an iron factory in Osaka. Hong recalled the day in his interview in 1991, in Alameda, California:

> Outside ... I was polishing my shoes. Then, my friends all came out to do their shoes, and I told them, "Leave them there." So I took some pairs, telling them "I can do your shoes, you guys do something else." So with many pairs of shoes, I sat down comfortably and kept on polishing them.[142]

His friends, "all Japanese," thanked Hong for his generosity. Strikingly, this scene of comradeship is what Hong remembered at the moment of the bomb's explosion. Of course, it is possible to see in this story a successful case of Japanese wartime indoctrination, even an embodiment of national betrayal by a Korean. Hong's interviewer was a Japanese American, which might have made him feel that he should say something nice about the Japanese. An American citizen at the time of the interview, Hong's recollection might also be seen as his insistence on cross-nationality as an immigrant. When I met Hong in 2011, he repeated a slightly different version of the same story. The memory lived on for twenty years, side-by-side with the memory of mistreatment by his Japanese classmates.

———◆◆◆———

Taken together, US survivors' memories do not fit the dominant understanding of one nation fighting another, one dropping the bomb from above on the enemy below. But survivors' memories continue to underpin the cities' residents' experiences of the bomb, suggesting that the history of the bomb cannot be separated from the people it immediately affected. If we keep them separate, we risk perpetuating a myth that Americans used the bomb to attack the Japanese. The people under the mushroom cloud included those who did not belong to a single state – those who possessed a layered sense of belonging that persisted through the war. Americans continued to express their cross-nationality through language, diet, and habits well into the 1940s. By making their cultural heritage visible and invisible inventively, Koreans in Japan kept ties to Korean culture at the same time as they adopted certain Japanese ways. Their cross-national ties were not strong in the sense of influencing political or military decisions made by nation states. These ties did not change racist and nationalist policies, either. But this does not mean that the layered belonging in Hiroshima and Nagasaki deserves a continuing neglect in history. Indeed, convergence, as well as conflict, between cultures may be seen as a fact about any population that nuclear weapons destroy. As the next chapter shows, nuclear weapons did not obliterate the history of immigration in the cities, either. Instead, the bomb brought the strength of weak ties into sharp focus, making it a both uniquely and universally remarkable experience for US *hibakusha*.

2 REMEMBERING THE NUCLEAR HOLOCAUST

US survivors have uttered countless words about the nuclear holocaust. In their oral histories, many recounted the incident eagerly, resolving to tell it as accurately and completely as they could. To forget to say something – names of their family members who had perished – was to do injustice to them. To tell all intimate details of unprecedented injuries with utmost clarity, too, was *hibakusha*'s compulsion.[1] They seemed to say: *You may not believe it, but this happened to me.* For some US survivors, remembering was a kind of obligation that they had taken upon themselves by giving lectures or public testimonials. For the rest, their oral history interviews were one of the first occasions to speak about their experiences with someone outside their circles. Despite their determination to recount events, nuclear death and destruction are not easy subjects. Often, survivors were at a loss for words at the cruelty of the words they had just uttered. A handful of American *hibakusha* refused to recall certain images or moments by flatly saying: *I do not want to remember this. Please excuse me for not telling.* Their speech and silence about what happened on the ground at Hiroshima and Nagasaki are revealing of their identities as survivors. To those of us who are not survivors, ways in which *hibakusha* recount the nuclear destruction become part of what little we can know about them. Memories wane and wax, but they do not go away. The identity of a survivor shifts and glows by breathing in this movement. At the same time, survivors' recollections (or refusals to recollect) remind us of a vast distance between the teller and the listener, by shedding fleeting light on the impossibility of fully knowing or remembering what *hibakusha* experienced in 1945.

Keeping an eye on both speech and silence, I recapture some of American survivors' experiences in an attempt to continue to trace the counter-memory of the bomb.[2] Building on their cross-national experiences as immigrants discussed in Chapter 1, I explore how Nikkei's layered sense of belonging to Japan and America (and in the case of Korean Americans, to Korea and Japan as of 1945) continued to shape their remembering of the explosion, destruction, and death. Simultaneously, I illuminate some of the most common, yet underexplored, aspects of the *hibakusha*'s experiences on the ground in Hiroshima and Nagasaki, by considering memories of bodies, clothes, medicines, care, water, and food. It is a cultural history of the nuclear holocaust that stays close to survivors' remembering. It is a history that exposes the mass, indiscriminate nature of the bomb by showing memories marked by both uniqueness and universality. Japanese American and Korean American survivors experienced the bomb's effects along with other survivors. At the same time, the cross-national meanings they found in these universal experiences reveal a striking uniqueness. Their burns were no different from Japanese or Korean survivors'. In most cases, they treated injuries in the same way as did everyone else. And yet, some American survivors felt as if they had more (or, in some cases, fewer) resources than Japanese *hibakusha* because of their cross-nationality. US survivors escaped, rescued, and survived just as others did after the bomb's explosion. There were fires to run away from, rivers to be crossed, and loved ones to be found. The meanings Americans attached to each step, though, often differed from those typically found by Japanese or Korean survivors. Sometimes, universality and uniqueness stood in sharp contrast; other times they merged together, as if to mirror the sweeping power of nuclear destruction that turned everyone alive on the ground universally into survivors regardless of their individual uniqueness.

The convergence of and contrast between uniqueness and universality in US survivors' remembering reveal a history that ran counter to national memories and commemorations that proliferated in Japan, the United States, and South Korea after the war. In fact, the cross-national history of US survivors suggests that memories bound by national interests offer only a limited path toward understanding the nuclear destruction and its indiscriminate ways. Many studies that highlight these nation-bound memories either assume or imply that all or most survivors were part of Japan's national polity, culture, and body.[3] These studies have rarely discussed non-Japanese victims whose number in the best estimate reached more than one in ten. A few studies that have analyzed non-Japanese *hibakusha* tend to separate them into different groups based on their nationality. None has fully focused on the coexistence and convergence of multiple national belongings and cultural affinities in survivors' remembering of the nuclear destruction.[4] To show that they included not only Japanese but also Koreans, Chinese, and Americans is one important way of illuminating the uncontainable force of nuclear weapons. Still, placing survivors in groups based on nationality, ethnicity, or race tends to highlight the distinctiveness of different groups of *hibakusha* while downplaying commonality among them and multiplicity within a given group. As a group whose history has been fundamentally shaped by Hiroshima and Nagasaki as cities of immigrants, US survivors' remembering brings to light the limits of categories based on citizenship, national loyalty, and cultural belonging in our understanding of nuclear destruction and its human costs. If we follow the path of US *hibakusha*'s remembering and see these categories through the lens of the history of immigration, they appear to be as fictional as they were real at ground zero.

I follow a loosely chronological order in my exploration, although an occasional back and forth in time is inevitable to show ways in which American survivors made sense of certain times, locations, and incidents. Beginning with the days before the bomb's explosion, I first examine how US survivors recalled the destruction of the two cities, often with a distinctively cross-national accent. I look at how this accent shaped US survivors' remembering of their escaping and rescuing. Next, I examine their bodies and clothes as they were fused together with foreign objects such as glass, soil, and heat in the bomb's aftermath. The third section is devoted to an analysis of medicine and care that survivors devised in the hours and days after the explosion. The last section examines water and food in US *hibakusha*'s remembering of ground zero. In my analysis of survivors' stories, three major trajectories of the nuclear holocaust's meanings emerge. First, the bomb was remembered as causing devastation common to all, regardless of their nationality, age, class, or gender. All the differences that normally separate individuals from one another appeared to be erased momentarily. And yet, shortly after survivors found each other, these categories came back powerfully. In some cases, survivors sought to express these differences as if to remind themselves of who they had been before the bomb. In other instances, survivors were reminded of these categories of difference by others who were shaken by survivors' seeming otherworldliness. Because American *hibakusha*'s national and cultural belonging prior to the bomb had been layered, what they regained after the explosion, too, was compound.

Secondly, survivors' remembering points to a particular significance of gender as a source of cross-nationality that came back after the bomb. Regardless of their nationality at the time of the bombing, many American *hibakusha* experienced the nuclear attack as an eraser of their gender. They felt that their identity as men or women was shattered by the bomb, and they made whatever effort they could to regain it. This was particularly true of older survivors, while younger ones remembered how adults struggled to act in distinctively gendered ways. Men felt as if it was their duty to rescue others at any cost, while women were expected to mobilize womanly resources to save their families. In this light, it is important to note that it was indeed mostly women who crafted medicine and offered care to the dying, ill, and injured. Using what little resources were left behind – tea, oil, vegetables, herbs, bones, and ashes – women became improvisational practitioners of folk medicine. To remember the care and treatment that women imparted was one of the most empowering actions that US survivors took many years later. Men's gender identity, too, took a particular shape. Despite their desire to protect families and communities in the bomb's aftermath, their resources were severely limited. How men might come to terms with their inability to protect without losing their sense of self-worth, then, became a central concern in 1945, as it did decades later.

The nuclear destruction may be seen as the beginning of a new gender awareness for both women and men, which in turn may explain the relative lack of gender in US survivors' remembering of times before the bomb. To be sure, as seen in Chapter 1, many of them were children in the 1920s and 1930s, making it unlikely that a clearly defined gender would play a central role in their remembering. Nonetheless, those who were still children in 1945, as well as those who were reaching their early twenties, noted things related to gender more frequently in their recollections of the bomb's immediate aftermath. Before the bomb, their gendered memories were about food cooked by mothers, clothes worn by boys or girls. Their remembering about times after the bomb, however, became more filled with acts and aspirations framed by distinct ideals of femininity and masculinity. It appears as if the bomb marked the end of childhood, as well as the beginning of their identity as survivors. Part of this identity was markedly gendered, signaling the coming of adulthood albeit at a young age for many. It is also likely that gendering the bomb added a universal tone to their remembering, making their experiences listenable to non-survivors. Consciously or not, *hibakusha* might have sought a way to be heard by recalling themselves as men and women who were, it was assumed, like everyone else.

Thirdly, I illuminate how the shifting ground of identity that emerged after the bomb's explosion created a realm of the unspeakable in American *hibakusha*'s remembering. Although survivors of any nationality might face the unspeakability of the nuclear holocaust, American survivors are distinct in that their layered sense of belonging unequivocally marked their experiences on the ground. The destruction's universality and its utter obliviousness to the uniqueness of the destroyed powerfully shaped things that cannot be recounted in US survivors' remembering. Often, conspicuous silence took shape in the midst of their remembering, although I found no silence that was merely empty. When and how it descended pointed to what was remembered but could not be spoken. Sometimes, the tension between speech and silence followed a trajectory similar to that of the visibility and invisibility discussed in Chapter 1. Cross-national experiences were difficult to speak, as much as they were to show. In a larger sense, though, unspeakable things that emerged after the bomb were unprecedented and unique. Arising out of a survival that shifted the meaning of life and death, things that US survivors did not speak became inseparably entwined with things that they did speak in their remembering. The coexistence of speech and silence, I argue, offered a structure to the counter-memory of the bomb. As later chapters reveal, the counter-memory of the bomb stayed largely private in the 1950s and much of the 1960s, while the following decades witnessed a conscious revelation of the memory in public. In this light, the immediacy of ground zero, recounted both in silence and speech by US *hibakusha*, signified the beginnings of their memory and identity, which in turn shaped the bomb's meanings in the margins of mainstream history.

Survive, Escape, and Rescue

US survivors' remembering of the bomb often started with the airplane that had dropped it, so it seems appropriate for us, too, to begin with the B-29 as we reach out to meanings of the nuclear destruction. In America's public memory of the war, the airplane has symbolized the technological advancement that led to a victory, an embodiment of national pride. In Japanese memory, in contrast, the aircraft seems to stay in the sky, a remote, dutiful yet emotionless carrier of the weapon that caused a national tragedy.[5] If we consider Hiroshima and Nagasaki as cities of immigrants as shown in Chapter 1, though, it is hardly surprising that the airplane provoked an entirely different set of meanings for many on the ground. Nikkei, for one, saw the planes not only from below but also at the same height as the aircraft. Given their attachment to American things, it was unsurprising that these airplanes embodied what they meant for the United States, as well as what they meant for people in Japanese cities. Often told unthinkingly yet with striking immediacy, US survivors' oral histories trace the beginning of the mass destruction in cross-national contexts.

By the summer of 1945, the B-29 was a familiar figure for many in Japan. Major cities such as Tokyo, Osaka, and Kobe had been heavily pummeled by incendiary bombs rolled out of the aircrafts' distinctively silver bodies. Because the bomber excelled in low-altitude aviation, many in these cities remembered how they could see the pilots' faces when running away from bullets raining down on them. For those in Hiroshima, however, the aircraft was a relatively benign figure, having flown high over the sky many times but hardly engaging in attacks from low altitudes. Not only Americans, but also the Japanese and Koreans familiar with the presence of Americans in the city, considered the aircraft's apparent lack of interest in bombing Hiroshima a proof of US awareness about its citizens there. Some Americans in wartime Japan knew that their families and relatives in the United States had been incarcerated. And yet, this fact did not necessarily lead them to believe that their country was ready to bomb its own citizens and their family members. For fifteen-year-old Haakai Nagano, the airplane was a constant presence but held no further meaning. He recalled how "during the last part of the war ... getting closer [to the end], and we could see the B-29s flying ... you see the B-29[s]. I don't know, hundreds, but there were a lot of them. But they never dropped the bomb. So you feel like there was just a bunch of planes flying out there."[6] The planes did not threaten to kill, although it was of course clear that they were from America. So it was that the airplane provoked a childhood memory for eight-year-old Katie Yanagawa from Washington state. She recalled: "Since our location was [near] Seattle, and there is a Boeing [factory] right in Seattle, we used to drive back and forth from Eatonville or Tacoma to Seattle, and were able to see all of these impressive aircrafts – B-29s and whatever. So Father knew that the war was coming." In fact, Yanagawa's father continued to insist throughout the war that "there was no way that Japan was able to win." This was "because he saw all of those resources in the United States before he left."[7] For Yanagawa, then, the B-29 was a reminder of both her belonging to her home country of America and the inability of her adopted country of Japan to measure up.

Fourteen-year-old Hayami Fukino described the B-29 in even more intimate terms. Like Nagano, Fukino did not feel afraid of the airplane. In fact, she used to think: "'Oh, yeah, they're from America!' ... [They are] part of me, you know. My friend."[8] Kazue Suyeishi, born in 1927 in Pasadena, California, and coming to Japan immediately thereafter, felt equally attached to the airplane, secretly nicknaming it an "angel." The way it flew was "so beautiful. It was silver-colored, and it looked like an angel in a beautiful costume dancing in the blue sky. I did not have any adverse feeling to it. I actually longed for it."[9] Such fondness for the US bombers was likely rare in wartime Japan. But the feeling that drew Nikkei close to America in fact coexisted with a sense or acts of belonging to Japan. Fukino had been participating in *teishintai*, Japanese girls' army corps. By 1945, she was working at a paint factory in Hiroshima, which made dryers for the Japanese Imperial Army's airplanes. Suyeishi, too, had been in the girls' army corps, although she happened to be off duty and at home on August 6, 1945, because of a fever. The B-29 on that day did not seem much different than usual, gliding high and quiet in Hiroshima's blue summer sky. Many went outside to watch the airplane, some even with a telescope in hand.[10] Suyeishi, too, stepped outside. A few moments after she greeted the "angel" with a silent "Good Morning!" Suyeishi felt her body flying. She landed across the street, in front of her neighbor's house and under the roof that came down on her.[11]

Some remembered a flash of bright white light. Others recalled seeing many colors such as blue, red, pink, yellow at the moment of the explosion.[12] What they recollected almost uniformly, though, was the monotonous, black-and-grey scenery that emerged in the bomb's aftermath.[13] Most thought that the explosion was an incendiary bomb or some sort of accident, but none of course understood that it was a special bomb. Everything was burnt and black, be it a building, tree, horse, or person. Things that escaped heat and fire still turned black, covered by ash or the "black rain."[14] In addition, everything was on the ground, transforming the city to a vastly flat space. People remembered being able to see all the way to the sea because there was nothing to block the view. For a moment, it was very quiet, with no one making any sound or uttering any word. In this strangely transformed world, a few things caught American *hibakusha*'s attention. Julie Kumi Fukuda heard "something funny," which turned out to be the mushroom cloud. It was the only thing yielding any color or sound: "... the best way I could describe it as I recall it was like it was a red smoke, and it was whirling around like a whirlwind. It was making such a NOISE. This is why I noticed it. And I thought: Wow, that was a great ball of firelight. And so I thought: If that falls on me, I'll really be burned." Although the whirlwind did not fall on Fukuda, she still was struck by "the heat [that] was so intense." She wondered if she was "burned to a crisp" or about to be. Reaching high temperatures, the air did not feel like the natural surrounding it used to be.[15]

Twelve-year-old George Kazuto Saiki remembered one thing that remained standing: a sewing machine that his family had brought back from Hawai'i in 1939, an old-fashioned, sturdy model made in America by Singer. About three-feet high like a little desk, it was "still standing, mysteriously." The only difference was that it was about twenty feet away from where it had been.[16] In the post-nuclear explosion's ground, implausible sights emerged anew, while familiar things were suddenly placed in unfamiliar surroundings. Changes were everywhere – in the sky, air, on the ground.

Katie Yanagawa's Singer sewing machine was not to be found where it had been, either. Ordered by mail in 1939 and coming to Japan for the first time in 1941 together with her family, on that day in 1945, the machine was found by the main entryway of her collapsed house in Hiroshima. Her father "spotted this Singer," Yanagawa recalled, "wooden portable, sewing machine sitting there." Not knowing where to put it, he "left it right by the hedge" outside the house, greenery that soon "burned down to the ground" when the house caught on fire.

Similar to how Saiki's remembering connected times before and after the bomb through a home appliance, Yanagawa's recollection of the bomb followed a small yet sturdy machine's whereabouts. It was her way of making sense of things familiar and unfamiliar, abruptly thrown together. The "machine caught on fire, but only charred the outside, and the inside is perfect," recalled Yanagawa. Then, her remembering freely stretched into the present: "I am still using that." Returning to the United States in 1953, she took the surviving machine with her. Now, she was considering if she could donate the machine to the Singer Sewing Machine Company. She felt sure that "this means a lot to them," evidently because the history of the machine meant a lot to her.[17]

Such elasticity of time in survivors' remembering was not unusual. Hayami Fukino, too, connected times in America and Japan early on, then linked them together with the present moment of remembering in the United States. Similar to Kazue Suyeishi, Fukino was blown off her feet, though in her case it was into a closet. She had to hurry out because the house was on fire. Then, something remarkable happened. As she left, she took only one thing with her, a blanket. "And that blanket . . . was the one that . . . [her family] took from America." In fact, it carried a very special meaning for her family, because her father had once used it to show hospitality when he was hosting an important visitor from Japan, a Buddhist monk, in 1929. Her father had put it on the backseat of his brand-new American car, so as to make sure that the guest felt comfortable. It turned out, then, that the blanket fulfilled another significant mission, this time at Hiroshima's ground zero. On their escape, Fukino's family had to cross a river at high tide. It was a struggle to climb onto the other shore, because it was hedged by a tall stone wall. The family managed to get over it, but there were many others still struggling in the river. So her father took out the blanket, and according to Fukino, "we used the blanket, so we saved lots of people. So that they could get up. That's the only thing I can remember."[18]

Although this was the only episode that Fukino could remember about her escape, the story did not come without hesitation. She talked easily about how she took the blanket, but then she wondered "if I should tell you this" before she went on to reveal the history that stretched back to her childhood in the United States. The reason for her hesitation might have been her modesty; she might have felt that the episode was too personal to share. She also might have been reluctant because she was struck by the unusual cross-nationality of this story. It did not fit into an oft-told national memory, whether in Japan or America. She did not know if her interviewer was invested in either or, if so, which. *Your American blanket saved Japanese people?* The question could lead to suspicion about Fukino's belonging, perhaps even her loyalty, in her interviewer's mind. Questions similar to this one frequently had this effect in wartime Japan and America. In this light, Fukino had reason to be cautious if she was to share the episode. Although a long time has passed since 1945, it would not hurt if she used caution when remembering things that could invite unwanted inquiries. The universal story of escaping was easier to tell, while a more unique history of the cross-national blanket might remain untold because of past tensions finding ways into the present remembering.

Fukino's hesitance revealed only one of many relationships that formed between silence and speech in US survivors' recollections. In some cases, cross-national experiences were such ordinary elements of US survivors' remembering that it appeared as if they did not even think to tell about them until repeatedly prompted. So it was with Masako B. Hamada, who came to Japan as a twelve-year-old in 1933. At one point during my interview with her, she explained how she had passed out after the bomb's explosion, and how she had remained unconscious until after her friend brought her to an air-raid shelter. But she needed some prodding before she acknowledged that her friend was also an American:

HAMADA: ... when I woke up ... they put me – my girlfriend put me in, in the cave, you know, uh, *bōkūgō* [air-raid shelter]?
WAKE: Right, right. ... Was it, was it your Nisei friend? When you say "girlfriend"?
HAMADA: Yeah, my group of friends. ... Sewing ... sewing friend.
WAKE: Right, okay. ... And then she was also a Nisei?
HAMADA: Y-yeah.
WAKE: Okay.
HAMADA: She's from Hawai'i.[19]

It was more important for Hamada to say that the friend was from the sewing school that she had attended in Japan than to acknowledge that the friend was also a second generation American. Earlier in the interview, Hamada had already told me that there had been many Nisei girls at her school in Hiroshima, so that was the reason why I asked. Unlike Fukino, Hamada did not show any hesitation in revealing her cross-national memory from the beginning of her oral history. By the time she was telling the story of rescue, it seemed as if she expected me to assume that the friend in question was an American. "My group of friends," including a girl who rescued Hamada, of course were Nisei. Unlike Fukino, who evidently hesitated to tell a cross-national history, then, Hamada expected me to know better. Clearly, it was *her* memory of the bomb before it was a cross-national memory as I saw it. It was I, not her, who was stunned by the image of Americans rescuing each other in Japan's post-nuclear holocaust landscape. *Of course, we were there.* She seemed to say. *Why do you even ask?*

Silence, then, could carry a range of meanings, including both hesitance and forthrightness. This also rang true in Korean American survivors' remembering. James Jeong offers a vivid example of how speech and silence might even converge to disclose a cross-nationality in an American *hibakusha*'s remembering. As discussed in Chapter 1, he was a Japanese-born Korean, twenty years old in 1945 and working for his older brother's company in Hiroshima. During my interview with him, Jeong abruptly began a story about how he helped a daughter of his high school principal in Hiroshima. "Ah, she was heavy!" exclaimed Jeong, with no context. Not understanding who this woman was and why he was talking about her, I followed up with questions. Gradually, it became clear that he was remembering a woman whom he had rescued immediately after the bomb's explosion. And yet, when I asked him to further explain what happened, he was reluctant to tell anything specific. "Where were you on the morning of August 6?" I asked, only to receive in response, "Yes, there really were so many terrible things." Clearly, he was hesitant, although he also wanted to tell the story of the woman. After some back and forth, reasons for his urge to speak the unspeakable began to emerge. To remember the woman was to bring back both pain and pride that Jeong felt as a Korean man. Moments after the bomb's explosion, Jeong found himself under a heavy wooden fence that had fallen on him. His back might have been broken. Soon after he crawled out, someone approached him to ask for help. Jeong described the incident:

> She said, "Excuse me, could you please help me? I am the daughter of the high school principal." Of course, a rich girl like her could not have known me, a Korea-boy, so I figured that she had mistaken me for somebody else. ... Regardless, I took her to a shrine.[20]

He went on to explain how he had helped not only her but also her father. She was severely burnt and could not sit down on a trailer that Jeong had found to carry her. So, her father held her to lift up her body, and Jeong carried them both, together, to a shrine nearby where many refugees congregated. Thanks to Jeong's assistance, the father and the daughter survived. Only after ensuring their safety, Jeong headed home where he was reunited with his worried father.

The heroic story carried darker meanings, which were cross-national as much as gendered. As shown by his use of the derogatory term "Korea-boy," Jeong was keenly aware of his precarious status as a Korean man in Japan at the time. The term suggested that not only his nationality, but also his manliness, had not measured up. It still came as a shock, though, when his father told him not to speak to the woman afterward. According to Jeong's father, "It is not an honor for a Japanese girl [to be rescued by a Korean man], so do not say a word about what happened unless they come to thank you. . . . Especially for an unmarried woman, there is nothing good to be said about getting to be known as a survivor." If Jeong went to check on them, the woman's reputation could be compromised not only because of her survivorhood but also her tie to a Korean man. Still dubious, Jeong waited for the father and the daughter to come to thank him. Such a visit would have been completely expected between Japanese families. But it never happened, prompting Jeong's father to say: "Here we go, just as I told you. Be kind and keep the secret of *those people*" by not revealing their survivorhood. Spurring his sarcasm was Jeong's father's pride as a Korean generous enough to shield his thankless rulers from disgrace. The "secret" of the Japanese, however, came to haunt Jeong long after the war, after he migrated to the United States, because of his marriage to a Nisei woman. His injury did not completely heal, which brought the woman back to his memory: "My back still hurts because she was plump. Even her father was kind of chubby!" he said. He also mentioned how his friend, a Nikkei man, had been urging him to get a certificate of survivorhood issued by the Japanese government. The certificate could offer him access to free medical care and monetary allowances that the Japanese government began to offer Japanese survivors in the 1950s and 1960s. But to obtain the certificate, he would need two witnesses to prove his presence in the city as of August 1945. Jeong thought of finding the woman and asking her to serve as a witness; still, he was reluctant. "I don't talk about the bomb, especially about women survivors," said Jeong. "She would be disgraced if it became known that she was a survivor." Now, Jeong was talking as if he were his father more than sixty years ago. Jeong of course understood that the woman, if alive, would be nearly eighty years old. Her survivorhood would not affect her chances for reproduction or marriage. His reluctance to have her be a witness, then, was not driven by a practical concern about her. Instead, he was driven by his self-respect, hurt by being unacknowledged by the Japanese and hardly repaired by remaining silent. As of 2010, the hurt was still palpable, the need to keep the repair urgent. As both a Korean and a man, he would continue to protect a reputation of a Japanese woman. In this way, he could stay on a morally higher ground. This act of self-respect, though, brought back to his mind Japan's gendered racism against Korean men, which continued to disadvantage him by barring him from the possibility of applying for a certificate.[21] To pursue the possibility, he would have to give up his role as a Korean man guarding a Japanese woman. The pain and pride that arose out of Jeong's cross-national experience were entangled with his gender identity.

Jeong's silence was burdened by his urge to speak, even as his speech was frequently fused with his desire to not attempt the unspeakable. This dynamism might not have revealed itself if he were not being interviewed by a Japanese national in the United States. I am also a woman, someone he could have easily placed in a similar category as his school principal's daughter. Remembering knows little boundary between then and now, connecting seemingly unrelated dots like a flash of light. His inclination to speak about the most universally known effect of the bomb – that it caused terrible things – only might convey his cautiousness about his listener, brought to the fore by the linkage across time made by the act of remembering. Similar to the way that Hayami Fukino was reluctant to tell the cross-national history of her blanket, Jeong might have hesitated because he was afraid of offending his listener's national loyalty, race, and gender identity. As the interviewer, I wanted to believe that my questions gradually made it clear to him that I could hear stories of Japanese racism against Koreans; I wanted to tell myself that this revelation explained why he eventually told me the difficult story of the rescue. Clearly, both the interviewer and the interviewee were Asian residents of America, aware that racism has been our common enemy regardless of great differences between the histories of Korean and Japanese peoples. But the fact may be that, simply, my family name did most of the persuading. My name is unusual for Japanese, as it sounds a bit Korean. Toward the end of the interview, Jeong asked me about my family name. When I answered that it most likely came from a man who had migrated from the Korean Peninsula to Japan many centuries ago, his response was enthusiastic: "I thought so!" Then, he went on to talk in great length, animatedly, about how Korean and Japanese peoples had been one and the same in ancient times. If only this were still true, there would be no need for a "Korea-boy." Or, there would at least be no need for Jeong to feel shy about revealing the name-calling. Gradually, I began to wonder if my national belonging throughout our time together appeared to him more uncertain, layered, than I had ever imagined. It might be that, as Jeong carefully assessed my identity during the interview, the balance between silence and speech shifted. When he finally spoke, his manhood, nationality, and race, diminished by the Japanese empire and further damaged by the American bomb, came back with lucidity. As someone who might have a family connection to Korea, his interviewer might be able to lend understanding ears to such a story.

US survivors remembered cross-national artifacts and experiences dear to their histories as immigrants. These histories, often provoked by American objects in the Japanese landscape, ranging from an airplane to a blanket, shaped their narratives of survival, escaping, and rescuing. Cross-nationality shaped remembering about ground zero by Koreans in Japan, too, showing the striking entanglement among gender, race, and nationality. These narratives in turn reminded US *hibakusha* of who they had been before the bomb, creating a counter-memory that resists a singular, nation-based definition of the meaning of Hiroshima and Nagasaki.

Body, Clothes, and Foreign Objects

The nuclear bombs developed by the United States after 1945 were many times more powerful than those dropped on Hiroshima and Nagasaki. I often think about this well-known fact. One of its implications might be that any future nuclear war would destroy more than one country, in effect making all of us survivors of a nuclear holocaust regardless of our nationality.[22] But what about the meaning of such a comparison between weapons now and then for survivors of Hiroshima and Nagasaki? Does the comparison make them think that the older weapons they confronted were less capable of mass, indiscriminate killing? In this regard, it is notable that some US *hibakusha* expressed a concern about more recent, powerful bombs and their capacity to ruin the world. Equally notable, though, is that such sentiment was revealed almost invariably toward the end of the oral history. When US survivors discussed *their* bomb and its effect on *them* in the midst of their interviews, virtually no one said anything that compared 1945 and thereafter. Instead, they told of strange things that had happened to their bodies and clothes. Stripped of normal clothes, unfamiliar-looking burns and cuts were harshly exposed. Humans did not seem like human beings anymore. Such was the common experience on the ground, prompting them to use whatever means were available to restore a semblance of normalcy. Similar to their memories of escaping and rescuing, US survivors' remembering of their transformed bodies was also accentuated by cross-nationality. In some cases, bodies marked by items of clothing brought from the United States became one of the most distinctively remembered aspects of US *hibakusha*'s experiences. Their bodies, literally fused with foreign objects by the bomb's force, become for us a pathway toward understanding the meaning of the coexistence of universality and uniqueness on the ground. In this light, the contradictory essence of the 1945 bombings comes to the forefront of our view of ground zero. Individual uniqueness was there, expressed in their memories marked by a range of cross-national experiences as immigrants. And yet, the bomb's force had universal effect, destroying Americans, Koreans, and Japanese alike. The convergence, as well as the contrast, between uniqueness and universality was intrinsic to the use of nuclear weapons in the modern world; their blanket power of destruction relies on nation states' disregard for people who move, live, and connect. The magnitude of the bomb recalled by US survivors suggests that a nuclear holocaust did not require a bomb a thousand times more destructive than "Fat Man" or "Little Boy." These weapons were powerful enough to nullify a comparison between the past and present, and to define all of us in the post-1945 world as survivors regardless of our nationalities.

John Hong, a Korean American survivor who, as discussed in Chapter 1, was a student at Japan's Imperial Army Weapons School in 1945, decided to run after he saw the flash. He dashed out of his classroom and darted down the hallway. To his right were classrooms, to his left were windows facing the city of Hiroshima. After a while, he noticed that his view was blocked by "water" dripping over his eyes. The water turned out to be his blood, which he did not realize because he felt absolutely no pain. In fact, though, his face and chest were covered by pieces of glass.[23] Such an unexpected, nearly inconceivable merging of a human body and foreign objects struck many as worth telling, attesting to the extraordinary time. Izumi Hirano, born in Hawai'i in 1929 and coming to Japan in 1933, was stunned to see a piece of glass deeply embedded in his father's chest. And yet, his father had walked from his house to a nearby air-raid shelter to see if his wife and children were there. Finding no one, he turned around and came back home. There, he was reunited with the family. Seconds later, he collapsed, his breaths visibly leaking from his lung. The injury was so implausible that he put it aside until he regained human contact.[24] For Joyce Ikuko Moriwaki, born in Japan and coming to Hawai'i after the war because of her marriage to a Nisei survivor, the foreign object was dirt. As she recalled, her grandfather was living in an old-fashioned, Japanese style house with walls made of mud. Although he was fortunate enough to survive the blast, his body was covered by pieces of dirt released by the wall's violent collapse. These pieces stayed so firmly affixed to his skin that Moriwaki could still spot them when she, who had been three years old in 1945, became old enough to remember them. For years, no one succeeded in removing the dirt from his skin.[25]

Fathers, mothers, sons, and daughters were stunned by burns, blood, and swellings that distorted their faces. Many had to call each other's names to confirm who they were, and some could not help saying that a loved one looked like a ghost.[26] Some refrained from commenting on their transformed looks, only to have others cry out. An eight-year-old in 1945, Masako Kawasaki recalled the severe burns that completely altered her younger brother's face. Nobody said anything about it for a long time, but a neighbor who had seen her family right after the bomb remembered it later: "His face looked like a baked potato. It was so blackened that it looked like it had been cooked on an open fire." Recalling this, Kawasaki seemed to feel both upset and impressed by the comment. "It was such a shrewd expression!" she exclaimed.[27] Born in 1931 in Japan, Kazuko Aoki was struck by the incredible patterns she found in burns. These patterns were made by *kasuri*, a fabric motif commonly used for *monpe*, Japanese wartime clothes worn by civilians. The *kasuri* motif consisted of various black and white segments. Black parts were burned into the wearer's skin, while white parts remained unfused. The remaining pieces of fabric hung from the body as if they were some sort of rags on display.[28] It was not clear if those wearing *kasuri* were better off than people wearing black only, although perhaps they were, according to Hawaiian-born Minoru Sumida. He remembered how people in wartime Japan refrained from wearing white clothes. White stood out too much for US bombers looking for a target. Many white or light-colored clothes were dyed black, gray, or dark navy. Although such precaution might have saved some from incendiary bombs or bullets, black clothes became something of a curse in the bomb's aftermath. The difference between old weapons and this new one was not missed by people on the ground, although they were yet to learn that the latter was nuclear. Sumida recalled how everyone, including "women, was naked after being burned by that flash." Some "were burned so severe that their arms seemed twice as long," because their arms' skin sagged down from their fingertips. These arms belonged to those who had chosen a dark shirt for the day. The more cautious they were, the more damage they suffered.[29]

It is notable that, in Sumida's recollection, it was skin, the surface, that transformed people's bodies and, by extension, the city's landscape. In the chaotic, immediate aftermath of the bomb, people were struck by visible signs of annihilation rather than invisible measures of contamination. What was visible then could lead to invisibility now, however. Like Sumida, Toshiaki Yamashita remembered seeing a type of burn that caused a person's facial skin to hang down from the chin. After explaining this, Yamashita recoiled from the image: "Well, I don't want to talk about this kind of thing." His hesitance seemed to bear both his and his listener's dread, suggesting earlier times when dread had stifled his recounting. Certainly, this was not the only time when "this kind of thing" that *we* find difficult to hear silenced survivors. As images of catastrophe took shape and became visible in remembering, the tellers fell speechless. The listeners, too, had no choice but to fall silent.[30] I wonder if this dynamism is one of the reasons why survivors' bodies have found a surprisingly limited space in the historical inquiry into the bomb. After briefly describing injuries, most scholars have steered readers to survivors' testimony in John Hersey's *Hiroshima* or Robert J. Lifton's *Death in Life* published a long time ago. Whether from respect, fear, or both, we have collectively recoiled from finding historical meanings in people's profoundly damaged bodies. Seeing their images or reading disturbing words about them, we have told ourselves that we already understood. But there are rich histories to be found in the immediacy of bodies.

Survivors' bodies were so drastically altered that they prompted sheer astonishment as well as an urge to bring back any sense of normalcy. When Kazue Kawasaki's younger sister crawled out of her house, she thought everyone had turned into "Americans." This was because everybody's hair was covered by dust and appeared "brown."[31] Izumi Hirano was astonished by how he could not tell men from women even though everyone was naked. Their hair was gone, and their bodies were unrecognizably disfigured by heat. Public nakedness was unusual in Japan, especially in middle- and upper-class neighborhoods, making suddenly naked survivors everywhere a strikingly otherworldly vision. Hirano thought that those who survived with underwear were fortunate.[32] Even more fortunate were people who managed to escape from the city with their clothes on. Born in Japan in 1937, Magohei Nagaishi, recalled how he felt too embarrassed to run outside without wearing any piece of outer clothing after the bomb fell on Nagasaki. It was a hot summer's day, and he was only wearing underwear. So, as he left his house, he grabbed a pair of slacks hanging on a clothesline outside. Thus, he was one of the fortunate few who did not have to feel ashamed of their appearance.[33] Both Hirano's and Nagaishi's remembering complicates the better-known story about how nakedness became the norm at ground zero.[34] Certainly, some US *hibakusha*, as well as their Japanese counterparts, recalled how they were stunned by naked people everywhere, seemingly unconcerned about how they looked. Thus, it was not surprising that some felt embarrassed or sorry about the fact they were still wearing decent clothes when they escaped.[35] Nagaishi's recollection of embarrassment about not being fully clothed, as well as Hirano's feeling that those clothed with anything were lucky, however, shows us that concluding too quickly that nakedness was the accepted norm only blinds us to how survivors remained capable of feeling the most ordinary feelings.

Assaulted by heat, glass, fabric, dirt, and deprived of clothes to hide their foreign-looking injuries, survivors grasped at normalcy and a command over their bodies that they had enjoyed only a few moments earlier. Such grasping, often strongly gendered, was urgent enough to mark a defining moment in US survivors' remembering. Atsuko La Mica's older sister, severely injured, insisted that her younger siblings not come to see her at the hospital. Although the hospital was equipped with sheets and blankets, they were too warm for hot summer days. The patients lay with their scars exposed, a state that La Mica's sister did not think to be tolerable as a young woman. Thus, it struck the twelve-year-old La Mica as good news when her sister asked for a freshly washed and ironed *yukata*. It sounded as if her sister was anticipating a much-awaited homecoming, which she wanted to celebrate with the ordinary clothes that made her a presentable woman again. Shortly thereafter, though, La Mica's hope was crushed. Her sister suddenly passed away, just before she was scheduled to come home wearing the prepared clothes. Her desire to make her body once again feminine, respectable, and presentable was so urgent that it kept the sisters apart at the moment of her death.[36] For Yasuko Ogawa, her desire to return to a state of normalcy by way of clothing created an equally intense memory. Because the bomb in Hiroshima exploded right after the "all-clear" siren had sounded, Ogawa was not taking cover but undressing her young daughter out of "her favorite satin dress." This was because she wanted her daughter to be in the most beloved outfit if and when "the worst happened." Now that the air-raid siren was replaced by the sound of safety, there was no need to keep her daughter in the dress any more. "I had just taken her dress and *monpe* off when we were bombed," recalled Ogawa. Everything was blown away, including the dress. "Afterward, she [her daughter] cried that she could not find [it]." She was further upset by the fact that she had to run naked, with no time to wear or take any clothes. For a little girl, this was a shocking embarrassment. It came as great news then, when Ogawa went back to the house about a week later, that she miraculously found the "dress . . . on the second floor roof. It had gone around from the kitchen and had been blown up to the roof."[37] The surprising power of the explosion was met by the daughter and the mother's determination to regain what had been lost to it. In fortunate cases like Ogawa's, survivors succeeded in finding not only clothes, but also the feminine intimacy they used to share in them.

As the stories of Hirano, Nagaishi, La Mica, and Ogawa show, virtually any clothes were desirable, sparking many recollections. But reasons for this desirability varied, illuminating both the universality and uniqueness of American survivors' remembering of the nuclear attack. In some cases, what appears to be a universal story contained surprisingly unique meanings. In Haakai Nagano's remembering, a padded cap he called *bōka zukin*, which he wore when escaping from the city of Hiroshima, protected him from both fire and radiation. It worked as if it were a "miracle coverage seal," a term that conveys his appreciation of his mother's cross-cultural resourcefulness:

My mother made that for me. It was so hot.... I had to do something, because otherwise I could never pass through all this heat. So I got this *bōka zukin*, and put it in a tub [of water] ... I put it on my body, and I just opened up a little hole so I could see. ... Those days, *bōka zukin* was made out of cotton ... I think when you wet it, it gets dense. So it's really a good shield. ... So that's how I traveled through Hiroshima with this miracle coverage seal. And I don't tell the story too much, because it may sound ridiculous, but I didn't even have my hair fall off.[38]

Embedded in this memory of the life-saving cap was his mother's education that taught Nagano how to use *bōka zukin* appropriately. Following the steps of many mothers in wartime Japan, she made the cap with thick cotton so that it functioned as a water absorbent shield against fire. She also taught her son that there were tubs of water called *bōka suisō* that could be easily found anywhere, because they were strategically located to put out fires caused by incendiary bombs. These instructions, commonly given by parents to children in wartime Japan, carried cross-national meanings for this particular mother and son. For Nagano's mother who had migrated from Japan to America as a young girl at the turn of the century and come back to Japan as a mother of three in 1941, *bōka zukin* and *bōka suisō* were new realities of her old country at war. She had to learn, then teach, these facts of life to her American son, who spoke fluently only in English. Indeed, Nagano "had a lot of problem" with Japanese after he had come to Japan for the first time in 1940. He went to a Buddhist temple to learn the language, but still, things were "very difficult in Japan" for him. In this light, it could have been truly a "miracle" for him to be able to escape from a factory only three quarters of a mile away from the hypocenter. His relative unfamiliarity with Japanese could have easily endangered him at ground zero. However, his mother's cross-national skills ensured his safety, as she had taught him Japanese customs in English, the chief language of communication between mother and son.

For other US *hibakusha*, too, clothes worked a kind of miracle, though in strikingly different ways. Both Tae Alison Okuno and May Yamaoka felt that they had benefitted from "American" clothes worn by family members. Unlike Okuno, who was born in 1921 in Merrillville near Sacramento, her young cousin, a girl, was born in Japan. But the cousin's connection to the United States remained palpable. On August 6, 1945, the cousin was "wearing a piece of American underwear with a distinctive stripe pattern on it." Indeed, the underwear had been "sent by her parents from the United States for her brother, but he was not in Hiroshima at that time so she was wearing it instead." Because of this underwear, Okuno's family was able to identify the cousin after the bomb took her life. Her American item of clothing made her body distinguishable from others lying on the ground. The underwear became the cousin's *katami*, a memento, which remained dear to the Okunos, another family of immigrants who understood its meanings.[39] May Yamaoka's remembering, too, was infused with a lived cross-nationality that quietly found its way into people's clothes. Raised in Lodi, California, Yamaoka was in Hiroshima in 1945 as a sixteen-year-old. Although she lost her sister Mana to the bomb, she thought that her family was "lucky." After searching for days, the family found Mana's body on the top of a pile of corpses. The family identified her by her "American slip," silky underwear unknown to most Japanese at the time. This made Mana, also American-born like May, stand out, making it possible for the family to bury her appropriately.[40] Both of these stories are similar to those of other survivors who looked for their loved ones relying on any sign of distinction, be it clothes, a name tag, or teeth (gold ones were frequently mentioned as identity markers).[41] These items did not have to be American; they simply needed to be recognizable by searchers. But both Okuno and Yamaoka show how their linkage to the United States distinctly made their memory of the bomb. In their remembering, their uniqueness as Americans becomes seamlessly integrated into a universal element of the nuclear destruction – mass, indiscriminate death. Their uniqueness as immigrants connected them to universal desires to recover and remember perished family members.

If clothes distinguished otherwise indistinguishable bodies in the nuclear holocaust, national origin, class, and gender worked to determine what clothes were worn by whom or if clothes were worn at all, suggesting yet another way in which universality and uniqueness related to each other. Indeed, in Pak Namjoo's remembering, the social standing of Koreans in wartime Japan, as well as the gender norms shared in their community, shaped her particular account of the mass death. As discussed in Chapter 1, Pak is a Japan-born Korean residing in Japan; thus, she is not a US survivor. And yet, her story offers a rare look into the experiences of Korean American survivors whose number is small. Although their migration histories diverged after the war, Korean and Korean American survivors had shared experiences as Korean subjects in the Japanese empire until 1945. As such, Korean survivors offer the best proxy for us as we reach out to Korean American *hibakusha*'s experiences on the ground. Pak's account of the bomb began in the Fukushima district in Hiroshima, a poor neighborhood of mostly Koreans. There, the nuclear holocaust occurred in the Fukushima River, where many children played:

> Children went to swim in the river. They were all naked – there were no clothes to wear anyway because of the wartime shortage. Girls refrained from going there because boys were naked. I mean, they were completely naked, not even covering their genitals. So those who were in water got their upper bodies burned, while those playing on the sandy bank got completely burned and died instantly. So I remember their mothers crying, shouting: "*Aigo! Aigo!*" [Korean word expressing shock and remorse]. These shouts never leave my ears.[42]

In Pak's account, these mothers' devastation was amplified by the fact that it was boys, not girls, whom they lost to the blast. Girls were neither in the river nor on the bank because they were avoiding the naked boys. In a Korean tradition of Confucianism, Pak continued to explain, boys were considered to be more important than girls for the continuation of family lineage. This gender differentiation, combined with the "wartime shortage" of clothes that had hit the Korean community particularly hard, shaped the tragedy. As Pak recalled, public nakedness was not unusual in the poorer neighborhood of Korean minorities; neither was it embarrassing for boys to be wholly naked, giving her a memory specific to her community. Pak indicated a unique way in which a common experience of being bombed was woven together with a cross-nationality of immigrants. Despite the bomb's universality, its effect could be discriminatory because of one's national background, class, and gender. The uniqueness and universality of the nuclear holocaust could be placed against each other, each elucidating the other's sharpness.

As survivors emerged from the bomb's indiscriminate destruction, they encountered people who were not directly affected and were troubled or offended by their presense. Indeed, non-survivors were often shaken by survivors because they seemed to annul human distinctions. To be sure, many survivors themselves were shaken by the lack of appropriate clothing because they retained their dignity as unique individuals; for non-survivors, however, survivors often seemed indistinguishable, ghost-like figures in a universal mass. Their apparent failure to act in gendered ways seemed to particularly disturb non-survivors. Takashi Thomas Tanemori's father could not find his wife in the bomb's aftermath. Feeling desperate after a long, fruitless search, he took his children to his mother-in-law's, located more than thirty miles away from the city of Hiroshima. "How dare you come back without my daughter?" was how he was greeted by his mother-in-law, whom he met in a park, where others could overhear the tense conversation. She berated him, Tanemori recalled: "What sort of man are you? Do you even have testicles?" In response, Tanemori's father went back to the ruined city in search of his wife. He became sickened by what we now know to be radiation, and he passed away shortly thereafter.[43] The pressure to fulfill his duty as a man and a husband destroyed him. Chisa Frank lost her baby son to the bomb, which created a feeling of distrust between her and her husband. In 1946, he requested a divorce from her, because he "blamed" her as an irresponsible mother. "I survived. Why, then, not rescue that helpless baby?" speculated Frank about her husband's reasoning.[44] Clearly, her apparently compromised motherhood, femininity, or both, was a good enough reason for him to abandon the marriage. No matter how severely wounded she was, she as a mother could have saved her child.

Mothers who survived with their children, however, did not necessarily feel fortunate. They suffered from their children's transformed bodies and unknown futures. Yi Jougkeun, a Korean survivor who stayed in Japan after the war, remembered how his mother cried every day when she picked maggots from his wounds. His face was severely burned, his body covered by scars that attracted flies. Her tears fell on his cheek, which made him cry, too. "I hope you die soon to be peaceful," she told him. "A person with this face and this body, infested by maggots, must not live. Please die soon, I beg you to die soon." For Yi, to recall these times was to see motherhood and childhood on a shifting ground. "I don't think that my mother really meant it," said Yi at one point in the interview. A few moments later, he thought of it again: "I don't think she really wanted me to die soon, but maybe she did, up to a point."[45] Powerful, too, in Yi's remembering was how the nuclear destruction appeared to override gender. As in Pak's earlier story, a boy's death was deemed more devastating than a girl's in the Korean community. That Yi's mother wished her son a death nonetheless meant that, in some cases, such a view failed to persist. While many called back gender eagerly, it could seem worthless for some in the face of nuclear holocaust.

Parenthood, childhood, femininity, and masculinity, once seemingly natural ground for meanings and purposes, became uprooted in

Hiroshima and Nagasaki. Oftentimes, young children were left on their own to survive, while adults struggled to regain normalcy. One way or another, survivors pushed back against the loss of distinct identities that made them look not worthy or capable of living. Pak Namjoo remembered how, in the air-raid shelter in which she took refuge, it was only she, a child, who attended other child-survivors. Someone had told her that crushed cucumbers and potatoes could help heal burns, so she took it upon herself to make and apply these "medicines" for children. It was also she who removed maggots from child-survivors' bodies:

> I was a child, so I went to help children of my age.... I don't remember helping adults, but I did help children. Especially because people used to have a lot of children, they tended to be left alone. It was as if people thought that it's okay if [a few] children were to die.[46]

In contrast to the Korean mothers grieving over the loss of their boys, adult-survivors here turned into a mass marked only by their disregard for child-survivors. Following Pak's remembering, then, one sees different meanings of nationality, gender, or age given by changing moments on the ground. In a matter of seconds, old distinctions could come or go; in no time, a new distinction might emerge. Kazue Suyeishi's younger brother seemed taller when he came back home soon after the bomb's explosion. It appeared as if he was wearing a brown Indian-style turban on his head. The turban turned out to be a fabric drenched with blood streaming out of his wound. Under the strong August sun, "he smelled awfully awful." Then, Suyeishi's remembering took a surprising turn, which pieced together her brother's coming-of-age and her cross-nationality as an immigrant in a single breath:

> My brother could not stand the smell, either. I used to be referred to as "Mary-chan," a nickname given to me by a white customer [of my father's business in Pasadena] who thought I was so cute but could not pronounce my name "Kazue." This was the origin of "Mary-chan," everyone calling me "Mary-chan, Mary-chan!" So my brother asked me: "Excuse me, Mary-chan, could you please bring me my mother's perfume?" He was a young man, and it was the first time he said anything like that.[47]

Figure 2.1 Kazue Suyeishi in a photo taken in Hawai'i, on her way to return to California. On the back of the photo Suyeishi wrote to her family in Japan: "Here is Mary in Aloha shirt." Kazue Suyeishi papers, 1949.

Suyeishi could not find her mother's perfume, so she sprinkled her brother with some wine that her family's acquaintance had left. Whether with wine or perfume, he was determined not to smell bad. The coming of adulthood for him – becoming aware of the way he smelled – came with the nuclear holocaust that he had narrowly survived. For his sister, it was a moment that brought together the person she had been before and the person she became after the destruction. *I was Mary-chan; and I still am.* No matter how her father felt about his American customer who could not pronounce his daughter's name "Kazue," at least he liked "Mary" enough to make it into a nickname by adding "chan," a Japanese diminutive commonly used for girls. That sweet baby girl in Pasadena was still Suyeishi indeed (see Figure 2.1).

Medicine and Care

There was no ready-made medicine for survivors. Most doctors and nurses perished with the bomb. In the city of Hiroshima, 224 out of 298 registered physicians died, and 46 more were injured or ill.[48] The total destruction of the cities' infrastructure blocked or slowed down rescuers from other cities and prefectures. It took even longer for hospitals and clinics to be rebuilt. These facts of destruction have created a blank spot in our understanding of people's immediate response to the bomb before the infrastructural recovery began months later. We know a few famous figures such as Sasaki Terufumi and Nagai Takashi, physicians who at ruined hospitals in Hiroshima or Nagasaki assisted in the care and treatment of survivors immediately after the bomb exploded.[49] We are also familiar with hospitals and research facilities that attended the injured or irradiated years later. The Atomic Bomb Casualty Commission (ABCC), which studied genetic and epidemiological effects of radiation in Hiroshima and Nagasaki, as well as Mount Sinai Hospital in New York City, which performed surgeries on Japanese women whose faces were disfigured by the bomb (as part of the famous "Hiroshima Maidens" project), are notable examples.[50] Here, I turn my eye toward the hours and days after the moment of explosion, which have been seen as a time of little to no medicine or care. A few patterns emerge in my inquiry: faced with the lack of ready-made medicines, *hibakusha* concocted medicines from virtually any materials available. The medicine makers and caretakers were overwhelmingly women, bringing to light a practice of folk medicine that has been overshadowed by the understanding of medicine that revolved around male doctors, Western science, and their institutions. Moreover, the medicine offered by women became one of the tenets of US survivors' remembering because it was one of the first reassurances they found in the bomb's immediate aftermath. If the bomb erased or diminished gender in certain ways, it came back powerfully in the folk medicine that women devised. This, in turn, made it possible for American survivors to reconnect times before and after the bomb by affirming a universal experience of surviving a nuclear holocaust. Compared to this kind of medicine sustained by universality, then, the medicine driven by national and institutional interests, which conspicuously marked the years after 1945, seemed desperately lacking. As I argue, then, it is not surprising that some US *hibakusha* became strong critics of the ABCC; most of them showed no interest in the "Hiroshima Maidens" project.

The experience of Junji Sarashina, a sixteen-year-old from Hawai'i, encapsulated some of these patterns. Soon after the bomb's explosion, he found himself "somehow, on the ground," miraculously unscarred. But when he went to the first-aid station at his factory, he found a nurse "standing there, and she was covered with blood. And she opened the mouth, and I saw a piece of glass ... in her tongue. So she was yelling at me, and I went over there, pull the piece of glass from her ... I was scared, too, I didn't know what I was doing, and she was scared, too." The shared moments of terror scrambled the roles expected of a nurse and a patient. Things did not seem any more orderly at the Red Cross Hospital, one of the few facilities that offered emergency care in Hiroshima on August 6. Sarashina recalled: "I went to the Red Cross building and I could not get in there. It was full of doctors and nurses, all hurt. All the nurses were hurt, all the doctors were hurt, they can't do a damn thing." However heroic, the care offered by a handful of soon-to-be famous physicians was not substantial enough to be remembered by any US survivors. Sarashina's experience was also similar to others in that it was his mother who cared for his injury. "Of course, when I walked in, my mother just cried, oh Junji-san. ... She tried to feed me but for some reason I couldn't eat. ... I had a diarrhea ... and she fed me all kinds of things, home remedy, she heard what's good, what's bad."[51] Clearly, the benefit of a mother's care was not only physical but also psychological. It was a huge emotional relief for Sarashina that his mother's knowledge about all sorts of "home remedy" survived the blast that transformed or erased so much else.

We do not know specifically what Sarashina's mother fed him, but we do know from others that various oils were used to treat burns. Yi Jougkeun (before he came back to his crying mother who wished him to die) applied engine oil to his facial burns. An employee of the Japanese Railway Bureau, he found the oil the only material that seemed therapeutic. Unfortunately, his pain greatly intensified. Yi also tried castor oil for his diarrhea. Not knowing that his condition was caused by irradiation, his mother, the caretaker, thought that the oil customarily used as a cathartic might be beneficial to him. It seems that it worked at least better than engine oil.[52] Toshiro Kubota, a Sacramento-born fourteen-year-old, seemed to have even better luck with the rapeseed oil that his family used to use for cooking. Because his parents were farmers in Hiroshima's countryside, at least food was ample. Not surprisingly, the food materials of yesterday were made to serve as the medicines of today, rapeseed oil being a good example. Meanwhile, his neighbor, an acupuncturist, was swamped by "patients" who flooded his office, although they could not receive anything better than what Kubota was getting next door. Here again, the distinction between homes and hospitals was erased.[53] Alfred Kaneo Dote, another Sacramentan, recalled how he, his sister, and his mother cared for his younger brother after they fled to Hiroshima's countryside. They burned rice straw and mixed the ash with vegetable oil. They applied the mixture to the boy's face until they realized that it was attracting flies. They removed maggots with a pair of tweezers, along with parts of skin that had dried and were causing the patient great pain. The caretakers then decided to apply vegetable oil only to see if it attracted less flies and reduced pain. Thanks to this improvisation, Dote believed, his brother was not heavily scarred, though one can still tell that his face had been burned.[54] What emerges out of the remembering by Yi, Kubota, and Dote is not only that people relied on their existing knowledge about the healing capacity of oil; they also revised or experimented with it when confronted by extreme injuries.

Solid vegetables and leaves that contain water were considered therapeutically valuable, too, serving as another link between traditional practices of folk medicine and what people invented anew to treat nuclear burns. Indeed, caretakers showed remarkable resourcefulness. As seen earlier, Pak used crushed potatoes and cucumbers to treat child-survivors. Some remembered using grated pumpkins, too. Various kinds of leaves were deemed effective, including those of tea, the chameleon plant, and poppy. Oftentimes, people used these leaves first to make tea, then to cover burns and injuries. Similar to crushed vegetables, these leaves gave burns a sensory relief, sometimes by working as a disinfectant. They also offered protection from direct contact with air. Nobuko Fujioka remembered a method of treatment that involved an application of used green tea leaves. They were particularly effective when placed on a maggot-infested wound. Fujioka was impressed by how they appeared to work as both a disinfectant and an anti-inflammatory medicine. Maggots disappeared and pus subsided. Although the healing power of green tea was known, this particular application of leaves was new to Fujioka's mother, the caretaker. In fact, a neighbor who had traveled on a hospital ship told her that they were good for reducing pus. Thus, the treatment consisted of a combination of old and new methods.[55] Jeremy Oshima's grandmother used potatoes for her daughter's wounds, although there was no known therapeutic value to the vegetable. "Of course we had no bandages and such," recalled Oshima, "so my grandmother baked potatoes, white potatoes – mashed them, and put them on the wound to absorb the juice that came out."[56] Here again, a new means of treatment (mashed potatoes) was adapted to an old technique (bandage). Mitsuko Okimoto's mother used to cut both ends off cucumbers and keep them in a jar to ferment. She believed that they made a good painkiller. To heal her nuclear burns, then, she dipped a piece of old *kimono* fabric into the fermented cucumbers and covered her wounds with it. Sure enough, the pain began to subside. The next step, to dry the burns, was entirely new: to apply ground human bones that she collected from a crematory. Okimoto's mother needed something solid and flexible, and human bones were one thing that was abundant in the nuclear holocaust's aftermath. Looking back on the episode, Okimoto seemed to feel somewhat ambivalent: "Bones have calcium in them, so they are good for you … [but] she was not at all concerned about radiation's effect. Now that I am thinking about it, she must have been doubly irradiated."[57] Though clearly concerned about her mother's possible exposure to the irradiated bones, Okimoto chose to say something reassuring about them: that they were a source of calcium. In Okimoto's remembering, then, her mother remained a remarkable caretaker, who fearlessly mobilized old and new ways at her disposal.

A similar method of treatment played a key role in Tokiko Nambu's account, suggesting yet another way in which the folk medicine invented by female caretakers shaped American survivors' understanding of the bomb's aftermath. Nambu's older sister needed urgent care; her eyes and face were so severely burned that at first her mother did not recognize her. Only her skirt and her feeble response to her mother's call allowed her to be identified. With no medicine at hand, her mother decided to go to a cremation site hurriedly set up and collect human bones left unclaimed. She ground them finely to apply to her daughter's face. According to Nambu, her mother "knew that it was wrong to take these bones, but her daughter was a girl with a burnt face. If left untreated, the skin would harden, and she would look pitiful. My mother also did not want the burn to fester." This emergency procedure,

Nambu believed, prevented the girl's face from becoming hardened except in the area around her eyebrows. Nambu's sister did not become a "keloid girl," a girl with highly visible, discolored scars, because she "got [her] mother's good treatment." As with Junji Sarashina's and Okimoto's, Nambu's account suggests that women's care imparted not only physical aid but also emotional relief. What Nambu's mother first thought to be "wrong" became "mother's good treatment" in her daughter's remembering. As recalled by her daughter in America many decades later, the account can also be read as a story of resistance. Thanks to her mother's inventiveness, Nambu's sister did not draw attention from American medical scientists after the war. Although Nambu did not explicitly mention this, her sister could have been asked to come to the ABCC or be chosen to be one of the "Hiroshima Maidens" to receive cosmetic surgery at Mount Sinai Hospital years later. Indeed, Nambu's other sister, whose legs were severely injured, was asked to participate in the study conducted by the ABCC, "even though she really didn't want to show her scars" to anyone. Her mother did not hide her outrage: "This is not to treat her. They [the ABCC] came to get her to help American research. It would be nice if they treated her burns, but they don't." In this light, the sister with healed facial scars was fortunate, as her mother's care helped protect her privacy, autonomy, and integrity. Here, it is notable that Nambu was only three years old in 1945. It is likely, then, that her family's accounts of the treatment shaped Nambu's remembering as much as her personal recollections. In both the mother's account and the daughter's remembering, the home treatment differed sharply from the institutional research, in no small part because of the gendered identity that the treatment protected.[58]

Because new ways of treating injuries caused uncertainty, unease, or even guilt, it was all the more necessary for survivors to find reassurance somewhere outside of the medical professions and institutions as they had known them. Often, reassurance came through caretakers who were their grandmothers, mothers, or sisters, suggesting the importance of intergenerational connections that imparted care. Their method of treatment might be unfamiliar, but at least those who used it were familiar. Women had been the chief caretakers of households, creating at least some sense of continuity between times before and after the bomb for those who received emergency care from them. These caretakers sometimes offered a folk medicine long forgotten but now revived out of necessity. Sue Carpenter did not appreciate the aid first offered by her mother: alcohol. Because her father was a physician, her house was equipped with a small assortment of modern medicines. This potentially enviable situation quickly turned into a nightmare when the nine-year-old Carpenter realized how painful alcohol felt as it penetrated the burns on her legs. She pleaded with her mother to discontinue it, to which her mother responded by trying a much older method: leeches. Although her mother clearly considered them to be inferior to alcohol, the blood-sucking creatures produced surprisingly soothing effects. Thanks to her mother's flexibility to use a folk method instead of a modern one, Carpenter believed, she endured the healing process and regained her ability to walk.[59] Michiko Benevedes, a Japan-born thirteen-year-old in Nagasaki, went with her family to Gotō Rettō, a small island off the city's shore right after the bomb. Severely injured and ill, her family sought the help of her grandmother who lived on the island. But the island was far away, exhausting the family who traveled in a rowboat for more than ten hours. Her cousins and mother died shortly after their arrival, and it appeared as if Benevedes was to follow. In particular, a wound on her feet, inflicted by a large nail, was angry, causing a high fever. No wonder, then, that she was greatly impressed by the effect of a medicine her grandmother made out of crab shells. Because she had not been particularly close to her grandmother, the medicine she concocted was unfamiliar to Benevedes. And yet, the grandmother's dedication as a family caretaker helped Benevedes to trust the medicine. This, in turn, offered Benevedes her first encounter with a previously unknown traditional medicine. She was delighted when a version of the medicine became patented many years later both as a disinfectant and an anti-inflammatory.[60] For Benevedes, the patent proved that her caretaker knew what was right all along. Care and trust conveyed across generations of women, in addition to the specific medicines employed, were an essential part of the medicine devised immediately after the nuclear holocaust.

In some extraordinary cases, survivors found a surprising reassurance in both medicine and its makers. Minoru Sumida, a Hawaiian-born eleven-year-old in 1945, received a mixture of oil and ground human bones. The caretaker was his older sister, and the bones were their mother's. His mother had passed away in 1943, so his older sister had been taking care of her younger siblings. The family also kept their mother's bones at home, in a compact Buddhist shrine, as many Japanese families customarily did (and still do) with the remains of their loved ones. As Sumida recalled, his sister decided to use this method of treatment because "people told her that if she used oil only, it would drip off" from the scar. She needed something to keep the oil in place, and she was told that ground human bones worked well for this purpose. Thus, this was a new method for Sumida's sister, which she decided to try with the help of their deceased mother. Because their house was only a little more than a mile away from the hypocenter, it is likely that the sister could have gone to a crematory as did Mitsuko Okimoto's and Tokiko Nambu's mothers. But she chose the bones that belonged to her dearest person, her mother, most likely because it was a way to make unfamiliar medicine familiar.[61] When his burns were nearly healed, Sumida received another course of treatment from a family member. This time, the caretaker was his father, although his method was far fiercer than what the term "caretaker" usually implies. Sumida's burns made his legs and arms unnaturally bent and bound together. Fearing that these disfigurements could disadvantage the son's future, the father tore the son's legs and arms apart by sheer force, so that they could be separated and moved freely. Sumida recalled how he screamed out of pain, stating: "In the end, my father became *oni* [a Japanese monster known for his ferocity]" at that moment. But then, Sumida continued: "Unless he became *oni* there was nobody else who would do that for me." The son regained an ability to walk, and his arms began to function more normally.[62] Faced with the lack of modern medicines, doctors, and hospitals, Sumida's family formed a chain of innovations sustained by communal advice, familial ties, and gendered divisions of labor. Women imparted care and continuity, while men seemed to be assigned to drastic, even violent, tasks of treatment.

The care and medicine offered to survivors in the bomb's immediate aftermath, then, were based on folk medicine practiced by predominantly female (and occasionally, male) caretakers. This was a medicine embedded in the community, and they felt personally compelled to use it because of the destruction of modern medicine and its institutions as they knew them before August 1945. Seen through our contemporary lens of medical science, the effect of the medicine-on-the-ground might seem dubious and rudimentary. And yet, its efficacy was striking in the context, distinctively shaping US survivors' view of the nuclear holocaust. Certainly, destruction was on an unprecedented scale, provoking terror, fear, and deep uncertainty among the injured and ill. But it is wrong for us to assume that the bomb created a medical vacuum; instead, the altered landscape of Hiroshima or Nagasaki was peopled by survivors making the best use of old and new resources to care for each other. The nuclear landscape refused human life, but there were humans left to live. For many, one urgent purpose of their life was to give care. One import of this experience of survivors as caretakers is that it shaped their views of institutional medicine in the years following the war. As will be shown in Chapters 3 and 4, US survivors' responses to medical authorities in both Japan and America, including the ABCC and the "Hiroshima Maidens" project, were complex and often critical. These responses need to be understood as not simply directed at the institution or US sponsorship of the project, but as more deeply rooted in the care and medicine *hibakusha* had created in the hours and days after the bomb.

So it was, that shortly after Japan's surrender, some US survivors already began to see the uneasy relationship between the medical care devised by their family and community members and its postwar counterpart delivered by medical and scientific establishments. The former was delivered by familiar faces, with a watchful eye toward patients' reactions. The latter, in contrast, was established by governments and served primarily national interests. Kazuko Aoki, for one, felt "fortunate" enough to be cared for by her neighbor, a female doctor whom she had known from her high school, even though the physician did not have the means to treat the rash that appeared on Aoki's skin. When the war ended and the occupation forces came to Japan, Aoki's father was called upon to assist the US Army military police. Because he had lived in America for decades and was fluent in English, he was tasked with the responsibility of a translator, visiting Japanese households with American MP officers to confiscate daggers and swords. He was dismayed by young US officers' lack of knowledge about Japanese culture. They did not remove their shoes when entering Japanese houses, and once, one of them broke a Japanese flute over his knee, mistaking it as a weapon. Aoki's father scolded the officer, and interestingly, the officer did not talk back. He apparently was willing to take some lessons from this cross-cultural man. In any event, her father's work made it possible for Aoki to receive medicine not readily available to Japanese civilians. Aoki recalled: "My father told the MPs that his daughter was injured by the bomb ... and had a rash. They started to come to my house to deliver a big tube of cream and apply it thickly on my rash . . . they also brought a brown bottle of medicine to take orally, which I think was Vitamin C now that I am looking back on it, but there was no label on it because it was a military supply." Thus, her father's cross-cultural skills and experiences made it possible for him to treat his daughter. But this does not necessarily mean that he gave institutional medicine a blanket approval. It is possible that he considered the MP supplies as much-deserved compensation for his service. Moreover, it seems clear that he felt he could decide what was acceptable care. For instance, he did not believe that participating in the study of survivors conducted by the ABCC would benefit survivors. Though a survivor himself, Aoki's father also refused to receive the certificate of survivorhood, the medical care, and the monetary allowances offered by the Japanese government years later. He was willing to negotiate for military supplies insofar as he was treated as an equal player in the negotiation. Beyond that, however, he did not want to be dependent on institutionalized support as he felt it would interfere with his autonomy.

Pak Namjoo's remembering also revealed a complex relationship between the folk medicine invented immediately after the bomb and the modern medicine brought by the end of the war. She had a relative in Osaka, one of the centers of opium poppy production in Japan before 1945. Japanese people found the plant effective for treating diarrhea. So, Pak's relative sent poppy extract to her family, who suffered from the condition shortly after surviving the bomb. But soon, the supply stopped, because of the occupation forces' intervention:

> Many people used to plant poppy plants [to treat diarrhea]. Then, the occupation forces came and pulled them out. . . . They said that these plants were dangerous, and they took them all away, down to the last one. . . . The plants had beautiful pink flowers, but they said that you could make opium out of these plants. They could see the color of the flowers from the sky, so they took pictures to spot them.[63]

Here, the distinction between the familial and commercial uses of poppy plants was ignored, resulting in the loss of a community medicine known to work. What came after, DDT, also provoked highly mixed feelings. Seeing that everything was infested by lice and flies, Pak was both appalled by the lack of cleanliness and impressed by the human ability to survive in such extreme conditions. Then came a new medicine in October 1945:

It was white, called DDT, and US airplanes sprinkled it over us. We all went outside. If this were done today, it would be a big scandal. But everyone said: "This will kill the lice!" So we all went outside and moved our bodies like this to get the medicine [Pak gestured to show how people made dancing moves]. Indeed, all the lice and flies disappeared. It was in October. ... I was so impressed. I remember thinking: this is awesome, this is awesome![64]

Obviously, Pak's youthful self in 1945 had been awed by DDT's ability to terminate harmful insects. And yet, she was also aware by the time of the interview that the substance was harmful not only for insects but also for humans. Neither did she fail to mention that people appeared to be fully capable of living with the insects. Her remembering, then, did not point to any conclusive judgment about the insecticide. Rather, it illuminated a shifting ground of medicine on which survivors must navigate their health, illness, and injury. Nation states dictated changes, sometimes literally from above, while people were left alone to figure out what these changing policies might mean for their families and communities. New caretakers were powerful yet remote, leaving survivors to wonder about their efficacy with no opportunity to negotiate the terms of care and treatment.

In the face of such complexity, the medicine offered predominantly by women across generations became a strong element of US survivors' remembering of the bomb. As they took familiar and unfamiliar medicines, American survivors' connection to caretakers who made and gave these medicines carried considerable weight in determining their efficacy in retrospect. Survivors' cross-nationality, too, shaped efficacy as they perceived it, leading some to define it sharply apart from any state-sanctioned medical authority. In the eyes of many, the latter was too narrowly unique to serve as a meaningful response to the universality of the catastrophe.

Water and Food

The landscape after the nuclear attack was a ground for new moral questions. Nothing raised more compelling ones than water. Water was not unavailable, perhaps surprisingly so given the intense heat and fire generated by the explosion. Hiroshima had seven rivers, and the water supply from some of them continued for a while after the bombing because of the water flowing from broken hydrants, spigots, and water pipes everywhere.[65] Nagasaki, too, experienced the same destruction of infrastructure, which ended up supplying not a few survivors with a much-needed drink of water briefly. A familiar story of survivors, however, tells of cries for water heard everywhere. In the outskirts of the cities where many sought shelter, there actually was a shortage of water, caused by the sudden flux of a large number of people.[66] Within the city limits, these cries likely arose as well from survivors' inability to walk to water and the absence of any container to carry it. With nearly everything shattered into pieces, it suddenly became a difficult assignment for those who were capable of walking to bring water to those who were not.[67] Moreover, a rumor quickly spread that it was dangerous to give water to those who were severely burned. Rooted in an accurate observation that many survivors passed away after drinking water, the rumor inaccurately supposed that death was caused by the water itself instead of burns or gastrointestinal injuries. Regardless of its erroneousness, the word about lethal water posed a moral question that was deceptively simple and difficult to answer: *Should I give this person water?*

Survivors recalled different ways in which they answered, sometimes more than once by revisiting it repeatedly over years. In a way, the question about water was similar to questions that survivors asked about other elements of the natural environment such as air and soil contaminated by radiation. Things that humans needed for life turned poisonous, one universally felt consequence of the nuclear holocaust.[68] And yet, the question that survivors asked about water was also unique in that doubt about water existed from day one, before most survivors became aware of radioactivity. As such, how survivors grappled with the question about water offers us a pathway toward understanding the convergence of uniqueness and universality in the nuclear holocaust, which brought all survivors to an uncertainty about their surroundings regardless of their nationality, race, or gender. George Kazuto Saiki first heard of the rumor about water at an elementary school in Hiroshima, which was set up as a rudimentary refuge station. He was told that someone from the Red Cross was taking care of survivors with merbromin solution, so he thought that his missing father and brother might be there.[69] He was pierced by numerous calls for water as he walked through the dead and dying on the school's ground. Though filled with pity, he was dissuaded from responding to the calls. As Saiki explained, "Doctors shouted at me: 'Please don't give them water! Please don't give them water!' Because they would die immediately if they were given water." Thus, it was medical professionals who directed him and relieved him of guilt.[70] Pak Namjoo, on the other hand, was not so free of guilt, although it was primarily her rescuers who decided not to give water to the dying. Unaware of the rumor about fatal water, she was fortunate enough to drink water she received from rescuers who came from Hiroshima's countryside. She recalled how the rescuers made snap decisions about who was likely to live and who was not. Those in the former group were first given water and hardtack, then they were transported to a relief center outside the city. The latter group, in contrast, was simply left to die. Pak recalled:

> I didn't give even a single drop of water to those who were lying and dying but still calling: "Water! Water!" I think that any survivor would feel pain when they remember such a time. I, too, wonder why I was able to ignore their calls. I don't know if I can say that I regret, but I think about it over and over.[71]

Pak was still searching for an answer to the question in 2013 when she was interviewed. This uncertainty suggests a lasting effect of moral ambiguity posed by the nuclear holocaust. Because of the nuclear weapon's ability to drastically transform the environment, what used to be the most natural act – to give water to the thirsty – became problematic. This, in turn, has opened a path for survivors to become double participants in the mass death. In their remembering, they might be both sufferers and perpetrators.[72]

Other survivors grappled with the question of water more solitarily, without intervention by others such as physicians or rescuers. Junji Sarashina found himself in one such struggle, showing another way in which survivors tried to make sense of the new moral universe presented by the nuclear holocaust. As discussed earlier, Sarashina stopped by the Red Cross Hospital near his school on his way back home on the day after the bombing. This was when he was confronted by the water question:

> When I walked in there, I saw one of the students [of my school] over there ... you could identify it [the school uniform], so I talked to him for a while. And, you know ... I talked to him

for a while, and he said I want some water. . . . You were told not to give water ... but I looked at him and [thought] he is not going to live. Because he was burnt. It's almost like twenty-four hours after the bomb and he was down to nothing ... he looked at me, and that was it. So yes, at least I gave him water.[73]

Unlike Saiki or Pak, then, Sarashina decided to give water. Although all their experiences contained deaths (in Sarashina's case, his classmate passed away right after drinking water), Sarashina chose to participate in the process of dying by giving water. This decision offered him at least some solace years later, separating him from Saiki, who felt he had no choice, or Pak, who wondered if she could have acted differently. As death overwhelmed life and the dead outnumbered the living, the question of how one engaged with the process of dying carried an enduring significance. When there was little chance for life, there was no option but to engage with death. This blurring of life and death coexisted and converged with the practice of folk medicine on the ground. As Yi Jougkeun's experience with his mournful mother has already shown, caretakers could feel similarly to Sarashina: that life might not necessarily be more desirable than death. For all parties involved – sufferers, caretakers, and perpetrators – the distinction between healing and dying was boundlessly unclear.

The blurring of life and death embodied by the choice to give or not give water permeated everything with which survivors came in contact. With striking frequency, survivors of all nationalities have talked about "poison gas" they breathed in unknowingly, by which they meant air filled with radioactive dust. Food, another essential for life, could contain elements of death if contaminated by radiation. In this light, it is notable that many food materials were nevertheless used as medicines. As might be imagined by the many calls for water, vegetables that contained water were highly desirable not only for healing but also for eating. Mitsuko Okimoto remembered a cucumber that she ate the day after: "I woke up early in the morning, and for the first time, I ate a cucumber that came from a cucumber field owned by the family [with whom she stayed on the previous night]. Ah, it was so cool and tasty!"[74] Akiyuki Sumioka, a Japan-born fifteen-year-old in 1945, remembered the tomatoes he ate after walking all day to get home. The owner of a factory in his neighborhood owned a lot that he used as a vegetable garden, so the tomatoes came from there: "You are so young but you look so miserable," said the neighbor.[75] This incident likely offered one of the first reminders for Sumioka of who he had been before the nuclear destruction. He was a teenager, and he could still be treated to tomatoes by neighbors if he looked hungry. Akiko Watanabe, on her way from the city to the countryside, also was given a "refreshingly tasty" tomato by a farmer. After all, it was the height of summer and the seasonal vegetables were plentiful in the areas that had escaped the blast and the fire.[76] But as survivors learned later, these seemingly benign vegetables were highly contaminated. Aiko Tokito, then a sixteen-year-old, captured a mixed feeling provoked by a delayed revelation:

TOKITO: So I went back to where my house had been, and you know, we used to home-grow vegetables. Pumpkins were in season at that time, and they were baked – perfectly baked.

WAKE: By the bomb?

TOKITO: I didn't know [about radiation] at that time. I remember thinking, "Wow!" And I ate the pumpkin. I remember that it was tasty (laughter).

WAKE: Was it right after the bomb?

TOKITO: Right after the bomb. . . . It must have been highly radioactive, and looking back on it, I think it is funny. But it was tasty.[77]

In a similar way that Okimoto worried about the irradiated bones ground up and applied to her mother's burns, Tokito here appeared somewhat concerned about the radioactive pumpkin that she had eaten unsuspectingly. At the same time, her laughter and her description of the episode's humor reveal a kind of resilience to which we have not given enough attention. In a horribly transformed environment, survivors were compelled to redefine meanings of life, dying, and death. This redefinition was mediated by some of the most fundamental elements of the environment such as water, food, and medicines. As survivors took these elements into their bodies as they must, they became part of the nuclear holocaust even as they survived it. One might reason that Tokito's dark humor arose out of this process of internalization. As the nuclear holocaust in a sense became part of her, the tension it provoked called for a relief and resilience. Too, the new morality that the destruction opened up demanded that *hibakusha* shed light on the uniqueness – the absurdity – of their experiences by way of universality. Survivors' laughter signals their desire to capture how uniquely the world was transformed by speaking the universal language of laughter; it turns their extraordinary survival into an act of all-too-common human blindness.

US survivors' remembering often epitomized a similar combination of humor, relief, and resilience, accentuated by their cross-nationality. Katie Yanagawa, who had a family memory of the B-29s from Seattle, recalled how her family had lost nearly everything in Hiroshima in 1945. The devastation struck her mother particularly hard. As Yanagawa recalled:

> They [her parents] had this beautiful bed purchased in the United States, brought home, you know, this art deco type, and brass, and all of those things. . . . And my mother said that she didn't even have the energy to cry. . . . All of these things that my father had worked for all his life, brought back to Japan . . . everything was just burned down to ground.[78]

But Yanagawa's story had a brighter side. Thanks to "the Japanese-style homes" made of mud walls, some pots and pans that had fallen under them survived the blast, and the family could dig them up, still in good shape. Then, miraculously, they found a chicken running around on the street. As Yanagawa recalled, "Japanese people [kept] a chicken for the eggs." But the Yanagawas saw the *chicken* as the meal; they were Americans, familiar with the American diet.[79] So they caught the chicken, "dug up all of the potatoes and carrots and onions" from the family's garden, and took sugar and soy sauce from an empty air-raid shelter that belonged to a rich family in their neighborhood. The Yanagawas then cooked the chicken and vegetables using a pot dug out of mud walls, and this made the family's first meal at ground zero. When she talked about this incident, Yanagawa could not help but laugh. She felt sorry for "this poor chicken" because it "survived the bomb and (*laughing*) then [was] killed by" these Americans, eager to put it in *sukiyaki*. Of course, she was aware by the time of interview that everything had been highly contaminated. And yet, it was this "means of survival" that made this episode "an amazing story."[80]

In Yanagawa's remembering, the speechlessly dismayed mother and the humorously depicted "poor chicken" were placed in sharp contrast. In both episodes, cross-national meanings are salient, allowing her to define her story of the nuclear holocaust by both universality and uniqueness. Her mother's disappointment over loss, a common experience to all, was given texture by the family's hard work in America. Her disappointment was about not only a loss of belongings in Japan, but also a loss of the material embodiment of the family history that bridged nations. Her distress notwithstanding, it was also the family's cross-national ties that offered them the first meal after the bomb. It was their familiarity with both cultures that served as the meal's ingredients. Thinking of how the pots and pans had been protected by the collapsed mud walls, Yanagawa exclaimed: "God is very fair."[81] Although their wealth accumulated in America was lost in Japan, their Japanese house made of mud protected utensils that allowed them to prepare a family meal, American-style chicken *sukiyaki*. Similar to Tokito's baked pumpkins, the Yanagawas' meal was contaminated, pointing to the common experience of forced ingestion of harm and, in some cases, of resiliently making laughter out of the experience.

Writing this, I do not suggest that the nuclear holocaust could be overcome by any individual's attitude or "approach to life."[82] Rather, humor was a pathway toward speaking the unspeakable. As US survivors found each other and sought water, food, and shelter, their cross-nationality came back powerfully. Their layered belonging, which had invited questioning of their national loyalty, offered them a way to account for the otherwise unaccountable aftermath of the nuclear holocaust. If cross-nationality were largely invisible in the bomb's history, humor offered a rare opportunity for it to become visible. In this light, it is important that Yanagawa's interviewers were in fact US *hibakusha*. Surrounded by fellow immigrant-survivors, she likely found it easy to laugh about the episode. US survivors' resilience might have been indistinguishable from other survivors', but the route US survivors took to regain it was uniquely shaped by the collective history of immigrants. Here again, both universality and uniqueness were part of the nuclear holocaust that did not discriminate based on distinctions such as citizenship, cultural belonging, and national loyalty. Seen from where US *hibakusha* stood, the 1945 weapons were grossly at odds with the idea that, in a nuclear war, one nation wins and another loses. By bringing together the uniqueness and universality of their experiences, US survivors' remembering indicates how this dualistic view holds only if we are fundamentally uncurious about the nuclear war's reality.

Korean American survivors' cross-nationality, too, came back forcefully in their remembering of food, but in much different ways than Nikkei's. Their layered sense of belonging did not necessarily bring back a uniform experience in their remembering, either. James Jeong recalled how he was denied a rice ball because he was Korean. After the bomb's explosion, those in the ruined cities relied on emergency food supplied by nearby prefectures. One day, there was a team of soldiers from Okayama prefecture, which came to Hiroshima "with a truck full of rice balls." While Jeong waited "with his hands open, just like everybody else" in line, a middle-aged man yelled at him: "You are a Korean! These rice balls are not for you." Because Jeong had been born and "living almost as a Japanese," he was stunned. Nobody should be able to identify him as *Chōsenjin*, or a Korean. As it turned out, though, the accusatory man knew about Jeong's national origin because he had worked at a wartime rationed food distribution center in Jeong's neighborhood. Because the food rationing was a national program, the roster of recipients included information about their national origins. But Koreans were considered Japanese, so the man could not discriminate against Jeong at the distribution center. The rice balls delivered right after the bomb were not rationed, however; it was emergency food. The man thus felt free to discriminate. Ironically, when Jeong went to receive rationed food days after the rice ball incident, the same man was attending the food distribution center. "He looked really uncomfortable," now that he had to give rice to Jeong.[83]

If food after the bomb was capable of calling up an arbitrary mixture of discrimination and nondiscrimination, it was also capable of revealing the persistence of ties between Japanese and Korean peoples. John Hong did not recall any discrimination surrounding food supplies after the Hiroshima bombing. Shortly after receiving treatment for his injuries at a military hospital "since I belonged to the army," Hong recalled, "we had surrendered" on the 15th, "and on the 25th we got the order" to be released from the military. When he found out that there was no ship to take him back to Korea immediately, Hong consulted with the second lieutenant of his unit, who took him in. Hong was allowed to stay with this second lieutenant until early September, when the passage to Korea was finally reinstated. As discussed in Chapter 1, Hong's superiors were aware of his Korean background. Especially after the bomb, "they had an opportunity to look through all the personal records and documents concerning the students," so it was easy for them to identify him as Korean. Still, there was no discrimination as Hong remembered it. Clearly, he was treated, housed, and fed well enough to survive around the same time that Jeong experienced the inconsistent attitudes toward Koreans after Japan's defeat. Many years later, Hong looked forward to seeing his classmates in Japan at reunions. Jeong, in contrast, realized "how much he hated Japan" after being denied a rice ball. He knew he could not live in Japan anymore.

The universality of the bomb's effects could rise over the uniqueness of an irradiated pumpkin or an ingested chicken, as seen in the cases of humor finding a way to speak about the unspeakable; in Hong's remembering, too, his unique situation as an immigrant did not limit his access to food, something universally needed by survivors. But uniqueness could also stand out conspicuously in the sea of universal experiences, as seen in Jeong's experience of being denied food. Unlike Japanese American survivors, their Korean American counterparts conveyed no humor in their remembering. The latter's resilience, at least when recalled in interviews by persons of Japanese ancestry, was not accompanied by laughter.[84] This suggests that US survivors might have been unwilling to speak the unspeakable unless they felt assured that their listeners understood an essential contradiction of the nuclear holocaust – that it fused together uniqueness and universality inconceivably and inhumanly. This unwillingness, in turn, likely shaped the structure of the counter-memory of the bomb consisting of both speech and silence.

US survivors' experience of regaining cross-nationality after the bomb became a source of empowerment for some. For others, it offered moments of doubt about what it meant to be an immigrant in a defeated country. Either way, food marked a turning point where the transformed morality of life, dying, and death in the post-nuclear world might begin to return to what it had been. Unlike water that could turn sufferers into perpetrators instantaneously, food could be consumed no matter how irradiated it was without showing any immediate impact. In a way similar to medicine, food's effect on humans was felt over a longer stretch of time than that of water. This likely made food more open to different kinds of remembering about how survivors reconnected to life, including stories told with humor or without. When given or denied, food frequently brought to the fore US survivors' cross-nationality, suggesting its centrality to immigrant life. Equally important, gendered meanings embedded in food became central to some US survivors' remembering. As discussed earlier, the bomb in many ways was an eraser of gender, because it destroyed gendered roles and infrastructures. US survivors did everything they could to regain these, as seen in their reactions to bodies and clothes, as well as their use of medicine. Neither did food escape people's desire for meanings framed by gender.

For Yi Jougkeun, the importance of a meal cooked by his mother a day after the bomb went far beyond the simple fact that he finally had something to eat. After walking many miles after the bomb's explosion, Yi found that his parents were not back home. His younger brothers said that his parents had gone to Hiroshima to look for Yi. When they came back, it was already early in the morning. Yi recalled:

> My mother said "Oh! You are alive!" and held me [*daite kuremashite ne*]. She had thought that I was dead. Then we ate ... because we hadn't eaten. My brothers hadn't been eating because mother had been gone. So mother cooked something [*nan ka tukutte kurete*] and we ate it – I remember it.[85]

In addition to the last words that accentuated the memory's vividness, Yi's use of "*kuremashite*" and "*kurete*" also conveyed his sense of gratitude toward his mother. It was not assumed anymore that mothers would hold their children or cook for them. It seemed as if these had become acts of kindness, something that needed to be reaffirmed in the bomb's aftermath. This memory about a meal prepared by a mother became particularly significant for Yi because it recalled a time before his injury became worse and his mother began to doubt if he should live. For Yi, then, his mother's meal might have offered something to hold onto as he struggled for his life days later. In this meal, he could find a glimmer of hope that he still was a beloved son of a Korean family.

If the destruction of Hiroshima and Nagasaki led to an erasure of gender, its return by way of food was greeted by a near-universal sense of relief. This relief, in turn, opened up an unexpected opportunity for US survivors to redefine their cross-nationality and find resilience in it. The family of Brazilian-born American survivor Fumiko Imai, a fifteen-year-old in 1945, was fortunate enough to have access to beans, meat, oil, sugar, and blankets (which they gave to farmers in the countryside in exchange for food) after the bombing. Her older brother had worked at the Japanese Imperial Army's Ministry of Clothes, where all of these supplies were relatively abundant. But it was not her brother of whom Imai was proud. She was proud of her mother who, equipped with these food materials, taught her neighbors how to cook a small amount of available food to satisfy a whole family. As Imai told it, her mother knew how to make bread out of beans or corn because she had lived in Brazil before the war. She used a Brazilian coffee grinder that had survived the bomb to make flour. Her neighbors, who had been eating pan-fried dried beans, were delighted with the many possibilities that flour opened up.[86] In particular, deep-fried, sweet cornbread was popular, and Imai recalled helping her mother prepare quite a few meals for neighbors in a big pot of oil. In Imai's remembering, her mother was a chef-in-chief at these cookouts, a role that likely fit into her being a wife and a mother. And yet, it was also her cross-nationality that made the story worth telling; her son obtained food from the Japanese military, and it was her Brazilian skills and utensils that pushed her to assert herself in the Japanese community struck by a food shortage. Clearly, she had something special to offer. Decades later, this story of assertion and assistance became something for her daughter in America to share. This story is in striking contrast to Imai's pre-bomb memory of her mother showing up at a school gathering wearing a pair of high heels. Nobody else wore such shoes, and Imai appeared to feel embarrassed. In the bomb's aftermath, however, the mother's cross-cultural skills were affirmed and approved of by the daughter. Being an immigrant woman meant being useful. As gendered remembering pieced together places and peoples across the ocean, cross-nationality became an extraordinary, yet ordinarily practiced, terrain of the bomb's history.

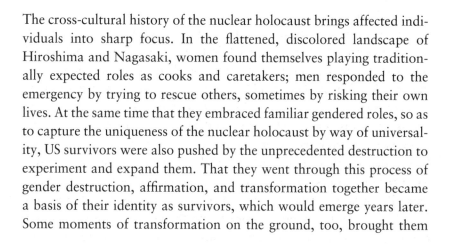

The cross-cultural history of the nuclear holocaust brings affected individuals into sharp focus. In the flattened, discolored landscape of Hiroshima and Nagasaki, women found themselves playing traditionally expected roles as cooks and caretakers; men responded to the emergency by trying to rescue others, sometimes by risking their own lives. At the same time that they embraced familiar gendered roles, so as to capture the uniqueness of the nuclear holocaust by way of universality, US survivors were also pushed by the unprecedented destruction to experiment and expand them. That they went through this process of gender destruction, affirmation, and transformation together became a basis of their identity as survivors, which would emerge years later. Some moments of transformation on the ground, too, brought them close to Japanese, American, and Korean cultural belonging, reminding them of the compound nature of their cross-nationality. Indeed, many memories told by US survivors were about cultural convergence marked by the shifting relationship between the bomb's uniqueness and universality, showing the striking diversity of experiences that the bomb attempted to destroy. Stripped of old meanings, survivors asked new questions about life and death. As they came back to life as immigrants and their children, American *hibakusha* recaptured or reinvented a sense of resilience and self-worth as people with cross-national ties.

Their remembering indicates how it extends into the present, as much as it is about the past. Nothing exemplified this ongoing nature of remembering more than the story of Yamaoka's sister Mana's "American slip" discussed earlier in this chapter. When she wrote a personal recollection of the bomb in 2008, Yamaoka simply mentioned how she "felt extremely thankful to have found" her sister because "she was on the top of a pile of corpses."[87] There was no reference to Mana's underwear. In her oral histories taken in 2009 and 2011, in contrast, Yamaoka revealed that her family had been able to identify Mana thanks to the "American slip."[88] As she talked to interviewers, it seemed, a more personal, closely held memory was revealed. But this was not the end of the story. When Yamaoka talked to her family, she included an even more intimate detail, embroidery stitched on the slip. This became clear when Yamaoka shared with me a copy of a 2006 essay by her granddaughter, then a college student. Her granddaughter wrote: "I know my grandma and her father found little Mana's body after searching through wreckage for three days and her father recognized her only by the embroidery on her undergarments; her face had been burned and bruised beyond recognition."[89] Here, the story is about the detail of family intimacy, which allowed a father's gaze to grasp his daughter's tiny identifier, the embroidery. That Yamaoka remembered the detail but chose not to tell me suggests her continuous interactions with the past that contain varying degrees of silence and speech. In speaking to me, too, Yamaoka did not indicate that Mana's face was so unrecognizable that the family had to rely on something other than that to identify her. But with her granddaughter, it was an indispensable memory to be shared. That Yamaoka gave me a copy of her granddaughter's essay suggests the shimmering boundary between speakable and unspeakable things.

US *hibakusha*'s cross-nationality that lives on today found little standing in Japan, Korea, or America in the following decades, when Cold War ideology spurred an increasingly narrow definition of national belonging, loyalty, and patriotism. And yet, as Yamaoka and others in this chapter show, their remembering never stopped. How they found a place to recollect in the difficult Cold War years was another story.

3 RECONNECTING FAMILIES

August 1945 marked the beginning of silent loss that persisted throughout the following decades. People continued to die mysterious deaths because of what we now know was radiation poisoning. Many who were left behind thought that the end could suddenly fall upon them just as it had on others. Death, illness, and poverty colored many US survivors' remembering of the time after the war. Someone was always ill in their families, which often ended with premature death. These losses led to material deprivation, which was omnipresent in postwar Japan but seemed to affect *hibakusha* more unexpectedly and persistently than others. Such was the tenacious nature of the nuclear holocaust. There was no clear end in sight. When US survivors began to rebuild their lives on the flattened cities of Hiroshima and Nagasaki, the uncertainty of the future carried specific meanings for them.

This chapter takes up the cultural history of the post-nuclear holocaust world that unfolded in Japan from 1945 to 1960, focusing on how US *hibakusha* responded to this uncertainty with a distinctive silence as they began to reconnect with their US families and friends before returning or coming to the United States. US survivors' silence was wide-ranging. Some found it difficult to talk about the bomb with other survivors because talking made their shared pain too palpable. Others found it challenging to tell their experiences to their family members who had stayed in America during the war. As it quickly became clear to many, these family members had no better understanding of the nuclear holocaust than any other non-survivors. It was a new phenomenon of a new age, and public information about the bomb was strictly controlled on both sides of the Pacific. Years of family separation, too, made it difficult for US survivors to recount the nuclear destruction. In their attempts to reconnect and rebuild families, it often seemed best if memories of terror were left unspoken. As was the case with US *hibakusha*'s remembering of ground zero, though, silence was not the opposite of speaking. Their silence signaled things known only through silence. By showing the many layers of silence that existed among US survivors and their families, this chapter continues to add to the memory study of the bomb, which has focused largely on political activism and cultural representation.[1] The silent remembering of US survivors that I explore here continued to connect Japan, America, and Korea across the oceans after the war, often in a way that countered memories construed mostly by national interests. These cross-national rememberings – the counter-memory of the bomb – too, are part of the history of the nuclear holocaust's aftermath.

US *hibakusha*'s silence about the bomb was occasionally broken by what I argue were unique historical circumstances that further illuminate limits of nation-bound responses to the nuclear attacks. Although no survivors felt eager to talk about the bomb in the decades immediately after the war, a few circumstances made it impossible for them to stay silent. Some felt it was their obligation to tell when they were asked to marry because of the widespread belief that survivors were unfit for marriage. They were thought to be physically weak and prone to illness, their offspring likely to be deformed or disabled. Many survivors thought that their assumed liability as future spouses must be revealed before entering matrimony. Similarly, some *hibakusha* felt compelled to reveal their survivorhood for the first time when they considered having children or became pregnant. Their concern about their offspring overrode their desire not to tell. Other US survivors broke silence when they fell ill, which they suspected was caused by the bomb. Their stay in a hospital, or bedridden time at home, was difficult to hide. Still others, female *hibakusha* in particular, revealed their survivorhood by simply going to work. Hiding their hairlessness with scarves, which in fact signaled survivorhood in postwar Hiroshima and Nagasaki, women who had surpassed the prime age for marriage and continued to earn wages embodied a post-nuclear way of living. It was not a time for them to stay at home; economic and social independence had become a necessity. Either by words or actions, then, US survivors broke silence even as they kept their experiences mostly unspoken. This reveals how the structure of the counter-memory of the bomb, discussed in Chapter 2, matured in the years following the war. Entwining silence and speech, the memory grew quietly by absorbing US survivors' experiences of poverty, illness, and loss as they explored the uncertain world after the nuclear destruction.

This counter-memory of the bomb healed US survivors as much as it kept their experiences hidden. To be sure, in the era when people expected that conflicting national interests and mutual hostility between the occupiers and the occupied would dominate life in the cities, US *hibakusha*'s cross-nationality remained largely invisible. But the counter-memory of the bomb also created a space where US survivors' sense of layered belonging might become a source of healing, if only in quiet ways. In this light, it is essential to see that US survivors' occasional speaking – about illness, marriage, pregnancy, and work – was inseparably connected to their encounters with authorities that shaped postwar national and international policies in the Pacific region. These policies brought US *hibakusha* a new awareness of their cross-nationality, offering them opportunities to reflect on their unique experiences as immigrants and to reach out to an emerging identity as survivors. When the US occupation forces arrived, for instance, US survivors found many familiar faces among the GIs. They were their brothers, cousins, or friends, including a number of Japanese Americans, some of whom helped US survivors to reconnect with their families. Through personal channels across the ocean, letters were exchanged, as were food, clothes, medicines, and countless other supplies. These goods and opportunities offered a sense of new beginnings for US *hibakusha*. In the deprived, black-and-grey landscape, connections that came through personal acquaintances lit up with warmth. Some men in the occupation forces became US survivors' family members because they married them, often in a great rush because of the limited amount of time allowed to US military men in Japan. The ABCC, established in late 1946 by President Harry S. Truman's directive for the purpose of studying radiation's effects on humans in Hiroshima and Nagasaki, also offered opportunities for US *hibakusha* to reconnect with their families. To some degree, US survivors shared with Japanese survivors a critique of the commission as invested only in conducting research on radiation illness. The ABCC was not interested in offering treatment to *hibakusha* when it was most needed. Many US survivors felt insulted when visited by the commission's representatives when they became ill or their family members passed away; these institutional folks looked too thirsty for materials to satisfy their scientific curiosity.

And yet, US survivors also found their neighbors and friends at the ABCC, which offered one of the largest number of employment opportunities for those equipped with bilingual skills and cross-national experiences in postwar Japan. Just as the US occupation forces were not simply a former-enemy-turned-occupier, American science of the nuclear age, embodied by the ABCC, was not simply a source of apprehension for many US survivors. In fact, these institutions affirmed important threads in their history as immigrants, rife with familial and communal meanings. By exploring these meanings, I show not only similarities but also crucial differences between the ABCC and the occupation forces as they affected the relationship among America, Japan, and Korea that took shape in Hiroshima and Nagasaki after the war. As I argue, the ABCC's approach to US *hibakusha* often pried opened their silence, a way of healing they had devised. In contrast, the occupation forces largely left US survivors' healing process alone, while offering numerous opportunities for new beginnings. Both the ABCC and the occupation forces contributed to the counter-memory of the bomb, as they both largely ignored cross-national effects of the bomb in their pursuit of national interests. Still, they did so in importantly different ways. By highlighting the distinction, I hope to move beyond the assumption that the relationship between former enemies was underpinned by mutual distrust, hostility, and fear, especially in the early phase of the occupation.[2] The cities of immigrants had more nuanced responses to the postwar era than an assumed national animosity leads us to expect.

As US survivors rebuilt their family and community connections across the Pacific, they became increasingly aware of the arbitrariness of citizenship defined and divided by national and racial boundaries. As seen in Chapter 1, some US-born *hibakusha* had obtained Japanese citizenship while keeping their American citizenship throughout the war. Others, including deportees, had gained Japanese citizenship in exchange for American citizenship. Still others had lost both citizenships because of inconsistent, constantly changing citizenship requirements on both sides of the Pacific. Those who found themselves lacking US citizenship or documentation for it after the war had to endure years of waiting before they could return to America. Korean survivors, like other Koreans, lost their Japanese nationality after the war. Although the loss symbolized Korea's liberation from Japan's colonial rule, it also deprived them of their rights as Japanese nationals.[3] For instance, Koreans after the war were not given access to Japanese national health insurance. Korean survivors who returned to Korea were met with the lack of not only medical treatment but also social understanding. Indeed, symptoms of radiation illness could easily be seen as signs of national disloyalty. The idea persisted that those who had left the Korean peninsula for Japan proper before the last years of the war had betrayed the homeland. Thus, whether migrating to the United States from Japan or Korea, Korean American survivors had a bewildering array of experiences of nonrecognition based on the lack of clearly defined citizenship rights by the time they headed to the American shore. Citizenship was a complicated matter, too, for people originating in Korea or Japan who tried to cross the ocean to America after the war because of their marriages. In the United States before the 1967 Supreme Court decision that found anti-miscegenation laws unconstitutional, the absence of citizenship rights was inseparable from a racism that curtailed *hibakusha*'s ability to marry and settle on the other side of the Pacific. Although the Alien Brides Act of 1947 made it possible for Asian wives of American soldiers to be admitted to the country, their marriage was not necessarily recognized by the state in which they wished to live.[4] Clearly, US survivors had to begin to consider regulations that were distinctively hostile to them even before they departed.

When seen through US *hibakusha*'s remembering, institutions and policies driven by national interests begin to look strangely warped. Their stated purposes did not seem to recognize the very people that they intended to govern, educate, assist, or study. In a larger sense, then, this chapter attempts to show how the gaps between the interests of national institutions and those of their assumed beneficiaries continued to shape US survivors' history in conflicted ways through the Korean War of 1950–1953 and beyond. In fact, the importance of this war in the history of the bomb cannot be overstated; it goes well beyond the geopolitics of the nuclear buildup during the Cold War. For one thing, the war brought a number of men in American uniform to the US military bases in Japan, offering more opportunities for them to meet US survivors. Some Nikkei men serving in the US Army in Korea took their military leave in Japan, facilitated by both the physical proximity of the countries and their family connections to Japan. Many letters and supplies now flew not only from the United States to Japan, but also from America to Korea, then from Korea to Japan. The still-restrictive immigration and marriage laws in the United States made this flow of people an excellent opportunity for marriage for Japanese American men in uniform. The US military intervention in the Korean Peninsula also planted seeds for some Korean survivors to move to America. Both in Japan and Korea, US men of all races serving the war fraternized with local women, including *hibakusha*. Some of these affiliations resulted in marriage, leading to survivors' migration across the Pacific eastward.[5] Here again, the making or remaking of cross-national ties was entangled with tensions created by nations where clear boundaries between peoples were a given. By leaving Japan, survivors became inadvertently ineligible for the benefits that the Japanese government was soon to offer to survivors. The Law Concerning Medical Care in 1957 offered *hibakusha* living in Japan government-funded medical checkups and treatment of radiation illnesses at designated medical facilities. Survivors who stayed in Japan became beneficiaries of the law, while those who left Japan – both Korean survivors who went back to Korea and American survivors who returned to the United States – were excluded from the law's coverage. For many decades to follow, not only the Japanese government but also its American and Korean counterparts devised no system for aiding non-Japanese survivors outside Japan.

As the nation states defined immigrants' citizenry during the early years of the Cold War based largely on their national and racial backgrounds, their history of cross-national linkages formed before, during, and after the nuclear explosions was nearly forgotten. The histories of those who faced a range of obstacles in marriage, employment, and migration, became too easily hidden behind stories about the Cold War that focused on America, the divided Korea, and Japan as actors defined by their respective national interests. US survivors' remembering indeed became the counter-memory of the bomb in this context, too, a reminder of Hiroshima and Nagasaki that continued to reverberate cross-nationally in the crucial fifteen years after the nuclear holocaust.

Loss, Illness, and Poverty in the Silent Remembering of the Bomb

Growing up, Kyohei Sakata never saw his mother out of bed. Always bedridden, she passed away three years after the war's end.

A family physician who frequented his home told the family that hers was not an isolated case. There were many others suffering prolonged illness without a diagnosis and being relieved only by an early death.[6] In Seiko Fujimoto's family, a misfortune fell on her younger brother. Diagnosed with leukemia as a four-year-old, he was the reason why the family moved from Hiroshima to Tokyo after the war. Their hope was to find a better doctor to treat him. Despite the family's effort, however, the boy passed away within a few years.[7] Yasuo Grant Fujita lost nearly all his family members when he was five years old. After his grandfather, then his mother, died within two weeks after the bomb, Fujita and his younger brother were taken to an orphanage. There, Fujita lost his brother to malnutrition. Fujita stayed in the institution for three years, until his father returned from a labor camp in Siberia.[8] For those left behind, the loss of loved ones meant that they, too, could face the beginning of the end at any time. Fujita wondered why he stayed alive while everyone else vanished. Sakata recalled how terrified he was when his father asked the family physician about the likely fate of the youngest of the family – Sakata himself. The doctor's response was that he might live "ten years if he were lucky." Sakata, then a five-year-old (who later became a leader in US *hibakusha*'s activism), took this statement to heart, thinking "this is it for me" every time he caught a cold. He also learned to shy away from making any long-term plans.[9] Fusae Kurihara, too, remembered obsessing about her symptoms and her imminent death. Since she had survived the explosion in an office just one-and-a-half miles away from the epicenter of Hiroshima, she suffered anemia. Seeing many in her neighborhood die although "they didn't even have any injury and were not burned at all," she felt she had to "face the possibility of dying at any time." Thus, it brought her extraordinary pleasure when August 6, 1946, arrived. She explained:

> I've heard if people survived one year from the day, this person would be okay. That's why, one year after the A-bomb, my aunt celebrated my survival with red rice. And she said to me, "Oh, Fusae, you will be okay. You can live a long life."[10]

The red rice was *sekihan*, a red-bean-and-sweet-*mochi*-rice dish that Japanese people prepared for special occasions such as birthdays. With illness and death so common, survival even for a year was a cause for celebration.

When people held sickness and death so close in their daily lives, reasons to talk about suffering disappeared. At least this was how many US *hibakusha* responded to the post-nuclear holocaust world. Who would want to talk about a girl with no hair and scars on her face, when there were so many others like her in her classroom, her neighborhood, and her city?[11] Her teacher had injuries on her leg, which caused her to walk with a limp.[12] When injury and illness were so prevalent, distinctions that usually separated people – young and old, teachers and students – mattered less. They did not dictate how people were affected by the bomb. Polite silence was gentle to all; to break it was to inflict pain everywhere. The existing literature about the bomb has highlighted various discriminations against survivors, and unwanted stares and whispers were certainly plentiful.[13] And yet, it is also notable that survivors with surprising uniformity remembered thick silence around the bomb, suggesting psychological and cultural significance of the reticence for *hibakusha*. In Keiko Shinmoto's mind, everyone was "in the same situation" and thus "they just [didn't] have too much to say."[14] Asked why there had been no talk of the bomb, Izumi Hirano offered a similar explanation: "Because everyone experienced the same thing." But wasn't the explosion worth talking about regardless? Hirano's thought was that the bomb was too shocking to talk about because of its momentary nature. "In Tokyo and elsewhere, the air raids came gradually, giving people at least some time to run. With the atomic bomb, it was just this one second that destroyed everything."[15] There was no time to grasp it, hence it generated no speakable things.

But silence was not an act of resignation; it was an act of reaching out toward healing. Even as Hirano remembered the silence in the years following the war, he also kept a sharp memory of rare occasions on which the silence came close to being breached. On these occasions, both illness and injury were turned into teenagers' jokes. Seeing a piece of glass protruding from Hirano's face, his classmates offered "to pick out that pimple." It was their way of easing their friend's pain, after being struck by shattered glass at the moment of explosion. The friends also pulled each other's hair to see if it came off, and they made a big deal out of a strand that did come off, not because of radiation exposure but simply because it was strongly pulled. As they shouted "It came off! It came off!" they were celebrating one more day of survival, where silence was still mostly in place but perhaps a small dose of fear was alleviated.[16] Toshiko Hishinuma's mother was determined not to talk about the bomb because she did not want to hurt Hishinuma's older brother Takeo's feelings. As Hishinuma recalled, early in the morning of August 6, 1945, six-year-old Takeo had asked his older brother Yoshio to go to school earlier than usual. When the blast hit the school, the younger brother survived while the older perished. If Yoshio were at home at 8:15am, as he would have been without Takeo's urging, he might have survived. Seeing that Takeo "secretly" reflected on this possibility, his mother decided that no talk of the bomb was a rule of the household.[17] Silence was keenly seen, and it became protected by another layer of silence. Survivors' will was busily at work, and its emotive power impressed them. Jeremy Oshima's aunt was severely scarred, and there was a time when she asked Oshima to "help her commit suicide." When "somehow, she came through" the difficult time, silence began. Oshima was amazed by its encompassing power: "Even when we meet each other, we never talk about it. We just kind of erase it out of our minds, that there was such a time." Although Oshima's aunt became active in an antinuclear group years later, the silence over this aspect of her suffering was kept watchfully between them.[18] It seems as if mutually recognized silence was a source of strength to speak at another time, another place.

US *hibakusha* remained silent for different reasons, most of which contained a desire for both hiding and healing. To be sure, there were some who recalled the silence imposed by the censorship of the US occupation forces. The press code prohibited the release of a range of materials related to Hiroshima and Nagasaki, curtailing publication of scientific papers, newspaper articles, literary materials, and films and documentaries about the bomb.[19] Seiko Fujimoto recalled how her schoolteachers "did not talk about the bomb *at all*" because of "the pressure by the country that won the war." "Because we lost the war," explained her teachers, "we must show perseverance" even as the censorship seemed to continue as firmly as it did during the war.[20] Some of those who moved out of the cities after the war found no one who lent a sympathetic ear, which they felt made silence their only option. Masako B. Hamada's family, as were many other US survivors', was separated by the Pacific during wartime. Soon after the war's end, in 1947, she went back to the United States, while her parents stayed in Japan for a few more years. So, she "didn't talk to parents that much," including about her memories of the bomb.[21]

More pronounced than these reasons related to an enforced or circumstantial hiding, though, were US *hibakusha*'s conscious efforts to heal by way of silence, by fending off the discrimination against survivors. As Tokie Akihara put it bluntly, "there was nothing to be gained by talking" about the bomb. If she came out as a survivor, she could be denied marriage or employment.[22] Every survivor seemed to know someone visibly scarred who missed a chance to marry. Unlike others whose scars were invisible, they could not hide their survivorhood. Why, then, make invisible marks of the bomb visible by talking, if the result was to be ostracized? Michiko Peters recalled how she chose not to tell when she learned of a rumor that radiation illness could spread out. To avoid being treated as a pariah by keeping silent struck her as sensible.[23] Isamu Shin echoed Peters's sentiment when he relayed his experience of being asked not to donate his blood. "Because you were bombed in Nagasaki, your blood might be contaminated by radiation," he was told. This ran counter to Shin's own sense of his health, which he thought to be good despite his exposure to radiation.[24] Keeping silence around the bomb, then, was his way not to lose sight of *his* sense of self-worth. Fumiko Imai, too, avowed *hibakusha*'s right to heal by keeping silence. She had a coworker who always wore a long-sleeve shirt, even at the height of Hiroshima's summer, because short sleeves would not hide his keloid. Looking back on the gentle silence that surrounded him – no one said anything about his odd choice of outfit – she thought that it was good that there had been little "fuss" about the bomb. Solitary though it might be, hiding also had a way of creating a collective place of healing. Compared to more recent times when even a relatively "small leakage of radiation is loudly reported" by the media, as was the case with the 2011 Fukushima nuclear plant accident, the years after 1945 contained more room for unspoken healing that involved non-survivors as well as survivors.[25]

One might argue that if survivors took a different route for healing and voiced their suffering more publicly, they might have received recognition from the Japanese government sooner. Despite the mounting number of inexplicable deaths and illnesses, survivors did not receive any state recognition of their losses until 1957. As Chapters 4 and 5 will discuss, Japanese survivors in Japan by then began to attain a conspicuous public presence through not only their own organizations but also antinuclear groups that sprang up across the country. When contrasted to these later developments, US *hibakusha*'s silence in the first decade after the war may seem lacking. But their remembering was surprisingly devoid of frustration over the quiet ways in which they went about their healing. That the silence was a result of survivors' considered decision to heal – and that it was a therapeutic effort they made consciously after the nuclear holocaust – becomes clearer if we consider other subjects about which they outspokenly expressed their feelings.

Mitsuko Okimoto, for instance, recalled how her family was angry with President Truman, the man who made the decision to drop the bomb. Although it is not clear if her family talked about their anger publicly, it still was more readily expressed than her family members' feelings about Okimoto's scars – a topic that hardly came up.[26] Many US *hibakusha* also expressed their anger rather freely about what they perceived to be arrogance among US occupiers or employees of the ABCC. When US survivors chose such Americans as their spouses, as many did, some of their families were loudly upset about sending their kin to the country that dropped the bomb. These families' resentment often intensified when the spouses were white, suggesting that the "country" of America could be externalized for some US *hibakusha*'s families when it took the face of the dominant race.[27] Thus, even when the state authorities prohibited release of any information about the bomb, survivors did not simply suppress their critiques of America. Instead, they chose what to say and when to say it. In this light, their silence shows their effort for autonomy, healing, and care as they grappled with the unknowns of the nuclear attacks' aftermaths.

There is some evidence suggesting that, in choosing silence, survivors continued to use some of the folk medicines discussed in Chapter 2. Seeing that her daughter continued to suffer difficulty in breathing, for instance, Okimoto's mother fed her with wheat flour dissolved in rice vinegar. The solution went down relatively easily, and had a soothing effect on Okimoto's chest.[28] A few years after the bomb, Isamu Shin's grandfather grew impatient with a burn that seemed to never heal. It appeared to remain inflamed, with an unseemly abscess. Someone told him that saltwater might help, so he started to drink it. It caused diarrhea, a reaction considered to have a decontaminating effect.[29] Pak Namjoo's mother also drank a special kind of purging drink, a strong herbal tea. Someone told her that the bomb was "poisonous" and that this was the reason for her hair falling out. Pak was impressed by how, shortly after she began the tea regimen, her mother's hair loss stopped.[30] Many survivors continued to use these home remedies even as they went to hospitals that began to return to the cities and offered Western medicine. Indeed, some early literary works about the bomb depicted the use of folk medicine alongside modern medicine in the years after 1945. Published in 1965, Ibuse Masuji's *Black Rain* revolved around a group of survivors who suffered radiation illnesses four years after the bomb, when the memory of the devastation among non-survivors seemed to be receding. Plagued by chronic fatigue, survivors eagerly sought "live blood of carp" to boost their energy. They took this folk medicine discreetly without telling anyone but their family members. Just as US *hibakusha* consumed their handmade medicines at home, then, these survivors in Ibuse's story infused hiding with healing.

Interestingly, another medicine used by Ibuse's survivors, aloe, was recommended by the physician treating Yasuko, the novel's heroine, as something to take together with Western medicine prescribed by the physician. Going to the physician's clinic was a publicly visible act, revealing Yasuko's illness to her neighbors. Taking aloe was an entirely different matter. Similar to the home remedies used by real-life survivors, this natural medicine was consumed discreetly, which fostered silence even among her family members. At one point in the story, Yasuko's uncle discovered that someone had been eating aloe in the garden; there were fresh cuts on the plant. The uncle at first thought that it was his wife. It was only much later that he discovered it was actually his niece Yasuko.[31] Both US *hibakusha*'s remembering and *Black Rain*'s depictions of folk medicine, then, suggest a relationship between Western medicine and its Japanese counterpart relatively free of tension. The years following 1945 brought back modern medicine and hospitals. But they did not eliminate home remedies; instead, they coexisted with modern ones, often in a complementary way. Whether to take a folk medicine was a person's decision, which might be seen but not necessarily commented upon. A survivor could make a decision without prompting others to make a "fuss" about it. In this way, folk medicines were important ingredients in the process of hiding and healing, protected by quiet observations made by all parties involved.

Poverty was prevalent in postwar Hiroshima and Nagasaki, made to look more so because much of the wealth remaining after August 1945 was carefully hidden. Farmers in the cities' outskirts made sure that their produce was kept in storage either for their families or black market customers. Landlords scrambled to divide up their properties among their relatives, so that they would not be bought up and distributed to former tenants, as was likely to happen under post-war regulations.[32] Much of the wealth in public view, then, belonged to the occupation forces. Beyond the well-known memories among the Japanese children of chocolate kisses and chewing gum that American GIs had given them, US *hibakusha* relayed many stories of US materials coming or returning to their lives as the beginning of their recovery. In a way similar to how their silence about radiation illness helped their healing, US survivors' experiences of poverty embodied not merely despair but also aspiration for a step forward. Chizuko Blakes recalled receiving a green military blanket distributed by the United States. Come winter, she dyed it brown using *habucha*, herbal tea leaves. An acquaintance of hers, a tailor, hand-stitched the blanket and trans-formed it into an overcoat. Looking back on this, Blakes said: "Yes, we wore *that*," as if to remind herself of its bleakness. But saying this also prompted her to recall her career as a tailor. In fact, the blanket-turned-coat was the beginning of her interest in tailoring, which soon expanded from women's to men's clothing. Following better-paid jobs, Blakes moved from Nagasaki to Yokosuka where the US Navy base was located. She met her future husband there, and their marriage brought her to America.[33]

Julie Kumi Fukuda's remembering, too, contained layered meanings she found in material abundance because of her intimate tie to the United States. A few months after the war's end, Fukuda was on her way from Hiroshima to Tokyo to take up a laundry job at General Headquarters, US Army. This position was made pos-sible by her mother's cousin, who had come to Japan as part of the headquarters' Civil Service division. Since Fukuda had been left without any other family members in wartime Japan, this cousin was the only person she could rely on. On the train to the capital she met a few American soldiers, with whom she interacted:

> We said, "Hi." And they said, "Hi." And we put our baggage in, and pretty soon they're looking and they said, "Oh, you're from the States." You know, we had [American] stickers on there, and stuff. And we sat up half the night talking with them, and they were so nice. They covered – when we fell asleep, they covered us up with blankets.[34]

Similar to Blakes's, Fukuda's memory is underpinned by material scarcity coming into sharp focus particularly when compared to the abundance of US supplies. At the same time, Fukuda's remembering was about one of the first encounters she had with her countrymen after the war. Being kept warm by a US serviceman's blanket was important. It symbolized something hopeful about the new steps she was taking – a kindness transpiring tenderly among those who shared home.

Just as Blakes's determination to make the best of the blanket marked the beginning of her life after the bomb, Fukuda's story conveyed a distinct turning point from which she began to rebuild herself. Despite the divergent meanings they found in the same object – a blanket – the significance of their ties to America was palpable in both. These connections were evident, too, in US survivors' remembering of the boxes from family and friends in America that began to arrive shortly after the war's end. These boxes, packed with supplies, linked families still separated by strict rules regulating international travels. Ships from Japan to America were not open to civilians until 1947; but packages made their way across the ocean well before then. So it was that George Kazuto Saiki received sugar, powdered milk, cocoa, sausage, and SPAM cans from his friend in Hawai'i.[35] Tokie Sakai, too, got boxes from her aunt living in Hawai'i. A lovely pattern of yellow flowers on a children's dress stayed in her memory. Brightly colored children's clothes had been absent in Japan for a long time.[36] Kiyoshi Mike Nakagawa received a box from his father in Sacramento, containing chocolate, aspirin, and tobacco. Nakagawa's favorite was Levi's jeans, which his friends envied so much that he agreed to give away a pair.[37] Kazue McCrea's sister received clothes and dolls from her aunt in Los Angeles. McCrea remembered how they looked different from – better than – their Japanese counterparts.[38] As Nakagawa and McCrea later learned, both senders had been in Nikkei concentration camps during the war. They had been stripped of their belongings. The contents of these boxes, then, were not what their senders could easily afford; instead, the contents were carefully chosen gifts.

These materials were shared or sold as well as directly consumed by their recipients. Seiko Fujimoto recalled getting saccharin from her neighbor who had a relative in the United States.[39] Nakagawa took the tobacco that his father had sent him to a local stationary shop. In exchange for the boxes of Lucky Strike and Camel cigarettes, he got a fair amount of school supplies.[40] Some US *hibakusha* who returned to America relatively early, in the late 1940s, relayed similar memories, suggesting how US supplies continued to cross the ocean westward even after survivors began to return. When Izumi Hirano was back in Hawai'i in 1949 as a twenty-year-old, he worked on a poultry farm where one of his duties was to feed the chickens. He was inspired when he noticed that the large bags of chicken feed, about twenty of which he emptied every day, were made of cotton and had a rather handsome print on them. He washed and ironed them, then sent them to his mother who was still in Japan. She sewed a few bags together to make children's clothes; the fabric could also be exchanged for a bag of rice. Regardless of its original use, cotton of decent quality was treasured. Remembering this story, Hirano's demeanor was matter-of-fact.[41] This does not erase a sense of humiliation that US survivors like Blakes felt about their poverty. And yet, remembering such as Hirano's suggests that humiliation did not necessarily boil down to a national animosity. US survivors' experiences as immigrants continued to shape the world after the nuclear holocaust, often serving as starting points to rebuild their lives amid death, illness, and poverty. As they practiced quiet hiding and healing, there arose moments of new beginnings.

Reconnecting through the Occupation Forces: The Return of Cross-Nationality

These moments of beginnings for US survivors did not wait for the occupation forces to arrive. They started right after the war ended, when hopes for family reunions were suddenly rekindled. When Yuriko Furubayashi heard of the Japanese surrender on August 15, 1945, her response was sheer excitement: "They surrendered ... for me, it was: 'Oh, what are we doing now? I can see my family!'"[42] Jeremy Oshima, too, felt happy about the war's conclusion. He might be able to see his family again, although at this point he still did not know where they were in the United States.[43] The remembering by US *hibakusha* brings a sharp focus to how Americans' joy of VJ-Day – an iconic image in US twentieth-century history – was not confined to one side of the Pacific.[44] Although Furubayashi and Oshima did not overtly express pleasure over Japan's loss, they shared a surging expectation for a family reunion with many other Americans on the other side of the ocean. As far as they knew, their parents had not been killed by the war, and now they would not be. As the weight of the war lifted, people's longing to see loved ones swelled. Korean American survivors, too, felt rising hope. John Hong eagerly waited for a ship to bring him back to Korea. His parents had been in Shanghai since the war's end. As former subjects of the Japanese empire, they were soon to be expelled from China. But they could not find a boat to return to Korea. After Hong arrived in Busan on September 10, 1945, his parents remained trapped in Shanghai for another year. When his parents finally made their way back in 1946, they did not know that they would soon be separated from their son again. The outbreak of the Korean War in 1950 brought Hong to the warfront; a few years later, he was ordered to attend a military school in Georgia, a move required by the Republic of Korea–United States Mutual Defense Treaty of 1953. The family reunion proceeded on ground kept unstable by the war's aftermath and the coming of the next war.[45]

As Hong's remembering shows, individual aspirations to bring families together invariably became entwined with America's early Cold War strategies in Asia. These strategies aimed to contain as much as to liberate, resulting in an array of policies in Japan, including racial segregation within the occupation forces, suppression of free speech among Japanese civilians, the granting of suffrage to Japanese women, and land and currency reforms that aimed to equalize the distribution of capital. In this particular mix of policies, US "liberal paternalism" began to congeal, with an eye toward global leadership soon to manifest itself violently on the Korean Peninsula.[46] It was in this era of unforeseen transformation that Nikkei survivors in Japan began reconnecting with their families. Indeed, opportunities to locate family members were brought about first by the US occupation troops, something that ran counter to the commonly held assumption that a mutual distrust existed between the former enemies in the early days of the occupation. As shown by scholars, Americans expected the Japanese to harbor hatred against those they had fought so unwaveringly. Often, the Japanese saw Americans in the streets as humiliating signs of defeat; some Japanese felt that these Americans might be vengeful.[47] Neither should Japanese American members of the occupation forces be trusted; they might be mediators who "transform former 'enemies into friends,'" but they could also "behave unsympathetically and arrogantly toward Japanese nationals." Lacking the obvious racial differences that distinguished Japanese civilians from non-Japanese American servicemen, some

Japanese American members of the occupation forces engaged in the role of "aggressive conquerors ... in the most 'undemocratic' manner"[48] so as to accentuate their status as victors.

Just how Nikkei survivors negotiated their relationships with Japanese American occupiers, then, reveals much about the interplay of race, citizenship, and national belonging in this transitional era. Indeed, US *hibakusha*'s cross-nationality varied in ways not obvious to the occupiers or the occupied, making it all the more necessary for them to make absolutely clear their desire for family reunion. Furubayashi, for instance, sent a letter to her parents in Hawaiʻi through the Red Cross, a godsend for family who had read about the Hiroshima bombing in US newspapers and thought her dead. When Furubayashi's brother was drafted as an "occupational," his father told him to "get assignment in Japan so that you can ... look and see if your sister is okay. She said it's okay, but you never know, maybe she's critically ill."[49] Sumie Kubota learned that her mother in Sacramento was safe and sound through a family friend, a Nisei, who had come to Japan as a captain of the US Army. Until then, she "did not even know if she [her mother] was alive," because of the lack of reliable means of communication.[50] Even with the postal service run by the Red Cross, sending letters across the Pacific was a shaky business, frequently marred by the dislocation of both senders and recipients.[51] The Furubayashis, who managed to get their letters through, were fortunate. Families like the Kubotas, who had to rely on a friend to relay a crucial piece of information about the family's whereabouts, were more numerous. Most important, neither Furubayashi nor Kubota encountered the kind of naked nationalism that often pitted Japanese and American citizens against each other in the occupation era.

This lack of antagonism, seen in Furubayashi's and Kubota's cases, might be explained by the fact that they were family and friends. But evidence suggests that Nikkei connections were a sound basis of trans-Pacific communication among strangers, too. Perhaps because of the shaky dependability of the Red Cross, Sayoko Utagawa's father in Seattle asked a Nisei officer assigned to a branch of the US occupation forces in Japan to deliver a letter to his daughter in Hiroshima. Albeit a stranger, a personal letter carrier seemed more dependable than a bridge offered by the faceless organization. Looking back on this era, Utagawa seemed amused as well as grateful: The Nisei officer who delivered her father's letter to her "was *not* our family friend or acquaintance. He was just *tōrisugari no hito* [a stranger who happened to pass by]." Her father was so desperate to locate Utagawa that he asked anyone who might be willing to help. Before too long, this "stranger" was delivering letters back and forth between the daughter and the father, which eventually made him a family friend. He became "Mr. Fukuhara" in Utagawa's remembering, a kind Nisei man.[52] This sort of story affirmed that familial and communal belonging had not been entirely broken by the war, something that US survivors felt necessary to remember. Despite the strengths of cross-national ties that carried them through the bombings, US survivors did not simply assume that these connections were there. Ties may be weakened if not seen, felt, and spoken; more urgently so after the nuclear holocaust had generated layers of silence. For many US *hibakusha*, the US occupation forces offered one of the first steps toward the reaffirmation of their cross-nationality. For Japanese Americans who came to Japan as part of the US military, an urge for family reunion expressed by Nikkei in Japan might have been a reminder of how, despite the war, their history as children and grandchildren of immigrants had not been erased. Strangers helped each other, while those who were fortunate enough to have families and friends relied on them to locate estranged Nikkei.

The coming of the occupation forces also offered US survivors and their families employment opportunities. In particular, those fluent in English were in high demand. Hayami Fukino recalled how her family hosted two military officers who were tasked with dismantling Japanese Imperial Army bombs still hidden in the mountains. As she recalled, "We were lucky [because] we [knew] a little English ... They got all kind of food ... [and] we were able to get their food. .... [English] was the reason why they came to our house." US officers did not go to Japanese houses more spacious than Fukino's because their residents would not be able to communicate.[53]

Katie Yanagawa's father (who had caught the chicken at ground zero) got a job as the US Army's interpreter without even looking for it. He was in the reception area of the army station in Kure, waiting for his second cousin who was there for a job interview. An "American soldier came in and said hello to my father," said Yanagawa, "so Father said, 'Hello.' And then of course he [the soldier] realized that the pronunciation of the 'hello' is not typical Japanese (*laughter*)." As shown by her laughter, this was a surprising moment when the most ordinary part of their family history – their cross-nationality – was suddenly made to shine. Yanagawa's father was "hired on the spot," bringing his family a good income.[54] US *hibakusha* could find themselves in an envious position vis-à-vis the Japanese who lacked cross-national skills.

And yet, evidence suggests that Nikkei in occupied Japan also faced racial boundaries hardened by the war. Early encounters between US *hibakusha* and US military personnel indicate that the latter were well aware of US citizens' presence in Hiroshima and Nagasaki after the war. Before bombing the cities, the US government was fully aware of the presence of "disloyals" and their families in Japan, who had renounced their American citizenship while under duress in Nikkei incarceration camps. As discussed in Chapter 1, their deportation was conducted under the auspices of the War Relocation Authority and the State Department. There is no record indicating that these former US citizens counted as anything but enemy nationals in the eyes of the US military and political leadership.[55] After the occupation forces came to Japan, however, it likely became more difficult for US authorities to see all Nikkei in Japan, including those affected by the bomb, simply as "disloyals." To be sure, it is possible that most US *hibakusha* who interacted with the US military around this time did not reveal their survivorhood. Silence was about hiding as much as healing, easing the way for US officials to keep the knowledge of US casualties of the bomb at arm's length. But silence did not mean that what was unspoken went unnoticed. Some US survivors' remembering suggests that both their cross-nationality and their survivorhood were easily noticed by many, including US military personnel.

May Yamaoka worked as a typist for several months at the Kyoto office of the US occupation forces before she left for Stockton, California, in April 1947. She spoke English and was able to type in the language. Too, she had suffered a leg injury, a cut inflicted on August 6, 1945, that required surgery before it started to heal.[56] Katie Yanagawa's father, whose pronunciation of "Hello" landed him an American job, sustained a six-inch cut on his back. He was from Hiroshima, and his workplace was nearby Kure.[57] Neither Yamaoka nor Yanagawa's father was a deportee whose loyalty was believed to lay squarely with Japan. US *hibakusha*'s cross-cultural skills, along with their resumes, likely made the fact visible to their employers.

Perhaps Yamaoka never let her scar be seen by any of her coworkers. It is also possible that the injury of Yanagawa's father was completely healed by the time he took the job as an interpreter, or, the scar was easy enough to hide under his shirt. But the sheer number of encounters that occured between US officials and US survivors suggests that, at least, the cross-nationality of the nuclear holocaust was not invisible. And yet, it was rarely mentioned, indicating that US authorities, too, contributed to the making of the counter-memory of the bomb. It could be that US military persons could see survivors only as Japanese nationals. The attacks had been so uniformly represented as being against Japan, that victims by definition had to be Japanese.[58] Perhaps, too, it was that the bomb's cross-national effects were noticed but left unarticulated because Nikkei were "perpetual foreigners." They had been deemed undeserving of citizenship rights no matter which side of the Pacific they were on. In this light, the Japanese as former enemies and Japanese Americans as racial minorities became easily conflated; their universal suffering of the nuclear holocaust made it even harder to distinguish them. These factors, combined with US *hibakusha*'s need to heal by hiding, likely kept the cross-national extent of the nuclear destruction difficult to grasp. If silence about US survivors arose out of necessity at first, it then created a setting in which US occupation authorities could believe that the bomb was a weapon targeting enemy nationals of the Japanese race. Or, that the bomb was directed toward the Japanese race that was, by definition, the enemy. These two conceptions became exceedingly blurred to the extent that there was no plausible space for Nikkei survivors. Some Japanese American GIs tried to carve out a space for themselves by exercising their power and privilege as American occupiers; Japanese American survivors' US citizenship, by contrast, seemed to lose its import in the face of racism and nationalism that pushed them together with Japanese citizens.

It is not surprising, then, that US survivors held a highly mixed view of the occupation forces despite the opportunities they brought. This led US survivors to perform somewhat of a balancing act. To be sure, some remembered it affirmatively; simultaneously, these memories are complicated by others that raised questions about the occupation's impact on US *hibakusha*. I will first look at the favorable memories, and then the more critical ones, both of which I see as significantly gendered. Here, it is important to note that, among US survivors, even those who had no history of living in the United States frequently took an American job in Japan. This was because many had a Japanese American relative or friend with a position in the occupation forces. These Nisei or Sansei individuals recommended US survivors for employment, something that proved convenient for both the occupiers and the occupied.

Kazue Kawasaki, a Japanese-born American *hibakusha*, started a position in the Etajima office of the occupation forces in 1946 as a sixteen-year-old. At that time, she still suffered from a leg injury, peculiar spots all over her body, and fatigue likely caused by her low blood count. But she also had a reason to be hopeful; she was a high school graduate, and this accomplishment, still rare for girls in Japan, made her feel that she might obtain a job better than cleaning or cooking. Her relative, a Nisei woman already working as a translator in the office, introduced Kawasaki to her boss, an Australian major (or colonel; Kawasaki could not recall which). Consisting of cleaning at first, Kawasaki's job took a surprising turn when the major found pictures that she had drawn during a break. Impressed by their meticulousness, he decided to train her as a draftsperson. He assigned a junior engineer to coach her, and he procured a drawing table especially made to fit her modest height. Kawasaki obtained not only career development but also an opportunity for marriage during the year in Etajima. Her future husband, a Nisei, was an employee of the same office. Her initial fear that a woman in ill-health like herself would not be recognized by the US military turned out to be unfounded.[59]

Rememberings like Kawasaki's are not uncommon, particularly among female US *hibakusha*. Jobs brought to Japan during the occupation era carried particularly compelling meanings for women, often breaking gender boundaries. They had spent the war years in Japan where women rarely worked outside of the household. Now, times were different. Material deprivation made it necessary for anyone able-bodied (and not so able-bodied, too) to find a job, and women were no exception.[60] Reasons for Nikkei survivors to find employment were numerous. Japanese Americans who had lost their families to the bomb were taken into relatives' homes, something that often made it necessary to contribute to the hosts' household income. For Nisei and Sansei children in Japan who had lost touch with their parents in the United States during the war, the need for financial security was equally urgent.[61] For Chisa Frank, who had lost her baby son to the bomb and had been divorced by her blameful husband, obtaining employment was nothing less than a means of survival. With no income or marriage prospects, she felt even more hopeless because her hair began to fall out. She believed the likelihood that this "bald-headed lady" would get a job was small, so she started a sewing business at home. But soon, she obtained a position as an English-speaking switchboard operator at a telephone company working with the occupation authority. She went to work with a scarf to hide her hairlessness, although she did not expect the scarf to make her survivorhood invisible; people would know what the scarf was hiding. More importantly for her, though, nobody made a fuss about it at the company, allowing her to just work. This position was an opportunity for Frank not only to gain "very good ... income" but also to refresh her "old-time English" that she had learned many years ago.[62] Out of loss, poverty, and silence emerged unprecedented paths to economic independence, particularly prized by women who had not experienced such an opportunity before.

These memories of new beginnings existed side-by-side with a different kind of recollection of an era that did not go so smoothly. As seen in Chapter 2, Kazuko Aoki's father was dismayed by US soldiers' lack of respect for Japanese culture. At least, these "mentors" of democracy could have learned to take off their shoes or tell the difference between a flute and a gun – but they had not.[63] The fact that US men in the occupation forces fraternized with Japanese women meant for some female American *hibakusha* a lost opportunity. Unlike Kawasaki and Frank, who were delighted by employment opportunities, Mitsuko Okimoto felt resentment toward the occupation forces when her aspiration to learn pharmacology at a junior college in Kobe was shattered by her father's concern about the presence of US soldiers in the city. Her cousin had seen a number of female college students "walking with soldiers arm in arm." This story of fraternization was alarming enough for Okimoto's father to prohibit her from going to a city that put her near these soldiers. Okimoto cried to no avail, and after finding no college in Hiroshima that interested her, she decided to take a position as a clerk at a local bank. Still, the occupation forces' presence continued to disrupt. Once, a friend who worked for the US military visited Okimoto's house accompanied by a GI. Her "old-fashioned" father was infuriated; he believed that nothing good could happen to families that socialized with Americans. Here, Okimoto seemed to feel a sense of irony about the rigidity of her father, while at the same time sympathizing with his determination to protect his family. She shared his indignation about the United States as a country that dropped the bomb; and yet, she did not feel any animosity toward American people.[64]

Such mixed feelings also shaped one of Katie Yanagawa's distinct memories of her father. Shortly after taking up a daytime job as the occupation forces' translator, Yanagawa's father began to assist local police officers in Kure in the evening. As she recalled, he was frequently needed because of the sudden influx of US military men:

> When it came to the night time, all of the American soldiers [were] out in the street and having their fun and getting in all kinds of trouble and the Japanese police had to control them along with the [American] MPs. But because of the English language difficulty, they had a tough time to be able to control whatever problems came up. So the police station at Yoshiura [in Kure] where my father was living was looking for someone to help them out.[65]

In this case, Japanese Americans functioned literally as mediators of US–Japan encounters. Although Yanagawa was not harsh on GIs – they were just having "fun" – she also saw them clearly as "problems." Her father might be assisting American MPs, but his employment was with the Japanese police. Nikkei like Yanagawa's father, then, helped protect Japanese civilians and neighborhoods by making use of his belonging to and familiarity with the United States.

Such balancing acts by Nikkei remained under-recognized by either nation's authorities, even when their cross-nationality was evidently beneficial. In fact, cultural mediations have been generally seen as originating from the United States. Whether directive, pedagogical, or philanthropic, Americans were deemed initiators of the acts of mediation. Japanese people responded by acceptance, rejection, or perhaps both, mixed with a desire to build and begin.[66] Seen from where US *hibakusha* stood, though, these acts were initiated actively by the residents of Hiroshima and Nagasaki, too. They were cities of immigrants, and they continued to be so throughout the occupation period. Sharing others' resentment toward the occupation forces, US survivors also felt they could offer, and gain from, their cross-nationality. Although the occupiers' racialized, gendered, and silenced "others," US *hibakusha* nonetheless found ways to reconnect with America as they knew it, and at the same time, insisted on Japanese ways. Their remembering shows how US survivors' silent era of hiding and healing comprised some of the most complicated work of postwar reconstruction. This task of reconstruction was sustained by a tacit collaboration with the occupiers who also kept silence around the bomb for their own reasons. With the ABCC, however, it was a different story.

Disconnecting through the Atomic Bomb Casualty Commission

Conflicted sentiments about America are evident in US survivors' remembering of the ABCC, too. Like the occupation forces, the ABCC, since its establishment in 1947 in Hiroshima and Nagasaki, was a major employer of US *hibakusha*, their family members, and their acquaintances. Although the occupation forces were much larger than the ABCC and thus offered more opportunities for rebuilding familial and communal connections, there still were a fair number of Japanese Americans working at the ABCC. For example, Helen Yokoyama, a Japanese American woman who played important roles in the famous "Hiroshima Maidens" project of 1955–1956, was an ABCC employee when she was recruited for the project.[67] The standard "exit interview" conducted at the ABCC after survivors completed all medical examinations was designed by Nisei physician Scott Matsumoto in 1951. There were other Nikkei doctors who worked at the ABCC, too, who drew Japanese media's attention as contributing to "a picture of the advancement in the scientific fields made by the Niseis which is especially noteworthy in America after the war." Matsuo Kodani was one such doctor at the ABCC in Nagasaki, where he collaborated with the chief geneticist James V. Neel.[68] Moreover, some US soldiers in the occupation forces in Japan, including both white and black soldiers, took civilian employment with the ABCC out of necessity; these American men had fallen in love with Japanese women, but they were "unable to wed as soldiers" because of the US military's restrictive policy on interracial marriage. Although the Alien Brides Act in 1947 permitted entrance to the United States of Japanese wives of American soldiers, the act was applicable only to those who had married within thirty days after its enactment. Given the military's unaccommodating policies, this limit made it impossible for many couples to benefit. Civilian institutions such as the ABCC, by contrast, had more permissive rules about marriage. In a way, then, the ABCC could have seemed a workplace where American men took their relationship with Japanese women seriously.[69]

Nonetheless, the ABCC with its specific scientific focus managed to provoke more objections than the occupation forces among US *hibakusha*. Here, it is important to note that the research institute had a mission largely unfamiliar and potentially harmful to *hibakusha*, more so than missions of the occupation forces. Scientists at the ABCC conducted studies of atypical changes in survivors' somatic cells, genetics, aging and mortality rates, and their interactions with survivors were driven by the purpose of collecting scientific data. In fact, it was mandated that ABCC medical researchers offer no treatment to survivors because treatment was seen as an act of apology or atonement. Studying radiation effects on humans, by contrast, was considered a Cold War necessity. Because the United States was the sole maker of nuclear weaponry as of 1946, US authorities found it essential to stay on the cutting edge of the knowledge about their capability.[70] The scientists' interest in long-term epidemiological changes, combined with their obvious lack of interest in treatment, made *hibakusha* feel that they were guinea pigs. More important, though, the commission's exclusive focus on research effectively pried open the gentle silence kept by survivors without telling them the information that it gained from them – unless there was a need for survivors to seek treatment immediately. At much as the ABCC's nontreatment policy itself, this imposed breaking of silence, coupled with the stiff secrecy that the ABCC built around what they knew about survivors, explains why US *hibakusha* expressed more resentment about the ABCC than they did about the occupation forces.

Kazue McCrea went to the ABCC twice in 1951, only to realize that scientists were conducting research "for Americans only, not for the Japanese," when her test results were not made available to her. In fact, she did not learn her results until 1978, when she became friends in San Francisco with a Japanese woman who had worked at the ABCC in Hiroshima. A friend of this woman, an employee of the Radiation Effect Research Foundation (RERF, a successor of the ABCC established in 1975), provided McCrea with a fifty-page report, after nearly thirty years of delay. Although she was relieved to learn that she had no abnormalities, McCrea's favorable impression of the ABCC, if any, appears to be confined to her gratitude for her friend. In fact, McCrea seemed to regret that her younger self had allowed the ABCC to examine her so easily when there had been no talk of the bomb elsewhere in postwar Hiroshima. She explained how she had gone to the ABCC only because "*yobidashi o kutta*," using the terms indicating both the imposing nature of the ABCC's request to come and her unwillingness to go. Moreover, her visits to the commission "made me realize, gradually," that, although free of physical injuries, she could suffer from radiation just like her sister who had sustained a severe burn or her neighbor who had been disfigured by keloid. By testing without telling the results, the ABCC broke open the silence and instilled a decades-long worry that she did not need to have.[71]

Yasue Monberg's remembering also suggests her complex feelings about the commission, though in a much different way than McCrea's. Soon after the ABCC's building was erected near her junior high school, Monberg found that one of her neighbors, a Japanese American woman, was working there. Although Monberg never spoke with this woman, she was memorable because "she looked so modern." The word also spread that this woman was well-paid by her employer. This rumor, combined with her "modern" outlook, constituted Monberg's impression of America: a country of abundance that compelled people to say something about it. As much as her remembering conveys a youthful look into power, it also contains an unmistakably critical edge. America was all about money and material things, with little care for have-nots. No wonder, then, the bomb made by such a country would widen the rift between the rich and the poor. Because there was no open discussion of the bomb in her village, this woman became the most visible and voluble symbol of the bomb's aftermath. Although the Nisei woman did not interact much with her neighbors, her presence sent a clear signal that, as far as the ABCC was concerned, there was a secret about the bomb among *hibakusha* that must be broken open. But there were no opportunities for her neighbors to learn what work she did at the ABCC, creating an imbalance between what she might know about her neighbors and what they knew about her.[72]

The unwanted disruption of silence was striking enough to "color" the ABCC in some American survivors' remembering. Indeed, the commission stood in stark contrast to the black and grey landscape of Hiroshima and Nagasaki. As Jeremy Oshima recalled, in Hiroshima "it seemed like there was no color, just black-and-white scenery like the old movies ... Nothing was colorful. Everything was dusty and dirty."[73] In this kind of landscape, the ABCC seemed extremely clean. Its employees, too, struck survivors as highly sanitized. Korean survivor

Pak Namjoo painted her first encounter with the ABCC in white, a color that disturbingly mirrored the death of her first child:

> The ABCC came to collect my child's body. I didn't understand why – we were all living in these barracks in this poor neighborhood. They came on a Jeep, in white, pure white, lab coats, carrying a box. They said, "We are from the ABCC," in their white lab coats – such clean lab coats. Then they said: "Please give us your child's body."[74]

Infuriated, Pak's husband asked with whose permission they made such a request and demanded: "Who told you this?" Their child was barely dead, but the ABCC came with such readiness, complete with a box to carry the specimen.

Sharp cleanliness in the sea of debris meant not only material abundance but also medical professionalism detached from *hibakusha*'s daily needs. Pak's husband was repulsed by what this professionalism brought to his family: it had the power to spread the rumor that their child's death was caused by a bomb-induced disease. Perhaps the word had already leaked out; if not, it soon would because these lab coat-clad folks advertised it to the entire neighborhood. Equally troubling, it might be someone in the neighborhood who had initially leaked the word to the ABCC, prompting its employees to come to the Paks. Instead of helping the family to heal, the person had exposed their hiding. Meanwhile, the ABCC would not reveal their source of information, keeping it behind the wall of secrecy. Examples such as Pak's are also numerous among US survivors, colored by their resentment toward the ABCC's intrusion into the process of hiding and healing.

For Yasuo Grant Fujita, the ABCC meant trouble for his marriage prospects. When he met his future wife, a Sansei, Fujita made no secret of the fact that he was one of the rare survivors from the area within one kilometer (0.6 miles) of the hypocenter. This revelation did not change her commitment to Fujita, no doubt a great relief for him. But her father objected. A Nisei, the woman's father was employed by the ABCC at the time and thought that a marriage with a survivor would have a "mal-influence" on childbearing. His daughter should simply forget about Fujita. Although her father was not a physician, his words still carried a weight. When she considered having a child, her father's words came back to her. Fujita, too, had to work hard "not to worry."[75] As in Pak's case, then, Fujita's experience shows how the commission's scientific inquiry, as well as the authority it afforded its employees, shook his sense of self-worth. The ABCC's effort to track survivors disrupted the process of hiding and healing, one of the few resources that they had devised. They were under a medical gaze. The medical authorities, in contrast, mostly kept their silence. If any leakage occurred, as in Pak's and Fujita's cases, it was likely to be partial, misleading, and hurtful for survivors.

When we consider the breach of silence instigated by the ABCC, we see more clearly the reason why it drew more criticism and resistance by US *hibakusha* than the occupation forces. Indeed, the occupation forces could have drawn more criticism from US survivors than the ABCC because of US soldiers' seemingly out-of-control fraternization with Japanese women. Many Japanese survivors took it as a national humiliation, and examples such as Okimoto's and Yanagawa's suggest that American survivors, too, felt anxious. Everywhere US military men went in this era – France, Germany, and Korea – tension arose out of their use of local women for their sexual pleasure, and Japan was no exception.[76] Still, the ABCC held a darker place than the occupation forces in US *hibakusha*'s remembering, suggesting how it was not simply national animosity that shaped US survivors' particularly tense attitude toward the ABCC. Neither was the nontreatment policy, largely featured by scholars, the only factor in US survivors' understanding of the institution. Their view also arose from how the institution ran counter to the opportunities that they felt they could find there. As was the case with occupation forces, US institutions in postwar Japan could, and sometimes did, offer genuine opportunities for rebuilding lives. Often, US survivors were active makers of these opportunities. And yet, the ABCC worked to reverse this kind of endeavor, something of which US survivors became keenly aware. By infringing upon silence, the commission embodied a failure of nation states to recognize acts of healing devised collectively by *hibakusha* of any nationality. In their interactions with the ABCC, the space that American survivors had carved out for Japanese medicines such as tea, aloe, and fish blood, seemed to shrink. As seen earlier, healing processes made up of these medicines could, and in many cases did, exist side by side with modern medicines offered at the cities' medical facilities. But the ABCC was not part of this modern medicine. In US survivors' remembering, the study of radiation effects conducted by the ABCC embodied a thread of medical inquiry incapable of coexisting with patients.

As shown by Pak Namjoo's remembering, a critical understanding of the ABCC was shared by Korean survivors who stayed in Japan, as well as by American survivors who returned or came to the United States after the war.[77] The critique was also shared by some Canadian survivors, suggesting a striking consistency of resistance to the ABCC across national boundaries. For Joe Ohori from Canada, for instance, the ABCC became memorable because it had opened up unwanted discussions about the bomb. Moreover, by following his remembering, we see how *hibakusha* used a series of tactics – ranging from literally "running away" from medical authorities to an assertion of their cross-nationality – to counter the ABCC's infringement on autonomy. Having survived the blast in Hiroshima, Ohori began to experience hair loss in November 1945. Knowing what had happened to many survivors who died mysterious deaths around this time, he began to check himself in the mirror every night. He thought he would be doomed if black spots appeared on his skin, a common symptom for *hibakusha* nearing death. But he did not talk about his worries with his families or friends, although most of them were survivors and likely to have shared his concerns. This remained the same after the ABCC was established right in front of his high school. Their "truck" began to come to "round up" student survivors. Not knowing the institution's sole focus on research, he initially complied. But when he learned that they wanted to draw his blood just so that they could examine it, he felt upset. He asked if the ABCC "had a permission from the Canadian government to draw my blood. ... I am not a Japanese but a Canadian. If you are to draw blood from a Canadian citizen you should get permission from the Canadian government."[78]

This resistance did not work, prompting him to ask if he could expect to be paid. When "there was no food to go around after the bomb," such reward seemed only fitting. Of course he could not expect it, so he concluded: "That means that they are testing us so that they can drop a bomb again. The blood work has nothing to do with curing us of radiation illness." After that, he wanted no relationship with the ABCC. Whenever their vehicle showed up, he hid himself in his school's bathroom to avoid being found out and taken away. Interestingly, Ohori was not alone in his resistance. Some of his friends, too, joined him in his hiding. Here, it is noteworthy that, in Ohori's remembering, his talk of the bomb was always directed to ABCC employees, not to his friends. By hiding together, they can be seen as affirming a shared silence without vocalizing it. In response to the ABCC's intrusion into silence, survivors came together to reaffirm their way of healing. It might even have been exciting – a handful of teenage boys playing hide-and-seek with the ABCC. Ohori's resistance continued to take the form of silence even after he returned to Canada in 1949. Since there was no media coverage of the bomb before the press code was lifted in Japan in 1952, he did not hear much about radiation effects that survivors like himself might suffer. Fortunately, he suffered no symptoms other than hair loss. This, combined with his successful hiding from the ABCC, freed him from excessive worries. Looking back, he felt he was "lucky" because his cross-nationality allowed both his escapes.[79] Given experiences such as Kazue McCrea's, Ohori could well be seen as truly fortunate; at least, he was not burdened by scientific procedures unrelated to therapeutic practices.

Just as Kazuko Aoki's father used his connections with the United States to obtain medicines for his daughter (Chapter 2), Ohori mobilized the best resource that he could – his Canadian citizenship – to protest against the ABCC. Ohori may even be seen as trying to privilege himself over the Japanese by bringing his non-Japanese citizenship to the ABCC's attention. By asserting this background, though, Ohori was also claiming, if implicitly, a larger cross-national history, something that neither US nor Japanese authorities were willing to recognize: that the bombs were not singularly dropped on the Japanese but on people from a range of cross-national ties. His cross-nationality further permitted him to maintain a sense of self-worth by allowing him to return to Canada, where there was no probing by a research institute or loud talk of radiation effects. As with many US *hibakusha*, his chosen way of healing remained silence, not science, about the bomb. Their remembering of the ABCC suggests how, if silence and science were to join, attention must be paid to the healing process formed by patients from a range of nationalities. This was a task of reconstruction created by the staggering power of nuclear weaponry – a task that mostly fell on survivors alone in the years following 1945.

Citizenship and Race on Shifting Ground: Through the Korean War

As American survivors became reconnected with their families, they began to think about returning to the United States. Japanese and

Korean people who got married to Americans, too, made plans for crossing the ocean eastward. Although it took until 1947, or later, to realize their aspirations, their commitment was unceasing. One of their most urgent concerns was to clarify their citizenship status. A brief look into their efforts reveals how US survivors negotiated the shifting demands of nation states. Some, such as Julie Kumi Fukuda, had lost all personal documentation during the war, not surprisingly given the encompassing effect of the nuclear attacks. Fukuda was chagrined whenever she ran into her "friends from Delano and Fresno and all over, from California, in Tokyo." They were in the occupation forces, and "every time [she] walked on the street [they said] 'Hey, what are you doing here?'" Still, she could not prove her US citizenship.[80] US *hibakusha* who were fortunate enough to keep documentation for their American citizenship during the war also met challenges. In fact, many US survivors acquired Japanese citizenship out of necessity even as they held onto their American citizenship. Without status as Japanese citizens, they were unable to obtain food rations. Because communication between the American and Japanese consulates had been terminated since late 1941, the attainment of Japanese citizenship did not negate their US citizenship. But US citizen status alone was not a sufficient basis for US survivors to return.

Jeremy Oshima recalled the lengthy process that he went through to prove his eligibility:

> It seemed like it took two years to get my paper processed. I went to Yokohama with my father a couple of times to get my papers approved ... to prove to the United States government that I was not in the military service. I was too young to start with. But ... at the age of 14 you could sign up for the *kamikaze* pilot school ... it takes about four years of training, so at 18 you'll be a pilot. There was that case [of citizenship rejection] too, [so] it could have happened [to me].[81]

Indeed, US citizens who wished to return to America had to show that they had not served in the army or attended a military school during their years in Japan. Although these requirements might have seemed logical for a US government that intended to continue barring "disloyals," the effectiveness of these rules was highly doubtful.

Izumi Hirano, for instance, was able to come back to America primarily because his English was *not* good enough to enter a military school in Hiroshima during the war. His family had come to Japan when he was four, so he did not have a chance to fully develop his English skills. The irony was clear: he tried to get into both the Japanese Imperial Army Academy and the Naval Academy, not only because he wanted to join Japan's war effort but also because these were considered the best schools for Japanese boys. On both accounts, these military schools were Hirano's first choices, which the US government could have easily defined as a sign of disloyalty to his country of birth. Still, Hirano came back to the United States relatively easily, because he did not get in to either school.[82] Thus, barring returnees based on their formal associations with the military was no guarantee that former Japanese patriots were excluded.

In some cases, those who complied with the US occupation forces' directives met more difficulties than those who did not. Yasuko Ogawa's remembering clarifies how this came about, particularly for women who were given a chance to vote for the first time after the war:

> After the war's end, under MacArthur's direction, even women over the age of 18 gained the right to vote. We were instructed by the neighborhood association that we had to vote. I cast my vote in that [first] election. That hung me up. I went to [the Consulate in] Yokohama many times. I was told that I couldn't regain my [American] citizenship. Two or three years after that, I heard that it would be all right to apply in Kobe [Consulate], so I began the process in Kobe.[83]

Voting required a family register – documentation of one's family – in Japan, in effect giving Ogawa a label of loyalty to Japan, which in turn became a record of disloyalty to America. In this way, women's liberation triggered a prolonged family separation, revealing a discordance between new regulations implemented by both the state and the military.[84]

Seeing this disparity, some US *hibakusha* made frequent inquiries to the US Consulate; others asked Japanese officials to write the American Embassy on their behalf.[85] But US survivors' own histories during their stay in Japan were not the only obstacle to overcome. Some, as if they were new immigrants, had to have a sponsor in the United States, posing a financial burden on Nikkei families whose resources had been thinly stretched.[86] Even when everything fell into place, the process of regaining American citizenship remained rocky. Haakai

Nagano lost his US citizenship because, as seen in Chapter 1, Japan's war climate made it difficult for Americans to reveal their citizenship. He was "not stupid [enough] to . . . say 'I am an American'" and report to the "consulate's office to register," said Nagano. This act of self-defense led to a lack of proof of US citizenship, and when he acted to reclaim it after the war, he noticed that his name had been misspelled on his US birth certificate. "It's [spelled] Haakai. But it's, in real English, Hakkai." Apparently, some recording officer had made a mistake registering his birth in 1930. Instead of asking that his name be correctly spelled and possibly causing further delay, however, Nagano decided to let the wrongly spelled "Haakai" stand.[87] The incident was at once a loss of American identity in Japan and a reminder of the tenacious foreignness of Japanese Americans in the United States. Their names seemed unfamiliar, and they could be easily misspelled.

Korean and Korean American survivors, too, experienced chaos arising from their loss of Japanese nationality following Korea's liberation in 1945, and from the Japanese government's failure to end its decades-long discrimination against Koreans. Although Yi Jougkeun stayed in Japan after the war, his experiences immediately after 1945 likely resembled those of Korean survivors who returned to Korea or went to America in the 1950s and 1960s. As Yi explained, he decided to stick to his Japanese identity, including his Japanese name, because it was a matter of survival:

> I wondered why. I was as Japanese as any other Japanese, and I was bombed just like any other Japanese. I continued to be a Japanese until midnight . . . then in the morning, I became a foreigner all of the sudden. . . . [When I applied for a job] I noticed that [my Japanese name] Egawa Masayuki was accompanied by a note in red, which said: "Korean." It was written by a pencil, a red pencil, because there was no such thing as a pen back then. So I thought . . . that I would be immediately rejected and become a laughingstock if I didn't do something about this. So I erased it. With an eraser.[88]

This split-second decision brought Yi a job, a sign of how arbitrarily Japanese officials continued to treat Koreans in Japan. They were to be treated separately, but the bloated extent of Japan's imperial rule had made it impossible to single them out consistently. In a sharp refutation of the discourse about racial differences between Koreans and the

Japanese, propagated by some Japanese colonialists, there was nothing that distinguished the peoples when the state-imposed demarcations were gone. Their names, language, and documents failed to tell any difference. By passing as a Japanese out of necessity, Yi held the nation-state's disarray at arm's length.

It was this dysfunctionality of national distinctions that prompted James Jeong to come to the United States and, at the same time, shielded him from family discord thereafter. Soon after he fell in love with Masae Kanagawa, a Nisei woman, in Japan, in the mid-1950s, she began to urge him to immigrate. "There is no point for you to suffer as a Korean in Japan," said Kanagawa: "Come to the United States – everyone is mixed up there!" To Jeong, jumping into an American "mix" sounded more appealing than being arbitrarily included and excluded in Japan. This awareness about the dysfunctionality of national distinctions also shaped Jeong's relationship with his in-laws. Although Kanagawa's father was supportive of their marriage and sponsored the couple to come to America, one of his brothers – Kanagawa's uncle – complained about the fact that Jeong had brought "Korean blood" into his "Japanese *ie* (family or family lineage)." Kanagawa's father countered by putting forward an entirely different way of setting national distinctions: "Why are you talking about *ie*? You are American! You don't have *ie*. And of course, he [Jeong] is not even coming to your *katei* (home or household)."[89] Here, Jeong's father-in-law highlighted his brother's American belonging to refute his attachment to Japan and Japanese *ie*. The rebuttal was made effective by reminding his brother of *katei*, a concept associated with a modern nuclear family. By using this term, he urged his brother to see families more individually than as part of an extended family. Jeong and Kanagawa will have *katei* of their own, and it will have nothing to do with *katei* of the Kanagawas. This was the American way, defined by the Japanese term. Equally important, this exchange took place between two Japanese Americans about a soon-to-be Korean American. Unlike Yi, who had to hide his Korean identity in Japan, Jeong was welcome to make an American *katei*; that was what immigrants in America did. A shift from *ie* to *katei* made immigrants who they were. Their shared cross-nationality helped to prevent national differences from dictating individual decisions.

As Jeong's experiences show, the problem of citizenship often intensified when US *hibakusha* made key life decisions such as marriage and migration. These decisions, in turn, opened up possibilities for speaking about the bomb. There were those like Yasuo Grant Fujita who did not show any reluctance about telling their sweethearts the truth. There were others who hesitated to reveal their survivorhood, even as they felt they should be honest about it. Still others, especially those who had suffered radiation poisoning briefly but were not physically impaired, were unsure about what to tell. Regardless, people's reactions to US survivors' telling of their experiences proved unpredictable. In some cases, the bomb was discussed but not treated as a pressing matter. Especially for *hibakusha* who married interracially, racial differences seemed to shape their relationship at least as importantly as their survivorhood. When Atsuko La Mica met her future husband in Nagasaki in 1951, she decided that he and his family "don't have to know about my history." Indeed, her experiences as a survivor rarely came up in the couple's conversation, while their racial differences created conspicuous family tensions. Her older brother in Japan was upset because he was the heir of the family and "didn't like Americans," meaning white Americans. Meanwhile, her husband's family in America "was strange to me," said La Mica. "They'd never seen an Asian girl before. But they had gone to a Chinese restaurant, you know."[90] She became a foreign person for whom the only point of reference was a restaurant.

Nobuko Fujioka, too, remembered racial awkwardness that she had experienced as a newlywed. Anticipating that her family would disapprove of her marriage to "a gentle, nice man" from Milwaukee, Fujioka decided in the late 1950s to get married without telling her parents. Her husband did the same with his. Fujioka had told him about her experience of the bomb, but the confession did not deter him from marrying her. Nor did it occupy a significant place in their discussion about their elopement. Clearly, they thought that their national and racial differences, not her bomb experiences, were the main reason why their families might object. Both of their families eventually accepted the couple, and Fujioka soon found herself at the center of her in-laws' attention. They were envious of the "beautiful skin" of "Orientals," something they had not seen before. Recounting the episode, Fujioka did not convey displeasure; still, their words of praise struck her as odd enough to remember. Further, she recalled how her mother-in-law was worried about radiation effects. In the end, the couple decided not to have any offspring, although Fujioka insisted that their decision was not because of her mother-in-law. Rather, it was "because I didn't particularly care for children."[91]

In these racially mixed families, then, US survivors' experiences of the bomb might be talked about but in a delicate balance with questions about interracial intimacy, a matter of urgent concern in the 1950s and 1960s. In comparison, the distinction between survivors and non-survivors did not seem so consequential. In the 1960s, Ayako Elliott felt it liberating that her Caucasian husband "didn't really care that I am a survivor." Unlike Hiroshimans who keenly, if quietly, tuned into radiation illness, American spouses did not seem to pay much attention to it. Even so, some survivors, including Elliott, decided not to have children. Strikingly, her remembering of the decision drew on a mix of racial and medical reasons:

> My mother told me that it would be better for me not to have a child. I knew that it would be difficult if I were to have a racially mixed child. I knew a child like that in Hiroshima. . . . He was bullied very much. I did not think that it would be wrong to have a racially mixed child, but my parents' generation . . . they were directly affected by the bomb, so they did not want anything strange to happen to my children. Although it was not as if I decided against having children because of what they said, it still lingered at the corner of my mind.[92]

Here, racial otherness was seamlessly woven into radiation illness. As will be seen in Chapter 5, an integration of racial and medical concerns became important grounds for US *hibakusha*'s activism in the 1970s. In the earlier decades, too, racial differences and their potential to cause social rejection played into decisions that US *hibakusha* made as people exposed to radiation. In turn, their identity as survivors could be expressed as their anxiety about racial discrimination. What would it be like to raise biracial children with disabilities caused by irradiation? How would American families respond, when their only knowledge about the Japanese was that they were "Orientals"? As US survivors sought answers, their concerns about racism and radiation became inseparable.

For US *hibakusha* who married Japanese Americans, race played an equally important role, although in a much different way. In most cases, these spouses of survivors had been confined in Nikkei concentration camps during the war. Others were either "no-no boys" (who had responded negatively to both of the national loyalty questions) or their underage family members who had been deported to Japan in 1944 or 1945. Still others had been in Japan because they, like US survivors themselves, had been trapped in the country since the war's onset. Some of them had been in Japan several years by the war's end; others had gone back to America at one point after 1947, then came to Japan for a brief stay for a range of different reasons. Still others came to Japan for the first time after the war. Here, I examine the remembering of US survivors who married Japanese Americans in Japan (I will discuss US survivors' experiences after they went to the United States in Chapter 4).

Some survivors who married another survivor talked about their bomb experiences more freely than those married to non-survivors. For instance, Joyce Ikuko Moriwaki, who was married to a Nisei survivor from Hawai'i, recalled exchanging stories of nuclear injuries with her husband. Such talk was in contrast to the overall silence about the bomb, suggesting that in intimate relationships, conversation about the bomb might have taken place with an ease that did not exist elsewhere. Although Moriwaki worried about the effect that they, as dual survivors, might have on their children, a marriage to Nisei still seemed highly desirable to her. Like many other Nikkei in Japan during the occupation period, her husband had US relatives who sent him many boxes full of a variety of things. He also had a good job because of his English-speaking ability. Clearly, Moriwaki "married up." Unlike Atsuko La Mica and Nobuko Fujioka, whose marriages were colored by racial tensions, Moriwaki felt as if her prospects could not be better.[93]

Such sentiment was not uncommon among *hibakusha* who married Japanese Americans whose families had in fact been shattered by the wartime imprisonment. Tsuruko Nakamura married a Japanese American man whose family had been held in the incarceration camp in Heart Mountain, Wyoming. Although he was her senior by sixteen years, everyone deemed the marriage highly desirable. Nakamura recalled how, as a twenty-four-year-old, she had been dreaming about traveling to a foreign country, especially the United States. When she met her future husband, what stood out was that he was from San Francisco. "I wanted to go, because I thought San Francisco was such a far-away, dream-like place!" said Nakamura. The image of a city on America's shore appeared in stark contrast to Hiroshima, where Nakamura and her three sisters continued to hide their survivorhood in order to remain marriageable. She did not imagine that there were restrictions about apartments they could rent, or neighborhoods they could live in, once she arrived in the dream city.[94]

Sachiko Matsumoto's remembering, too, pointed to hopefulness. A marriage to an American man could bring Matsumoto and her family more material comfort, which was why her stepmother had eagerly arranged a marriage with a Nisei. Matsumoto's stepmother had a sister in Hawai'i who had sent her a package of candies before the war's beginning. If she had a stepdaughter in the US mainland, she might be able to get more. These assumptions were made despite the fact that the future husband had renounced his US citizenship and had been sent to the camp in Tule Lake, California, one of the most tightly watched sites of confinement for "disloyals." Although he escaped deportation to Japan, this label dealt him a legal challenge (he had to apply to regain his American citizenship), as well as financial struggles. All of these became clear to Matsumoto only after she married and migrated to America in 1956. For the first time, she realized that her husband had no business or property.[95] Similar to Moriwaki, both Nakamura and Matsumoto initially thought that they had taken a step up the social ladder with their marriages. The difference between bomb-stricken Japan and post-incarceration Japanese America was believed to be obvious by all, perhaps too hastily. Obscured by the assumed difference was the racism that continued to push Japanese Americans into the socioeconomic margins.

Nakamura's and Matsumoto's remembering also differed from Moriwaki's, revealing how not only the camp but also the bomb became part of the silence around racism against Japanese Americans after the war. Unlike Moriwaki, both Nakamura and Matsumoto continued to keep silent about the bomb through their marriages, something that seemed reciprocated by former inmates' reticence about the camps. Nakamura, by the time of her oral history in 2011, knew that her husband had known of her survivorhood before their marriage. His friends had found out, urging him to rethink the marriage. Nakamura's family rallied for her, showing her medical records and insisting that she was perfectly healthy. All of this took place without Nakamura's knowledge; she learned this only years after marriage. Given this troubled history, it is not surprising that the Nakamuras hardly talked about it. "He didn't know what the bomb was like, so there was nothing to talk about," Nakamura explained. In return, her husband did not tell her about his experiences at Heart Mountain. "Until I came to America, I did not know how Japanese Americans had survived" the war, said Nakamura. "There was no talk of that in Japan," although the silence about the camps gradually broke after Nakamura came to America.[96] Clearly, the memories of both the camps and the bomb remained fragmented in Japan, requiring many years for those who experienced only one of them to uncover.

Matsumoto, too, decided not to reveal her survivorhood to her husband: "It's not relevant. He did not ask, and I did not tell," said Matsumoto flatly, showing how she felt justified in her nondisclosure. Meanwhile, she was greatly disappointed by the living conditions she found once she came to the United States. Her husband's employment as "a cleaning person at a white American's house" led her to conclude: "He is a *genan*," using a derogatory, gendered term for a male house-keeper. Despite the fact that she was well aware by the time of the interview that he had been in Tule Lake, Matsumoto did not make connections between his incarceration and his profession. What she stressed instead was that she had been surprised by his less-than-desirable socioeconomic standing, a failure of manhood.[97] This suggests how the assumed class difference between the Japanese and Japanese Americans might have steered the latter away from any talk of the camps. Racist policy could become a story of personal failure, some-thing that needed to be kept hidden. Similarly, some survivors felt it necessary to hide their bomb experiences, so as to protect their mar-riageability. If careless, their experiences in August 1945 could become part of their personal liability, a reason to be treated as outcasts. In these ways, silence around racism became entangled with silence around the bomb, quietly engrained into histories of US *hibakusha* as they crossed the ocean.

These marriages and migrations might not have surged without the Korean War and, more broadly, the US preoccupation with the East Asian theatre of the early Cold War. Fujioka's husband, for one, came to Japan from Milwaukee because his company had a military contract requiring him to be stationed there.[98] La Mica was married to "a military," from whom she was frequently separated before marriage. He "had to go to Korea" many times from the time they met, in 1951, until they got married in 1956. Even after the marriage, she found herself living with her in-laws because of his continued deployment to the peninsula.[99] Kazue Kawasaki's husband, whom she initially met at the occupation forces' Etajima office, might not have married her if it were not the Korean War. Soon after US civilians were allowed to travel from Japan to America in 1947, he returned to see his father in Stockton. His father had been in a camp, and the son had been worried about his health. It turned out that his worry was not misplaced; the older man passed away while his son was waiting for the US Embassy to process his travel application. Devastated, the son still planned to go to college in America, a plan that unfortunately was shattered by the military draft for the Korean War. Finding himself alone in Korea and away from his family, he wrote a letter to his former colleague, Ms. Kawasaki of Hiroshima. Letters rekindled their acquaintance, eventually leading to their marriage in 1953.[100]

The Korean War was a hotbed of these encounters, making the composition of the US survivors gender-skewed. The vast majority of US persons who came to Korea or Japan beginning in 1950 were men, hence their marriages added a substantial number of women to the total number of US survivors. For Japanese Americans and Korean Americans in the pre-*Loving* v. *Virginia* era, these encounters were great opportunities to meet legally marriageable persons. Marriages between Asian and white persons were still prohibited by anti-miscegenation laws in many states, including Arizona, Texas, Missouri, Georgia, and Virginia, before the Supreme Court declared them unconstitutional in 1967. Even in the states where interracial marriages were legal, Japanese Americans and Korean Americans could easily be subject to harassment if married to white persons.[101] Interracial marriages between Asian and non-Asian minorities were legally permissible but not socially favored, often provoking family and community disapprovals from all parties involved. John Hong, who came to an army school in Georgia in 1953 and then again in 1955, was probably fortunate to have been already married to a Korean woman by then. The Asian and Asian American women's population in Georgia in the early 1950s was miniscule.[102] Among all male US survivors whom I interviewed, there are no cases of interracial marriage as it was defined by US laws as unions between white and nonwhite persons; all their marriages were with women of Asian origin. This was in contrast to female US *hibakusha*, a number of whom were married to white males. This, combined with the assumed class difference between the Japanese and Japanese Americans, clearly indicates the gender dynamism that cut across racial boundaries. If men were to marry women from lower social or racial hierarchies, it was more socially acceptable than men marrying women from a higher status. In this light, the very existence of Japanese survivors who became American survivors after the war was shaped by the racial and gender orders underpinning the early years of the Cold War. The Cold War logic of alliance-building, containment, and conformity thrived on this underpinning.

Simultaneously, US survivors' remembering revealed a range of cross-national meanings that did not fit into any single logic. These meanings disrupted a nation-bound understanding of the bomb, leading us to see US *hibakusha* as much more than a mere casualty of the Cold War. In their remembering, they emerge as people who continued to turn their experiences as immigrants into a source of their resilience and identity as survivors.

Take, for example, Korean American survivor Hye-kyo Lee. Her remembering of the bomb contained stories of loss, illness, and poverty so compelling that, at first glance, it was difficult to see her as anything but a victim of endless wars. She lost both her grandparents to the bomb in Nagasaki, and shortly after returning to Korea, eight more members of her family, including her parents, perished. After being sent to her aunt's home at the age of seven, Lee "was abused" and beaten because she was "half Japanese." Although this was because her mother was Japanese and her father, Korean, there was also some hostility against all Koreans who had returned from Japan, especially those affected by the bomb. The fact that they were injured or sickened by the bomb became a scarlet letter of a sort that marked them as "disloyals." In the eyes of "Koreans who had stayed in Korea" throughout the years of Japan's rule, Koreans who came back from Japan after 1945 were seen as "those who had escaped Korea to Japan in spite of the hardship that the Korean Peninsula endured."[103] Supposedly, their "escape" was a sheer act of self-preservation prompted by selfishness. In this light, it was not unsuitable that survivors were afflicted with an incurable disease, and the dearth of information about the bomb in Korea fueled the misinformation about radiation illness.

As a returnee and an orphan, Lee had worked many backbreaking jobs, including gold mining, dishwashing, cleaning, and babysitting for a circus, by the time she was twelve. When a marriage proposal came from an American GI assigned to Korea shortly after the Korean War's ceasefire in 1953, she turned it down. But when he came back a few years later, she felt she did not have much to lose, having no other marriage prospects. By then, she also had seen enough of the war's turmoil. She had been giving shelter and care to a few elderly Koreans who had lost their families to the war. She did this without assistance from any public or private agency – she worked at six different restaurants during the day and made *kimchee* at night for extra money. When one of her charges passed away under her care, she felt that marriage with an American soldier offered a chance to break away from days filled with crying.[104]

Did her marriage offer her such an opportunity? In many ways it did, although her marital relationship after she migrated to America reveals how her husband took advantage of her by treating her as a housekeeper (Chapter 4). Nonetheless, Lee's story also suggests that her endurance through the wars had earned her the ability to make decisions independently from unsympathetic state authorities or a society that labeled her as both disloyal and disabled. Similar to many other Korean and Japanese military brides who came to the United States in the 1950s and 1960s, Lee's story as she tells it is not simply that of a woman whose life was tormented by American racism and sexism. She thought about not getting married, then chose to give it a try, making considered decisions. Nation states had always injured her; she had no reason to trust her fortune to one country or another. Her decision to come to America, then, was her own as much as it was structured by the Cold War that defined Koreans as America's weaker, if eager, allies.

Similar evidence for *hibakusha*'s resilience and resourcefulness within the Cold War's asymmetric alliances is evident in Pak Namjoo's remembering, told from the position of a Korean survivor who remained in Japan through the Korean War. As Pak recalled, Koreans in postwar Japan were "barred from employment in the government." No reputable companies would hire them either, regardless of their qualifications. She also recalled how she had to carry a registration card as a "foreigner" all the time, or risk being fined. Most difficult of all was the lack of access to national health insurance. When her father was afflicted by liver cancer, he had to pay for treatment out-of-pocket. This ruined the already fragile family finances, making it impossible for his daughters to attend school. As Pak recalled: "I was in the first year in my junior high. My sisters were in the fifth and third grade [of an elementary school]. We did not go to school after [then]. . . . We could not." Ironically, the only bright spot in this era of neglect was the 1957 Law Concerning Medical Care, which offered medical tests and treatments for survivors at designated hospitals in Japan. The beneficiaries included Korean residents, in effect offering them the first publicly funded health care after the war. Although she felt "jubilant" about the benefits she was receiving in Japan, Pak quickly became concerned about *hibakusha* in Korea who were not covered by the law. She was aware that they had been "harshly discriminated against in Korea" since they had returned with "no family to rely on, no house to live in."[105] Pak's remembering traced her growing awareness of those who fell between the cracks of national interests. Using her cross-national experiences inventively, she developed her identity as a survivor by assisting others whose lives also had been marked by many histories of immigrants.

———————◆◆◆———————

In both Japan and Korea, the era between 1945 and 1960 was ripe with opportunities for immigrants to question rigidly defined national policies. Variously yet consistently, these policies excluded histories of immigration from their parameters. This exclusion was not because of ignorance on the part of state authorities. Authorities in the United States, Japan, and Korea had abundant opportunities to become aware of immigrants inside their national borders, including those affected by the bombs. The ABCC had learned that Joe Ohori was a Canadian survivor before he decided to hide away. The Japanese government explicitly defined Koreans in Japan as ineligible for national health care unless they fell in the parameters of the 1957 law. Korean survivors in Korea were considered social and national pariahs, something provoked by how many of them returned to Korea after the war. At the same time, both Pak's and Lee's remembering show that these neglected *hibakusha* began to take critical action, though not in ways as vocal and visible as they would become in later decades. Lee sheltered elderly survivors of the Korean War when she hardly had means to support herself. Pak became aware of the discrimination against Korean survivors in Korea, something that decades later led her to serve as a translator for those who wished to visit Japan for medical treatment.

These survivors' experiences of negligence, originating in their histories as immigrants, opened up a possibility to address the limits of state policies and practices. In this way, during the decade of silence, their identity as survivors distinctively unfolded. Although the counter-memory of the bomb of this era was mostly hidden from public view, it offered US survivors a space to heal from illness and loss, and to nurture cross-national ties for the future. US *hibakusha* in Japan saw various Americas after the war. Their remembering took equally various forms, marking the first decade-and-a-half after 1945 as an era of quiet hiding and healing, as well as a beginning of cross-national identity as US survivors. As they looked to cross the ocean to America, their remembering and identity took yet another turn.

4 WAR AND WORK ACROSS THE PACIFIC

US survivors began to move again after 1945. The move was partly spurred by the presence of American troops in Japan and Korea. As seen in Chapter 3, some of these American men on duty married Japanese or Korean women who were survivors, generating a small flow of soon-to-be American *hibakusha* coming to the United States. In other cases, it was returnees who moved. Having been dislocated by the war, deportation, and colonial expansion, these returning immigrants sought to reunite with peoples and places they called home. Nikkei who stayed in Japan during the war crossed the ocean eastward, anxious for reunion with families they had left years earlier. Koreans who had been in Japan proper in the colonial era crossed the ocean westward. For Koreans born in Japan, the move was about coming to a home that they had not seen before.[1] *What happened to my family? Will they recognize me? Are they the same as I remember?* Questions abounded. Unique as they were as people who had been affected by the bomb, US survivors felt anxious and aspirational just as countless other immigrants did after the war. US *hibakusha*'s sentiments, then, illuminate an era when the history of the bomb became most conspicuously integrated into the postwar history of immigration in the Pacific region.

Just as their citizenship was marred by the war, Japanese Americans' return home was complicated by the state refusing to grant rights to "aliens ineligible for citizenship." Because of the lack of medical knowledge about radiation illness, none were denied entrance to the United States outright because they were survivors. And yet, reasons for the state to watch its gates closely were many. Before the passage of the 1952 McCarran–Walter Act, the race of Nikkei made it nearly impossible for them to reenter the country. Not only for Issei, but also for Nisei and Sansei who had lost their citizenship (or its documentation) in the war's chaos, the immigration restriction based on race proved a major obstacle. The only way for them to return home was to reclaim their connections with families in America or to create ties anew by marrying US citizens. Until 1965 when the Immigration and Nationality Act removed the national origin quota, only a small number of immigrants were allowed from Asia to America, making US survivors' struggle to return a prolonged process.[2] For women who married internationally and had children, questions of citizenship created additional layers of uncertainty. What happens to children's citizenship when their parents' belonging is in doubt? Do these children belong to Japan, America, or neither? In some cases, to secure children's citizenship became a chief impetus for women to cross national boundaries. As much as nation states dislocated people, they generated peoples' aspiration to belong.

Simply traveling across the ocean did not truly return US survivors home; nor did it bring stability to Korean *hibakusha* in Korea. After a long separation, some families needed time to become families again. Plans had changed; feelings of intimacy had drifted away. People confronted language barriers, a daily reminder of states' propensity to both connect and disconnect. Moreover, those who received returnees often found them a financial burden. In Korea, the division between South and North Korea in 1948, followed by the war of 1950–1953, sundered families again, giving them little to no time to recuperate.[3] Japanese Americans who had been incarcerated during the Pacific War were not in a position to easily take another person into their families.[4] For female US *hibakusha* married interracially, the racist policies concerning immigration, marriage, and work limited where they could live and participate in public life.[5] For male US survivors who returned early, in the late 1940s, the presumption of their foreignness became a reason for the US Army to recruit them for the Korean War.[6] Many Japanese Americans who were not fluent in either Japanese or English were nonetheless employed as translators. The long shadow of war, nationalism, and racism persisted in ways that constantly reminded US survivors of their status as "perpetual foreigners."[7]

Building on the analysis of hiding and healing discussed in Chapter 3, I continue to explore in this chapter how US survivors returned or came to America, made or rebuilt their families, found work, and served the country in silent, consequential, ways. The chapter discusses the same decade-and-a-half as the previous chapter, from 1945 to approximately 1960, but the location where US *hibakusha*'s histories unfold shifts from Japan to America. For most Korean American survivors, their history on American soil was preceded by their return to the Korean Peninsula. So, first, I look at survivors' travel from Japan to the United States, or from Japan to Korea, and then on to America. By showing a range of reasons to eventually come to the United States, I illuminate how citizenship, defined tightly by the nation states, was a driving force for US *hibakusha* to move. As I argue, the more narrowly officials construed citizenship, the more inventively immigrants found ways to protect their cross-national connections. By exploring this inventiveness, I highlight how, just as it did in the nuclear holocaust, survivors' cross-nationality continued to shape familial and communal ties, bringing together Asians of different backgrounds in America. These ties, nurtured in racialized communities, became essential resources for US survivors to try to heal from the war and to rebuild their lives.

At the same time as illuminating the "strength of weak ties," I also show how these cross-national bonds were severely challenged by the Cold War culture that demanded clear distinctions of friends and foes along national, racial, and gender lines. The Lucky Dragon Five incident in 1954, for example, in which twenty-three Japanese fishermen were irradiated by the US Castle Bravo test in the Bikini Atoll, stirred national and international debates about the definition of Cold War allies around questions of nuclear fallout.[8] The "Hiroshima Maidens," twenty-five Japanese women whose faces had been disfigured by the bomb in 1945, who came to America in 1955 to receive "corrective" surgeries, raised similar questions of what it means for people from different cultures to fight the Cold War on the same side of the iron curtain. *Should nuclear warheads be made at all costs? Could their human consequences be forgotten? What does it mean to be women and men living with such consequences in America?*

Faced with these questions, US survivors carved out a space of silence in Asian American communities, where an unspoken, yet eloquent, counter-memory of the bomb thrived. As before, US survivors' silence was intertwined with speech, both of which pointed to healing. Overall, however, the process of hiding and healing became less visible in America than it was in Japan. Although the process was still ongoing, it was consequential that US survivors were not surrounded by other survivors; there were fewer people who partook of the process in America. Resultantly, US *hibakusha*'s acts of healing became less audible in their remembering, too. As I argue, the process of hiding and healing became submerged by racism colored by nationalism, which significantly shaped how Asian Americans were perceived by mainstream US society. Their race, not their survivorhood, became the primary lens through which US survivors were defined. Unless highlighted by presumptions about their racial and national characteristics, their bomb experiences became paradoxically a matter of insignificance in Cold War America, highly preoccupied with nuclear issues.

Nothing revealed US survivors' submerged, if eloquent, silence more tellingly than Japanese Americans' connected remembering of the atomic bombs and the incarceration camps. As US *hibakusha* sought to rebuild their lives, it became a principal requisite for many to push aside their memories of both the camp and the bomb, at least on the surface. As seen in Chapter 3, their oral histories attest to the compelling need for silence they experienced in Japan; in the United States, too, silence permeated Asian Americans' remembering of wartime not only in their public but also in their private lives. As families came together in America, their tendency to remain silent about the camp and the bomb intensified.[9] On rare occasions when silence was broken, memories were presented either matter-of-factly or in a gently positive light. So, camp life might be mentioned as giving women a relief from household chores; no one had to worry about paying bills.[10] Likewise, spoken memories of the bomb often featured individual bravery or miraculous survival. Surprising things happened, and they saved lives; there were not only unspeakable but also speakable things about the bomb.

But these spoken memories did not represent all that was remembered. Unspoken remembering conveyed different sorts of experiences. Here again, silence was not empty or purposeless; it was about understanding conflictingly cross-national experiences of the war without dividing families and communities. This healing process became uniquely important in the early Cold War years when US survivors faced both inter- and intraracial discrimination in the United States. US *hibakusha*'s remembering both with and without spoken words had to be circumscribed, so that hostility could be kept at arm's length both inside and outside their communities. The problem, though, was that this dynamism remained largely invisible outside Asian America and, sometimes, within Asian America, too. In fact, these inter- and intraracial disconnects surrounding silence might have been a seed of the "model minority" myth, helping to shape the mainstream society's understanding of Asian Americans as quiet, compliant, and able before the rise of the Asian American civil rights movement.[11]

As I illuminate a range of meanings ascribed to silence, I pay close attention to spoken remembering that also signaled variety. Not all memories vocalized by American survivors were positive ones, such as the bravery or resourcefulness that marked their actions in Hiroshima and Nagasaki. Sometimes, US *hibakusha*'s silence was broken by circumstances that took them by surprise, prompting them to say what they usually did not say. Some recalled how their families' recollections of the camp made them feel as if bomb survivors like themselves were the *un*lucky ones; compared to their experiences of being bombed, their families' remembering made the camp appear enviably safe and stable. The bomb's shadow was also keenly felt when US survivors tried to enlist in the US Army during the Korean War. Indeed, their experiences indicated a surprising inconsistency in the US military's handling of *hibakusha*. Some were treated with curiosity shaped by the nuclear age, while others met outright rejection because of their bomb-inflicted injury or their assumed proneness to illness. I explore these spoken experiences, often spurred by US survivors' contacts with US authorities, with a careful attention to gender difference.

Chapter 3 explored discussions about the bomb triggered by US *hibakusha*'s interactions with authorities such as the ABCC. This chapter focuses on US survivors' relations with authorities in spheres more sharply separated by race and gender. While US survivors who served in the Korean War were men, many female survivors at this time embarked on work outside the home for the first time. For men in the military, the war offered yet another opportunity to articulate race, citizenship, and belonging under the scrutinizing eyes of the state. Similarly, I am struck by how female survivors remembered their work as a reason why they remained silent about the bomb. In surprising ways, their work and bomb experiences were bound together, often with their working lives as immigrants serving as a reason for their bomb experiences to remain invisible. By exploring how these seemingly disparate experiences – men's military service as Asian Americans in Korea, and women's work as racial minorities in America – were linked to their bomb experiences in Japan, I illuminate uniquely gendered relationships in racialized communities in the early Cold War. Unlike the more public and political changes in gender roles that occurred in the 1960s and 1970s, the transformation of gender in the 1940s and 1950s took place mostly in private and personal arenas. Nonetheless, these changes were felt and formed daily by US survivors, rendering them a significant force in the making of the counter-memory of the bomb.

Deciding to Come to the United States

For many US survivors, coming back to America was simply a thing to do. Haakai Nagano felt nothing but eagerness when he thought about returning. Although his name could not be "Hakkai" as it should have been in "real English" (Chapter 3), the English-speaking country was still his. "I just wanted to get back," said Nagano. "Japan was a place to stay [for a while], ... you are in a wrong place, you've got to get back." His uncle, who had been in America during the war, became his sponsor. So it was that Nagano in 1947 got on the first ship to return US citizens to the United States after the war, called the *Marine Link*. Barely seventeen years old, Nagano felt thankful that he could leave poverty-stricken Japan, where everybody was getting "tomorrow's food [out of] ... garbage can."[12] For Japanese-born Keiko Shinmoto, travel across the Pacific did not take place until much later, around 1960. More than anything else, she wanted "to go to school" in the United States. But her parents could not afford to pay for her education. She started to work at a bank, but her passion for college did not diminish. One of her US-born sisters who had gone back to America proved to be the key for making Shinmoto's dream come true; the sister's husband agreed to sponsor Shinmoto. At age twenty-three, she got a ticket to America along with a three-year visa, one long "enough to go to school." Crossing the ocean eastward for the first time, she was "not scared of anything. Because my brothers and sisters were here." It surely made a difference that Shinmoto's mother reassured her: "I know America ... it's not like a horrible place," she said before her daughter embarked. After all, Shinmoto's mother had lived for years in Portland, Oregon, where she had raised three older siblings of Shinmoto's. The youngest Shinmoto was "happy" to be in America, not least because her brother-in-law who lived in Torrance, California, agreed to pay for her college.[13]

Nagano and Shinmoto's stories, which, roughly speaking, bookend the period under consideration, appear to confirm the image of the United States as a country full of opportunities. In America, it seemed, no one starved to death; higher education was open to anyone aspirational. But a deeper look into their remembering complicates the bright images. Nagano traveled with his brother John, but not with his parents. Seeking opportunities to fend for himself meant family separation yet again. Boarding the *Marine Link*, Nagano could not help feeling a resounding sense of loss. "Here we were, coming back on a military ship," said Nagano. "I remember what ships used to look like – *Tatsuta-maru*, *Kamakura-maru*, all of those beautiful ships that the Japanese had. But this is the wartime ship that we came back on."[14] It was difficult to miss that his status as Nikkei had been transformed. Similarly, Shinmoto told of difficulty. The money that Shinmoto's brother-in-law paid for her college did not come easily. After serving in the Korean War, "he was struggling." He found a job at a Safeway supermarket, but the future seemed dim. He took advantage of the GI Bill to attend a business college. The degree, however, did not bring enough to support his family, not to mention its new member Shinmoto. Soon, she found herself serving "Mr. and Mrs. Brookes" in Los Angeles as a "schoolgirl" maid. They did not pay for college, but they did pay for other expenses in exchange for tasks that she performed for them, which ranged from babysitting, to cooking, to dishwashing.[15] Shinmoto's and Nagano's experiences, then, were similar to those of others who migrated from Japan to America after the war because of economic hardship. US *hibakusha* were determined to earn their living in the country they claimed as home, although they understood that it was far from accommodating. Neither Nagano nor Shinmoto thought of themselves as survivors, suggesting that, in their determination to succeed, there was little room to reflect on their suffering caused by the bomb.

Still, memories of the Pacific War were not erased easily. Even as they made plans to cross the ocean, US survivors began to learn, in many cases for the first time, about Nikkei experiences of incarceration during the war. While Nikkei remained largely silent about the camps, their memories nonetheless seeped quietly into their conversations. This seemed particularly true when they needed to bring up a camp to claim ties among war-torn family and friends. For Hawaiian-born Izumi Hirano, word from a Nikkei family in Hilo marked the beginning of his return to the United States. The family had been incarcerated in the same camp as Hirano's father, where they had become good friends. When Hirano's father passed away shortly after the war, the family asked if Hirano would be interested in coming back to Hawai'i. For the family, this was to "return the favor" that Hirano's father had done for them during the war. Although the family had not met the younger Hirano, the older Hirano's kindness was reason enough to be generous. Moreover, as it happened, Hirano's cousin from Honolulu, who had been serving in the US military after the war, came to Japan in the late 1940s as part of the occupation forces of the Allied Powers. With his cousin's assistance, Hirano made his way safely to Honolulu in 1949.[16] Family connections, made precarious by the war, became reinvigorated as Nikkei began remembering their war experiences in the early years of the Cold War.

Sumiko Yoshida's remembering also indicates how the camp was intimately intertwined with the bomb among Nikkei of the time, adding layers to the history of immigrants across the Pacific after the war. Born in Japan in 1930, her coming to America in 1956 materialized because her aunt's recovery from wartime losses had finally taken shape. The owner of a thriving nursery before the war, her aunt went to work at her friend's nursery after leaving the camp. Unlike Yoshida's aunt, her friend was fortunate enough to retain the property's ownership through the war. When the war ended and Yoshida's aunt learned that her mother, nephew, and another niece had been lost to the bomb, she still was not ready to assist Yoshida's coming to the United States. Only when she had finally saved enough to purchase a nursery in Anaheim, California, did the aunt ask if Yoshida would like to come. The expectation was that, in America, Yoshida would have a better chance for marriage. As we will see, her marriage to a Nisei created a rare occasion for Yoshida to speak about her bomb experiences. Early on, however, stories of Nikkei's recovery from the camp were the catalyst for Yoshida's travel across the Pacific. These stories became fuller when her cousins Bob and George came to see her in Hiroshima during the Korean War. Her cousins, serving in the US Army at that time, had also acquired a nursery in Anaheim.[17] Not only the mother but also the children of the camp became modestly successful. Here, remembering like Yoshida's seems to trace the early history of Japanese Americans as "model minorities" who remained loyal to their country against all odds. After release from the camp, hard-working Nikkei families rebuilt their lives by sticking together and duly serving the country.[18] Hidden in such narratives is the fact that, often, they were helping *hibakusha*. The recognition of hurt, as well as the need for hiding and healing it, occurred in families and communities, although it was invisible to mainstream society. They were not putting the past behind as the "model minority" myth would have it. They were engaging in acts of healing from the past largely neglected by nation-states.

Inside the silence among Nikkei about the camp and the bomb during the 1940s and 1950s, then, were quiet currents of talk about them. As families and friends became reunited, they did mention damage caused by the war, although hardly as a featured topic of conversation. As seen in Chapter 3, this kind of talk about the bomb was often prompted by major life events such as illness, marriage, and employment, as well as by US survivors' contacts with authorities such as the ABCC. This pattern persisted as US *hibakusha* faced another major life event – immigration. Only when absolutely necessary, then, they mentioned the bomb and the camp in passing, a tendency that became more pronounced in America than in Japan where survivors were surrounded by many other survivors. In the United States, Nikkei experiences diverged widely between the bomb and the camp, adding to their cautiousness. Furthermore, US survivors' remembering such as Yoshida's and Hirano's indicates that words could be matter-of-fact, seemingly devoid of feelings. They did not recall discussing fear, emptiness, or outrage. No doubt, many had these emotions; their oral histories unmistakably reveal them.[19] And yet, Nikkei did not voice these feelings either publicly or privately. This kind of reserve was hardly rare in Asian America, where silence was valued as an expression of care, articulateness, and resistance.[20] The socioeconomic status of Nikkei immediately after the war, too, likely contributed to circumspection both inside and outside of families and communities. With memories of the mass incarceration fresh, many Nikkei were understandably unwilling to make waves.[21]

But none of these factors fully explain Nikkei's measured talk about the camps and the bomb. Rather, US *hibakusha*'s remembering indicates that they felt as if enough was conveyed by being succinct. Having survived losses on both sides of the Pacific, a simple reference to an experience denoted suffering. Listeners might not have understood speakers fully, or they might have even misunderstood each other because their words were scant. Chapter 3 has already revealed how silence about the camp caused some *hibakusha* to have erroneous expectations about the socioeconomic status of their American suitors. As Yoshida's and Hirano's cases show, many Japanese Americans relied on their relatives in the United States for support, furthering the perception that Japanese Americans in America were better off than the Japanese in Japan. Nonetheless, US survivors' remembering strongly suggests that they cultivated a sense of mutual understanding in the era. This was an understanding that contained healing, a task that a flood of words may not have been able to achieve. Indeed, on rare occasions when they expressed their feelings about their wartime experiences, personal or family discordances erupted.[22] Nikkei's words about the bomb and the camps remained few and far between, creating a space in which a shared appreciation of losses might be formed. This appreciation, in turn, facilitated assisting hands to extend across the ocean.

Inside this particular kind of silence, Nikkei survivors quietly made a decision to come to the United States. In some cases, the chaos surrounding their citizenship became a chief reason for their move. Women, in particular, faced a complicated task because of a myriad of laws and customs concerning women in both Japan and America. Takeko Okano's remembering offers a striking example that illuminates the gendered meanings of silence, citizenship, and cross-nationality.[23] Born in Japan in 1925, Okano married a Nisei whom she met in postwar Hiroshima. Okano was warmly welcomed into his family, perhaps in no small part because a Japanese woman from a good Japanese family was considered the most desirable spouse for a Japanese American man. But her marriage quickly became shaky after her husband returned to the United States. Okano was at first reluctant to leave Japan; he, on the other hand, was eager to go back to America where he had been born and raised. In the Japanese custom of the time, a wife was expected to follow her husband's wishes, so Okano's reluctance attracted little sympathy. Soon after Okano went to America in 1951 to join him, however, it became evident that he had been unfaithful to her. "He felt like he was a college student," said Okano. It was as if "he grew wings" to fly free, because there was "no parental oversight" as in Japan.

Pregnant with her second child, Okano soon decided to divorce. The question was whether she would stay in America where she was still a newcomer or return to Japan. Her ex-husband's mother, as well as his grandparents, wanted her back in Japan.

Okano's own extended family, too, was there. Okano was torn; if she were to return to Japan, she would lose her US citizenship, making it necessary for her and her children to become Japanese citizens. At this point, she would be officially noted as divorced from her husband on both of their Japanese family registries, making her legally ineligible for a place in her ex-husband's family lineage. But her children would still be considered heirs of her ex-husband's family because of the Japanese customs that esteemed connections by blood. This might prompt her former in-laws to claim their right to legally adopt at least one of her children. This would mean that Okano would be separated from her older son, a likely favorite of her former in-laws. If she stayed in America, on the other hand, she would simply be a person who also happened to be a parent. With no former relative nearby to claim her children, she would be able to continue to parent them. Okano decided to stay stateside.

Okano's remembering revealed how gender-skewed laws and customs propelled people to cross national borders and stay. If a nation state held onto its citizens tightly, as Japan did in Okano's case, it might stir them to move away from it. Equally important, Okano found a source of strength after her divorce in her former mother-in-law in Japan, whom she "admired" as her "*sendatsu* [someone who had done it before]." Although Okano had never learned her former mother-in-law's life story fully, Okano was able to figure it out by "connecting pieces of puzzles together" and by imagining what might have lain in her silence. She was indeed Okano's *sendatsu*, because she, too, originally came to America following her marriage to a Japanese American man. The couple was separated by the war; she had been in Japan to accompany her oldest son, soon to be Okano's husband, who attended a Japanese college. Her husband, in contrast, stayed in America and was sent to a camp, passing away shortly after his release. His death struck a particular blow to her, as she had always felt that continuing her family lineage was her responsibility; she was the oldest child of her biological family that had daughters only. As a matter of fact, she had married him into her family by listing him as a member of her biological family on the Japanese family registry. In this way, men, not women, continued family lineage as they should in families with no biological sons. Born in America and unconcerned about how his name appeared on a foreign, that is, Japanese, record, her husband readily agreed, despite the fact that he, too, was the oldest offspring of his biological family. He simply kept his family name on his American records.

Unaware of all this, Okano once asked her mother-in-law how it was possible for the oldest son of a family to be married into his wife's family. In Japanese families, such an arrangement would have been nearly unthinkable; it would break male lineage, one of the most cherished traits of Japanese families. Okano's question was met by her mother-in-law's silence. Okano began to understand the meaning of this silence only years later, when the news of her father-in-law's death arrived. His death certificate arrived from America, with his family name before marriage on it. Seeing this, "her mother[-in-law] cried." As Okano recalled, her mother-in-law was ordinarily "a *cool* person," but this time, things were different. "He did not protect my family to the very end," said her mother-in-law, meaning that her husband never really became part of her biological family as she had hoped. Men's responsibility for continuing family had fallen upon her, and she failed. Although her husband likely did not intend to disappoint his wife, his insistence on his biological family's name, shown by the US death certificate, still felt like a deception to her. The mundane difference in record-keeping practices across the Pacific became a spiteful part of her life history as an immigrant.

When Okano mentioned how she respected her former mother-in-law as her *sendatsu*, then, she was imagining ties connecting generations of immigrants. These ties might not be easily visible, but they felt strong when Okano reached out for them. The most immediate tie was that both women had experienced family separations across the ocean. But Okano's respect for her former mother-in-law was also shaped by their gender; they both had been tasked with a family responsibility tightly defined by Japanese customs affecting women. Though in different ways, neither of them fulfilled the responsibility prescribed by a patriarchal society. But their words suggest that they did not see their experiences simply as a fault of Japanese culture. Quietly, they both claimed that American customs, too, disappointed them. In Okano's mind, the United States was the carefree country that led to her ex-husband's extramarital affairs. For his mother, America shattered her hopes twice, first by causing her husband's premature death, then by affixing a name other than hers to his death certificate. Her tears were not in resignation, but in protest. Her layered feelings, suddenly bursting into visibility, made her words memorable. Here again, words were met by silence, although it was Okano who fell silent at this time: Okano gradually understood her mother-in-law by putting together "pieces of puzzles" over many years. Clearly, Okano did not ask the crying woman why she cried.

Indeed, the contrast between silence and speech was sharply drawn for Okano; she had experienced something similar as *hibakusha*. Before she got married, her mother-in-law "probably had been worried about" radiation effects that might plague Okano or her children. But the worry had never been talked about, creating a quiet space where these concerns might slowly dissipate. Just as her mother-in-law "did not talk too much about the camp," she did not pry open Okano's experiences of the bomb. Okano had lost her father; he was so close to the hypocenter that no one could find his remains. This appeared to be the extent of what these women put into words in a matter-of-fact way. When her mother-in-law lost her "*cool*," then, Okano treated her with equally respectful silence. All of these meanings, both spoken and unspoken, were embedded in Okano calling her former mother-in-law *sendatsu*. "She was an utterly reliable person," Okano said twice in her oral history, unprompted. Okano insisted that she learned from her mother-in-law more than she did from her own mother, surprisingly strong praise for someone who could have taken Okano's older son away. Silence ran through the women's relationship like an invisible thread, giving them force to go across national and gender boundaries.

US *hibakusha* Natsumi Aida's remembering further illuminates surprising conflicts caused by strict regulations of citizenship on both sides of the ocean, amplified by her status as a wife and a mother. If Okano's case highlights why some survivors decided to *stay* in the United States, Aida's experiences show why others might have *moved* to America because of their gender. Like Okano's, details of Aida's story are unique, yet her remembering reveals the centrality of gender in the history of so many US *hibakusha*, and the power of their gendered experiences as immigrants to refute the distinction between "loyal" and "disloyal" citizenries propagated by the states through the early years of the Cold War.[24] Born in Sacramento, California, in 1930, Aida did not come back to America until 1952. The chief reason for her prolonged stay was that, despite the bomb, she was doing well in Japan after the war. Although she had lost her birth certificate and her passport to the bomb, her aunt and uncle planned to adopt Aida as their daughter. They were also looking forward to arranging her marriage, especially because all of their biological children were sons. Surrounded by a loving, relatively well-to-do extended family, there was no reason for Aida to hurriedly return to America simply because the war had ended.

This relatively fortunate circumstance brought Aida an unexpected challenge when she married a Japanese national in 1949. At that point, her uncle and aunt had not yet adopted her. This, combined with Aida's lack of US documentation, rendered her stateless. Only after marriage did her extended family realize that this would preclude registering her as a member of her husband's family. The problem became further complicated when Aida's first child arrived. Because he was a boy, everyone was especially overjoyed. He would be her husband's family's heir. It came as a disappointment, then, when it turned out that he could be registered only on his mother's side. In Japanese laws of the time, children's citizenship was determined according to their mothers'. This was to protect the purity of their fathers' bloodlines, especially in cases of children born out of wedlock. Aida's child became his mother's boy, not his father's, because of this paternalistic rule. This was not the only problem; what was the citizenship of Aida's child, when her citizenship itself was undocumented? Desperate to do anything to change this situation, both families made frantic inquiries, and they found a surprising solution: to register their marriage in America, using the father's name as their family name. In this way, a Japanese family's lineage could be continued, with the only requirement being that they all became US citizens. In America, there were no family records, only marriage and birth certificates, making the business of bringing together the family easier. This pushed the couple to move to the United States. Aida's mother assisted her daughter by helping her regain US citizenship and by sending her tickets to cross the Pacific in 1951. In 1952, Aida's husband followed as a US citizen's spouse.

Listening to Aida's oral history, one easily recognizes how greatly she cherished memories of being treated well in Japan because of her US citizenship. It was not only that her connections with America facilitated the Aidas' efforts to build a legally recognizable family. Both before and after marriage, Aida had been granted many privileges. "My younger brother's friend came to see me every week" after the war, recalled Aida. "He was part of the occupation forces ... he gave me many different things. Cheese, candies, and chocolate. A lot of clothes, too. Everyone was envious." After marriage, these supplies continued to come, which the couple sold to make money. Eventually, the saving allowed her husband to purchase a truck. Her economic advantage was furthered by cultural resources she brought to her marriage. Indeed, the person who found the solution to the family lineage problem was Aida's relative, a Nisei working as a translator for the US occupation forces. Fluent in English, he offered to look into a myriad of regulations about citizenship. Once he found that an international marriage was the solution, he accompanied the Aidas to the US Embassy in Kobe. There, the man helped them find a "white witness" to create a birth certificate for their son, without which the entire plan would have been moot. The witness was "white," meaning not only that he was someone legally endowed to serve as a witness, but also someone whose name did not indicate any connection to Japan. Such a person was likely to be deemed "loyal" to the United States in a way that a Japanese American might not be. The witness's words would be trusted, and Aida's son would be born again as an American citizen. The couple's goal might have been to continue *his* family lineage, but *she* was the only one who could make that happen, pushing their relationship toward gender equality.

Both Okano's and Aida's experiences pointed to their layered sense of national belonging, as well as to how it brought or kept them stateside because of their gender. US *hibakusha* were the first to be surprised by where they landed. When they found it nearly impossible to coordinate gender expectations, family laws and customs, citizenship, and national belonging, US survivors mobilized their cross-national resources by seeking the assistance of Nikkei on both sides of the Pacific. As Aida's story shows, they even took advantage of the racialized distinction between those who were likely to be considered "loyal" and those who were not. If they did not challenge the distinction, they were determined to navigate through it. In so doing, US *hibakusha* discovered new meanings of cross-nationality, those more formally gendered than before. Okano's story, for one, suggests how her identity as a Japanese woman paradoxically gave her reasons to stay in America. Unlike her American husband who abandoned his children, Okano was determined not to let go of them. "Because he grew up in America," said Okano about her ex-husband, his "morality was different than that of ours who grew up in Japan."[25] Emphasizing the difference between American and Japanese morality, Okano implied that she could be a Japanese parent – a mother who stays with her children – only in America. Aida, in contrast, felt proud of being an American particularly because she was in Japan. Being a woman there firmly established her motherhood; this, in turn, made it possible to bring her whole family to her country of America. In a sense, both their experiences embodied the power of nation states: it drew people closely to belong and, at the same time, it gave them powerful reasons to leave one country for another. By going beyond national boundaries in the Pacific, US survivors were crossing gender boundaries, too. Theirs were not political acts, but they were acts of defiance driven by the power of gender. Potent yet adaptable, gender offered US *hibakusha* a possibility to rise above deadlocked national interests. This possibility helped build the foundation for their persistence when they were treated as "aliens ineligible for citizenship" once they embarked upon their journeys in the United States.

Crossing the Ocean, Finding Home, and Rebuiding Family

As shown in Chapter 3, racism became integrated into discrimination against US *hibakusha* while they were still in Japan. We have seen that for those US survivors who married interracially, health concerns became intertwined with their need to cope with their in-laws' scrutiny of racial differences. For Japanese spouses of Japanese Americans, assumptions about class differences between the wife and the husband obscured the racism that was to affect them both after they arrived in the United States. As Nikkei survivors boarded ships to cross the Pacific, however, the legacy of the Pacific War as a race war came to the surface more prominently. Similar to Haakai Nagano, *hibakusha* on the boats could not help but notice their fellow travelers' desperation. "They were all Niseis," recalled Kazue Suyeishi, a Nisei who came back to America in 1949. "If they had a lot of money, they would not have needed to go back to the country. So, people who returned were without a job, without hope." Having a hopeful plan of pursuing education in America, Suyeishi recognized that she was extremely fortunate among Nisei who seemed thoroughly worn out. She also learned that, regardless of her fortune, she would be treated as a second-class citizen. Although Suyeishi was ready to pay for a private room on the ship, her request was declined. "Only US military men were allowed," a Japanese American man on the ship told her.[26] George Kazuto Saiki, who was lucky enough to get on a ship with more amenities called the *President Wilson*, found that all of the other passengers were white (see Figure 4.1). After arriving in Hawai'i in 1949,

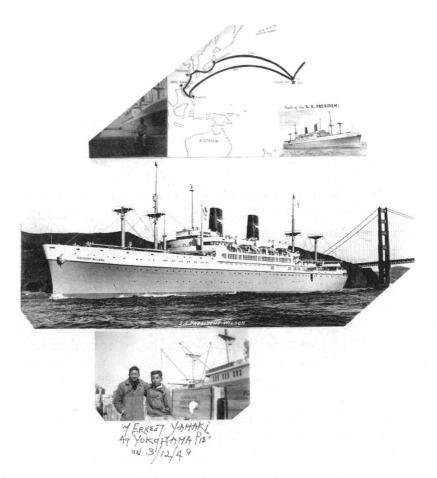

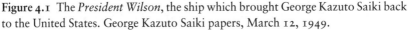

Figure 4.1 The *President Wilson*, the ship which brought George Kazuto Saiki back to the United States. George Kazuto Saiki papers, March 12, 1949.

he learned that nonwhite persons were supposed to book a lower-class ship, the *Golden*, on which his Nisei friends had traveled.[27] May Yamaoka, who came back on a cargo ship, had to laugh about the room she was given, which was supposedly in first-class. "They were all bunk beds, all Niseis," said Yamaoka of her roommates, recounting the poor treatment they received.[28] Whatever socioeconomic status they occupied in Japan, they would be treated as racial minorities from now on.

Lower-class ships for nonwhite passengers came with a price, as well as with further opportunities for US *hibakusha* to discover meanings of their layered national belonging. Fusae Kurihara remembered how she got seasick on her way to America in 1950 because of terrible odors on board. "Because the ship was a cargo ship, not a passenger ship, and smelled bad, for 14 days going to the United States I couldn't eat anything ... I was exhausted when I arrived in San Francisco." After her mother, brothers, and uncle drove her to Welby, Colorado, where they lived, she stayed in bed for fourteen more days.[29] Hayami Fukino, too, became ill on her way back to America in 1951. This probably had something to do with the fact that she "was in where you put the luggage in." As she recalled, "there were thirty people in that one room, one place." When the ship stopped in Hawai'i, she was given a lemon by a worker on the ship, a boy. "Then I felt good. I felt good," said Fukino. The taste of the fruit was a vivid contrast to the ship's stagnant air. Also, her brother's friend in Hawai'i took Fukino around the island. These were just two of the many beginnings in her return to America. "When I was on the boat," recalled Fukino, "one thing that impressed me was [that] all the different people ... on the boat, only one language that [they] ... could get along with [was] English." Not only Nikkei, but also people from China, where her ship had stopped before Japan, shared the language.[30] If this tacit agreement among passengers to use English pushed US survivors to become Americans, other incidents reminded them of their belonging to Japan. On its way to San Francisco in 1948, Alfred Kaneo Dote's ship stopped in Hawai'i. He was treated to some ice cream by Issei who had stayed on the island through the war. "They were old folks," said Dote. "They bought ice cream for four or five of us [returning Nisei]. Then they asked us if it was true that Japan had lost the war." The twenty-year-old Dote responded: "I wouldn't have been going to America if Japan won. I am going to America because Japan lost; because it is better to get rid of even one mouth to feed." The older men cried like children.[31] Dote's words sounded authentic because someone from Japan pronounced them. Dote clearly knew the power he held. By the same token, the Issei men understood the power they held over the Nisei returnees. Their memories of Japan would be solicited over an American cup of ice cream, a delight for those who had been long deprived of such luxury. To cross the ocean was to be pulled into multiple national belongings.

US *hibakusha*'s cross-nationality continued to shape their lives once they arrived home, which turned out for many to be a surprisingly unfamiliar place. Indeed, homes were not easy to come by. When Yasuko Ogawa, who had difficulty regaining her US citizenship because she had cast a ballot in Japan (Chapter 3), finally returned to America, she realized that her travel was not yet over:

> My husband's uncle was in San Jose. . . . [From there,] I first went to Newcastle and worked on my nephew's ranch. . . . [Then,] we learned from the newspaper that a carnation grower named Shibuya in Mountain View was looking for a couple to work, so we went there. . . . We stayed there for two years, and then about one year at Mr. Satake's.[32]

Just as her travel across the ocean was facilitated by her relatives in the United States, her travel on the ground was dotted by Nikkei families, friends, and strangers. Those who had come to the country earlier helped the newcomers, something that rewarded both.

Indeed, Mitsuko Okimoto's remembering reveals how assistance in Nikkei communities was mutual for older and newer immigrants:

> I did alterations after coming here. . . . Although one of my acquaintances recommended that I work at a bank [as I used to in Japan], the job would have required that I leave my child in someone's care. My income would not have been as good as it was in Japan – not enough to pay for a babysitter. So it was better not to work. At that time, I had a friend, a cleaner. So, although I had never done sewing, I decided to do it to help our income. My husband had never done anything domestic in Japan, but he worked hard. I initially opposed, but there was nothing else that a Japanese could do. He eventually became a gardener, and found that there were a lot of [Japanese American] gardeners with a university degree. There was no job that allowed them to work together with Caucasians.[33]

Although the employers of Nikkei domestics or gardeners were likely white, Okimoto's remembering makes it clear that they did not count as people with whom Japanese Americans "worked together." In a racially segregated work environment, then, it was necessary for Nikkei to rely on each other when they needed to "work together" either as coworkers or employees in family businesses. Ogawa needed Mrs. Shibuya and Satake, but they, too, needed laborers like the Ogawas.

Unlike Japanese schools and neighborhoods in the 1930s where Nikkei children enjoyed a relative lack of racial and national divisions,

American workplaces in the 1950s left no doubt that these divisions would be enforced. Okimoto's memory also suggests a class boundary that Nikkei crossed now that they were in America. She had never done hourly paid alteration work; her husband had had no experience as a domestic. The sudden shift in her remembering from a reference to a friend who was a "cleaner," to a talk of her "sewing," sheds light on how difficult it was for her to vocally acknowledge her husband's line of profession. Instead of saying that her husband was a "cleaner," she indicated only that his work required additional income earned by his wife. He then became a "gardener," a trade that still struck her as below him. But, at least, other university graduates were doing it, so "gardener" was easier to pronounce than "cleaner." If Nikkei on trans-Pacific ships began to understand how class was assigned to their race and national origin, their experiences after arrival confirmed it as a daily reality.

US *hibakusha*'s lives generated not only the close "work together" ethic of Nikkei, but also intraracial tensions. Family separations during the war had compelled many parents, children, and siblings to concentrate on family members who stayed together. Many of those who were apart received only restrained attention from family. Tim Nakamoto's remembering made this painfully clear:

> You don't automatically from day one create the same family atmosphere that you left six years ago. I found that out. I [had] expected to be embraced fully as before ... but in many instances it was almost like coming back to ... strangers' home.[34]

George Kazuto Saiki, who returned to Hawai'i on the upper-class ship *Wilson*, experienced similar alienation. Although he was taken into his older sister's family, he was not treated well. In his oral history, memories of family rejection surfaced:

> It is funny for me to tell you this, but there is no love among us, brothers and sisters. We live separate lives. This is a bad family story. When I came back, my sister did not welcome me. This was because she [already] had three children. She owned five houses, where she used me as a servant. I took her children to a bath. I washed dishes. I also took out five houses' worth of trash, and cleaned their yards.[35]

Saiki's frustration about being treated as a "servant" was made worse by the ridicule that he received from his neighbors. After he returned to Hawai'i as a sixteen-year-old, his neighbors began to taunted him. They were all Japanese Americans, he said, who spoke only English:

> I didn't understand English. ... No wonder, then, did everyone ridicule me. This was because Japan lost [the war]. ... They were all Japanese Americans, but they had become Americans. For, all Japanese language schools had been closed down during the war. They gave me a nickname "Japan." It was my name at that time, "Japan."[36]

One consequence of wartime persecution of Nikkei, then, was the discontinuity of language, which caused a cultural schism within the community. Even in Hawai'i where most escaped incarceration, suspicion about their national loyalty was widespread. For instance, community leaders, including teachers in Japanese language schools at Buddhist temples, were taken away by officials for questioning. After 1945, these cultural institutions did not promptly bounce back. In fact, many never did. This created considerable gaps in Nikkei communities. When a Japanese-speaking person like Saiki returned after the war, there were few bridges between new and old immigrants. Clearly, the former were deemed inferior to the latter, just as many first generation Japanese immigrants with strong ties to Japan lost authority over their US-born sons and daughters during the war. Younger generations with stronger familiarity with American culture were valued more than older ones who did not speak English fluently nor regularly eat American food. This kind of rupture existed side by side with the need for new and old immigrants to "work together."

US survivors dealt with intraracial discriminations in many ways. Dote, for one, accepted the lack of affection from his parents as a matter of fact, and decided to distance himself from the family as a way to cope with it. "There were brothers and sisters who had been born" while he was in Japan, who held "a stronger connection to their parents" than Dote. "So, I went to a house of a white family" for whom he worked as a domestic while attending school. This allowed him not only to be away from his parents, but also "to learn English."[37] This "schoolboy" or "schoolgirl" was a form of employment frequently adopted by Japanese Americans, shaped by socioeconomic disparity and underpinned by racist policies that confined the Japanese in America to the status of "aliens ineligible for citizenship" until 1952.[38] Seeing this arrangement from where US *hibakusha* stood, however, it might have also been a way for them to keep family and community rejections at arm's lengths. For Dote, being a "schoolboy" was an option that served multiple purposes, including an escape from intraracial discriminations and an ability to survive amid interracial inequality.

Natsumi Aida, by contrast, took a more outspoken route in confronting her parents: "You sent me to Japan because you did not want me," said Aida to her mother shortly after she returned to America. The mother in response scolded Aida, saying: "I have no children that I don't want." Although this exchange lifted the cloud somewhat, Aida also felt that it became more difficult for the family to discuss anything related to the war after this conversation. Her mother was worried about Aida's fragile health, but said nothing about its possible connection to the bomb. When asked if her family members told her about their experiences of the camp, Aida responded: "They told me this and that, as if they remembered the camp by accident or when they were talking about something else. There was no direct talk. ... [After I confronted my mother] we did not talk about many things."[39] Spoken words, especially those that exposed hurt, brought silence.

Amid these tensions, some US survivors began to see their wartime experiences in Japan as more devastating than those of their families who had lived out the war in America. Although much of Nikkei's talk of the camps and the bomb remained matter-of-fact, some of their remembering suggests that camps were more readily recalled, often with an emphasis on ties that they brought to the community. Kazuko Aoki, for example, remembered how she had been enthusiastically welcomed into her husband's group of friends – his fellow inmates at Jerome, Arkansas, during the war – when she had come to Hawai'i in 1959. Her husband had lost his brother to the bomb, so Aoki felt that he understood her pain. But when it came time to get together with his friends from the camp, his concern for Aoki's health appeared to diminish. Aoki remembered:

> The friends were closer to each other than they were to their parents and siblings. They got together all the time. But it was a bit hard on me ... because I could not take a rest even when I wanted to. So, although I didn't want to go to their gatherings,

I couldn't tell Gene [my husband] because he was so looking forward to it.[40]

Especially after her daughter Carole was born, everyone wanted the baby to come to the gathering, too. But it meant that Aoki had to prepare and pack not only food for the gatherings but also all sorts of baby stuff. At that time, Aoki was struggling with her health. She felt extremely weak, spending five to six hours a day bedridden. Compared to her physical and psychological suffering, what Jean's friends told her about the camp sounded lighter, at least in spirit. "It was in a desert-like place," said Aoki, of what Gene's friends had told her about Jerome. "They found sea shells. When they found driftwood, it was treated as a treasure. They smoothed it with sandpaper and applied wax, and made it into a piece of artwork." In their narrative, the camp was a self-sufficient community where everything from school to hospital was available, as if it was a well-sustained small town. The residents even celebrated *bon'odori*, a summer festival, in *yukata*, a summer-style Japanese *kimono*.[41] Although they might have suffered psychologically, it seemed many left the camp physically intact. Remembering the camp as a community, they seemed to have recovered psychologically, too, with the passage of time.

As the camp and the bomb became juxtaposed against one another, some US *hibakusha* and their family members began to develop an image of the camp as relatively benign, even benevolent. Tsuruko Nakamura did not recall hearing about Nikkei experiences in wartime America before she came to the United States in 1963. But she began to learn about them from her in-laws once in San Francisco. Strikingly, a conclusion she drew from their stories was that incarceration had helped Nikkei survive the war: "Compared to those in Japan who did not have anything after the war, those in internment camps were able to eat well. So, I realized that they were fortunate to be in internment camps in the United States," said Nakamura. Her husband, who had spent three years in the camp in Hart Mountain, Wyoming, and accompanied Nakamura to the oral history interview in 2011, agreed:

I thought that the food given at our camp was poor. But then, I was conscripted in 1946 and sent to Japan as part of the US occupation forces. I stayed in Tokyo three years. In 1946 and 1947, many people were sleeping on the street, and it was difficult to tell who was sleeping and who was dead. It was that kind of era. So, ... I thought that, although food at my camp had tasted bad, I had been more fortunate than the people [of Japan].[42]

Such cross-national comparison likely helped create reserve among former inmates in expressing their anger or anguish about the camps. No matter how critical they might have been, their damages seemed to pale in comparison with those of the nuclear holocaust. Whether this comparison was appropriate was beside the point. What mattered was that remembering benign sides of the camp offered an opening for everyone to heal. This healing was not only about recovering from personal losses, but also about rebuilding families and communities. Their silence about harm caused by the camp, then, did not necessarily indicate a lack of critique or a beginning of a "model minority." Rather, Japanese American silence grew from urgent purposes: to repair family estrangement felt by returnees; to help recover everyone from psychosocial injuries; and to keep ties made in the camps for rebuilding Japanese America.

US survivors, in turn, seemed to accept the view that the bomb was worse than the camps, although many recognized that the camps obviously had caused much suffering among Nikkei. The suffering extended broadly from psychological to physical, and yet the desire to heal pushed remembering of it to a back seat.[43] Tim Nakamoto's oral history, conducted in 1991 when the successful accomplishment of the Japanese American Redress generated an excitement among many in Japanese America, offers a case in point. As discussed earlier, Nakamoto had a difficult time being accepted by his family. A long separation had created not only a sense of alienation, but also a feeling that he had been unfairly treated. "I was kind of torn inside as to – why me? Why did I have to face this situation?" said Nakamoto of his survivorhood, shared by none of his family members in America. Feeling like a stranger at home, he explained:

> That's why I don't really have any sympathy for people – oh, you know, they talk about the redress situation now, that the people were held in the various camps in the U.S.A. I really don't – I'm sure within their own mind they, mental anguish and all that [is there] – but I really don't have that much sympathy over their struggle, so to speak, because, you know, ... they didn't have to dodge bombs every night like

I did, you know. I was not under any protection. You can look at ... barbed wire in two ways. Yeah, I didn't have that barbed wire, but I didn't have that [safety] net. So, you know, the bombs were falling somewhere [else].[44]

Here, the camp became something more than its own benign place. It was literally a protection from being bombed. Although no bombing occurred on the US mainland during the war, the idea of bombing Americans in the United States was not entirely outlandish for Nikkei. They were aliens at best, enemy nationals at worst. Before and after incarceration, they were subject to physical and psychological violence.

And yet, as their remembering went, they might have been fortunate compared to Nikkei in Japan. *It was only mental anguish that they suffered from.* As seen earlier, Tsuruko Nakamura's remembering pointed toward the image of well-fed inmates who fared better than starving survivors, while Kazuko Aoki's recollection highlighted the difference between sick survivors and healthy inmates. As Nakamura's husband indicated, these contrasts helped downplay former inmates' remembering about maltreatment in the camps and its resultant physical and psychological injuries. Meanwhile, bomb survivors such as Aoki continued to find it difficult to explain their radiation illness to former inmates, who seemed mostly uninjured to *hibakusha. Would they understand my injury?* Defining the bomb as more destructive than the camps did not open a frank discussion about either. As Nakamoto's remembering suggests, the former inmates suffered only "within their own mind." They did not share their agony with Nakamoto. Neither did Nakamoto share his lack of sympathy with his family members. Calling them "lucky" to have not been bombed, he was quick to say that his was "a very argumentative point" of view. If not prompted by a sympathetic interviewer, who assumed that his family "knew yours [the bomb experience] was worse," Nakamoto might not have made the cross-national comparison.[45] Divisions within families remained difficult to speak; among Nikkei, these divisions were, and continued to be, bound up with the camp and the bomb.

The task of keeping their family ties intact by way of silence fell particularly heavily on female *hibakusha* who were interracially married. For many, though, this was not because they did not try to speak. Miyuki Broadwater, who came to America shortly after the war because of her marriage to a US military man, recalled how her father-in-law did not believe that she was a survivor. "Yes, I even saw the mushroom cloud," Broadwater insisted. Even her husband found her experience difficult to believe wholeheartedly. "He is in the military, so he knows about nuclear tests. But the actual bombing, he can't grasp it. He doesn't ask about it, either. Perhaps he doesn't want to know," reasoned Broadwater. She decided not to press him. She felt "happy" about her marriage, so she did not want to reveal her "differences" by talking about the bomb.[46] Lisa Gendernalik, another female *hibakusha* who came to America because of her marriage to a US army officer, also found it difficult to discuss the bomb with her husband. He listened "up to a point," but then appeared uncomfortable and she began feeling guilty. Maybe she would "have been a wife of a *zaimokuya* if there were no bomb," meaning that she would have had no choice but to marry a destitute Japanese man if no bomb were dropped and no Americans came. She should be thankful for the bomb. Gendernalik found silence the best way to put aside such thoughts, even refraining from telling her children.[47] Both Broadwater and Gendernalik, then, tried to find a place in their marriage for their spoken remembering of the bomb. But their efforts were unsuccessful, in effect keeping the American memory of the war untouched by Japanese American memories. While Nikkei families were caught between the bomb and the camp, interracial families were gripped by the assumed differences in loyalty, belonging, and gender. White men embodied American loyalty, dutiful carriers of the nuclear attacks. Japanese American women had been victimized, but for good reasons; they had been disloyal to America, and they were fortunate to be saved by US men.

Both Broadwater and Gendernalik's remembering revealed a dynamism that has not been highlighted enough by scholars. In the postwar era, as scholars have shown, US–Japan relations were rebuilt by a discourse of alliance-building. America extended its helping hand to a Japan struggling to rebuild itself; Japan, in turn, became a mostly willing pupil of this trans-Pacific guidance. This discourse became conspicuously gendered around issues of the bomb; innocent Japanese female victims caught American imagination as particularly deserving of US assistance.[48] But within family relationships, a view of *hibakusha* as deservingly punished by the war might have been persistent. In this view, survivors did not need assistance, because they already had been rescued by their marriages to Americans. Kazue McCrea's remembering poignantly revealed racism and sexism that shaped silence about the bomb. Married to a marine and coming to the United States in 1964, she soon found herself in a small town in Nebraska, where she would not meet another Asian person for a long time. Her life seemed to be off to a good start. Her husband was dedicated to her, and his parents seemed supportive at least initially. A few days after her arrival, they threw a welcome BBQ party where all her husband's family relatives gathered. McCrea recalled:

> These American women were talking among themselves, blah, blah, blah, ... I was stunned, but I could not speak back. I felt so resentful, and I cried and cried.[49]

Listening to her, it was unclear to me what, exactly, was the source of her resentment. It could be her inability to speak English, or something that her in-laws said, or both. It was much later in the oral history when it became clear what had troubled McCrea. Her daughter, present during the interview at her mother's request, explained the incident quite differently than her mother:

> Unfortunately, my grandparents, my dad's parents, they are still calling her names, they wouldn't write her letters ... I could not understand, it's like okay, they call my mom Jap bitch, what about my brother and I, it put, it really put my father in a hard spot.[50]

At this point, I finally realized that the name-calling was what McCrea had referred to. The initial lack of specificity in her remembering indicated the depth of her pain and her still-persistent habit of silence, which made not only talk about nationality, race, and gender but also a conversation about the bomb difficult.

As seen in Chapter 3, some US survivors who married interracially were concerned about both racial discrimination against, and radiation effects on, their children. McCrea felt strongly that unsettling the family's stability by bringing up either one of the subjects would not be right for her children. Uncomfortable memories were to be avoided at all cost. This was made clear in her daughter's remembering:

> When I was growing up, she did not talk about it [the bomb], so I didn't ask. It was kind of unspoken. But I knew it. And when I went to Japan ... and she has a sister, [and] she has a scar. You don't go and question it, you just know it, it's out of respect, you

don't stare. And so five of us are walking, and my mother said, yeah, it's a scar, it's from the bomb. That's the only thing that I remember I heard about the bomb in my childhood.[51]

It was many decades before McCrea's daughter finally learned about her mother's bomb experiences. When it happened, McCrea's remembering seemed to come out of silence easily: McCrea's granddaughter asked questions, opening the door for her grandmother's remembering. Still, McCrea's daughter marveled at the persistence of silence: "It's ironic, because my daughter [was] eleven, and she [my mother] was that age at that time" of the bombing. A long time had passed. While racism after the war generated purposeful silence among Nikkei families, it rendered many interracial families fragile. Compared to silence around the bomb that persisted in Japan, silence in America was more tightly entangled with racism and its everyday, intimate effects. Children grew up hearing racial slurs, and some marriages broke. McCrea's came to an end in 1982.[52]

Other families stayed together, although their histories, too, were affected by the race war's long shadow. Setsuko Thurlow, for instance, immediately encountered difficulty after she came to study in a college in Richmond, Virginia, in 1954. Not only was her antinuclear sentiment taken as "un-American," which led to hate mail being sent to her, she found that her prospective marriage to a white person was legally impossible in the state. Thurlow was engaged to a Canadian, whom she had met in 1953 in Hokkaido. Their initial plan was that, after graduation, they would move from Richmond to Toronto to get married, so as to be close to her husband's family. Canada, however, prohibited the entrance of Japanese persons without Canadian citizenship, making the couple's plan moot. Now, they had to get married before going to Canada, so that she could become a Canadian citizen eligible to enter the country. Because marriage for them was not possible in Virginia, they had to find a way to marry elsewhere before going to Canada. Thurlow went to Washington, DC, where interracial marriage was permitted, got a marriage license, applied for Canadian citizenship, and finally crossed the border.[53] The era's perception of Nikkei as racially undesirable defined a narrow path toward the goal of keeping families together and finding home.

Hye-kyo Lee, as discussed in Chapter 3, became a Korean American survivor after she migrated to the United States because of her marriage to a GI. Shortly after settling in San Pablo, California, she discovered that her marriage had made her the ninth wife of an alcoholic man. His domineering manner affected many aspects of their marriage: he refused to pay for their children's clothes. He also expected his wife to "serve" him: "He sat down, snapped his fingers to have the coffee brought to him," said Lee. Nonetheless, she was determined to stay in the marriage. "At that time, I already had my daughters. I figured that I never had a parent" because she had lost both of hers to Nagasaki. She wanted to give her child a complete pair of parents. This determination propelled her to make money by selling household items. She bought old furniture, fixed and sold it at yard sales to pay for her children's education. Meanwhile, she suffered from unexplainable pain. "I can't stop the pain," she said, since that August day in 1945. "I have pain every night, every day. I can't sleep. I can't lay on my back because I feel like somebody is sticking a knife in me." Her perseverance, though, brought her respect from her in-laws. Although her oral history does not reveal much about her relationship with his family in the early years of their marriage, everyone (including her husband's twelve children, of whom two were hers) in its final years agreed that she took excellent care of him. "No one [else] took care of him," said his children, when their father became critically ill in 1988. When he became brain-dead, the children agreed that the decision to end his life should be hers. "You make the choice. [It will] be the right choice," they insisted. Lee was taken by a sense of accomplishment. As she "let him go free," she thought: "I've been through a tough life, but another way I look at it is, I had two daughters. I had a husband, at least."[54] Racism and sexism brought ends to some marriages, while fighting the prejudices quietly opened ways for US *hibakusha* to take root.

As US survivors formed families and communities anew, they experienced both inter- and intraracial tensions. Now, they were not only immigrants but also racial minorities in America, something that forced their survivorhood to recede from their daily lives and their remembering. Consequently, both male and female *hibakusha* deepened their silence about the bomb, though often in gendered ways. US survivors' oral histories suggest that many of them were cognizant of their inclination to hide their bomb experiences, and that they tried to make the best of it by turning their silence into a process of healing. But the results varied; some found the lack of communication stifling, while others appreciated mutual understanding nurtured by silence. As the next section shows, racism and sexism also shaped US survivors' experiences of radiation illness as not only physical but also psychosocial illness. This broad, if largely invisible, definition of illness shaped US survivors' experiences extensively – in their lives in the workplaces and on the warfronts of Cold War America.

Illness, War, Work, and the Rise of Ableism

One legacy of the Pacific War that unfolded during the Cold War was radiation illness. It affected US *hibakusha*'s relationships with war and work not only racially but also in distinctively gendered ways. Kazuko Aoki's remembering of her bedridden days in Honolulu in the 1950s has suggested the inexplicable conditions that struck some US survivors. Born in Monterey, California, in 1926, Fusae Kurihara came back to America in 1950, afflicted with anemia. Her condition worsened over the years, striking her with frequent episodes of fainting. But her physician did not see any connection between her symptoms and her irradiation: "I told the doctor I was the victim of the A-bomb. But the doctor couldn't understand," explained Kurihara. "My doctor used to say to me, 'Eat more meat.' And the doctor just gave me a shot and medicine."[55] Kazue Kawasaki, too, felt weak after she came to the United States in 1954. Earlier, she had expected that US physicians would have a better understanding of radiation illness than their Japanese counterparts "because it was America that dropped the bomb." Soon, she found out that "it was absolutely untrue. They [American physicians] had no idea what radiation illness was." Concerned about many occurrences of an irregular pulse, she instructed her four-year-old child to be sure to let her neighbor know if she ever lost consciousness.[56] Not only medical difficulties, but the tension between victors and victims also persisted. Born in Fresno, California, in 1925, and returning there in 1962, Asako Gaudette recalled: "When I first came to America, I never wanted to say I was from Hiroshima. Occasionally … it slips and the Americans would make such a terrible apologetic face." Gaudette felt sorry about making American physicians feel "so bad."[57] Physicians might be sympathetic or not; either way, US *hibakusha* grappled with the lack of understanding about radiation that brought them into frequent contact with medical professionals in the first place.

As will be seen in Chapter 6, the difficulty that US survivors had with their American physicians continued to occupy an important place in their remembering of the bomb throughout the 1970s and 1980s. US doctors were unfamiliar with radiation illness, quick to dismiss it as medically nonexistent. In earlier decades, though, US survivors' experiences appear to be more distinctively colored by the lack of sociocultural understanding, a lack that exposed the fallacy of the Cold War international and interracial alliance driving American hegemony. Supposedly, both the alliance and the hegemony were justified by America's democratic capacity to understand others. It was not only physical illness that affected US survivors. Psychological and social difficulties, too, shaped their understanding of their conditions, a point that appeared to be entirely missed by most physicians especially when they interacted with racial others who did not have a white-collar job or a social safety net. For Sumie and Toshiro Kubota, both Nisei who had returned to Sacramento in 1948 and 1953, respectively, the fact of irradiation itself was not a chief concern. Neither suffered any serious physical condition. Nevertheless, it became something of an unspoken rule for the Kubotas not to reveal their survivorhood. The secret needed be kept especially from their doctors. If they understood (or misunderstood) risks associated with irradiation, the Kubotas feared, the physicians would report it to the couple's insurance provider. The provider, in turn, would raise their premium.[58] Radiation illness for the Kubotas, then, was not a physical illness, but a medical and social liability.

When the liability was exposed, it could cause both psychosocial and physical damages. Sumiko Yoshida, as discussed earlier, came to America after marrying a Nisei man (see Figure 4.2). Although the bomb remained an infrequently discussed subject, her fear of it could suddenly come to the surface. One such outburst of memory occurred when she went out with her future husband for the first time, to Disneyland. As Yoshida entered the haunted house, she lost control. She could not look at the skeletons, and she started to shake violently. This incident was followed by a fear of sleeping alone and frequent nightmares, something for which she apparently did not seek medical treatment. Psychological or psychotherapeutic treatment was not readily available outside the affluent class in America, and as will be seen in Chapter 6, mental health care remained largely inaccessible to Asian Americans through the 1960s and 1970s. Exhausted, Yoshida

Figure 4.2 Sumiko Yoshida in front of Genbaku Dōmu (A-Bomb Dome), shortly before she went to the United States. Sumiko Yoshida papers, circa 1953.

lost her baby to a miscarriage. Although this loss could not be medically proven to be related to irradiation, it was clear to Yoshida that it was triggered by psychosocial tensions brought on by the bomb.[59] Experiences such as Yoshida's, then, indicate that the medically or statistically defined "radiation illness," established (though incompletely and inconclusively) by the studies conducted by scientists at the ABCC, did not comport with US survivors' experiences of illness. For them, what mattered was not "radiation illness" linked to exposure to a specific dosage of radiation. Rather, it was the "bomb illness" or the "illness related to the bomb" that arose out of stigma, liability, and loss.[60] Particularly because medical knowledge about irradiation was imperfect (and remains so), its sociocultural contexts filled the vacuum.

Ironically, the US–Asia alliance propagated by the Cold War accelerated this process of *hibakusha* hiding their illness in psychosocial contexts. May Yamaoka was caught by surprise when she was working as a typist in a federal government office early in the 1950s. Although she had not told her coworkers about her experiences of the bomb, the Korean War brought it out rather unexpectedly:

> They [her coworkers] never asked [about the bomb], and I never volunteered. Never volunteered. But when, I think after the Korean War, all the veterans were coming back, . . . they showed an atomic bomb movie one day. And I, that's when they knew. Because I could not stand it, I ran out. I could not watch. They were showing it to the employees, and I said I could not watch it. So they wondered why, so I told them why.[61]

As the era's preoccupation with nuclear weaponry became intensified by the war in Asia, Asians in America were reminded of their difference – cross-nationality – that separated them from others. Just as Nikkei in occupied Japan were not recognized as *hibakusha*, they remained a kind of absent presence in postwar America. Any association with the bomb furthered their otherness, putting a limit on their remembering. Yamaoka reiterated: "I guess they ... could not believe that I was in there [Hiroshima]. But I guess I don't really remember, I don't, I didn't say too much."[62] Their illness following the bomb's explosion – physical, psychological, and social – thrived in this atmosphere of stifled remembering. As much as US survivors' silence helped to heal by making their otherness invisible, this invisibility risked making silence seem a racial trait.

Indeed, US survivors' oral histories near-uniformly suggest that their inability to speak about their bomb experiences was inseparable from their understanding of their illness, which in turn was shaped by the Cold War culture dividing racial groups by their national origins. Tadachi Kohara, who came back to America in 1950, remembered the reason why he felt it necessary to keep his survivorhood secret. "White people believed that we survivors had a bad disease," said Kohara. The disease was contagious, so went the rumor, something that Kohara believed was evidenced by a peculiar way that white people acted: "On a bus, they escaped from a seat next to a Japanese." Although these "white people" were likely unaware of Kohara's survivorhood, it is striking that Kohara took their (most likely) racially motivated actions as a sign of their fear of secondary irradiation.[63] Racism fueled a hidden fear of radiation, weighing heavily in US *hibakusha*'s understanding of bomb illness.

Takashi Thomas Tanemori, who had migrated to America in 1955 as an eighteen-year-old, was in Minneapolis to register his marriage when he encountered prejudice against radiation illness intertwined with racism.

> I went to the [city's] office to obtain a certificate of marriage. I was denied it, so I asked why. They told me that it was because I was a survivor. They said: "We do not know what kind of children you would have, and we do not want to be burdened by them."[64]

His survivorhood was known to the office clerks because of his medical history. Shortly after coming to America, he was sent to a mental hospital because of what his employers deemed erratic behavior. Although the condition was likely caused by food poisoning that struck his workplace at the time, a grape ranch in Fresno, Tanemori could not make this understood by physicians. Language difficulties were just one of many problems. During a stay at the hospital that extended to six months, his survivorhood became known, and he was subjected to examinations he did not agree to, including electroshock therapies and repeated cerebrospinal fluid examinations. Their purpose, as Tanemori understood it, was to see if his conditions were caused by irradiation. His medical records shaped by racism left a mark on his record, a mark that in Minnesota denied him marriage. After he completed a degree in theology, Tanemori encountered difficulty in keeping a position as a minister. Predominantly white church members whispered loudly enough for Tanemori to hear their complaints: "If only our minister could speak better English, we would be able to be proud of him." The whispers followed him from one church to another.[65] His illness, race, and otherness were bound up with Tanemori's endless search for acceptance.

While US survivors felt mistreated at hospitals, churches, and on buses, their relationship with the military was uniquely complicated by the state's need to mobilize the utmost resources for the Cold War. US *hibakusha*'s experiences as immigrants, and in some cases, their experiences of the bomb, could be assets to fight communism. Many male US survivors were drafted and sent into military intelligence because of their bilingual ability. Their remembering, though, suggests that the ability was largely a product of stereotypes. Keiko Shinmoto's older brother Shigeru, who came back to America a few years after the bomb, was quickly drafted to the US Army at the onset of the Korean War in 1950. This struck Shigeru as peculiar, because "he couldn't speak English. So he said 'I don't know why I was drafted.'" During the war, the number of US military personnel across Japan multiplied, making translation an urgent necessity. The problem, though, was that Shigeru was barely able to comprehend English, technically his mother tongue. No wonder, then, that his family thought him extremely fortunate to survive the war; he did so without understanding the language of command.[66] Behind this story of good luck is the recognition that the military was not concerned about risks to Shigeru's ability to survive. He was assumed to have an ability to be useful for the war, and that was all the authorities needed to know.

George Kazuto Saiki, who as I discussed earlier had been ridiculed as "Japan" because he could not speak English, further illuminated the stereotype about race and ability that rose in this era. Saiki was at first rejected as a "4 F" during an induction examination in 1951. His English fluency simply did not match up. A year later, in 1952, things were different. Although he still struggled with English, which he spoke by mixing it with "gestures and Japanese," Saiki was judged as good enough. The examiner asked Saiki in English what time it was; Saiki answered in English, which immediately resulted in a "pass." The irony, however, was that Saiki had to take another language examination in Tokyo. This time, it was a Japanese, not English, examination. Doubtful of Nisei's Japanese fluency, his superiors were determined to station only the truly fluent speakers of Japanese in the capital's headquarters. The rest of military intelligence would be sent to Korea. This surprised Saiki, who thought he would be exempt from duties in Korea. Serving in Japan as a translator was the main, perhaps only, reason why he was inducted despite his shaky English. Having failed to stand out as an excellent Japanese speaker, however, Saiki ended up spending sixteen months on the battleground, where he continued to struggle to understand English.[67] Both Shinmoto's and Saiki's cases suggest how Japanese Americans might be recruited for the military on racial assumptions that did not match their ability. As a result of this racially specific ableism, which likely contributed to the formation of the myth of Japanese Americans as a "model minority," US *hibakusha* served in the Korean War unsure of what they could comprehend or contribute.

Their experiences of the bomb, too, complicated US survivors' relationship to the Cold War military. The scars left by the nuclear explosion carried conflicted meanings in the nuclear age, eliciting not only outright rejection but also curiosity driven by national interests. Minoru Sumida's remembering offers an example of a rejection based on survivorhood. As seen in Chapter 2, he suffered severe injuries in August 1945, which left large, visible scars on his extremities. These scars led to his prompt rejection at the medical examination for conscription. Although in his oral history Sumida did not indicate resentment about the rejection itself, he certainly conveyed a sense of having been misled. This was because he had returned to America in order to enlist in the military. Without enlistment, dual citizens like Sumida would lose US citizenship by their twenty-third birthday. So, he crossed the ocean in haste, heading to the examination only a week after his arrival. Found to be "4 F," he felt as if all his effort was wasted. Although he was able to maintain his US citizenship by a different route, he could not shake off his frustration: "It was on March 3rd [in 1957] when I enter the United States," said Sumida. "A week later, I went to a medical checkup for conscription. They looked at my bomb scars ... and I failed to pass."[68] If the bomb had made him disabled and disqualified as of 1945, why did he have to make such a great effort to come to the examination? There was no clear answer.

For Alfred Kaneo Dote who, as discussed earlier, had been working as a schoolboy, the treatment by the military also seemed irrational and intrusive. Merely two years after he had come back to the United States, in 1948, he was back in Japan again, serving as a translator at military trials. In six months, he was transferred again, this time to Korea. Unlike Sumida, Dote's experiences of the bomb solicited curiosity instead of dismissal. Indeed, one of his superiors asked him to share his experiences as a survivor with the entire unit. Dote figured that the reason was that this officer wanted to know what surviving a nuclear bomb was like; he probably wanted to educate his unit about its effects as well, in case it became a reality on the battleground. Dote discussed this request in a matter-of-fact way in his oral history, but he did not hide his irony when he recalled another unique experience that his survivorhood had brought. Before discharge, he was given a special examination. He was told of the result, as he recalled with a sly smile: "Well, there is nothing to worry about at this time!"[69] Somehow, the new war healed the scars of the old one. Disabilities – both physical and psychosocial – inflicted on Americans in Japan during the Pacific War were erased by their service to the American military in the Korean War.

No matter how reassuring (or not) this test result might have been for Dote, a revelation of survivorhood subjected male US *hibakusha* to unwanted attention. Exposed, they could be seen as disabled, unfit, and disloyal, especially given the era's intertwining of military service and national loyalty. If they were to assist America's survival in the nuclear age, by contrast, US survivors might become able, perhaps even loyal, citizens. The former fueled the view of Japanese Americans as "perpetual foreigners," while the latter comported with the nascent "model minority" myth.

Some US survivors sought a third way by expressing their bomb memories in art. But it was a struggle. Jack Motoo Dairiki, a Nisei survivor who returned to America in 1948, offers a case in point. While attending a city college in Los Angeles in 1951, as a student majoring in architecture, he drew a colorful mushroom cloud for his art class when the assignment was "free drawing" (see Figure 4.3). His teacher became interested in his drawing, which resulted in some media attention. Subsequently, in 1952, Dairiki was interviewed by a radio

Figure 4.3 Jack Motoo Dairiki's drawing of the mushroom cloud. Jack Motoo Dairiki papers, 1951.

program sponsored by the California Civil Defense, which used his story to assure state residents that "[even if] an atomic bomb [were] dropped over the city, ... many will survive *if* they simply observe the fundamental rule of survival." Thus, the horrors of what Dairiki witnessed just outside of the city of Hiroshima in 1945 became neatly summarized as stories of "training" that prepared him to cover his eyes and ears at the time of explosion, and of the "civil defense" that taught the Japanese how to take care of themselves in case of injury. In this narrative, Dairiki's remembering was construed as that of a man ready for nuclear emergency, something useful for citizens who had not experienced nuclear attacks.[70]

Cold War culture favored an unambiguous distinction between allies and enemies, effectively stifling the cross-nationality central to Japanese American remembering of the bomb. Consequently, the nation-specific definition of survivors prevailed. The underlying assumption was that, if you were a survivor, you must be Japanese. There cannot be survivors who are American. Even Dairiki, as his story was told by Civil Defense, became a representative of the people of Japan. What made him available for the radio program in the first place – the fact that he was a US-born citizen living in America – was not mentioned. It was obvious that US *hibakusha* were in the United States. Their scars and illnesses were visible as they came into contact with authorities. Instead of speaking out against the way the California Civil Defense program altered his story, however, Dairiki stopped talking. He did not start to talk about his experiences in public again until the late 1970s. Although he did not articulate the reasons for his silence in the oral history in 2010, a clear tension existed between his remembering and how his country had used it.[71] Only an absolute hiding seemed to offer a measure of healing.

A similar tension is found in Kiyoshi Mike Nakagawa's remembering, with a vivid illumination of how US survivors experienced a shift from speech to silence, a narrow path toward healing by hiding. Unlike Dairiki, Nakagawa was willing to discuss brighter aspects of the bomb. After explaining how his body was blown away by the explosion and how he felt "sorry" for his classmates who were killed, he began to talk about the "clean up":

> So we entered the city to clean up, which continued every day, for about ten days. Although, by then, soldiers had already done

their clean up. . . . Then we found our music teacher. We found his puttees sticking out on the ground at first. We disentangled it, and found his name, Yamamoto, on it. That's how we found that he was there. If we didn't, he would have been burned black.[72]

Death and destruction were given only a few words, while stories of recovery occupied much of Nakagawa's remembering.

The relative lack of words about dark aspects of Hiroshima did not mean that Nakagawa did not have dark thoughts about it. In fact, his understanding of the Pacific War appeared to crystalize while he was serving in the Korean War. Part of military intelligence stationed just north of the thirty-eighth parallel, he found himself in active combat in the early months of 1953. He kept a photo diary through these months, offering us a glimpse of his remembering. In March, his unit confronted "about 2000 of the enemy (human sea) [as they] tried a break through of our front line." Fortunately, "B-29s from Okinawa later unloaded more than 500 tons of bomb on the hill" in assistance. Nonetheless, he later received "sad news . . . an entire company was listed KIA [killed in action]." It was not only the silver airplane that provoked a jolting memory of the Pacific War in the midst of the Korean hills. Another entry from this period began with a quote in large letters: "NO BIG DEAL." Accompanying this abrupt statement was a picture of bullets, one of which had struck Nakagawa. "They [the Chinese army] are hitting us with shells which WWII Japanese military had left. . . . This one – vintage 1941," wrote Nakagawa (see Figure 4.4). He was injured by a bullet made in Japan, where he had been bombed by a B-29 eight years earlier. These ironies were not lost on Nakagawa. "This was my birthday," said Nakagawa, showing me a picture of himself, standing in front of an army tent. Looking at the image, he had to say: "I was just a young boy. No ability to think, full of stupidity. So many failures."[73]

What did Nakagawa mean by this? Was he being sarcastic about surviving one war, only to be nearly killed by another? Despite my repeated attempts, his response to my questions such as "What did you think when you realized that the bullet was made in Japan?" remained elusive. "It was not funny," he said, nothing more. Instead of elaborating on his feelings about the bullet, he began to talk about the disability compensation he received after the war. Nakagawa lost hearing in one of his ears, making it

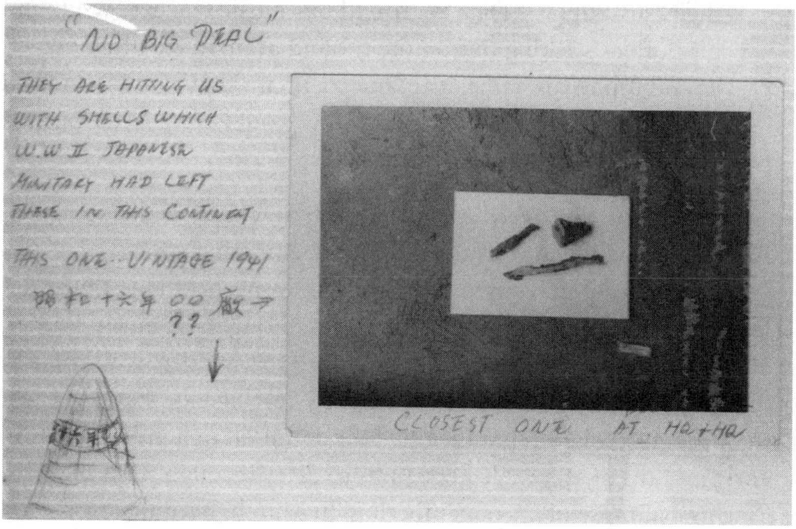

Figure 4.4 A page from Kiyoshi Mike Nakagawa's album showing his memory of Japanese bullets in the Korean War. Kiyoshi Mike Nakagawa papers, 1953.

necessary for him to purchase a pair of hearing aids. Upon learning that it cost US$5,000, he began to seek veteran's compensation. His effort was successful, and he became entitled to a monthly allowance, too. Meanwhile, his response to my questions about B-29s and the bomb remained unspecific. He explained that he had not thought of himself as a survivor until he was recognized as such by the Japanese government many years later. But he would not hold a grudge against this delayed recognition. "It was a wartime," reasoned Nakagawa. "I don't want to say anything [about the war]. I don't try to think about it. It's history." Toward the end of the interview, he again expressed his appreciation for the monetary compensation he has been receiving as a disabled veteran of the Korean War.[74]

Nakagawa's detachment from history seemed labored in light of his comments about "stupidity" and "failures." Following his narrative, it is likely that the compensation he received, first as an American soldier in Korea, and second as an American civilian in Japan, explains his reticence. He was disabled and then compensated for it; nothing more needed to be said, he was telling me. If there was any damage done to his manhood, the nations at least recognized it. The rest of the story needed not be taken out of hiding.

Nakagawa was not alone in becoming reticent about the bomb after serving in the Korean War. Junji Sarashina, as seen in Chapter 2, suffered acute radiation sickness in 1945. Still, returning to the United States in 1949, he was promptly inducted into the army. His service became a catalyst for his remembering of the bomb:

> I didn't have any resentment against the United States. I hate the fact that the bomb was dropped and people got killed. But maybe because I served in [the US Army], during the Korean War, and saw quite a bit of actions, too, maybe because of that ... my mind is so soft, maybe I am not committed to anything 100 percent, maybe I was born as a flexible person, in fact, maybe too flexible, too soft, maybe.[75]

Although Sarashina did not suffer any injury or receive any compensation, he still developed a sense of belonging to America by serving in the war. He positioned this against his feeling of "hate" toward the bomb, which suggests that he also felt a sense of belonging to his experiences in Japan. Indeed, he was quite capable of belonging cross-nationally. For male US *hibakusha* who served in the Korean War, then, their "flexible" sense of national belonging, coupled with services to or compensation by the US government, might have sanded the sharp edges off their remembering of the bomb.[76] Compared to raising questions about their illness, ability, race, and loyalty, placing the bomb in a benign light or being silent about it seemed preferable. Being "soft" offered a reasonable way forward: not 100 percent loyal but not disloyal; disabled but maybe able if successfully serving the country. That Sarashina internalized this process by calling it part of his imperfect "person" shows how difficult it was to be a US survivor without falling into one of the stereotypes – disabled and disloyal "foreigner" or loyal, able "minority."

While the Korean War chiefly affected male survivors' remembering of the Pacific War, daily work as immigrants shaped female *hibakusha*'s experiences considerably. Because many had not earned wages before, and also because many jobs that they held were physically demanding, work became a dominant fact of their lives. Work also became an oft-cited reason why they did not think or talk about the bomb, even when an opportunity presented itself. After the Lucky Dragon Five incident in 1954, for instance, US survivors' response to the crisis remained surprisingly muted. In this incident, twenty-three

Japanese fishermen on a tuna boat were irradiated by the nuclear test US Castle Bravo in the Bikini Atoll. Soon after, the national and international outcry about the danger of fallout intensified, in no small part because of the antinuclear movement spurred by Japanese women's organizations. These women were particularly concerned about radioactivity that threatened food safety.[77] The outcry led to a rising concern about the contamination of food, soil, and water on and around the Marshall Islands. Shortly after the test, those living on the atolls of Rongelap and Utirik suffered symptoms of radiation poisoning, and doubtless, the effect was not limited to humans. Eventually, the US government recognized the problem and began to issue compensatory payments in 1975.[78] And yet, the incident was rarely discussed by US survivors then or in their oral histories. Isamu Shin, the only US survivor who mentioned the incident in his interview, recalled how the "knowledge about this and that effect of radiation" did not become widely available until "that incident of the ship, the ship that encountered the bomb." He did not immediately recall the name of the ship.[79] For Shin, then, the incident was something that made him aware of radiation effects for the first time, but it did not make any strong impression. Otherwise, US *hibakusha* seemed not to notice; nor did they participate in the antinuclear movement. This was in contrast to Japanese women who initiated the movement across the Pacific. Too, US survivors differed from their Japanese counterparts, some of whom became outspoken participants of the test-ban debate in the mid-1950s.[80] US *hibakusha*'s oral histories confirmed their lack of participation and interest with a striking uniformity. When asked why, they frequently mentioned how they were busy raising families and trying to make ends meet by working. Simply put, they seemed to say, they did not have time for the antinuclear movement.

A similar lack of engagement was found in US survivors' responses to the "Hiroshima Maidens," young Japanese women whose faces had been severely disfigured by the bomb. Receiving more than 300 cosmetic surgeries in total at Mount Sinai Hospital in New York City, in 1955 and 1956, these women drew intensive media coverage. Reportedly, they were grateful for American modern medicine's miracle, and they willingly served as ambassadors of goodwill exchanged by America and Japan. Privately sponsored by the editor-in-chief of *Saturday Review* Norman Cousins and Kiyoshi Tanimoto, a Methodist minister from Hiroshima, the project also had the potential to provoke antinuclear sentiment in America.[81] And yet, US *hibakusha* did not see the project as particularly relevant to them. Satoshi Fujiyama, for instance, recalled that he "read something in the newspaper" about the project, which he spoke of as "an assistance for a former enemy country" that did not have advanced medical technology.[82] Fujiyama's recollection mirrored the media representation of the program at the time, playing on the image of feminine, innocent, and helpless victims in a country still reeling from the war. Japanese victims, not American survivors, were to be beneficiaries of the Cold War alliance. A project that in fact involved significant participation by Japanese Americans such as Yuri Kochiyama and Halen Yokoyama, the "Hiroshima Maidens" program nonetheless failed to elicit broad support from Japanese American communities. US media featured "suburban bliss reportedly experienced by the young bomb victims recovering in East Coast homes" of white, middle-class families, downplaying and discouraging Japanese American presence. With the memories of incarceration and questioning of national loyalty still fresh, many Japanese American leaders felt cautious about supporting a program that might associate them too closely with Japan.[83] This, in turn, likely shaped the lack of interest in the program among US survivors. In this way, even the high level of attention that the "Hiroshima Maidens" brought to the bomb did not help break the silence among US *hibakusha*. For them, these women remained distant figures. They were fortunate enough to obtain monetary and medical assistance; US survivors, by contrast, had to generate both of these outside the limelight in order to heal from the bomb.

US *hibakusha* were busy at work, and women excelled in remembering busyness particularly as they balanced work with the task of caring for a family. When asked if they thought about the bomb or were concerned about its effects, the majority of female survivors answered no, and explained that they were too busy to worry. This does not mean that they did not reflect on the bomb. Several decided against having children, showing that their concern about the bomb's effect lay only skin-deep.[84] Still, it is important that many chose to mention their employment in the same breath as talk of the bomb. Indeed, work for women was something new on both sides of the Pacific. In Japan, women who came of age after the war found that they were expected to work, at least before marriage.[85] For female *hibakusha* who faced little prospect of marriage, work might well be a life-long necessity. In America generally, work remained a fact of life for immigrant, working-class, and nonwhite women, even as their white, middle-class counterparts felt pressured into making a "homeward bound" turn.[86] Joyce Ikuko Moriwaki's remembering illuminated how female US survivors experienced this change on both sides of the ocean. She enjoyed working at an amusement park in Hiroshima after the war, but she also noticed that there were hardly any desirable jobs available for women. Before Moriwaki was old enough to work, her mother took a position as a cleaner of public parks. Ironically, one of the parks assigned to her was the Hiroshima Peace Memorial Park, near which she had been injured in 1945. Billed as a symbol of new, peaceful Japan, the park stood in sharp contrast to the lack of support for survivors. Resources were generously allocated to ideological and infrastructural rebirth, while care and treatment of survivors remained a non-priority. "She had to sweep the street and weed the park," said Moriwaki. "It was the lowest kind of job." When she came to Hawai'i in 1961, Moriwaki was pleasantly surprised by the treatment she received from her employers. "I thought I liked the job at the amusement park [in Japan], but things were even better in America," said Moriwaki. This was "because there was no discrimination" against women.[87]

During the era when many white, middle-class American women felt confined by the "feminine mystique," a statement such as Moriwaki's might have sounded overly optimistic.[88] And yet, many female US *hibakusha* experienced work in the United States as liberating. Katie Yanagawa's father, fortunate enough to obtain a position as an interpreter in an office of the US occupation forces in Kure, took a job as a janitor in Seattle after he returned to America in 1953. Although he worked hard and was well-respected by his coworkers, the job clearly was a step down for him. Her mother also took a blue-collar job, as a maid at a hospital, changing sheets and cleaning rooms. According to Yanagawa, her mother had been a "very spoiled person," but she was compelled to work to help the family's income once she was in America. Although we do not know how the older Yanagawa felt about this, the younger one thought that "there were definitely more opportunities to develop" oneself in the United States. "I realize," she claimed, "that Japan is a very, very difficult place to run a business, and especially [for] women."[89] Similar to Moriwaki, then, Yanagawa deemed women's status in America as better than in Japan, although the difference did not work to benefit men in jobs without any upward mobility. The same kind of low-paying jobs that women took, in contrast, could be a step toward the betterment of women's status. Instead of being "spoiled," women could achieve economic independence.

Fumiko Imai, too, experienced something of a liberation in her job as a self-made tailor. When she was in Japan, she could not get a position at a bank. She had been schooled in accounting and felt more than qualified for the job. Because she had lost her father to the bomb, however, she did not have male business acquaintances she could rely on, leading to many rejections. When she came to America in 1952, she continued to feel the presence of "discrimination" against the socially marginalized, though in entirely different ways. Her Japanese American friend could not buy a house because of her race. The friend's husband, who was white, made an offer on a house. After the offer was accepted, it became known that his wife was a Japanese American. The deal was summarily withdrawn. Incidents like this made Imai feel cautious around white people. At the same time, Imai was proud of her ability to build a career by navigating through interracial relationships. Because she wanted to be at home while her children were little, she looked for stay-at-home work that combined caring and earning. "Then, I thought I liked sewing," said Imai. Her children wore clothes she had made to school, telling friends and teachers that these were their mother's handmade items. Gradually, requests from the children's white acquaintances began to arrive, asking her to finish hems and adjust sleeves. She described the pleasure of earning income: "I thought, 'Five dollars! They will bring *a lot* of meat!'" Gradually, Imai also became outspoken about the skill she did not have a chance to practice in Japan. Because of her training in accounting, she was good at calculation. Once, at a bank, she caught a mistake that a teller made. The teller insisted that it could not be a mistake because a computer did the calculation. Imai responded by asking: "*Who* is going to use the computer?" The teller pushed back once again, so Imai declared that she would then terminate her business. She transferred all her funds to another bank.[90]

By working, earning, and caring for the family, women learned to stand on their own. Their income might have been modest, but their feelings of self-worth were no less tangible. Often, their sense of accomplishment arose not only from their work, but also from gender, racial, and national confines they felt they overcame, elements of which we have seen in some male US *hibakusha*'s rememberings of the Korean

War. Clearly, US survivors' pride of having "made it" in America furthered their sense of belonging to America and tamed their desire to recall the bomb. Imai was not alone in suggesting this dynamism.[91] In Julie Kumi Fukuda's remembering, too, her work served as a catalyst for crossing gender and national boundaries. Returning to the United States in 1947, Fukuda was unsure about her marriage's future. As seen in Chapter 1, her husband had been deported to Japan in 1942 because he had become a "no-no boy" at the camp in Arizona. Unlike Fukuda, he had no desire to come back to America after the war. Although Fukuda did return to America, she was still not ready to end the marriage. Their son Paul was young, and the bias against female divorcees could be dire. When she realized how her marriage would influence her work in America, however, she made up her mind to let go of her husband in Japan. The benefits that came with her employment as a medical stenographer in Los Angeles, including those for retirement, would have to be shared by her husband if she stayed married to him. "No way! No way!" was Fukuda's response when she realized this. She promptly filed for a divorce. As her friend attested, she "work[ed] hard" and had no reason to have it reduced by half.[92]

For Takeko Okano, a divorcee discussed earlier, too, work became a reason to discover a sense of belonging to America, a country she had thought helped destroy her marriage. Working first as a seamstress, she found the job detrimental to her health. As a single mother of two children, she began to look for something else. Her friend, a Japanese American woman, encouraged Okano to go to college and get a certificate for keypunching. After completing night school at Heald College in San Francisco (see Figure 4.5), she landed a job at a bank:

> At first, I applied for a job at a Japanese bank [in San Francisco]. But they didn't like a divorcee with two children. They also had a plenty of employees who had a college degree and were bilingual. But when I went to a bank operated by white people, they did not care about those things. They were happy that I had a certificate. The manager of the bank I went to had been in the US Army and stationed in Japan, in Sendai, so he understood Japan well. He helped me with my job interview ... he said he would read [difficult parts] for me.[93]

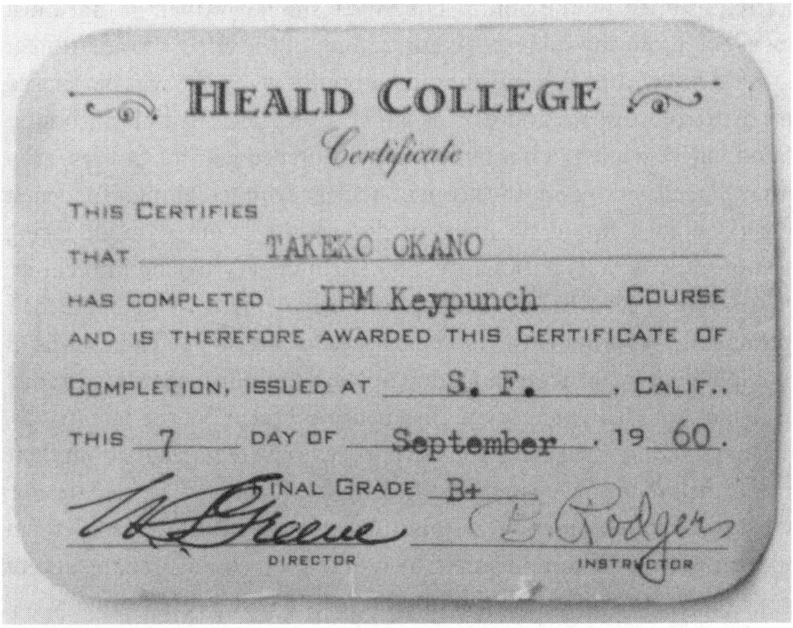

HEALD COLLEGE
Certificate
THIS CERTIFIES
THAT TAKEKO OKANO
HAS COMPLETED IBM Keypunch COURSE
AND IS THEREFORE AWARDED THIS CERTIFICATE OF
COMPLETION, ISSUED AT S. F., CALIF.,
THIS 7 DAY OF September, 19 60.
FINAL GRADE B+
DIRECTOR
INSTRUCTOR

Figure 4.5 A certificate issued to Takeko Okano by Heald College in San Francisco, which led to her employment at a US bank. Takeko Okano papers, September 7, 1960.

Her remembering makes clear several key negotiations she had made across gender, racial, and national boundaries. As she had relied on her mother-in-law as her *sendatsu* earlier, Okano relied on her network within the Nikkei community to train herself. Applying for jobs, it turned out, required a different kind of negotiation. Banks in the Nikkei community did not want her, while she found better acceptance at a bank operated by a white man. "I should not be saying this," said Okano cautiously, during her interview in 2012, then, going on: "I think that non-Japanese people were nicer than Japanese people to me." These "nicer" people brought her a decent job and a surprisingly generous retirement plan. She also became friends with Chinese American and African American colleagues, some of whom stayed in close touch after retirement. Asked about her concern about radiation illness, she laughed: "I have lived until I am eighty-seven."[94]

Racism driven by national origin, then, did not shape US survivors' remembering in any uniform way. Undeterred by racism, female US survivors like Imai and Okano made a living without becoming overtly unsettled by the bomb. They were similar to men in that most kept silent about the subject. "I didn't think of the effect of radiation at all," said Imai (although she did think about it when she was diagnosed with a thyroid disease and cancer later).[95] Unconcerned about bomb-related illness while young, Fukuda, too, pursued gainful careers, even as they placed her outside the norm of nuclear families. Similar to men, it seemed, women found no place to discuss the bomb without facing questions about race, nationality, ability. In effect, they had no choice but to plant a seed for the "model minority" myth by keeping their mouths shut, working hard, and being able to carry it all. Their mode of accomplishing social acceptance and upward mobility seemed to predict the Asian American stereotype that became potent by the late 1960s. Moreover, unlike their male counterparts who were reticent about their sense of belonging being transformed by the Korean War, female survivors were more outspoken about how working life offered them opportunities to belong. Thanks to work, they could prepare decent meals; thanks to work, they could take care of children. In some ways, these kinds of remembering by women pointed to the "model minority" myth more straightforwardly than men's recollections, likely contributing to the feminization of the myth.[96] But in other ways, work connected women of different racial backgrounds as seen in Okano's case, planting a seed for the critique of the myth that was to flourish in the era of the Asian American civil rights movement in the 1970s.

Men, too, formed interracial ties in their work, but men's opportunities for making these ties were more limited. Reasons for this difference were several. Unlike women, men did not experience the breaking of gender boundaries in socially uplifting ways. Moreover, many Japanese American men took employment in family-owned businesses, keeping interracial interactions to a minimum. In certain lines of work such as factory and office work, however, it was more likely that employees would mingle – "work together" – with people from different backgrounds. These kinds of employment, in turn, compelled some male US *hibakusha* to reshape their racial identity and national belonging in a way that countered the ableist myth.

Revealingly, the man who explained this transformation most affirmatively was James Jeong, a Korean American survivor who had experienced multiple incidences of Japanese racism against Koreans. Jeong found unexpected moments of cross-racial and -national bonding at the Greyhound Bus Company, where he was hired as a maintenance worker. Some of his white coworkers mistook him as Japanese, and told him to "remember Pearl Harbor." Others realized that he was Korean because of his family name, and they tried to bad-mouth Japanese employees with him. Words such as "Jap" and "poor" were frequently used. In response, Jeong said he considered himself to be in the same boat as the Japanese employees. They all struggled with English in an unfamiliar work environment. Jeong also found himself lecturing white workers about how they, too, should think of migrant workers as their equals: "You are an immigrant, too. Your grandfathers did not come to America to enjoy sightseeing, right? They came because they were poor and desperate." In his oral history, Jeong explained that the reason behind making such statements was his identity as a "Korean Japanese." In Japan, this identity brought him unforgettable incidents of racial discrimination. In America, however, the identity became a reason to join together with other Asian immigrants. Whites, too, would be welcome if they were to leave racial animosity behind.[97] His cross-national belonging was foundational to his belief that, in America, one should, and could, go beyond racial borders. Although his emphasis on his ties to the Japanese might be partially explained by the fact that he was interviewed by a Japanese person, his remembering is a striking indication of a new dynamism in Asian American history in the 1940s and 1950s. Silence about the bomb contained a thread of history that lay outside the stereotypes of "perpetual foreigner" and "model minority" and pushed for the coming together of people from different racial and national backgrounds by highlighting the cross-nationality of America as a country of immigrants. That this particular thread was most lucidly explored by women and Korean Americans suggests how those who had been marginalized during wartime because of race, nationality, or gender, were more likely than others to pursue the thread. Crossing boundaries placed US survivors in a precarious status; and yet, their acts of border crossing also opened the possibility for ties to be formed anew.

In the first fifteen years after 1945, the counter-memory of the bomb continued to shape US survivors' history as it became entwined with constraining assumptions about their nationality, race, loyalty, ability, and gender. As they rebuilt their lives in the shadow of racial conflict and nuclear weaponry, both inter- and intraracial discriminations shaped their remembering of the bomb and the camps. In silence, radiation illness became tightly bound up with biases against immigrants and racial minorities. War and work in the Cold War era solidified silence in gendered ways, while major events that exposed the nuclear danger – the Lucky Dragon Five incident and the "Hiroshima Maidens" program – failed to open the door for speaking. On the one hand, US *hibakusha* felt as if they needed to keep their remembering of the bomb hidden in order to heal from it, because the process would help them to (re-)build their sense of belonging to the United States; collectively, they wished to eradicate the image of Asian Americans as foreigners who never belong. On the other, silence was the means that allowed them to steer clear of the most blatant racism and sexism on either side of the Pacific. Men who served in the Korean War felt caught up in their layered sense of belonging. Women (and some men, too), found a ground for belonging in their working lives, sometimes by forming inter- and intraracial alliances. Although these connections offered opportunities for individuals to take root in America, one consequence of their collective silence was that US survivors missed a chance to learn that there were others like them – a fundamental basis for taking collective action. Striking, too, is that their remembering of this era lacked discussion of the medical care and treatment that the Japanese government started to offer to Japanese and Korean survivors in Japan by the mid-1950s. As will be discussed in the following chapters, these medical services were supplemented by monetary aid for survivors by the mid-1960s. That US survivors did not talk about these developments in their remembering indicates the weakening of their cross-national ties across the Pacific in the 1940s and 1950s, especially in the public sphere. For the strength of the ties to return and for the counter-memory of the bomb to become audible, US survivors needed to find each other. For silence to be finally broken, family and community needs must come together with a broader public's demands for change. This coming together was precisely what took place in the late 1960s.

5 FINDING SURVIVORHOOD

In the fifteen years beginning in the mid-1960s, US survivors witnessed a series of dramatic changes in their self-perception. Many of these changes were unforeseeable when a handful of survivors got together for the first time in Little Tokyo, Los Angeles, in 1965. Six years later, in 1971, this group became a nonprofit organization called the Committee of Atomic Bomb Survivors in the United States of America (CABS), with strong support from Los Angeles County Medical Examiner-Coroner Thomas Noguchi, a known figure in the Asian American civil rights movement. Soon, emerging leaders of the era's Asian American effort for social justice and racial equality, including those who played important roles in the early stage of the Redress Movement for former inmates of Japanese American concentration camps, began to back CABS's efforts to obtain recognition from the US government. These included Yuji Ichioka, Karl G. Yoneda, and Wayne Horiuchi, all of whom signed on as CABS supporters. Japanese America's most powerful civil rights organization, the Japanese American Citizens League (JACL), also assisted CABS's efforts to obtain access to medical treatment of radiation illness by, among other things, testifying in a congressional hearing that Americans should listen to the plight of "forgotten" *hibakusha*.[1] Not only Japanese American US representatives such as Norman Mineta and Patsy T. Mink, but also liberal politicians such as Edward R. Roybal, Mervyn Dymally, and George Moscone offered support for US survivors.

The rise of the US *hibakusha*'s activism in this era is striking, especially given the silence and circumspect telling that marked their remembering earlier. US survivors' reserve in the 1950s turned into a growing outspokenness in the 1970s, which in 1974 led to their cause being featured on the front page of the *New York Times* in a sympathetic article, "29 Years Later, Hiroshima Haunts Survivors in U.S."[2] In the same year, a CABS-sponsored bill in the state of California made its way to a public hearing by a Senate committee. By 1978, CABS and its supporters were pushing for a US Congressional bill written on their behalf, which was optimistically featured by *Hokubei Mainichi* (*North American Daily*) in San Francisco as "likely to pass."[3] In many ways, this was the most hopeful time for US survivors, with the possibility of gaining what they thought to be fair treatment by their own government coming within reach. This chapter explores the growth of that possibility – first, of obtaining formal recognition from the US government that there were such people as "US survivors of Hiroshima and Nagasaki," and second, of obtaining monetary support from the government for care and treatment of radiation illness – in US *hibakusha*'s remembering. As I argue, their remembering itself became transformed in this era from an individual to a collective process, bringing the counter-memory of the bomb out in public. Among US survivors, there were a few who took notable action that drew widespread attention and admiration. They became the public face of US survivors, by contributing columns to newspapers and participating in public education programs about peace, war, and nuclear proliferation.

Equally important was the work of ordinary *hibakusha* who came forward to share their remembering, usually without any fanfare. They created a setting for others to talk as well. Many were women who cooked and brought food for CABS gatherings. They kept connections among survivors by writing, calling, and seeing each other frequently. At first glance, such efforts seemed to occur effortlessly. As I show, some survivors were long-time friends or acquaintances from their time in Hiroshima or Nagasaki, and they were able to rely on the existing network of people when they began to come together in America.

And yet, extraordinary things had to happen for personal remembering dependent on "weak ties" to take on "strong," public and political meanings. Prior to the 1970s, the Hiroshima and Nagasaki bombings had been commemorated in California, but for the most part only by the Hiroshima Kenjinkai, a group of US residents who originally came from Hiroshima prefecture. By the early- to mid-1970s, in contrast, the bombings were commemorated not only by CABS and JACL but also by groups of younger Asian Americans such as the Asian-American Ad-Hoc Committee on Hiroshima and Nagasaki, the Bay Area Asian Coalition Against the War, and the Northern California Peace Action Coalition. Clearly, the significance of the bomb had outgrown a narrowly local context and began to draw a broader engagement. Here, I consider the coming together of the older and the younger generations as a key to understanding how US *hibakusha*'s remembering rippled outward from a small gathering for themselves to a larger sharing that extended across the community. This was the time when Asian Americans, the younger generation who came of age in the mid- to late-1960s in particular, were beginning to be aware of the silence and invisibility imposed on their community. They were learning about the racist, anti-immigration policies that had culminated in the incarceration of Nikkei during the Pacific War. The lack of appropriate social services and health care in Asian American communities, as well as the absence of educational programs about Asian America at colleges and universities, were becoming more critically examined. The escalation of the Vietnam War, too, caught Asian Americans' attention, as the war seemed to embody yet another example of violence against Asia by America. President Richard Nixon's statements about the possible use of a nuclear weapon in Vietnam might not have seemed to America's general public to be as threatening as the Cuban missile crisis several years earlier; for Asian Americans, however, the race of the people who might become a target of US nuclear warheads sounded an alarm.[4]

As Asian Americans' race consciousness soared, they became more keenly aware of trans-Pacific ties and tensions. This awareness pushed Asian Americans to articulate their citizenship in more broadly and critically cross-national ways. It was no coincidence, then, that US survivors around this time began to build affiliations with antinuclear groups, including organizations of other *hibakusha* in America: those who suffered radiation illness after laboring in uranium mines on Native American reservations, or after unknowingly being exposed to fallout near one of the nuclear test sites in Nevada. It became increasingly evident that some American citizens were affected by the bomb while in Japan, whereas other US citizens became irradiated while in the United States. This implausible constellation of universal and unique survivorhood could be comprehended only by thinking about the bomb beyond national boundaries.

This was a time of reflection about the troubled past, as much as it was an era that generated an unprecedented passion for reform now. In survivors' efforts to link the past and present across the Pacific, collective, intergenerational, and gender-transformative remembering played crucial roles. To be sure, some elements of individual remembering, typical of the 1950s and much of the 1960s, remained constant. Many female survivors in the 1970s stayed largely invisible, their voices hardly audible. And yet, some of them began to take on more public roles, most notably by serving as witnesses during the hearings for the aforementioned 1974 California Senate Bill and 1978 US Congressional Bill. Male survivors, too, signaled a shift in their remembering. Contrary to the earlier images of men acting with courage to help others on the ground, men in their remembering in the 1970s more freely conveyed their physical and psychological hurt. Both male and female *hibakusha* challenged the feminine prototype of "model minority" discussed in Chapter 4 built around the image of Nikkei women not only earning but also caring for their families uncomplainingly. US survivors began to tell a broader range of stories regardless of how they might go against established gender expectations or racial stereotypes. And they had an increasingly eager, and larger, audience.

This growing audience made a considerable mark on how and why US *hibakusha* remembered the bomb. Very few offered detailed recollections of the legislative efforts in the 1970s, a fact that might have been shaped by the nature of oral histories and their tellers. Most of the histories were told in one-to-one settings, which likely prompted recollections of personal, rather than public, events. Too, many informants were women, who tended to see their collective actions in individual light. For these reasons, survivors' remembering during this era was more frequently recorded in the proceedings of the congressional hearings, newsletters of CABS and its support organizations, and newspapers within the Asian American community and beyond. Now, US survivors' remembering was to be heard by a large audience. This, in turn, defined their mode of speaking about the past, as well as my approach to their remembering in this chapter. In some ways, the private process of hiding and healing, discussed in Chapters 3 and 4, was replaced by the public assertion that *hibakusha* desperately needed the government's "aid."[5] Clearly, they were making demands, though often in modest language. In response, my mode of analysis diverges from the focus on speech and silence. I focus instead on US *hibakusha*'s speaking as an act of personal determination to join political processes. By so doing, I show how US survivors' personal stories reflected the increasing propensity in the Asian American community to claim civil rights rooted in cross-national experiences. Rather than highlighting a national belonging as a proof of loyalty, Asian Americans of the era began to assert that their belonging to the United States arose out of their critique of America's fraught relationship with Asia. This assertion, which featured the strengths of cross-national ties, was distinctively echoed by US *hibakusha*'s remembering. In fact, it merged with the communal remembering of Asian America, the counter-memory surging into the national remembering. This makes it essential to consider non-survivors' remembering of the bomb as much as survivors'.

As their identity as survivors emerged out of a remembering that went beyond national boundaries, US survivors inevitably raised questions about the definition of the bomb as a weapon of war between nations. Nations might be distinguished by man-made borders, but not necessarily by their peoples; this history of immigration was brought to light by nuclear weapons' blanket power of destruction. As far as their oral histories tell, no survivors in the era covered by this chapter explicitly questioned whether the bombs were a military necessity or legally permissible. Nonetheless, their remembering brought to the fore questions about the morality of nuclear weaponry. Their stories not only contributed to the more publicly told counter-memory of Hiroshima and Nagasaki, but also became a fertile ground on which one might raise questions about US nuclear policies after 1945. Now, it was abundantly clear that these policies left scars on both sides of the Pacific. It is notable that the coming together of old and young generations in Asian America proved a primary site for this critical revelation. No longer were they silenced "aliens ineligible for citizenship." That this transformation occurred at the same time as the "model minority" myth took hold suggests US survivors' subversiveness. Equally important, however, the failure of both the 1974 and 1978 bills to pass – or even to come to a full vote by lawmakers – showed the persistence of the belief that the bomb was a necessity for protecting US national interests.

Breaking Silence: From Personal to Communal Remembering

As survivor Kazue Suyeishi remembered it, it was in Los Angeles, in 1965, when a "private" gathering took place among survivors who wanted to talk in a "friendly" way over a glass of *sake*. This gathering marked the beginning of a small group that was to become CABS in 1971. Suyeishi was a friend of one of the several men attending, who had an older brother in San Francisco. A childhood friend of the brothers, she was especially close to the older one, Kanji Kuramoto. Both Suyeishi and Kuramoto were born in America, and they had grown up in Hiroshima "like a brother and a sister," calling each other by their nicknames – Japanese style "Kan-chan" for Kuramoto and "Mary" for Suyeishi which, as noted in Chapter 2, was a moniker that a customer of her father's grocery store in Pasadena gave her when she was still a newborn.[6] Unlike CABS meetings several years later, these early gatherings were not about what support US survivors wanted from the American or Japanese governments. Rather, they talked mostly to "encourage each other," according to Toshiko Hishinuma, a survivor in Los Angeles. Hishinuma did not attend these meetings, but she later heard about their supportive spirit from the first leader of the group, Tomoe Okai.[7] Sachiko Matsumoto, a *hibakusha* in San Francisco, recalled a similar story about the early gatherings of survivors in that city around the same time. Kanji Kuramoto was the initiator, and he booked a small room at the back of a modest bank building in Japantown, available for community members free-of-cost. "There were no proceedings" of the meetings, said Matsumoto. Rather, they were for US survivors to "console" each other by sharing stories of where and how they had "met" the bomb.[8] Although there is no decisive record of how many came to these early gatherings, none recalled that it had been much more than a handful.

There were reasons why these meetings were close-knit gatherings, ranging from US *hibakusha*'s concern about being seen as "disloyal," to their desire to heal by way of hiding. Ayako Elliott, one of the early participants in San Francisco, did not want any publicity, fearing that her status as a US resident could be jeopardized if she were suspected to be participating in radical antiwar or antinuclear activism.[9] This was 1969 and 1970, when such activism seemed to be common in cities and campuses across coastal California. The rising radicalism, especially in communities of racial and ethnic minorities, seemed to make them an easy target for state surveillance and police harassment. Yet Elliott did not have to worry. Kuniko Jenkins, another survivor in San Francisco, made it a habit to arrive "heralded by friends lugging boxes and a big coffee pot ... [and to] spread out doughnuts, cakes, cookies, senbei [Japanese rice crackers]." Sometimes, she "even brought whole chickens, mounds of sushi, potato salad and coleslaw." She was also generous enough to bring a nice bottle of *sake*, still hard to find in the United States. The rumor was that Jenkins "sneaked" it from the collection of her husband Richard, who was nonetheless supportive of Kuniko's participation in the gatherings.[10] Natsumi Aida, of Sacramento, also remembered preparing rice balls and side dishes for these early meetings in San Francisco.[11] These contributions, among others, helped make the gatherings amicable, not overtly assertive or angry. At least for the participants, who were eating and drinking together, remembering the bomb in the United States was not an act of political or moral questioning.

These seemingly casual meetings were the first important occasion for many US survivors to find and talk to each other. Their memories often highlight the intimate atmosphere of the occasion (the sharing of *sake* gets frequent mention), perhaps reflecting a special kind of relief they took in the gathering and also a lingering concern that they might be seen as a group critical of, and thus disloyal to, their country. Most learned about the meetings by word of mouth, thanks to friends who were also *hibakusha*.[12] Others heard about the group through their local Hiroshima Kenjinkai, which of course included many survivors on its membership roster.[13] Without doubt, many of those who started to gather in the mid-1960s had known that there were other survivors in America. But that awareness had not led them to share their memories easily. But now, there seemed to be ample reasons why they needed to come together.

Sachiko Matsumoto, for one, decided to go to the meetings because of what her mother in Hiroshima had told her before she came to America in 1955: "You vomited after wind brought it [radiation] on us. You must take especially good care of yourself." Matsumoto thought that she might learn how others were taking care of themselves by being part of this group.[14] Masako Kawasaki's and Kazue Suyeishi's reasons were more immediately urgent. Kawasaki had a tumor, hernia, and anemia that kept her bedridden. Finding no local doctors who understood her conditions as related to radiation, she was considering a trip to Japan to see a radiation illness specialist. Kawasaki was curious if others had a similar plan.[15] Suyeishi had been trying to forget about the bomb and be a good wife. But her husband told her he was alarmed by her frequent nightmares. These dreams prompted her to wake him up by "pulling him up" in the middle of the night and shouting: "Wake up, wake up! Take cover, take cover!" Come next morning, though, she remembered nothing. No doubt she needed care, now that her marriage seemed to be threatened in spite of her efforts to protect it.[16] For these and other reasons, US *hibakusha* began to gather, and the size of the Los Angeles and San Francisco groups quickly increased from a little more than a handful to a few dozen. By the early 1970s, the number of both groups combined reached an estimated 200.[17]

Once survivors came together, for the loosely set purpose of remembering the bomb, the reticence, fear, and guilt that had been associated with US survivors' memories seemed to lift, though only gradually. No one in their oral histories said that *they* were the ones who talked about the bomb, suggesting that the feelings that had shaped silence before the mid-1960s never went away completely, even at the time of the interviews many decades later. *Someone* was talking, though, and many vividly remembered what it meant for them to listen. For Toshiko Hishinuma, to listen was to recall her own experiences: "Everyone was talking, saying that this happened, that happened. Listening, I felt as if my memory began to come back to me." This left a strong enough impression on Hishinuma that she begin to help others recall and release memories, although she understood that remembering also "made us feel dejected." One of the survivors with whom Hishinuma became acquainted confessed how her attempt to remember caused her recurring nosebleeds. The bomb memory was too "exciting" for her.[18] Ayako Elliott, an in-utero *hibakusha*, began to ask questions that she had never asked before. "It was after I joined this group of US survivors that I began to ask my mother" about her bomb experiences, said Elliott. "Sometimes, she would tell me a whole story, while other times she would skip and jump around. But everyone told me that it is better to ask." So Elliott asked, and later, like Hishinuma, she began to help others remember, making sure along the way that their memories were recorded.[19] A story generated many stories to be told, making those who listened want to know more. Yasuo Grant Fujita, an early participant of the Los Angeles meetings, had no health concerns, a rare fortune of which he was keenly aware as someone who had survived less than a mile from Hiroshima's hypocenter. He did not want to hear stories of radiation sickness at all, nor did he feel that it was right for US survivors to ask for anyone's help. What Fujita wanted instead was for "America to understand that the atomic bomb was a horrible thing."

Although he had steered clear of illness, he had lost most of his family members to the bomb. As discussed in Chapter 3, both his grandfather and his mother, seemingly uninjured by the explosion, died within two weeks after August 6 because of acute radiation sickness. Thus, part of what Fujita wanted "America to understand" was that mass, indiscriminate death had left him wholly alone. It also impressed Fujita that he had been surrounded by many children just like himself at the orphanage to which he was sent. Although he felt no "grudge" against America, he thought that a catastrophe of this magnitude should be remembered "for the sake of future."[20]

As Fujita admitted, his unwillingness to talk about ill-health or to ask for help was rare among US survivors, a majority of whom wanted to discuss their "pain caused by the bomb," "health effects of radiation," and in a few years, what assistance they might want from either the American or the Japanese government.[21] Because there are no records of these early talks, we do not know if the kinds of memories about the bomb discussed in earlier chapters were also shared on these occasions. The earliest records of oral histories suggest that they were, as do the memories of Hiroshima or Nagasaki that a handful of US survivors shared with newspapers in the 1970s.[22] They both have narrative arcs similar to those of later oral histories, in that most featured gendered stories of ground zero and stories colored by immigrants' cross-nationality. At some point in the late 1960s or early 1970s, though, US *hibakusha*'s remembering began to carry a desire for some sort of recognition. They were not sure where to begin or exactly what they wanted, but they realized that their group needed a structure. The Los Angeles group selected Tomoe Okai as president and Kazue Suyeishi as vice president, both women. Their counterpart in San Francisco was Kanji Kuramoto, Suyeishi's long-time friend. When these two groups came together in 1974, Kuramoto became president of the expanded CABS, and in the following year, Kuniko Jenkins and Ayako Elliott were selected as vice president and secretary, respectively.[23] By choosing leadership significantly consisting of women, both groups revealed an important gender dynamism that continued to shape their activism in the following years. As Suyeishi recalled, the women became the first leaders of the Los Angeles group more or less by default because "men did not want to be the president." Although "the majority of those who started the group were men, all of them were owners of good business," and they did not need or want to be a boss elsewhere.[24]

Elliott offered a slightly different explanation, with which many others concurred: "[Many] men could not be the president because they had a job. They could not take a day off to attend to the group's business. They also did not want their names in public because publicity might interfere with their work. . . . There were those who came out [as *hibakusha* at their workplaces] only to see their health insurance policies canceled."[25] Many insurance companies defined radiation exposure as a "preexisting condition," so these cases of cancelation sent a ripple through US survivors, especially men who were the sole earners and carriers of family health insurance policies. (This did not concern Kuramoto, though, because as a state employee, his insurance policy was secure regardless of his health condition.) In different ways, both Suyeishi and Elliott highlighted men's importance as breadwinners who felt they must attend to more serious business than survivors' organizations. Thus, on the one hand, the survivors' group could not be taken as seriously as a man's job. On the other, men's ability to conduct men's business might be compromised by revealing their survivorhood, meaning that survivorhood was a serious enough subject to potentially cause them trouble. Women eased this contradiction by recalling that they took leadership roles not because of their skills but because of a void created by men. This gender dynamism suggests that, at its inception, CABS members considered the organization to be tenuous. It was not clear if it would be strong enough to sustain itself and accomplish any goal. This perception made women, not men, the choice as leaders.

But this was not the whole story. As seen in Kuramoto's presidency, some men did pursue leadership in CABS, especially after it became a bigger organization that brought together the San Francisco and Los Angeles groups. His leadership did not simply fall into his lap; he sought it deliberately. Thomas Noguchi, the Los Angeles County coroner, who learned about the *hibakusha* group around 1970 and assisted in its application for nonprofit organization status in 1971, initially urged Suyeishi to become CABS president. Noguchi thought that Suyeishi had a talent as an organizer, while Okai seemed too dependent on him.[26] Most survivors in Los Angeles agreed and, soon, Suyeishi and Kuramoto emerged as contenders. Without consulting Suyeishi, though, Kuramoto declared himself to be the president of the newly integrated CABS in 1974. According to Suyeishi, Noguchi tried to explain Kuramoto's action by relating it to his modest social standing: "Although he is a public employee, he is not assigned to any administrative duty. It is understandable that he wants a title." And a title sounded better if it were a president of a state, rather than a municipal, organization. Once he gained the "title," Suyeishi recalled, Kuramoto made it clear to her: "[I] want others to defer to me. I am the main person of the organization, and I want you to stay quiet." His understanding of his leadership was expressly gendered; he explained how he was taking up the presidency "as a man," and how Suyeishi should understand this because she inhabited the "women's world as a woman."[27] These statements suggest that, despite the belief that CABS was not as serious as men's business, it nevertheless had a potential to augment men's status. This potential gradually became a reality as the US survivors' group grew in its scale and scope. Survivors were no longer simply telling personal stories; they were also trying to take political action. In some survivors' minds, CABS might be thus ready for men's leadership.

Here, it is important that Kuramoto received sympathetic support from a number of US *hibakusha* despite his unilateral approach. The sympathy partly originated from his status as a Kibei returnee. Kyohei Sakata, for instance, felt eager to assist Kuramoto when he realized that Kuramoto was leading the group "in his broken English." Because Kuramoto left Hawai'i when he was still young and spent much of his childhood in Hiroshima, he never gained native-level fluency in English. This characteristic, shared by many if not all US survivors, struck an especially sympathetic chord for them. As returnees or newcomers of Asian heritage, many did not acquire a respected profession or social status in America. To yearn for it seemed legitimate, particularly when the desire for upward mobility was paired with a vision and a willingness to act on behalf of others as in Kuramoto's case. Thus, US *hibakusha*'s activism by the early 1970s embodied transitional gender relationships. Women's leadership took shape when CABS activities were associated with personal remembering of the bomb. Men, in contrast, rose to the occasion with a hope for uplifting their social standing, especially as the group became more publicly outspoken. Women who had filled leadership positions earlier made room for men, because of a shared understanding that Asians in America lacked opportunities. But these patterns, familiar to scholars of gender relationships among racial minorities, became complicated in the later 1970s by two circumstances that made US survivors' history unique.[28] First, a majority of them were women who were more available and willing to remember in public than men. Breaking silence around the bomb continued to depend on women's participation, even predominance.

Second, as seen in Chapter 2, these women understood themselves to be caretakers of the injured and ill, which was complementary to the image of courageous rescuers that shaped many male survivors' remembering of the bomb. The remembering divided by gender, firmed up by war and work in the 1950s, in many ways seems to have fit well into Cold War culture. Nonetheless, it was increasingly unclear if this gender distinction would carry a relevance for US *hibakusha*'s remembering in the 1970s, the era of the Civil Rights and the Second Wave Feminist Movements. As their remembering took on more public dimensions, especially in their fight for legislation supporting American *hibakusha* in 1974 and 1978, these gender dynamisms had to be redirected for CABS's purposes.

In this regard, it is important to note that CABS from the beginning benefitted from the support of Noguchi, a first generation immigrant from Japan who became a respected figure in the Asian American civil rights movement and, for many, a role model promoting racial and gender equality.[29] Beyond assisting CABS to obtain status as a nonprofit organization, Noguchi played a key role in spreading the word about US *hibakusha* – that they were US citizens and residents, and that they needed access to medical care and treatment for their radiation illnesses. His political allies in California, including Edward R. Roybal, Mervyn Dymally, and George Moscone, became steadfast supporters of US survivors chiefly at Noguchi's urging. As supporters of immigrants and workers' rights, racial equality, and gay rights, these politicians of color helped align CABS's efforts with the 1970s politics of the New Left. This, in turn, led the way for Japanese American organizations to support the 1974 and 1978 legislation for US survivors without fear of being accused of national disloyalty. Most importantly, Noguchi was a hero of a sort for Japanese American youths, successfully bringing in their support for CABS along the way.[30] By the late 1960s, Noguchi had shown some of the qualities most admired by Sansei, including the ability to work cross-generationally, to speak forcefully for one's rights when challenged, and to reject racism and sexism. For Sansei born during or shortly after World War II and who learned about racial injustices of the past and present as politically conscious young adults in the late 1960s, these qualities were essential for moving the nascent Asian American movement forward. When Noguchi offered support for US survivors, his Sansei affiliates backed it by mobilizing their own organizations. Similar to Kuramoto whose "broken English" drew CABS members' empathy, Noguchi successfully turned his cultural belonging to Japan as *Shin Issei* into a source of his political strength in America. As such, Noguchi's story embodied fruits of cross-generational collaboration, that is, the breaking of silence around subjects previously considered a liability. Something that once might have been seen as a sign of national disloyalty, surviving Hiroshima and Nagasaki, became a past that belonged to, and was owned by, Asians across national and cultural borders. No longer should a discussion of American experiences of the nuclear holocaust in Japan suggest otherness. Instead, such a discussion indicated a confrontation with racism and sexism directed against Asians on both sides of the Pacific. Noguchi's story, more of which follows, helped define a path forward.

Connecting the Community through Generations: (Shin) Issei, Nisei, and Sansei

Before Noguchi became perhaps the most important supporter, facilitator, and alliance builder for US *hibakusha*, his career went through an upheaval. Born in Japan in 1927, Noguchi was a graduate of Nippon University School of Medicine in Tokyo and completed his internship at both Tokyo University Hospital and Orange County General Hospital, California. In 1953, while still a medical intern in California, he met his future wife Hisako Nishihara, a Nisei from Los Angeles. His success in obtaining appointments at reputable hospitals, and, in 1967, the position as chief medical examiner–coroner of the county of Los Angeles, solidified his status in America. One of the early generation of Shin Issei, he was a rare success as one of the "firsts" for the Nikkei community. Nobody before Noguchi had occupied a public office of such importance. His career was endangered, though, when he was suspended, then fired, from his position as the examiner–coroner in early 1969 based solely on the accusations of Lindon S. Hollinger, the county chief administrative officer. Hollinger claimed that Noguchi was mentally unstable, used drugs excessively, and behaved erratically.

According to JACL, this was a clear attempt at "character assassination."[31] Although these assertions were found baseless, the hearings of Noguchi's case generated bellicose expressions of prejudice against Asians, Nikkei men in particular, turning his struggle into a fight for the entire Asian American community. Even after cross-examination quickly proved the accusations against Noguchi thoroughly unfounded, the hearing continued with a host of problematic claims about his "erratic behavior," colored by racism and sexism against men of Asian heritage.[32]

One of the most contentious questions concerning Noguchi's "erratic behavior" was whether he was "sympathetic" enough to his coworkers, especially his junior colleagues. One witness claimed "He was not sympathetic; he's an Oriental. And he's a hard-working man and he expected everybody else to work as hard as he worked."[33] This claim was made in support of one of the charges made by Hollinger: that Noguchi had driven one of his inferiors to death by "overworking him."[34] Prejudice toward Asians as emotionless and mechanical was abundantly clear. Another witness made an even more straightforward connection between the accused and the wartime history by drawing "a picture of Noguchi as a 'stereotyped World War II kamikaze pilot.'"[35] These assaults struck JACL as requiring a substantial response, and this largely Nisei organization created J.U.S.T., or Japanese United in Search of Truth, in Southern California, in order to offer Noguchi moral and legal support. Soon, the J.U.S.T.–Noguchi Defense Fund was created in Chicago, so as to solicit financial support for the embattled doctor. As J.U.S.T. perceived him, Noguchi was portrayed by his enemies as "strange" because, as a recent immigrant, he raised powerful questions about racism. For instance, he "did not understand that a cop-killing of a black youth was supposed to be reported as an 'accident' and not the way he saw it. Nor [did] he understand the role of Japanese Americans as being generally a passive one."[36] Instead, he stood up to defend himself. At the same time that Noguchi's case brought prejudice against Nikkei men as machine-like and aggressive out into public scrutiny, the hearings also offered opportunities to refute stereotypes of Asian Americans as mute and docile.

Notably, JACL was not the only Asian American organization that saw an opportunity for a breakthrough in the Noguchi case. Organizations of younger Asian Americans, too, offered support. *Gidra*, perhaps the most widely read Asian American youths' newspaper of the era, featured the case on the front page of its inaugural issue in April 1969. Noguchi did not recoil in silence, stated the article's author proudly. Instead, "he decided to fight for what he thinks is right. And in taking this stand he has bolstered the Asian community by showing that yellow people do not always roll over and play dead."[37] After Noguchi won the case and was reinstated in his position, the newspaper featured him and his wife in a full two-page article entitled "Rebel With a Cause." This of course was a play on the famous film, with the message that "yellow" youths in America had ample reason to rebel though in a different way than their white counterparts. The title conveys a confidence that Asian Americans are part of American policy. Simultaneously, by speaking out in a clearly defined "cause," Asian Americans asserted a position that distinguished them from their white peers in the 1950s. Having been on the receiving end of racism, Asian Americans knew exactly what problems they faced.[38] Just as leaders of the Black Power Movement of the time such as Huey Newton and Bobby Seale defined blackness as a source of power and pride, Asian Americans positioned yellowness at the core of their identity from which their resistance was derived.

Three critical observations about the Noguchi case and the Asian American response to it help us understand the significance of US survivors' collective remembering within the broader community. First, although the case reached a satisfactory conclusion – the reinstatement of Noguchi – only several months after he was fired in early 1969, the intensity of his case powerfully united different generations of Asian Americans. JACL was the oldest, mostly Nisei organization, whereas those who published *Gidra* were largely third generation college students and younger community members. To have the support of both was no small feat, given how the older and younger generations often held sharply conflicting views about issues ranging from the Vietnam War to the budding Gay Rights Movement. As a successful Shin Issei, Noguchi moved more than one generation. Indeed, this making of intergenerational ties, spurred by racist incidents in the past and present, was hardly unique in Asian America. For instance, one of the chief concerns among politically active Filipino Americans and Chinese Americans in the mid-1970s was the International Hotel (I-Hotel), a low-cost apartment for first generation immigrants at the intersection of San Francisco's Manilatown and Chinatown. The I-Hotel's tenants faced an eviction order in 1977 when the municipal government decided to redevelop the neighborhood by demolishing the building.[39] When the community's youth began to organize anti-demolition, anti-eviction rallies, their talks with elderly tenants proved a crucial source of activism. One community newspaper, for example, published "Interviews of Tenants," featuring a seventy-nine-year-old immigrant from the Philippines. When asked "about his past, he told ... that [he] took a job as a dishwasher and a busboy" when he first came to San Francisco in 1926. It was the only position available at that time, and when the job disappeared, he started to work as a hired hand on a farm. As a long-term resident of the I-Hotel who had struggled his way through, he felt that the tenants "have to resist" the eviction.[40] Clearly, the older man's life story as an immigrant spurred the younger activists' desire to act on his behalf. Noguchi's 1969 case and Nisei and Sansei Japanese Americans' responses to it show that such intergenerational connection already existed in the community a decade earlier, when the Asian American civil rights movement was still in the making.

Second, and contributing to his intergenerational appeal, was Noguchi's decision to speak out, which was an aspired to, yet elusive, act of courage in Asian America. According to J.U.S.T., "being ... passive" when "basic civil rights of an American citizen" were violated as they initially were in Noguchi's case – he was not allowed an opportunity to respond to "slanderous" charges before his dismissal – was exactly what had happened in the imprisonment of Japanese Americans during the Pacific War.[41] The breaking of silence around today's racism led to speaking out more forcefully about past racial injustice. For younger Asian Americans, particularly those who were growing critical of America's ongoing war against Asia, breaking silence was the foremost accomplishment of Noguchi. When a group called Asian Americans for Peace organized a peace rally in January 1970 in Los Angeles, six months after Noguchi was reinstated in July 1969, it was not only the first public assertion of anti-Vietnam War sentiment in the Asian American community, it was also a continuation of the work started by Noguchi. "The Asian community has shown once before during the Noguchi hearings that it is no longer a 'quiet' minority," declared the antiwar group's organizers.[42] Now that silence had been broken, Asian Americans should be able to assert their opposition to the Vietnam War without fear of being labeled as disloyal, a fear that had haunted them well after the era of being "aliens ineligible for citizenship" ended by law in 1952. By the 1970s, it was time for them to change this fraught dynamism of fearful silence. Rather than acting defensively by accentuating their national loyalty, Asian Americans should outspokenly criticize US policies as acts of citizen participation.⁴³

Intimately connected to such outspokenness without – or despite – the long-held fear of being seen as foreign is my third observation about the significance of Noguchi's case, namely, how the process of breaking silence was shaped by racial and gendered meanings. In a refreshing repudiation of the earlier generations' main tactic of fighting racial prejudice, which was to highlight their national loyalty,⁴⁴ Asian Americans in the late 1960s and early 1970s were becoming more forthright about the connection between Asians and Asian Americans through their critique of racism. Instead of asserting their belonging to America, as most JACL leaders did in response to Japanese American imprisonment during the Pacific War, the organization decided to defend the Japanese-born Noguchi as one of them.⁴⁵ This was a courageous, if calculated, act of solidarity. It was not only that younger Asian Americans took a further step toward the alliance between Asia and Asian America by seeing in the Noguchi case a pathway toward speaking out against the Vietnam War. A coalition between Asian Americans and African Americans, too, flourished in the era's antiwar, antinuclear movements. In a statement prepared by Newton and read by Seale in 1967, in Sacramento, for instance, a linkage was made between "the enslavement of Black people," the "dropping of atomic bombs on Hiroshima and Nagasaki," and "the cowardly massacre in Vietnam."⁴⁶ One of the Hiroshima commemorations held in the Bay Area in 1971 included a program called "Speak Out for an End to War, Racism, Repression, and Poverty," which featured Rev. Ralph Abernathy, the president of the Southern Christian Leadership Conference, and Sallye Davis, the mother of Angela Davis.⁴⁷ Clearly, the era's new awareness of the Third World was beginning to make interracial coalitions in both national and international domains an urgent necessity.

The Noguchi case also offered an opportunity for articulating gender relationships. It is unmistakable, for example, that the "Rebel With a Cause" article in Gidra, by featuring Noguchi's wife Hisako along with her husband (her pictures and those of the couple surround the article), was making a point about gender. As the article carefully spelled out, Hisako earned her MA in Zoology in 1948 at the University of California, Los Angeles (UCLA), and her PhD in Medical Science at

Tokyo University in 1954. She gained these credentials despite the fact that her college education was interrupted in 1942 when she was sent to the incarceration camp in Amachi, Colorado. When Thomas met her in 1953, she was a medical researcher at the Bartlow Sanitarium. In the following decade, she held an appointment as a research biochemist at UCLA, a career followed by faculty positions at smaller collages in the state. Clearly, she was a woman with a long resume, not the kind of person who would partner with a "kamikaze pilot" in the imagination of those who spoke against Noguchi. Far from being a typical Japanese man married to a traditional stay-at-home wife, then, Noguchi found an equal partner. Or, at least, this was the image his younger supporters projected onto him.

These observations suggest how, when Noguchi met CABS leaders in 1970, he was bringing into the organization a potential for connecting different Asian American aspirations for change, be it for more intergenerational collaboration, the breaking of silence, or a critique of racial and gender stereotypes associated with Asians in both Asia and America. This possibility for change was what Noguchi hoped would be a favor to the community that had mobilized to put him back in the examiner–coroner's position.[48] Indeed, US survivors – aptly called "quiet Americans" by CABS leaders – came to embody all these aspirations by the end of the 1970s.[49] US survivors gained support from different generations by speaking out in public and by shifting expected gender roles for Asians as a racial minority. By delineating how Noguchi served as a bridge between survivors and non-survivors in Asian America, I do not suggest that his influence was the primary reason for the rise of US *hibakusha*'s activism. Their remembering of the bomb, too, inspired their community members to make critical connections across time. Nonetheless, it is important to note that Asian Americans, especially those of younger generations, were the foremost audience for US survivors beyond their small gatherings. What these listeners wanted to hear mattered as much as what tellers wished to say. If the 1950s built layers of silence around the bomb, the 1970s witnessed a gradual coming together of personal and political recollections. They were not identical, but these trails of remembering certainly echoed each other, even when they were in tension. Especially because CABS relied on Noguchi's assistance from its beginning, his and his community's concerns naturally found their way into US *hibakusha*'s remembering. Equally important, unlike the 1950s when Japanese Americans kept the bomb and the camps in silence, the 1970s witnessed both subjects recounted personally and collectively. This did not mean that all that *hibakusha* remembered in the later decade was a composite reexamination of the bomb and the camps. Nonetheless, they became a conspicuous pair in US survivors' remembering.[50]

Taking Kazue Suyeishi's oral history as an example, it becomes evident how US survivors discovered a new relationship between the bomb and the camps. She recalled how, when she was working with Noguchi in the early 1970s, his wife and her husband, both Nisei, facilitated their collaboration. Both spouses were former inmates "who experienced similar sorts of things" and thus felt at ease immediately when the four of them began to socialize. Suyeishi noticed that her husband shared with Noguchi's wife memories that he had not shared with Suyeishi: "My husband began to say, well, when I was in Cleveland [after being released from the camp] I did this, then when attending a school in New York City I did that. . . . I knew that he was in a camp, but I did not know how much he suffered. But Mrs. Noguchi understood."[51] Indeed, Hisako Noguchi went to Boston University shortly after she left the camp and before she was able to return to her alma mater, UCLA. In both of their life histories, unexpected displacements in youth were salient. As Suyeishi recalled, this friendship between the former inmates had greatly facilitated her relationship with Thomas Noguchi, which in turn had moved forward US *hibakusha*'s thinking about what they wanted. As with many Asian American women of her generation, Suyeishi did not have a driver's license. That her driver, her husband, could also look forward to seeing the Noguchis offered Suyeishi great encouragement. Spending a considerable amount of time outside the home in order to assist a social organization, too, was still a novelty for Asian American women, especially those married with children. By sharing life histories, breaking the gender boundary in remembering both the bomb and the camps became a reality.

In this regard, it is striking that Suyeishi's oral history indicates how a changing gender relationship was intertwined with a shifting balance between cross-national ties and tensions. Unlike memories that we examined in the earlier chapters, in which the image of emotionally unflappable men frequently shaped family conversations about the bomb and the camp, Suyeishi's story of her husband included tales of his "suffering." As much as the illness and injury caused by the bomb, the pain inflicted by the camp called for a better recognition regardless of the sufferers' gender. No longer did it matter that the camp had not caused as much physical illness as the bomb; both were united in a recognition of psychosocial suffering. Suyeishi's remembering, then, revealed the persistence of cross-national tensions that nonetheless began to be better recognized as such in the early 1970s. Earlier, she "did not know" how much her husband had suffered in the camp. Thanks to the conversations that took place between him and Hisako, she now understood it better. The tension between bomb and camp experiences, which had persisted in Nikkei families, might not be gone; but at least, silence around it was beginning to be chipped away. Seemingly small steps, these acts of remembering brought substantial results.

Thanks to many meetings between the Suyeishis and the Noguchis, CABS launched a campaign to encourage more US survivors to participate in the organization. With support from key senators and congresspersons, which US *hibakusha* obtained because of Noguchi's endorsement, they also began to attract broader sympathy from Asian American communities and beyond. As will be discussed, this sympathy culminated in political campaigns for legislative action in the state of California in 1974, and in the US Congress in 1978. As Asian Americans discovered more ties and tensions between the events separated by the Pacific but connected through Asian casualty, US survivors began to speak about their experiences with a clearer sense of purpose.

Other oral histories suggest different ways in which US *hibakusha*'s remembering shaped a new relationship between the bomb and the camps. Trans-Pacific ties and tensions around them persisted, but their balance seemed to shift subtly toward seeing ties by recounting tensions. For instance, Jeanna Oshima was a Nisei, a former inmate married to a US survivor. While her husband was trapped in Hiroshima, Oshima was confined in the camp in Topaz, Utah. Just as he did not talk about the bomb when the couple was getting to know each other in the mid-1960s, in San Francisco, she did not discuss much about her camp experience except to say that her mother appreciated some aspects of it (she did not have to wash dishes or pay phone bills anymore). Regardless, Oshima in her oral history recalled how she had lost her privacy in the camp and thought that this should not happen to anyone. These memories of the camp made Oshima feel conflicted about the bomb, especially when she thought about her husband's active participation in CABS beginning in the early 1970s. As Oshima recalled, she had felt "ambivalent on the issue of A-bomb dropping":

> I'd say yeah, maybe it was okay to drop it because it shortened the war, without too many more people [in the United States] getting killed, but on the other side of that fence is all the civilians that got killed … it killed so many innocent people. … But the question I have asked a couple of my Nisei counterparts, I said, you know, we were talking about camp. And I said, you know, what if Japan never bombed Pearl Harbor? Would we have been sent to camp? No one can answer that for me.

She felt even more troubled by the absence of a clear answer because her husband had suffered by way of the camp even without having been there: all his family members had been confined in a camp, and he lost his younger brother because of the lack of appropriate medical care.[52] Oshima's question was one for her husband to ponder, too.

Compared to the silence around the camps and the bomb during the 1950s, sustained in part by a sentiment that survivors had suffered more than inmates, the 1970s brought a stronger assertion of suffering by the camp survivors. This did not stop remembering about the bomb – as seen in Suyeishi's case, talking about the camp facilitated *hibakusha*'s coming together. In Oshima's remembering, her conflicted thoughts about the bomb and the camps led her to decide that she supported her husband's participation in CABS. This decision was not only a political one, but also part of a personal struggle having to do with family. After much thought, the Oshimas decided against having a child:

> There were some negative aspects to it [the bomb]. And yet he [my husband] has an aunt in Hiroshima who bore three children, very healthy kids. And she really was a survivor because she got half of her body burnt. But she had children and they are all very healthy. … You know Ayako Elliott … I think when she was growing up her mother told her if you were to get married don't ever have any children. That was her mother. … I remember her telling us that … even if they [survivors] could have children, how would they be grown, would they be deformed [or] … have a health problem later. So the same thought must have been going through on our mind, too. … So, anyhow, we never had kids.[53]

To talk about this decision was clearly difficult for Oshima, as she momentarily teared up during the interview, the only time she showed such emotion. In addition to feeling conflicted about the bomb because of her camp experience, then, Oshima faced a new relationship with the bomb as it began to seep quietly into her marriage. Families, including non-survivors like Oshima, became participants in *hibakusha*'s remembering. Their composite telling might not lead to an easy resolution; trans-Pacific tensions were still there. But at least, they were beginning to say what they wanted to say about their ties. In this light, memories accentuated by gender divisions, as in the 1940s and 1950s, carried much less relevance. Regardless of how bravely or gently they might have rescued or cared for others in 1945, men and women were both affected by the fear of radiation more than twenty years later. If this were the case, there was no point to ask who suffered more. They all suffered. This shift fore-shadowed a change in gender dynamism that was to take place by the end of the 1970s – a change that transformed US survivors into compelling, even subversive, witnesses of the nuclear holocaust.

As Noguchi's story has shown, breaking silence around issues of racial and gender inequality carried an urgency in Asian America. As survivors' personal remembering became shared by the community, they began to draw younger generations' interest. Initially, collective remembering began around issues of war, nuclear war in particular. Especially after CABS became accredited as a nonprofit organization in 1971, the existence of US survivors began to be noticed by word of mouth within Japanese American communities in California. In response, non-survivors, including those from different generations than survivors, began to participate in collective remembering. Some were clearly inspired by US survivors' coming together. Karl G. Yoneda, a Communist Party member and labor activist, is perhaps best known for his testimony in the early 1980s before the Commission on Wartime Relocation and Internment of Civilians, a federal commission formed by the Congress to review facts about the wartime incarceration of Japanese Americans.[54] Less known is that Yoneda ten years earlier had donated to and otherwise supported CABS, participating in the group called the Asian-American Ad-Hoc Committee on Hiroshima and Nagasaki that aimed to better understand the bomb's political significance for Asian America, and offering his own memories of the bomb at antinuclear marches. Some of his speeches in the early 1970s reveal reasons for his support for antinuclear causes:

Hiroshima was a beautiful city as I remember. I spent my young days from age 7 to 20 there. When Hiroshima was bombed, I was stationed in Kunming, China, as an enlisted man with the China, Burma, India Psychological Warfare Team of the US Army. My immediate reaction was "Why did they do it? What happened to my mother?" ... Many months after the bomb, the International Red Cross Informed me that my mother was alive and safe, but the home in the center of the city was gone.[55]

Yoneda's biography contained crucial similarities to US *hibakusha*'s, in that his family history came into crushing conflict with the history of the nations at war. It is likely that Yoneda recognized these similarities when he heard about US survivors. He closely followed CABS activities in the 1970s and 1980s, reading articles featuring US *hibakusha* such as Okai, Kuramoto, Jenkins, Suyeishi, and Elliott. When FOH, a support group for US survivors, was established in San Francisco in 1982, Yoneda promptly joined.[56]

Yuji Ichioka, a Nisei founder of the Asian-American Ad-Hoc Committee on Hiroshima and Nagasaki in which Yoneda participated and the associate director of the newly created Asian American Studies Center at UCLA, offered an equally compelling memory of the bomb in the early 1970s. Ichioka's statements suggest a different kind of conflict between personal and national histories than Yoneda's, although remembering – both his and bomb survivors' – played a similarly important role in his reflections:

In early August 1945, ... I myself was still in Topaz, Utah as a youngster of nine years. I can remember raising crude questions about the reasons for being there. But of Hiroshima and Nagasaki, events which were contemporaneous with our camp experience, I cannot remember anything. ... Indeed I cannot even remember hearing the news that they had been dropped over these two cities. ... Some people might take the position that there is no need to raise such questions now. ... But I strongly disagree with this kind of position. Just as we should insist upon raising questions about our camp experience, I think that we should also raise questions about the bombings.[57]

Similar to the way in which the "kamikaze pilot" reference in the Noguchi case in 1969 led JACL to revisit the Japanese American incarceration, the memory of the camps in the 1970s drove leaders of the Asian American movement to critically reflect on Hiroshima and Nagasaki as a history closely related to Asians in America in the present. Here again, the trans-Pacific connection was considered critically instead of anxiously brushed aside.[58] When the ad-hoc committee held a bomb commemoration in August 1970, the event was the first of its kind in Asian America. No longer was the bomb contained within the largely apolitical confines of Hiroshima Kenjinkai. The meaning of the destroyed cities of immigrants was to be articulated on the street, in the newspapers, even in the classroom. Equally important, the commemoration's program included a "community meeting" featuring "Miss Nobuko Ueno, Hiroshima survivor."[59] Although it is not clear if Ueno was a local resident or a Japanese person who happened to be visiting San Francisco, her presence in the program clearly indicated that survivors' voices were a driving force of communal remembering. The bomb's meanings should not escape Asian Americans' attention simply because the event took place in a country far away. Indeed, ties among Asian Americas would become clearer if they broke silence and reflected on their history's cross-nationality.

The growing awareness of the trans-Pacific connection not only found expressions in rallies and marches, but also took place in personal and familial conversations; now, these conversations included survivors and non-survivors across generations. As US survivors' remembering became more audible, their cross-nationality was no longer a reason for being labeled as "aliens" or "disloyals." On the contrary, it was essential for their community and its history, which must be more firmly recognized as part of American society, culture, and policy.

Expanding the Community, Building Alliances: 1971–1974

In the years spanning 1971 to 1978, US survivors achieved a remarkable rise in public presence and activism. Their efforts initially revolved around CABS membership drives. Simultaneously, they began to gather support from key politicians and organizations, a necessary step for crafting medical legislation to pay for their healthcare needs. The years 1974 and 1978 stand out as especially critical, as US *hibakusha* pushed for laws on both the state and national stages. What they wanted from this legislation was moral and material support, first in 1974 from the state of California, then in 1978 from the US government;

CABS by-laws since 1971 stated that their purpose was "to promote health and welfare of the members" by establishing a "government program ... to provide financial assistance to all victims" and a "special clinic in the US with focus on nuclear radiation problems and treatment."[60] Exactly what the program and the clinic would entail, however, remained elusive. As they began to build alliances with others, US survivors' demands seemed to shift from one draft of a bill to another. This was largely because of calculations made by more politically and legally experienced supporters, who chose features based on what appeared most likely to pass. Virtually no US survivor's oral history contained a detailed recollection of the 1974 and 1978 bills and their changing contents, suggesting that they were not chief architects of the legislation. Or, that they did not think of themselves as leaders; they did not wish to reveal their political acts in personal recollections. Regardless, their emerging collective identity as survivors, as well as their increasingly public counter-memory of the bomb, left a vivid trace in the legislative hearings, during which they served as witnesses. In this process, US *hibakusha* discovered what they wanted to tell publicly. Their distinctively cross-national remembering as immigrants pushed both racial and gender boundaries in a way that furthered their connection to the Asian American community. Although neither of the bills passed, the more outspoken identity that US survivors expressed comprised an unprecedented era of visibility for the counter-memory of the bomb.

CABS's most urgent initial task was to find how many survivors were living in America. No one knew their exact number, although a report in late 1971 stated "there are at least 200 atomic bomb victims in California, and more living in other parts of the United States."[61] Within a year, the estimate went up to "500–700 survivors"[62] and then to "over 700 survivors ... living in [the] U.S."[63]; by 1974, the number reached about "1,000 victims in the United States."[64] The number 1,000 was picked up by the August 1974 issues of the *New York Times* and *Wall Street Journal*.[65] The dramatic increase in the estimated number was a result of expanded communication. By 1976, CABS had started to collect ten dollars per member annually, funds mostly spent on communication. Many factors contributed to CABS's growth, and here I focus on the increase in US survivors' visibility led by survivors themselves (whereas in Chapter 6, I will discuss the efforts led by the ABCC, the Oak Ridge National Laboratory, and the Atomic Energy

Commission). Survivors' network of acquaintances remained an important factor, although this network transformed into a more systematic membership drive in the mid-1970s. To continue the most immediate form of communication – meetings – phone calls were made and letters had to be sent. Sachiko Matsumoto, a member since the mid-1960s, played a central role in keeping in touch with members by calling them to ask how they were doing and sending letters about meetings. This was particularly important for *hibakusha* outside California. For Lisa Gendernalik, residence in Arizona made it difficult for her to keep in touch. "But with Mrs. Matsumoto I occasionally talked over the phone ... I would call her when I have a question, and she would explain a variety of things for me."[66] Matsumoto never occupied a formal leadership position in CABS, so she was a notable example of how women took care of important things subtly.[67]

Kanji Kuramoto, CABS president since 1974, began to distribute a handwritten newsletter to members a few times a year. Kuramoto's children soon discovered their father's new habit of disappearing into his study after work. He sometimes would not come out until midnight. When his wife asked the children "What is Daddy doing?" their answer was "The Atomic Bomb!"[68] It was as if the bomb became personified; his engagement with it seemed to have become bigger than himself. CABS also began to put notifications in Japanese American (and, a few times, in Korean American) newspapers about its meetings.[69] These notifications also asked US *hibakusha* to contact CABS and become members. George Kazuto Saiki, of Honolulu, noticed one of these notifications and began to make donations sometime in the early 1970s. He felt CABS's decision to "seek support from the US government for those of us who were getting sick" because of radiation exposure was completely legitimate. "We have US citizenship, so I wonder why we don't have medical help," wrote Saiki in one of his letters to Kuramoto. CABS leaders such as Kuramoto and Suyeishi appeared on local radio and TV programs to discuss the organization's aims.[70] The media visibility spread the word. Atsuko La Mica would not have known about CABS if it were not broadcast. She lived in Carmel, California, away from any sizable Japanese American communities. But her daughter in San Francisco happened to see a TV program featuring CABS, and thanks to this, her mother became a member.[71] Communication among US *hibakusha*, which had relied almost entirely on word of mouth, spread more widely.

Nikkei newspapers in California also began to feature more personal stories of US survivors, gingerly at first, then more confidently. One of the earliest of these stories appeared in *Hokubei Mainichi* in San Francisco in 1972, which featured US survivor "Mrs. Emiko Komatsu." Although the article emphasized how Komatsu suffered from acute radiation illness in 1945 and how, after she started to work for the ABCC in Hiroshima in 1950, she was impressed by "people who [were] still suffering from the bomb," the article left it ambiguous how she came to be living in California by 1968. Aspects of Komatsu's life history made it seem likely that she was born in America or had a family member in the country. But these details remained hidden.[72] In contrast, when *Nichi Bei Times*, also in San Francisco, featured another survivor, Alfred Kaneo Dote, in 1974, his cross-national life history was made abundantly clear by the title "American 'Hibakusha' ... Sacramento Nisei Remembers First Atomic Bomb Blast at Hiroshima." After explaining how Dote was not "the enemy ... [but a] Native Sacramentan," the article highlighted how US *hibakusha* struggled with radiation illness and how they deserved medical care because they are "not even strangers ... they are neighbors, friends." Such sympathetic depictions, as well as the power of a life story with a person's face attached to it (the article about Dote was accompanied by his close-up photo, still a rare act of courage for US survivors at this time), likely prompted more to come forward (see Figure 5.1). The Sacramento chapter of CABS came into existence in 1974, and Dote became the "default" president.[73] Another survivor, Fumiko Imai, remembered a "small meeting" that took place in Pacific Grove in the mid-1970s. The meeting was made possible by another survivor, a woman who recently had come to America thanks to Imai's sponsorship. This woman operated a beauty salon, and she hosted a CABS meeting there, informing the participants of the organization's future plans. Similar meetings occurred in San Diego, San Jose, Pasadena, Fresno, and Seattle, and as we will see, a chapter in Hawai'i formed by the end of the decade.[74] Thus, *hibakusha* in cities beyond San Francisco and Los Angeles began to gather, and their meetings in turn increased CABS membership. This geographic expansion fueled a sense of purpose, especially when CABS requested legislative action by the US Congress in 1978.

As more local branches were created, it became increasingly necessary that CABS had the capacity to handle legal documents and procedures. None in the organization had such expertise, but Noguchi's support helped US *hibakusha* to gain it. Recently reinstated to his

American 'Hibakusha' . . .

Sacramento Nisei Remembers First Atomic Bomb Blast at Hiroshima

By PHIL JORDAN
In the Sacramento Bee

SACRAMENTO, Aug. 5 — Remember Hiroshima? It was a long time ago — 29 years on Tuesday and far away. The victims were Japanese, "the enemy," then.

Right?

Wrong. Native Sacramentan Al Dote remembers Hiroshima. Along with hundreds of other Americans stranded in Japan by the Pacific war, he was there the first time an atomic bomb was used on human victims.

He's an American "hibakusha," one of hundreds of thousands exposed to atomic explosion or resulting fallout radiation at Hiroshima and three days later, Nagasaki.

Al Dote remembers vividly . . .

At 46, Alfred Kaneo Dote has his family, his health and his work. Short, husky, sun-tanned, in the words of one acquaintance, "he looks like a really happy man."

But at 8:15 a.m. on Aug. 6, 1945, Al Dote was just a mile and a half from "ground zero" when the atomic bomb was dropped. He survived uninjured, without ill effects

— so far.

American occupation officials put the Hiroshima toll at exactly 129,588 killed, injured and missing. Japanese sources give a different, longer-view figure: Of some 420,000 persons in Hiroshima that day, more than 260,000 were dead as a result within five years. The deaths continue, 2650 last year alone.

Recalls Nightmare

Those are statistics, factual, cold, ready for the computer. Al Dote is a warm, good-natured human, not a computer.

He recalls a nightmare of blinding light and darkness, uncountable dead and dying, the stench from tens of thousands or rotting bodies, a different stench from tens of thousands of funeral pyres.

"I was a high school student but working in a shipyard," Dote recalls. "So many men were in the army, we were taken by classes to work at production jobs. My class started work at 8 a.m. We'd just arrived and were waiting in a workers' eating room.

"There was a tremendous flash of light, then the noise. For an instant, I thought it was lightning,

then I realized that lightning moves down. This light had moved along the ground.

"I knew there had been an explosion, so I dived under a table.

ALFRED DOTE

"After a while, I looked out, but couldn't see anything. There was darkness, and the air was thick with black dust."

Five hours later, Dote's teacher told the boys to go home as best they could.

I rode my bike right through the most badly destroyed area," Dote says. "It was the most direct way and the easiest — most buildings were gone. In other areas, the streets were blocked by blown-down buildings.

Many Thousand Dead

"But there were thousands — more than thousands — of people dead and dying. I saw many people I knew, friends.

"One man I remember was the richest man in our neighborhood. He asked me to tell his family where he was. I did on my way home, and they went after him. He died while they were carrying him home."

Dote's family home was on the outskirts of the city. It was still standing. His mother and a younger brother were alive, though his brother's head was badly burned.

"My older sister and my nephew
(Continued on last page)

position, Noguchi by 1971 had a number of acquaintances among Japanese American lawyers and community activists. When FOH began to solicit membership in 1974 with the purpose of assisting CABS, the support group immediately attracted Sansei legal experts.[75] This was because a chief source of FOH membership was the Asian Law Caucus (ALC), established in 1972 and serving low-income, largely first generation Asian Americans in the Bay Area. ALC translated English materials for CABS members not fluent in English; they also translated CABS information spoken or written in Japanese into English for wider distribution. Both FOH and ALC were small grassroots organizations; FOH membership at any given time did not exceed a few dozen, ALC a few hundred in the 1970s. Nonetheless, they exhibited the "strength of weak ties." When there was a matter that required immediate action, these organizations mobilized their members quickly and effectively. Their assistance was offered with little to no cost to beneficiaries.[76] When Noguchi urged his ally, a man he called his "friend" – Mervyn Dymally, a Democratic state senator from Los Angeles and the first black person to serve in that capacity – to author a bill on US *hibakusha*'s behalf (which eventually became the 1974 bill considered by the California Senate), these Sansei lawyers were instrumental in providing input to CABS for the bill.[77]

JACL's open support for US survivors came more gradually than ALC's. Indeed, the *Pacific Citizen*, JACL's organ that began to report on US *hibakusha* in 1972, did not acknowledge their US citizenship at first. Throughout 1972, 1973, and much of 1974, US survivors were "atomic survivors now residing in Southern California" or "Hiroshima and Nagasaki A-bomb victims now living in this country."[78] The uncertainty about their citizenship lingered. One of the largest civil rights organizations in Asian America (and the most powerful in Japanese America), whose membership included many who had been incarcerated during the war, JACL looked upon issues of national belonging with extreme caution. For the first time in September 1974, however, survivors in the *Pacific Citizen* became "Japanese American ... 'hibakusha' citizens," and in October of the same year, "American citizens by birth, marriage or naturalization."[79] Both reports indicated JACL's more forthright recognition of US survivors' citizenship and, by extension, their cross-nationality as part of the US history of immigration. Most likely, JACL's earlier conservatism was changed by a public hearing concerning US *hibakusha*, sponsored by Dymally in the California State Senate in May 1974.[80] In August, the Task Force on Atomic Bomb Survivors was formed under Dymally's direction. The task force's members included Noguchi as the chairman, Suyeishi, Kuramoto, and Dote as CABS representatives, and James Okutsu (of Japanese Community Services) and George Takei (a former member of the *Star Trek* cast) as notable members of the Japanese American community.[81] The developments facilitated JACL coming out in support of CABS when the bill was introduced in December. Just as Nikkei newspapers began to perceive US survivors as their "neighbors," one of the most influential civil rights organizations in Asian America came to recognize CABS members as their fellow Americans.[82] These organizational supports – both by community-based groups such as FOH and ALC and by a national group such as JACL with a much larger membership[83] – no doubt moved more US *hibakusha* to join the effort to gain recognition of and support for their illnesses and injuries.

The growing antinuclear sentiment, too, played a role in encouraging more US survivors to come forward. As previously mentioned, when Asian Americans for Peace (AAP) organized a peace rally in January 1970, the event was dominated by a strong anti-Vietnam War sentiment. This sentiment was augmented by "President Nixon's recent argument to justify the invasion of Cambodia: 'It will shorten this war. It will reduce American casualties.'" What troubled the rally's organizers was that, unlike US deaths, Asian casualties were deemed irrelevant. In their speeches and flyers, AAP members also cited repeatedly a statement made by an Iowa woman about the 1968 My Lai Massacre in South Vietnam, which cast Asians as expendable and made multiple headlines in Asian American newspapers for its breathtaking flagrance: "Asia is over-populated anyway. It's no real loss." In the AAP supporters' view, this kind of belief, expressed by political leaders and ordinary citizens alike, had facilitated America's mainstream understanding of the bomb since 1945 as an acceptable tool of war, and fostered public support for using nuclear weapons against Asians in the imminent future. Such concern was amplified by the revelation between the mid-1960s and early 1970s that Okinawa could well become a permanent launching pad for America's nuclear warheads in Asia. As America and Japan negotiated the return of Okinawa to Japan, it became evident that nuclear weapons had been brought to the island during the US occupation. Initially, America insisted on keeping the nuclear bases in Okinawa even after its projected return in 1972. This would have been a clear violation of Japan's no-nuclear weapons policy, provoking impassioned protests among the Japanese and the Okinawans.[84] Across the Pacific, too, the conflict over nuclear-equipped military bases elicited outrage, prompting detailed media coverage in Asian America.[85] It was no coincidence, then, that the early 1970s witnessed a surge of Hiroshima and Nagasaki representations in art. Artists Maruki Toshi and Maruki Iri's "Hiroshima Panels" were shown in eight cities across America for the first time in 1970. That same year, JACL bought copies of the film *Hiroshima–Nagasaki* produced by the Center for Mass Communication at Columbia University and made them available to JACL chapters for local showings. This prompted numerous requests for the film from the chapters in Southern California, including those in Fowler, Santa Barbara, and greater Pasadena.[86] On both political and cultural fronts, the antinuclear cause occupied an important place in the rise of Asian American political awareness. As much as the rising awareness about the connection between the bomb and the camp, the soaring concern about nuclear proliferation in Asian America shaped US *hibakusha*'s remembering of the bomb.

Indeed, although a majority of US survivors did not actively participate in antiwar or antinuclear movements because of the lingering fear that they might be seen as disloyal, some did come to CABS or FOH through their opposition to nuclear weapons.[87] Kyohei Sakata was one such survivor for whom nuclear issues were a catalyst for activism. A Nagasaki native, Sakata lost his mother, sister, and brothers to radiation illness. Still, he came to America in 1969 to complete his graduate degrees in theology. At the university that he attended in Japan, it was difficult to focus on study because of the anti-Vietnam War, anti-imperialism movements that raged across the campus and caused frequent class cancelations. Although Sakata learned about CABS soon after settling in Alameda, California, he felt ambivalent about joining. But when he heard about FOH sometime in the 1970s, he felt freer to participate. The younger members of the group, including those from ALC, shared his politics. Besides, FOH's mode of activism felt like an old shoe to Sakata. He had witnessed public speeches and demonstrations regularly in Japan, common expressions of 1960s activism. His remembering of the following decade, the 1970s, on the US

West Coast, shows how the convergence of activisms across the Pacific allowed him to become a survivor:

> I felt that it is okay to say what I wanted to say, as long as I am a member of Friends of Hibakusha. So I began to give speeches on [University of California's] Berkeley campus as if I am putting out an *ajito* (*laughs*). Everyone was thinking about the need for nuclear-freeze at that time; and because college students were particularly well-informed about those things, my audience was really interested in what I had to say. . . . So I came to the issue of US survivors through my opposition to nuclear weapons and wars. . . . I realized that peace and antinuclear movements could become more persuasive if they were not just about logics but about people who actually suffer the nuclear weapons. . . . Survivors were here, and I thought I could not avoid being one.[88]

By referring to "agitation" by a Japanese term, *ajito*, Sakata was imagining a cross-national solidarity, something that others in Asian America such as Noguchi, Yoneda, and Ichioka were discovering. For reasons that he did not fully reveal, Sakata decided against joining CABS. He left me with an impression that he may have felt as if his self-respect would be hurt if he asked for public assistance for himself. FOH, in contrast, allowed him to help US *hibakusha* who wanted assistance. Also, he likely felt that joining CABS would bring the bomb too close. As discussed in Chapter 3, a worry about radiation illness had not left Sakata's mind since 1945. Whenever he had a minor symptom, it struck him as the beginning of a nuclear death he had witnessed countless times. But as a FOH member, he felt fine to come out as *hibakusha*. This was one of many ways in which they broke silence and expressed their identity as survivors.

California's 1974 bill stood as another marker of the diverse routes that US survivors and their supporters took to come forward. In May, a hearing for the bill was called to order by the California State Senate Subcommittee on Medical Education and Health Needs chaired by Dymally. The hearing's purpose was to "explore the possibilities of using existing publicly funded programs to assist the Hibakusha in obtaining the treatment that they need." If existing programs such as Medi-Cal and Medicaid could not be applied, the bill's supporters would explore the possibility of creating a new program for US survivors. Additionally, the bill, SB-15, aimed to establish a clinic at UCLA, where survivors could be certified as such and be treated free of cost by radiation specialists and counselors fluent in Japanese and English.[89] The clinic's staff would include not only American physicians but also Japanese doctors from Hiroshima or Nagasaki, who had more experience in treating radiation illness than physicians in California. The proposed annual budget for this clinic was US$750,000. Although ambitious, what US *hibakusha* asked for also contained elements of cautiousness. Instead of demanding a new medical insurance system, US survivors requested that one of the existing programs be extended to cover radiation illness. Their demand was modest, too, in comparison with their original vision. There was no mention of the financial assistance that had appeared in CABS by-laws a few years earlier. Redefined as a problem pertinent to the entire Asian American community, the bombings of the Japanese cities as a subject of American legislation still required a careful test-drive.

Dymally's opening remark at the hearing made it clear that he was aware of the need for caution. He had formed a rationale to deter objections to the bill: "Whatever one may think about their military necessity, the only two atomic bomb attacks in the world were in Japan and they were tragic. We have now added irony to tragedy in that the native born Americans who bore those attacks are the only survivors for whom no program or treatment has been provided."[90] Here, Dymally was referring to the striking contrast between American and Japanese *hibakusha*; for the former there was no publicly funded assistance, whereas the latter had been beneficiaries of national legislation. First introduced in 1957 and amended in 1968, these Japanese laws offered Japanese survivors a range of monetary aid in addition to free medical care and treatment for radiation illness.[91] Dymally also tried to deter objections to the bill by those who supported the US decision to use the bomb on the basis of military necessity argument. Regardless of what one thinks of the US decision to use the bomb, he argued, the lack of comparable support for "our survivors" was disturbingly obvious for "all men and women of good will."[92] Interestingly, in a press release about the hearing, Dymally did not feature universal humanitarianism; instead, he used language more unambiguously critical of the uniquely American problem of racial injustice: "As a nation we have all but eliminated our discrimination against Asians. We should now take this last step to wipe away one of the last remaining scars of World

War II" in America.[93] To offer medical assistance to "forgotten" survivors was to do away with racism against Asians in America. The assistance should not be taken as an all-out, humanitarian critique of the US decision to drop the bomb. Although different in emphasis, both his statement at the hearing and his critique of racism in the press served to deflect objections based on the military necessity argument, and altogether avoided raising moral questions about the bomb's use. Along the way, both of Dymally's statements downplayed US survivors' cross-nationality. Although the reported percentage of US-born persons among CABS members at this point was 30–40 percent, Dymally singularly highlighted this group as if its members constituted the only profile of US survivors.[94] This accentuation of national belonging among racial minorities, not Hiroshima and Nagasaki as cities of immigrants, stood as a more effective strategy.

And yet, SB-15 was not only for US-born citizens but also for Japanese-born citizens who had come to America after 1945 and become naturalized citizens or permanent residents. Clearly, this was because of US *hibakusha*'s insistence on the layered citizenship that shaped their history as immigrants, a citizenship taking on more import in Asian America. In US survivors' testimonies, this insistence on cross-nationality found a range of expressions. During the May 1974 hearing, seven survivors offered testimonies before the subcommittee. Four of them were born in America, whereas the remaining three were Japanese-born – including at least one permanent resident.[95] On the one hand, this accurately reflected US survivors' diverse backgrounds. On the other, the mix of citizens and noncitizens caused some tension. Some were at pains to explain how they were not blaming American doctors as generally incapable; they simply were unfamiliar with patients with radiation illness, so they would be able to better assist *hibakusha* by collaborating with Japanese doctors at the proposed UCLA clinic. No witnesses wanted to be seen as overtly critical of US medical professionals. Others stressed the helplessness of survivors by highlighting their femininity. CABS president Kuramoto, for instance, insisted: "Most of the victims are women. They are not aggressive and insistent, but reserved and hesitant. They speak only Japanese and they are unable to explain and express their own feelings or desires to the public or to their own medical doctor. They come from low- to middle-income classes so they cannot get large contributions for their cause."[96] These traditional images of women as the weaker sex needing more help than men were invoked as a way to cover the bomb's cross-nationality. Although some hailed from Japan (as indicated by their monolingualism), these women in Kuramoto's statement were the "model minority" of America. This gender dynamism was both affirmed and contradicted during the hearing. One of the three female witnesses among the seven, Shigeko Morimoto, decided not to speak for herself because she was "too nervous to speak to you [the subcommittee's members] today." Her husband George Morimoto, "a United States citizen," presented himself to speak on behalf of Shigeko, who had become "a permanent resident" in 1962 after marrying him. When George told the subcommittee that Shigeko was worried about losing her status "as a dependent on [her] husband's medical insurance plan" after her husband retired, this concern was presented as an understandable concern for female survivors in need of male protectors. Here, US *hibakusha*'s citizen-guardians came to the forefront of the fight for the bill's passage.[97]

While George's speech on Shigeko's behalf likely elicited sympathy, an entirely different expression of gendered, cross-national survivorhood also provoked a strong reaction from the hearing's attendants. When the last witness, Kazuo Tosaka, a male survivor from Gardena, California, took his turn, it became quickly obvious that he had too much to say and too little time to explain. His remembering revolved around his failure to rescue his mother:

> My mother kept screaming, and I saw ... one-third of her body was caught in between [the debris]. I grab her and I could hold my mother's hand, but I couldn't pull her free. ... I had to make a decision ... I would have to chop her arm off or do something for her. She was screaming and the flames were getting closer and closer. I had the axe in my hand ... my knees started shaking, I just couldn't do anything. In the meantime, the flames were right on the top of her and she was burning (*Mr. Tosaka's voice breaking ... getting very emotional*). Then I don't know, I fainted I guess.[98]

As if to reiterate the stenographer's note about Tosaka's voice, Dymally interrupted him soon by stating "I don't mean to cut you short, but Dr. Noguchi has to testify before he leaves, and he has to go." Although this probably was a necessary intervention for the hearing's smooth progression, Dymally's statement nonetheless struck the witness as disapproval. "Yes, sir. I am sorry that my testimony was bad," said Tosaka.[99]

The audience applauded as he stepped down, indicating that Tosaka had garnered their moral support. Nonetheless, his embarrassment was palpable. This may be because his remembering of the bomb was about his personal pains, not about heroic acts. Unlike male rescuers who made frequent appearances in US *hibakusha*'s memories in the prior decades, Tosaka failed to save his mother. In a way similar to Suyeishi's husband accepting himself having suffered in the camp, Tosaka identified himself unmistakably as a sufferer of the bomb. As much a sufferer of the nuclear holocaust as anyone else, he was not at the hearing to speak on behalf of female survivors; he was there to speak about himself. In showing this, Tosaka's testimony was a remarkable rebuttal of the image of Japanese men as emotionless, the stereotype that the bill's supporter Noguchi had confronted a few years earlier. Just as Noguchi was not a "kamikaze-pilot," Tosaka was not to be mistaken for a Japanese soldier who had fought against America. Instead, he was a citizen hurt by his own government, something confirmed by the fact that he was "not receiving any treatment" for his radiation illness. As an Asian American, too, Tosaka's decision to come forward and speak about his suffering carried a particular significance. Noguchi, a Japanese-born Shin Issei, decided not to "roll over and play dead"; neither would Tosaka, an American-born Nisei, hide behind a shield of silence all too familiar to Asian America. Tosaka was not afraid of revealing his cross-national history as an immigrant. Born in America and bombed in Japan, he told his experiences forcefully in accented English. His testimony, then, signaled an important shift in gender relationship and national belonging among US survivors, refuting both their personal remembering in the postwar years and the public image of survivors as feminine as they had been portrayed by way of the "Hiroshima Maidens" project. Tosaka's testimony revealed a simple, yet formerly downplayed, fact that men could be survivors, and that they sometimes felt wholly helpless indeed. Their American or Japanese citizenship at the time of the bombing did not change this helplessness. In this light, there was little division among *hibakusha*.

US survivors' remembering illuminated a range of gender identities, national belonging, and race consciousness throughout the hearing, bringing in more supporters for CABS along the way. Indeed, as US *hibakusha*'s efforts became more firmly based in the expanding community of supporters, the bill's contents became more capacious. By the end of 1974 when it was introduced again into the Senate's subcommittee, the bill's beneficiaries included not only Hiroshima and Nagasaki survivors, both citizens and noncitizens, but also employees of the power plants in California who were accidentally exposed to radiation. In the minds of SB-15 sponsors such as Dymally, the expansion of beneficiaries made the bill more broadly appealing. It is also possible that the bill's sponsors thought that its expansion ameliorated the tension generated by the 1974 hearing. Despite Dymally's earlier effort to define the bill as a case of humanitarianism or racial justice, survivors' devastation was so palpable in their testimonies that they came close to raising questions about the bomb's morality. In particular, the power of the bomb to override gender and national differences, shown in Tosaka's testimony, signaled its moral gravity. Such was the force of personal remembering that it did not fit neatly into the discourse serving political goals. And although these moral questions might be legitimate, they might make the bill's passage difficult. By including irradiated employees in California, the bill would be seen more clearly as a measure to aid citizens rather than as an atonement for the decision to use the bomb. The bill's scope, then, included cross-nationality by embracing citizens and noncitizens alike; simultaneously, the inclusion of power plant workers was an attempt to make the bill more straightforwardly nationalist. Thus, it was national and cross-national at once, a difficult balance to strike. Here, it should be noted that the bill's scope expanded for practical reasons, too. A discussion arose in CABS around this time about the possibility of assisting *hibakusha* across the country. An effort to push forward a similar bill in the US Congress had existed since 1972, because CABS had begun to draw members from outside California.[100] There were survivors in Washington, Oregon, and Hawai'i, Nebraska, Arizona, Colorado, and Illinois. They needed recognition as much as their more numerous counterparts in California. Inclusion of workers irradiated on the job, as well as all US persons affected by the bomb, appeared a reasonable basis for a future, more encompassing, piece of legislature.

FOH, too, began to expand its reach beyond California in the mid-1970s by building alliances with *hibakusha* outside of Asian America. Some "atomic veterans" – US Marines who had been irradiated after entering the bombed cities to clean up the debris – got in touch with FOH. Nevada's "downwinders" – people irradiated by nuclear tests in the 1950s and early 1960s – and Marshall Islanders, too, began to come together and sought an alliance with FOH. Native Americans, Hopis and Navajos specifically, who had been irradiated in uranium mines in the reservations, came to FOH around the same time. As Ayako Elliott and others recalled, CABS was receptive but cautious about expanding the definition of survivors.[101] The leadership was concerned that more claimants might make CABS's purposes unfocused, its identity diffused, the bill more difficult to pass. Thus, these outreach efforts were chiefly led by Sansei supporters of CABS, most of them members of FOH, ALC, or both, not necessarily US *hibakusha* themselves. Eventually, CABS and its supporters reached a middle ground of a sort. Neither the California state bill in 1974 nor the US Congressional bill in 1978 explicitly included uranium miners, downwinders, or atomic veterans as its beneficiaries. However, CABS and its supporters maintained the alliance with other *hibakusha* throughout the 1970s and well into the 1980s, helping to expand public support for US survivors. At the same time, CABS's concern that expanding who counted as *hibakusha* might threaten the bill's passage proved not unfounded.

Remember "Forgotten" Survivors: 1974–1978

Between 1974 and 1978, US survivors acquired unprecedentedly broad support, although the fact remained that they did not succeed in passing the legislation they pushed forward. The 1974 bill in California went through some revisions (whose purpose was to control the cost; benefits were to be paid by Medi-Cal and were applicable only to those who had exhausted their own medical insurance) and came to the State Senate's subcommittee in May 1975. The hearing for the revised bill drew a sizable crowd of supporters. The room was "packed," with those who did not find a seat "overflow[ing] into the hallway."[102] Although the bill was dismissed again because of the "present economic situation" that did not favor public spending, the strong turnout indicated the considerable distance that CABS had traveled since its formative years.[103] It is worth noting that two out of eleven subcommittee members were hostile, insisting that US survivors were the "enemies" during the Pacific War. The image of Asian Americans as alien remained tenacious. But another member stood up in response and pointed out what should have been obvious, that most survivors were American-born citizens trapped in Japan because of the war; in no sense were they "enemies."[104] The 1975 bill also garnered support from liberal Democrats, politicians of color in particular. Because Dymally was elected lieutenant governor of California in 1975, he could no longer be the bill's sponsor. Alfred H. Song, the first Asian American to serve as a state senator, and Bill Greene, Song's African American colleague and a long-time friend of Dymally, came forward to push for the bill's progress.[105] George Moscone, then a senator and soon to be the mayor of San Francisco, also supported the bill. Greene had been a freedom rider at the height of the civil rights movement in the South, and after he became a state senator in 1975, he became a champion of union rights and worker compensation.[106] Moscone, too, was a rising liberal Democrat, and an early proponent of gay rights. He was instrumental in repealing the state's anti-sodomy law in 1975, keeping the senate session open after it had reached a dramatic tie vote until the newly minted lieutenant governor – Dymally – returned on a private jet to break the tie.[107] Patsy T. Mink, a Nisei congressperson from Hawai'i, penned in 1975 a letter of support for the bill. Moreover, she urged the early introduction of a similar bill in the US Congress by stressing the difference between the support given to American and Japanese *hibakusha*. To her frustration, "the U.S. has spent a total of $81.5 million on the atomic bomb casualty commission since 1948, but for the victims . . . who live in America, no help has been offered." The congressional bill that Mink supported had been sponsored by Roybal, another "first" – the first Latino congressperson from California since 1878. Beginning in his freshman year in the congress, 1962, Roybal had been a supporter of bills for bilingual schools and community centers for immigrants, as well as health care, housing, and meal programs for low-income seniors.[108] Just as antinuclear activism generated inter- and intraracial collaborations, US *hibakusha*'s legislation brought together political leaders dedicated to building coalitions among racial minorities. US survivors might not have been the politicians' top priority, but they constituted one of the focal points at which the politics of the New Left, especially those concerning social justice, gathered force.

In this light, it is notable that the support from Japanese American politicians such as Mink, and a few years later, Norman Mineta (California) and Daniel Inouye (Hawai'i), came almost simultaneously with JACL's unambiguous support for CABS. JACL's backing of CABS at this time went well beyond extending better recognition of the organization as "American" in their organ *Pacific Citizen*'s coverage of US survivors. In fact, the support for US *hibakusha* began to carry a parallel, if not equal, significance in JACL's agenda to the Redress Movement for former camp inmates. Wayne Horiuchi, for instance, was JACL's Washington, DC, representative and one of the chief Sansei activists who worked to gain a broad consensus within the Japanese American community about the reparation.[109] When Richard Nixon again caused an uproar in Japanese America in 1976, this time as an ex-president who during a congressional committee hearing on Watergate referred to "the 1942 Evacuation of Japanese Americans as an example of illegal action which the President *can* perform in an emergency," Horiuchi immediately protested: "To say that ... other presidents committed such illegal acts implies that those acts were necessary and tolerable. The internment of the Japanese Americans was neither necessary nor tolerable, but rather reprehensible."[110] Shortly before issuing this statement as a JACL spokesperson for redress, Horiuchi attended a CABS meeting in San Francisco as a JACL liaison, reporting on the progress of the congressional bill for US survivors. Indeed, he was an apt person for this assignment; he had been lobbying Democratic congresspersons to introduce the bill for at least a year by then. He was well versed in US *hibakusha*'s needs and purposes, taking the lead in collaborating not only with CABS but also with SANE (National Committee for a Sane Nuclear Policy) to request support for the congressional bill.[111] Horiuchi's support for CABS was a key element in JACL's official endorsement of the organization. By early 1975, JACL's Northern California–Western Nevada and Pacific Southwest Councils passed a resolution to support the bills.[112] In August 1976, the thirty-first anniversary of Hiroshima and Nagasaki was jointly sponsored by CABS, JACL, and the Japanese American Religious Federation (including both Christian churches and Buddhist temples in its membership), and its meeting was held at the newly designated JACL national headquarters on San Francisco's Sutter Street.[113] By then, the consensus in Japanese America seemed to firm up: the lack of the government's recognition of US *hibakusha* indicated a lack of understanding about racial discrimination. In this framework, JACL found a way to express a more determined support for US survivors.

By the late 1970s, then, the Japanese American community was prepared to claim US survivors as belonging to them, whose civil rights as Asians in America must be defended without reservation. When CABS president Kuramoto wrote a letter to President Jimmie Carter in 1977 asking for his support for the congressional bill, and got a disappointing response in early 1978 from the Office of Japanese Affairs instead of the Department of Health, Education, and Welfare as expected, JACL took it as an offense related to that inflicted on Japanese Americans in 1942. Harry I. Takagi, JACL's representative in Washington, DC, along with Horiuchi, wrote a letter of protest, reiterating that US *hibakusha* are "loyal American citizens [who] wish to be recognized and treated as such, and not confused with citizens of a foreign country" as the referral of US survivors' request to the office handling Japanese affairs indicated.[114] The earlier coming together of different historical strands, including those of the camp and the bomb, continued to be expressed publicly and went beyond the work of Horuichi, Takagi, or any other individual. *Pacific Citizen* issues in 1975 had already noted how some of the racist slurs that had driven Japanese Americans into the camp – "You, born here or not, Japs are always Japs" and "You Jap go home" – were also directed at US survivors.[115] Three years later, *Pacific Citizen* pointed out a more immediate link between the camp and the bomb: "[Some] Nisei went to Japan with their immigrant parents before the war to avoid the internment camps."[116] Such critique of the questioning of immigrants' national loyalty, which had shaped the history of both the camp and the bomb, strongly colored JACL's activism by the late 1970s. In fact, by 1978, JACL was drafting legislation to redress the mistreatment of former inmates, just as the organization became a more outspoken supporter of US *hibakusha*. Although CABS welcomed JACL's support, the latter's increasing involvement in US survivors' cause also brought to light a tension in ties among their varied organizational histories. For some, like members of FOH and ALC, to remember intergenerationally was to enliven cross-nationality that made immigrants strong. For others, as seen in Horiuchi's letter of protest, the older politics based on an assertion of national loyalty and supported by many JACL members remained potent. These positions converged and conflicted. The ties and tensions between different expressions of citizenship, as well as the changing gender dynamism among survivors, became dominant factors in the debate over the congressional bill in 1978.

In March and June 1978, the federal bill cosponsored by Roybal and Mineta, HR-8440, made its way to hearings in Los Angeles and

Washington, DC, with the aim of establishing federal support for survivors' medical treatment.[117] This bill stipulated that US survivors first exhaust their own insurance, but the law would be applicable to those without their own coverage, too. Unlike the earlier drafts of the California bill, this federal bill did not include as beneficiaries those irradiated on the job.[118] By focusing on individuals exposed to "the radioactive fallout from such explosion [of the bombs dropped in August 1945]," however, this 1978 bill opened up a possibility not only for US civilians but also for US soldiers irradiated in Hiroshima or Nagasaki in 1945 during the cleanup, to become its beneficiaries.[119] If this made the bill more clearly about the Pacific War and its American casualties, the bill also illuminated aspects of Hiroshima and Nagasaki as cities of immigrants. American civilians residing in the cities were treated in the same way as those in the US military. US survivors also insisted that the federal bill, like its state counterpart, apply to both US citizens and permanent residents. Their insistence created a potential for disagreement between JACL activists who wanted to see a bill based on a relatively clean-cut definition of citizenship, and US *hibakusha* and their ALC and FOH supporters who insisted on acknowledging the cross-nationality of immigrants and their children. Although the scope of the bill was still more limited than the Japanese laws for *hibakusha*, in the end it reflected survivors' demands for recognition of their cross-nationality instead of others' preference to limit its beneficiaries based on a single nationality.

By early 1978, there arose a sense of excitement among US *hibakusha* that the bill might finally become a reality. Although the aforementioned tension persisted, US survivors felt as if they had come a long way since the first days of coming together in the mid-1960s. They were a much bigger organization, with many more allies. One detail that concerned Kazue Suyeishi, though, was that the March hearing in Los Angeles was set for a Friday. She knew that many working Japanese Americans would not come to an event during a workweek. A hearing marked by empty seats was the last thing Suyeishi wanted, so she went to dinners for Issei retirees hosted by the JACL in order to solicit their participation. JACL further assisted her efforts by chartering a bus, knowing that many Issei did not have a driver's license. This delighted Suyeishi who also did not drive. On the day of the hearing, the bus went back and forth between Japantown in downtown Los Angeles and the county's administration building.

This "piston" of a bus eventually filled the hearing room with an impressive audience of 300. Most of the Issei retirees in attendance were not survivors and were not fluent in English; it is likely that they did not fully understand the hearing. And yet, they were willing to be there because they felt "sympathetic" to survivors such as Suyeishi, who asked for American assistance in halting English. Just as Sachiko Matsumoto served as a bridge of communication among US *hibakusha*, Suyeishi functioned as a behind-the-scenes keeper of alliances between different generations. CABS women's invisible work on the ground remained essential for the success of more visible events.

At the same time, female survivors began to take on more public roles, to a greater extent than four years earlier. CABS and its supporting politicians selected three female survivors, Tsuyako Munekane, Judy Aya Enseki, Kuniko Jenkins, and one male survivor, Kanji Kuramoto, to take the witness stand during the March hearing. Kuramoto again highlighted the difference between the care survivors were given in Japan and America, as well as his US birth, citizenship, and loyalty to America. He also articulated the connection between the bomb and the camps by pointing out how many "Nisei had returned to Japan with their Japanese immigrant, Issei, parents immediately before the war, due to anticipated 'precautionary' measures that eventually resulted in the placement of west coast Japanese Americans in relocation camps." As much as his testimony was a message to the committee members that US survivors are American patriots, it was also a message to Asian Americans who were becoming increasingly cognizant of their cross-nationality as part of their identity. Overall, as the president of CABS, Kuramoto's testimony followed a trajectory similar to that set by JACL.

Enseki, another witness, personified cross-nationality more prominently by explaining her family story: that she had gone to Japan with her husband who repatriated to Japan after refusing to take the loyalty oath in 1943. Shortly after her brief testimony, Enseki took the witness stand again to speak on behalf of Jenkins, who could not speak for herself "due to doctor's orders." Jenkins's prepared statement, read by Enseki, marked the subtle and subversive shift in the gender dynamism and expressions of cross-nationality among US survivors. At the same time as highlighting Jenkins's unemployed status, which had enabled her to come to the hearing, the Jenkins–Enseki testimony made Jenkins's simultaneous presence and absence (due to her inability to speak because of her illness) abundantly clear, a living witness of the nuclear holocaust:

> **Ms. Enseki:** I would like to mention that she [Jenkins] was not able to travel here by air today, because the airline would not accept her with her oxygen tank, so she had to drive from San Francisco to be here, 3 days ago, and she brought her father and mother with her, and her father sat in the back seat with the oxygen tank, so she could have oxygen during the trip while she was driving. [Reading:] My name is Kuniko Jenkins, and ... I was asked to speak ... partly because I am a housewife, and have more time than some of the others in the group, and also because some of the others are afraid to identify themselves for fear of losing their jobs. Many employers would not hire survivors because they would be concerned about time they might miss from work due to illness.[120]

As *Nichi Bei Times* reported, Jenkins was "assisted to the speaker's platform [with] her portable green oxygen tank beside her."[121] Her disability was in a plain view, bespeaking nuclear war's power of destruction hauntingly (see Figure 5.2). Until recently, she had been bringing sushi, doughnuts, and *sake* to CABS meetings to lift others'

Figure 5.2 Kuniko Jenkins with her oxygen tank, about a year before the 1978 congressional hearing concerning US *hibakusha. Committee of Atomic Bomb Survivors in the United States of America Newsletter,* July 5, 1977, Tokie Akihara papers.

spirits. Now, she was debilitated by radiation, a shadow cast by the nuclear holocaust.

Jenkins' narrative was similar to the stories of Ayako Elliott, Kazue Suyeishi, and Sachiko Matsumoto, in that it acknowledged that women played important roles but only in the background – in the void created by men. Being a housewife, she had more free time and less at stake than men to speak in public. And yet, Jenkins' determination to attend the hearing by driving herself three days to get there subverted any view of women as content with expected gender roles. Clearly, she was the only person capable of driving in the family; otherwise, one of her parents would have driven her. *Her father sat in the back*, while, presumably, her mother sat in the passenger's seat *as Jenkins drove*. She was adept at the American way of life, although she had grown up in Japan and became an American citizen only after marriage. Equally striking, her history was told by Enseki, a Nisei who had gone through incarceration, expatriation, and repatriation, all of which were results of US policies subjugating American citizens of Japanese ancestry. Though Enseki belonged to a younger generation than Jenkins, their affinity and alliance was made abundantly clear by their presence on the witness stand. Together, they embodied the cross-nationality of the bomb's effects, as well as a counter-memory that contained the bomb's uniqueness and universality. Arising out of different generations, Enseki's and Jenkins's divergent histories as immigrants that shaped the bomb's history also shaped their coming together as witnesses. To be sure, American legislators might have read John Hersey's *Hiroshima* or seen the Marukis' "Hiroshima Panels." They might have also seen films such as *Them!*, *On the Beach*, or even *Hiroshima–Nagasaki* by the time of the hearing. But most of them had not seen or heard survivors in person with such immediacy. Despite her inability to speak, Jenkins did not excuse herself from the witness stand. Her trusted ally, Enseki, would speak on her behalf, not because Jenkins did not have the courage but because she counted on the intergenerational tie intrinsic to US survivors' memory, identity, and history. No matter what citizenship was theirs at the time of the bombing, they were now all US survivors who had had their share of suffering. In the face of the indiscriminate destruction, distinctions such as (Shin) Issei, Nisei, and Sansei, rooted in one's citizenship status in the past or present, did not divide. The uniqueness of survivors was inseparable from the universality of the bomb.

The Jenkins–Enseki testimony in 1978 brought the collective, cross-national, and gendered remembering of the bomb to the fore as much as the Tosaka testimony had in 1974. More than Kuramoto's account, which blended the proclamation of national loyalty with the critique of racial injustice, Jenkins and Enseki embodied the mass, indiscriminate ways of the bomb by riding over national, gender, and generational divides. Together, they showed how the bomb was understood by immigrants and their children, for whom citizenship was often determined by chance. The bomb for them was an example of how arbitrary it was when and where nations came down on persons with a great force of destruction, capable of obliterating individuality and identity. Indeed, unique individuals were universally attacked. By revealing these meanings of the bomb, Jenkins and Enseki also embodied a new gender relationship among US survivors and, by extension, Asian Americans in the era of the "model minority" myth. Women might be silent, but no longer did they remain an "absent presence." Their injured bodies would speak as lucidly about the bomb's meanings as any word of suffering spoken by men. More than twenty years after the "Hiroshima Maidens" came to America to repair their faces so that they might become marriageable, US survivors brought to light scars inside and outside, unhealed regardless of their marital status. Nearly twenty years before the Enola Gay exhibit controversy at the Smithsonian Museum denied Americans an opportunity to see the bomb's artifacts, US survivors brought their injured and irradiated bodies into Americans' consciousness. All were diminished by the bomb regardless of who they were. It was only suitable, then, that both women and men carried this message. Certainly, they were not asking for Americans' assistance; US survivors were claiming their rights as Asians in America. These were rights that they believed belonged to them, as much as the decision to use the weapons had belonged to their country.

Despite the testimony and activism, the 1978 hearing resulted in two subtly different, but equally tenacious, dismissals of US *hibakusha*'s claims. Most immediately, some subcommittee members objected to the bill's inclusion of permanent residents. This inclusion seemed to bring the bill too close to atonement for the use of the bomb.

Questions about the bomb's morality persisted throughout the 1970s, in no small part because US survivors' remembering made these questions difficult to dismiss. Implicitly, the bomb's morality remained an undercurrent of any discussion about US *hibakusha*. For those who wished to stem this undercurrent, the military necessity argument became a useful means. This argument failed to work for the camps, leading to a sound refutation of their moral and legal legitimacy.[122] In contrast, the bomb continued to be seen as a military necessity, effectively stifling questions about its morality or legality. In this light, the bills' inclusion of US citizens might have been just as problematic as the inclusion of American residents of Japanese origin (although no supporters or opponents of the legislation explicitly articulated this). Noncitizen survivors were easy to dismiss because they had been enemy nationals. In contrast, citizen *hibakusha* might raise questions about the legality and morality of the US military decisions – if only implicitly. Indeed, by the mid-1980s, the reparations extended to veterans of the Vietnam War, particularly those affected by Agent Orange, began to chip away at the automatic legitimacy of weaponry used by US armed forces for military purposes. Although the payment was made only to veterans and their family members, its impact on the military necessity argument was not negligible.[123] As of the late 1970s, however, the US government did not let go of the argument as it pertained to Hiroshima and Nagasaki survivors including both civilians and soldiers. When CABS finally received a response to their second letter to President Carter late in 1978, the reply reiterated the US government's position "not to pay claims ... arising out of the lawful conduct of military activities by US forces in wartime."[124] This position remains unchanged today.

Forceful testimonies such as Tosaka's, Jenkins's, and Enseki's made it difficult for their Asian American supporters to maintain a united front that US *hibakusha* were pursuing racial justice. Although they certainly pushed boundaries, US survivors' pursuit of racial justice was often in an uneasy tension with their cross-nationality. Racial justice was first and foremost a civil rights issue; cross-nationality, by contrast, raised questions about US survivors' standing to claim rights. Questions such as *Are you an American? Are you loyal to America?* worked to undermine the bills. Unlike the camps, which became a prime example of America's racial injustice, the bomb remained an action taken in America's national interest; it never became a racial problem of cross-national import. Here again, the military necessity argument effectively preempted further consideration of the rights of Nikkei immigrants in the United States. If the bomb was a military necessity, those affected by it must be enemy nationals. US survivors' insistence on their cross-nationality fed into this logic. This logic, which pays no attention to the history of immigration extending back to the era discussed in Chapter 1, defined US survivors' cross-nationality simply as a sign of their foreignness. This kind of misconception might have been more effectively countered if there were more consideration of both nationalism and racism evidenced by cases like Enseki's. Yet, this was 1978, a decade before Japanese Americans led the Redress Movement to success by painstakingly delineating the racism that had caused the wartime incarceration. The Civil Liberties Act of 1988, which granted US$20,000 to each of the former inmates, was applicable to both US citizens and residents. If this act had preceded CABS's effort in the late 1970s, US *hibakusha*'s cross-nationality might have been better recognized.

Ironically, the second reason for the bill's failure arose from the growing alliance among different *hibakusha*. As irradiated people from Nevada and the Marshall Islands, as well as soldiers and civilians, joined forces, the bill for US survivors began to be seen as a dangerous opening for hundreds of thousands of individuals to claim compensation from the US government. This would be a huge increase from the thousand or so initially under consideration. There was also a concern about the potential need to pay for the medical needs of the second generation *hibakusha*, something which many congresspersons felt could become unaffordable. As the bill's scope expanded, a heretofore underexplored legacy of the nuclear age across the Pacific became illuminated; this, in turn, brought up the possibility that radiation illness and injury might be never-ending. To take on a potentially open-ended responsibility for the acts of the "Good War," continuing into the Cold War, seemed to many legislators to be insupportable. For them, moral and legal questioning of the bomb's effects, underpinned by the critique of racism and nationalism against immigrants, became reinforced as a taboo throughout the 1970s and much of 1980s. The 1978 bill was tabled, and stayed in limbo in 1979, and again in 1980 when Roybal tried unsuccessfully to reintroduce it. In 1983, ALC members explored the possibility of lodging a lawsuit on behalf of US survivors based on the fact that many of them were US citizens at the time of the bombing, and also because "there have been other examples of suits for nuclear related injuries such as those brought by US atomic veterans."[125] But the lawyers knew that they were unlikely to prevail. Indeed, the possibility of the endless increase of beneficiaries stalled any discussion of legal action by the mid-1980s. For a small group such as ALC, a pushback from the government seemed overwhelming. Since then, the bill or the lawsuit has not made any comeback. Here again, US *hibakusha* found their predicament much different than that of former inmates. Although compensation for former inmates and their heirs was costly, their number could be counted with a relatively clear end in sight; after all, the camps had been closed. The case of US survivors was different. Their number could grow endlessly if the cause of their suffering – the effect of nuclear weaponry and the nation's reluctance to recognize it – itself were found liable legally or morally. The bomb remained essential to US national security, military might, and international hegemony. As such, the bomb could not be abolished.

These limitations notwithstanding, the alliance among different *hibakusha* brought ways for US survivors to continue to pursue their goals. Their coming together since the mid-1960s allowed them to discover each other, as well as define whom they wished to be collectively. Many newsletters were written, calls were made, and snacks were prepared to make and maintain ties among them. These ties also generated new relationships in families whose members included both former inmates and bomb survivors. Indeed, by coming together, US survivors helped create a new mode of remembering throughout the Asian American community. Personal stories converged with collective remembering; this invoked a composite understanding of the past and present, bringing together people of different generations and political inclinations to publicly share the counter-memory of the bomb. In this regard, it is no mistake that CABS created a new branch in Hawai'i in 1980 thanks largely to the help of antinuclear activists. Mae Oda, a non-survivor in Honolulu, became involved in the Nuclear Free and Independent Pacific Movement in the late 1970s after learning about the Marshallese *hibakusha* and their forced removal from the islands because of nuclear contamination. In 1980, when the group held a conference on Oahu, Oda met a woman from Los Angeles, an acquaintance of Suyeishi. This woman put Suyeishi in touch with a survivor in Honolulu, Izumi Hirano, who then agreed to help establish a CABS branch in Hawai'i. At that time, the Hawaiian group's aim was not legislation for federal medical assistance. Rather, the group's goal was to organize the biannual health checkups offered by Japanese physicians and paid for by the Japanese government.[126] By the early 1980s, these checkups became the most reliable form of care that US *hibakusha* received from any government. Examinations by Japanese physicians were broadly appealing because they were well-versed in radiation illness. It is unlikely that these examinations would have occurred if US survivors had not come together with others in the 1970s.

How US *hibakusha* created such a trans-Pacific system of care is one of the next chapter's subjects. As was the case with US survivors' activism examined in this chapter, their effort to create medicine cross-nationally was shaped by the antiwar, antinuclear sentiments that arose out of the Asian American civil rights movement. But US survivors' approach to issues of health, illness, and medicine also contained uniquely trans-Pacific elements, pushing CABS to collaborate with survivors and their supporters in Korea and Japan. Unlike the legislative efforts in America, the collaboration across the oceans bore more substantial fruit, as much as it raised questions about US *hibakusha*'s identity, belonging, and gender in cross-national contexts.

6 ENDLESSNESS OF RADIATION ILLNESS

US survivors' identity formation from the mid-1960s onward could not be separated from their concerns about health, illness, and medicine. No matter how much they believed they were free of radiation illness, there always remained a possibility that medical problems would strike them in the future. Having seen their families and friends succumb to not only acute radiation sickness but also delayed afflictions such as leukemia, thyroid cancer, and microcephaly, many US *hibakusha* worried that they, too, could face the beginning of the end at any time. The distance and difference between Japan and America added to their burden. After the Japanese government established hospitals that specialized in the treatment of survivors (called A-bomb Hospitals) in the late 1950s, it became evident to US survivors that they were not getting care equal to Japanese survivors. US *hibakusha* heard of free exams, medicines, and surgeries that their families in Japan received, and wondered why they had nothing similar. After Japanese survivors in the late 1960s began to receive monetary allowances from their government to help them maintain their overall health and well-being, the international gap widened. These allowances, like the treatments offered at the A-bomb Hospitals, were available to all survivors. Not only conditions clearly caused by radiation, but also illnesses not directly related but difficult to fight because of survivors' overall ill-health, received coverage.[1]

Moreover, as their testimonies for the 1974 and 1978 bills suggested, US survivors found their family physicians in America unfamiliar with radiation illness. As they came together in meetings to form CABS, US *hibakusha* learned that they were not alone in their frustration; others, too, experienced that uncomfortable moment when they told their physicians that they were survivors. In some ways, US survivors recalled stories of illness from the 1960s, 1970s, and 1980s that were similar to those they had experienced in the 1940s and 1950s. One way or another, they were treated as "others" beyond medical understanding. Women married to US military men had a particularly difficult time, because their family doctors were often assigned to them at a Veterans' Hospital. As some recalled, physicians who had experienced the war in the army seemed to have a hard time understanding patients who suggested that they were ill because of what they had experienced on the other side of the "Good War": the bomb. Their physical and psychosocial concerns as patients did not seem to carry any validity for physicians for whom the bomb was unequivocally a legitimate tool of war.[2] US *hibakusha* did not recall the racism shaping their struggle with radiation illness between the 1960s and 1980s as being as prominent as it had been in earlier decades. And yet, racial inequality continued to shape US survivors' illness, as they tried to create medical treatment programs across Asian American communities where, they hoped, they could receive more empathetic care. As they soon found, however, these communities were generally deprived of medical facilities. In this sense, race remained an important factor in US *hibakusha*'s understanding of radiation illness and, by extension, of the bomb's long-term effects in a society unwilling to recognize them.

In response to the challenges they faced in America, US survivors began to seek supporters in Japan. At first glance, US survivors' efforts to obtain access to Japanese doctors, radiation illness specialists particularly, seem straightforward. These efforts took place in tandem with US survivors' legislative activism between the mid-1960s and the early 1980s. As seen in Chapter 5, US survivors tried to obtain recognition by the US government by collectively sharing the cross-national history of the bomb. As this chapter shows, their efforts during this era were not confined to the United States. Aspiring to be cared for and treated by experienced and, they hoped, sympathetic, physicians from Hiroshima or Nagasaki, some US *hibakusha* literally began to cross national boundaries by traveling frequently to Japan and lobbying politicians, physicians, and activists there. If what we have examined in Chapter 5 was a history that took shape mostly within US borders, the history that we examine here may seem like its trans-Pacific twin.

Although this contrast certainly holds, I also emphasize how US survivors' activism across the ocean had US roots and formations. Some of the dynamisms that emerged in the Asian American community, including the articulation of both the Vietnam War and the Asia–Pacific War as race wars, remained crucial for *hibakusha*'s efforts to build trans-Pacific ties. Asian Americans were subject to increased psychosocial and physical violence during the Vietnam War, which made them think of what their immigrant parents and grandparents might have experienced in earlier times. In this context, the lack of appropriate medical care for Asians in America was a local embodiment of global conflicts, racial injustice, and socioeconomic inequality. By offering only limited health care access in Chinatown, Little Tokyo, and Manilatown (and soon, Little Saigon), many Asian Americans believed US mainstream medicine was defining the poor, people of color, immigrants, and women as expendable.

Gender continued to affect US survivors' cross-nationality as they became more outspoken as patients, caretakers, and activists all at once. These coexisting, if potentially conflicting, roles needed to be performed with care when US survivors sought medical assistance from both the Japanese and American governments. These governments defined civil and human rights quite differently; indeed, the difference could not be greater when these governments dealt with radiation illness. Some of the tension concerning citizenship, national belonging, and gender discussed in Chapter 5 reemerged as Japanese American survivors worked with Korean American survivors. As American survivors' collaboration with Japanese supporters of Korean survivors deepened, the cross-national tension became sharp enough to cause some discrepancies within CABS. Partly because of these challenges, US *hibakusha*'s identity, shaped by their collective remembering, became less publicly discernable within the United States as the end of the century neared. In the 1980s and 1990s, there were no more public hearings that featured compelling stories of the bomb woven into many histories of immigrants. No longer were there legislators and lobbyists who tried to propose bills on US survivors' behalf. This is not to say that they lost their identity or that the counter-memory of the bomb disappeared; some reached out to others who were also ill and neglected, most notably to HIV/AIDS patients. Others began to pursue better recognition of illness solely by the Japanese government, using tactics ranging from pleas for humanitarianism to assertions of equality among all survivors regardless of their citizenship and residency. On the one hand, it was undeniable that the hopeful era of the 1970s had ended. On the other, the dimmed prospect for obtaining support in America made a space for US *hibakusha* and their supporters to express their gender identities creatively. Especially after reaching a certain dead end in the United States, US survivors' gender expressions in some ways took a more liberal turn toward equality and diversity than before.

By exploring trans-Pacific ties and tensions with an eye toward the racial, national, and gender dynamisms that shaped them, this chapter continues to analyze the counter-memory of the bomb between the mid-1960s and -1980s with a specific focus on survivors' identity as shaped by their concern about radiation illness. Then, I examine their history in the rest of the century, after nongovernmental organizations on either side of the Pacific became the only willing allies of US survivors. Particularly because of its elusive nature – we still do not understand fully the effect of radiation on humans – radiation illness remained psychosocial as well as physical. As seen in Chapter 4, the illness became entwined with not only racism but also ableism in the 1940s and 1950s. Between the mid-1960s and the early-1980s, the illness additionally took on explicit political meanings, as it became redefined by the Asian American activism of the Vietnam War era and the antinuclear activism that peaked in 1980 and 1981. Intergenerational connections and collaborations, some bringing together activists from the Pacific Islands as well as the US mainland, continued to shape US survivors' history, as medical professionals, social workers, and community activists came together to deliver equitable health care. Their demand that priority be given to community care over scientific research shaped an alternative way of practicing medicine. Women (and some men, too) played critical roles in defining and delivering care and treatment most needed by US *hibakusha*, continuing to place their counter-memory of the bomb at odds with the medical discourse about radiation illness generated by research institutions largely staffed by men. As I argue, all of this suggests that, similar to their efforts discussed in Chapter 5, US survivors' counter-memory of the bomb had the potential for being integrated into the national memory of the war in the United States. And yet, their remembering was marginalized significantly because of the influence of medical authorities. By the end of the century, US medical professionals helped push US survivors out of US history, making it a past that counts only as a foreign history.

Noteworthy in this regard is that questions about the responsibility for radiation illness – who is responsible for defining, treating, and caring for it – were raised increasingly by and for survivors of different nationalities in America, Japan, and Korea throughout the decades covered by this chapter. The various governments' responses to these questions shifted considerably and influenced US survivors' identity, memory, and history. For instance, the ABCC, the research institution in Japan originally founded by America, conducted preliminary research on the health conditions of US *hibakusha* in the early 1970s. Yet the ABCC's interest and investment in offering medical treatment for US survivors receded quickly. Initially, in the early 1970s, a handful of individual scientists at the Oak Ridge National Laboratory (Oak Ridge), one of the key sites of nuclear weaponry development in the Manhattan Project, as well as at the US Atomic Energy Commission (AEC), supported the idea of federally funded medical assistance for US survivors. However, their voices proved temporary and became mostly inaudible within a few years. The scientists' support for treating US *hibakusha* was an expression of their personal opinions, not a change in the nontreatment policy established in the 1940s by the ABCC. Few scientists denied that US survivors were ill or prone to be, a fact confirmed by a persistent interest in their radiation illness among American and Japanese researchers. Indeed, medical science's fascination with radiation illness was one of the most abiding constants throughout the decades discussed here, continuing to this day. Still, no clear consensus emerged in this era in response to the questions about the responsibility for radiation illness. This lack of consensus, shaped by medical and scientific expertise backed by US national institutions, powerfully denied the entrance of the counter-memory of the bomb into the national memory of the war.

In this light, it is striking that US *hibakusha* successfully established a system of biannual medical checkups in America, conducted by Hiroshima and Nagasaki physicians, in 1977. The checkup program began to receive funding from the Japanese government in 1983, opening a door for the universality of radiation illness to become recognized by at least one country. Simultaneously, though, it is unmistakable that day-to-day care and treatment were largely left to survivors and their supporters who belonged to nongovernmental organizations in local communities. Caretakers, frequently female survivors, showed remarkable resilience by continuing to build alliances and assisting fellow *hibakusha* in need. Simultaneously, though, what they could accomplish was limited by the lack of a full-fledged recognition of US survivors by any government. In the 1960s and 1970s, the lack of access to facilities such as A-bomb Hospitals was the foremost cause of frustration among US survivors. In the 1980s and 1990s, the lack of monetary allowances for non-Japanese survivors became a particular concern for them. The Japanese government had less regard for American survivors than for Korean survivors, furthering the former's perception that discrimination continued to be based on nationality, residency, and belonging. Many Japanese supporters of Korean survivors supported American survivors, too, but Japanese enthusiasm seemed to be more focused on Korean casualties of Japanese colonialism. Compared to Korean survivors, their American counterparts seemed to Japanese supporters to be less clearly defined as victims. Thus, both the limit and the possibility of their cross-nationality became illuminated as US *hibakusha*'s remembering reached out to one of the most unsettled aspects of their identity – radiation illness – toward the end of the century.

The Making of Trans-Pacific Medical Research

Ignorance was not bliss for US survivors by the 1960s. In earlier decades, radiation effects remained largely unknown or unspoken, which might have helped some who wanted to "forget" about the bomb.[3] But gradually, the lack of knowledge became an affliction of its own. When in pain, not knowing a diagnosis provoked *hibakusha*'s anxiety and distrust of physicians. The absence of doctors familiar with radiation illness brought back memories of symptoms such as nausea, diarrhea, hair loss, fatigue, and bloody stools that US survivors experienced at ground zero. Surely, they were irradiated; what would be the consequences now? Although Kazuko Aoki was more fortunate than others in this regard – as seen in Chapter 3, her father worked as a translator for the US occupation forces, and so was able to obtain some military-issued medicines for her – she still experienced disappointing episodes with her US doctors. When Aoki came to Hawai'i in 1959, she was chronically ill with dizziness, fatigue, and fainting spells. Her symptoms were so severe that she was bedbound for several hours a day. Her daughter was born in 1961 with a heart problem, which kept the baby in a hospital for four years. Shortly afterward, her brother-in-law, another US survivor, died of cancer at age forty, fueling Aoki's worry about her and her daughter's health. She was particularly disheartened when her family physician casually dismissed her concern that her conditions might be related to radiation. The doctor's response was: "Oh, you think that the bomb is the reason? It's a long time ago!" The conversation did not go any further, leaving Aoki frustrated: "Well, for the doctor, it has been fifteen years [since 1945] and it may be a long time ... but because of what happened 'a long time ago' I soon developed a tumor in my thyroid." It was not her doctor in Hawai'i who discovered her cancer. Instead, a Hiroshima doctor happened to find it during her stay in Japan. She recalled: "A medical checkup in Hiroshima carefully scrutinizes conditions related to radiation ... it was such a small tumor that it was difficult to spot. But the doctor said yes, there is a tumor." This Hiroshima physician wrote a letter to alert her Hawaiian doctor of the condition, and a swift surgery fortunately saved her voice and likely her life. Now, Aoki had to laugh: "So I went to see my doctor here [in Hawai'i], to tell him that a tumor is here ... yes, here, feel a bump? ... The doctor touched it and went 'Um? Ah, Oh!'"[4]

By reiterating in her 2013 oral history how funny this physician looked, Aoki turned more than a half-century-old episode into a larger question yet to be answered: Why can't doctors treat us better? Another question implicit in Aoki's remembering is why no country has trained medical professionals to truly care for them. To be sure, Japanese doctors seemed better qualified than their American counterparts to see *hibakusha* as patients. But these physicians in Japan were far away and not easily available for day-to-day sickness. For Sue Carpenter, these concerns were entangled with the unresolved questions undercutting the medical legislation in the 1970s: the bomb's morality and the national loyalty of survivors. Carpenter, a Nagasaki *hibakusha* who married a US Navy officer in 1966 and came to America shortly thereafter, has endured cataracts, miscarriages, and vertigo, in addition to head and leg injuries that she suffered right after the bomb. Her illnesses were endless, due to both delayed conditions and also immediate injuries sustained right after the bombing. Glass pieces continued to come out of her leg over the years, forcing her to walk with a limp; the head injury remained unhealed (there was an undetected bone fracture), causing a life-threatening inflammation. When she finally asked her physician at a Veterans' Hospital if these conditions were related to the bomb, "his attitude changed drastically." He told the symptom-laden Carpenter that "there are atomic bomb hospitals in Japan, so please go there." After this incident, the doctor refused to set up appointments for examinations.

Having supported her for many years, sometimes feeling "on the edge," Carpenter's husband Lonnie conveyed his bitterness about doctors both in America and Japan that Sue had seen in the mid-1980s:

> Navy doctors can't say it is not a problem, but they can't explain why it is a problem. So you see the government thinking that if you begin to say that [it is a problem], all of these people [here] are a part of what happened in 1945. Now it's been forty years, and doctors can't still figure out what her problem is. But her problems are real. I mean, they can't figure out why. In Japan, they keep her in a hospital for two weeks, [run] a lot exams, and if they can't find out why, then it kind of excuses. Make it go away, and wait until we go away.[5]

The striking disparity between the Carpenters' and physicians' perceptions of radiation illness seemed to originate from medical professionals' reluctance to see the bomb as a source of illness, to see survivors as patients. If "what happened in 1945" was legitimate, in the logic of these doctors, radiation illness could not be real, nor could survivors' claims be trustworthy. Even if they were, the fact that they were Nikkei made it seem dubious that they were worthy of medical attention. They were encouraged to go to Japan regardless of their US citizenship, a judgment that echoed the view of Asian Americans as "perpetual foreigners." Japanese physicians did not strike the Carpenters as particularly understanding, either. Lacking any medical diagnosis, her symptoms lacked legitimacy; this, in turn, "excuse[d]" physicians from the responsibility to treat.

The oral histories with Aoki and the Carpenters were conducted in 2013 and 2005, respectively, but their frustration was still fresh many years after the period discussed in this chapter. Indeed, as I argue, US *hibakusha*'s history from the 1960s to the 1980s was shaped by their efforts to close the gap between doctors' and patients' understanding of radiation illness, by speaking out about their experiences and by building alliances across the Pacific. They resisted the perception that radiation illness did not exist and, in so doing, they continued to insist on their identity as survivors. For US survivors, the challenge was twofold; one, long-term radiation illness was still being studied at the ABCC, and except for conditions such as leukemia, thyroid diseases, and cataracts, whose rate of occurrence increased rapidly after 1945, the illness's relation to irradiation was not fully established. Nonetheless, US survivors' experiences strongly indicated that radiation illness existed beyond these diagnoses. Second, US survivors continually grappled with what they perceived to be US physicians' insufficient attention to radiation-related conditions. Not only yet-to-be established categories such as cancers, heart conditions, and liver diseases, but also more established categories such as thyroid diseases, easily escaped medical attention. This oversight struck US survivors as particularly problematic: many were aware that, since the late 1950s, Japanese *hibakusha* had been receiving comprehensive care for conditions including those that might not be directly related to radiation, including respiratory diseases, motor disorders, and psychiatric illnesses. In comparison, the definition of radiation illness was extremely narrow in the United States.[6]

In response to these challenges, two groups stepped up to support US survivors in the 1970s: Asian American communities and medical professionals on both shores of the Pacific. At first, these groups worked in loose collaboration, with a hope to not only establish access to Hiroshima and Nagasaki physicians but also further the medical legislation in the United States. The early sign of a collaboration came in 1971, when Tomoe Okai, acting on behalf of CABS, announced the Hiroshima Peace Friendship Center's plan to send Hiroshima physicians to examine US *hibakusha*. Established in 1965 by Barbara Reynolds, a US antinuclear activist, for the mission of peace education, the center's purpose at this time was to have Japanese doctors offer American physicians "first-hand information on the sufferers' conditions." As Okai told Nikkei newspapers, "doctors in Los Angeles dismiss atomic radiation complaints such as anemia and fatigue as mere neurosis," highlighting the need for more thorough diagnosis, treatment, and care in the United States.[7] In the summer of 1971, the plan drew in more collaborators, changing the focus of the doctors' visits from the "education" of American physicians to the "study" of US survivors. The ABCC in Hiroshima agreed to supply physicians to "conduct exams" in California. The Hiroshima City Council, as well as Mayor of Hiroshima Yamada Setsuo, signed on to assist. In response, Hiroshima Kenjinkai in Los Angeles, County Coroner Thomas Noguchi, and Mayor Samuel Yorty agreed to help prepare the US setting for the examinations.[8]

By mid-1972, Maki Hiroshi, deputy chief of the Hiroshima ABCC, was selected as the lead scientist to conduct the examinations in Los Angeles. The Los Angeles County–University of Southern California (USC) Hospital promised to offer a space for the exam. Maki would be joined by a US scientist who had studied radiation illness in Japan, and by "three Japanese American physicians," in evaluating forty-three US survivors.[9] This "examination" did not include any treatment. From a legal standpoint, a Japanese physician without an American license was not allowed to practice medicine in the United States. Even so, the medical visit was billed in a range of different, potentially misleading, ways: Japanese experts will "test," "examine," "evaluate," "interview," "advise," "assist," "consult," "comfort," or "treat" US survivors, as it was reported in Japanese American newspapers.[10] The examination was projected to take place at "an Atomic Bomb Survivors' Clinic . . . set up in" the USC hospital, suggesting something akin to Japanese A-bomb Hospitals that *did* offer treatment. Evidently, no treatment took place in Los Angeles, but it appears that "preliminary tests," consisting of a fifteen-minute interview and a range of medical examinations including X-ray, blood work, and urine analysis, were conducted for the purpose of comparing this data to that of the Hiroshima ABCC to determine if further tests and treatment might be necessary.[11] Thirteen out of forty-three US survivors were found to require immediate medical attention, and they were hastily called back to the USC hospital for reexaminations.[12] At the completion of these preliminary tests, which were given media coverage in both America and Japan, a member of the Japanese Diet "promised the hibakusha [that] he would urge Premier Tanaka to discuss their plight with President Nixon" when they were to meet in a summit scheduled later in the year.[13] These promises, which combined the language of research, treatment, and care, as well as attention to physical and psychosocial aspects of radiation illness, encouraged US *hibakusha* to come together. CABS had only recently been established, and it could use this examination as an occasion to attract members. At the same time, the ambiguity about what specific benefits might be offered to US survivors planted the seed for their future discontent with medical professionals and government officials on both sides of the Pacific.

In the following few years, additional medical examinations were conducted on US survivors with promises of future treatment offered by the US government through the ABCC. In March 1974,

Noguchi helped CABS conduct a medical survey with *hibakusha* in the San Francisco and Sacramento areas.[14] This was both to supplement the earlier examinations in Los Angeles and to assist the passage of the medical legislation that was, as discussed in Chapter 5, then in the making. These additional examinations were conducted in the two cities' public health buildings, creating an impression that the US government was somehow backing this endeavor (which it was not). By August, though, a plan firmed up for George Kerr, a physicist at Oak Ridge, to visit the Hiroshima ABCC with the approval of the US AEC. His mission was to bring some 160 medical histories of US survivors collected by the ABCC and CABS at that point for "analysis in cooperation with specialists of the US atom bomb casualty commission in Hiroshima." Kerr found that about half of US survivors' records were already registered with the ABCC, while the remaining half was missing. This both corroborated the authenticity of US *hibakusha* – that they had indeed been in Hiroshima in 1945 – and indicated the need to collect more data from yet-to-be registered survivors.[15] Quickly, a plan developed for a researcher from the Hiroshima ABCC, Yamada Hiroaki, to be dispatched to Oak Ridge to survey the health conditions of US survivors more thoroughly. Fluent in both English and Japanese, Yamada was scheduled to visit California and a few other states for about a year beginning in October 1974. He was specialized in epidemiology and medical statistics, and his responsibility included reporting his findings to Oak Ridge to determine each *hibakusha*'s radiation exposure dose. Both CABS and JACL deemed all of these research programs helpful for securing public support for the medical legislation.[16] *Hibakusha* in California, said a JACL official, could "assist in the survey" by participating in the study designed to determine if they needed any medical aid.[17] Here, medical research and treatment remained closely intertwined; finally, it seemed, US survivors should feel no need to hide in order to heal.

While the involvement of the ABCC, AEC, and Oak Ridge in CABS's efforts offered hope that US survivors would become formally recognized, some of the statements made by US officials suggested that radiation illness might be considered broadly in medical and social contexts. William Doub, an AEC commissioner, explained the agency's involvement in the research in highly sympathetic terms: "I felt we had a humanitarian responsibility to ... survivors" in America, especially given how "research has shown that survivors with high radiation doses are 20 times more likely to develop leukemia and other forms of cancer" than non-survivors. If properly examined by specialists, Doub contended, US *hibakusha* would be better informed about whether they needed to "get cancer checkups" regularly and, as a result, be "reassure[d]." It is "not only the actual radiation dosage we are concerned with . . . but the mental torture that some of them might have suffered thinking that they were exposed to radioactivity," he added.[18] Sidney Marks of the AEC's biomedical and environmental research division also spoke to psychosocial aspects of illness by discussing a "sort of stigma attached [to survivors] . . . that their children might be looked down upon." All indications were that US medical scientists were beginning to listen to US patients' understanding of radiation illness, sometimes by framing it in social terms, other times by calling for a humanitarian response.[19] The remaining question, though, was if these understandings would translate into treatment programs. There was a subtle, yet important, gap between the medical scientists' statements and the sentiments expressed by survivors such as Kazuko Aoki and Sue Carpenter. These survivors already suffered illness, which they believed was caused by irradiation. For them to "be reassured," they needed more than information about radiation dosages. Their doctors must be supplied with resources to offer tests, treatment, and care imme-diately. Moreover, their doctors needed to be better educated about radiation illness, so that they could identify symptoms more promptly and assess what tests and treatment may be offered. The core of the problem was that illness did not wait until studies at the ABCC confirmed a causal relationship. As the experiences of Aoki and many others show, US survivors might pass away before science caught up.

Notwithstanding the uncertainty, US survivors mobilized their ties with Japan as the critical foundation for the development of the preliminary measures. For instance, the initiator of Japan–US collabor-ation, the Hiroshima Peace Friendship Center, came out in support of US *hibakusha* because of Ayako Elliott's affiliation with the institution. A few years before coming to America in 1968, she volunteered for the center's program that assisted Korean survivors in Hiroshima. Most Korean survivors in Japan were trapped in ghetto neighborhoods, struggling to find jobs in a depressed postwar economy. They were left out of national health insurance coverage; they also often lacked extended families to rely on in case of illness. Despite her family's objection to her assistance of those who were "looked down upon,"

Elliott was inspired by Reynolds' work to raise funds for Korean survivors. When she moved to the United States and became a CABS member, it seemed only natural to keep in touch with the center. After all, US survivors were yet another group of neglected *hibakusha*.[20] Others from CABS, too, made use of their ties with Japan. Tomoe Okai had been meeting with the mayor of Hiroshima since 1967, four years before the city announced its support for the study of radiation illness among US survivors.[21] Kazue Suyeishi by the mid-1970s had met with a handful of physicians, the mayors of Hiroshima and Nagasaki, sympathetic members of Japan's National Diet, and eventually, the Ministry of Health and Welfare (MHW).[22] In making contact with political and medical leaders, both Okai and Suyeishi relied on their personal acquaintances, including their family physicians and friends who had friends who worked for the government. Junji Sarashina, a member of Los Angeles CABS, had a sister, Nisei like himself, who had worked at the ABCC in Hiroshima after the war. At the commission, she had been a colleague of Yamada Hiroaki, who led the medical examination that started in California in 1974. At that time, Sarashina recalled, "Mr. Yamada came here and came to my house. And you know, we took him up. And [he said] please come to our meeting, to come to talk to us. So I said okay, for my sister's sake I went along."[23] In his remembering, it was his sister's friend from Japan who prompted Sarashina to meet other *hibakusha* in America. At every turn, their trans-Pacific ties were crucial in making the first series of medical examinations. The "strength of weak ties" seemed to be back in force.

US survivors' participation in the exams was further amplified by the assistance that they received from the Nikkei community. From its beginning in 1972, the ABCC's preliminary work was facilitated by a few Japanese American physicians in addition to Thomas Noguchi, who served as a chief organizer of the US settings. Although we do not know these physicians' identities, we do know a handful of medical professionals and social workers who volunteered for the biannual health checkups beginning in 1977. As we will see, the ABCC-sponsored exams in 1972–1974 morphed into this larger, Japanese government-sponsored program in 1977, one that continues to this day. Many Japanese American medical professionals who joined the program between the late 1970s and early 1980s had built their careers in the Asian American community in the 1960s and early 1970s, when the community was going through significant sociopolitical changes discussed in Chapter 5.

Their commitment to assisting CABS in the 1980s and 1990s, then, was of a piece with that of Japanese Americans who practiced medicine during the earlier era of transformation. For Fred Yutaka Sakurai, one of the Nikkei physicians who conducted the medical exams in Torrance, California, the relationship with US *hibakusha* began shortly after he was discharged from the US Army in 1963 and started his appointment as a practitioner at the City View Hospital. About 90 percent of the patients there were Japanese speaking. A Japan-born American citizen who came to the United States after the Korean War, in 1953, he held both American and Japanese medical licenses and was fluent in both languages. In the US Army, he served as a surgeon during the time when "the Vietnam War and the Cuban Missile Crisis ... were making the demand for physicians urgent." Meanwhile, Sakurai's older brother in Japan, a survivor, suffered from radiation illness and endured multiple surgeries for cancer. When the request came to the City View Hospital that it serve as the examination site for US survivors, it struck Sakurai as an incredible opportunity. Now he could care for someone "instead of my brother" who was too far away to benefit from his younger brother's medical skills.[24] John Umekubo, another participating Japanese American physician, did not have any family connection to the bomb. He was a San Francisco native and a 1977 graduate of St. Louis University, Missouri. He took an internship at St. Mary's Hospital in San Francisco after his degree, soon to be the second site of the exams. Upon completing the internship, Umekubo began his practice as a primary care physician in Japantown. By the time the medical exams came to St. Mary's, he had returned to the hospital as an internist.[25] For Umekubo, then, helping US *hibakusha* came naturally as part of a career trajectory that revolved around Japanese America, still not rare for Asian American professionals whose work often stayed within ethnic enclaves. They did not have many role models who built successful careers outside Asian America; meanwhile, the need for professionals within the community was urgent, prompting many in Umekubo's position to return to respond to its need.[26]

While Umekubo's engagement with US survivors indicates how firmly they were embedded in the Nikkei community, Sakurai's relationship with them suggests that US survivors were part of communal remembering not only by FOH, ALC, and JACL, but also by medical professionals who crossed national boundaries after the war. US-born Umekubo and Sakurai, Shin Issei, belonged to different generations, but they both became dedicated supporters of US survivors for decades to come. In these regards, Asian American doctors had the potential to differ considerably from the ABCC, AEC, and Oak Ridge-affiliated scientists who grappled with the tension among medical research, treatment, and care. Unlike research scientists at the government's institutions, physicians such as Umekubo and Sakurai were community practitioners focused on patient care. In Umekubo's case, his commitment to the underserved community became organically integrated into his career. As for Sakurai, his bilingual ability and bicultural fluency made him a suitable person to conduct the examinations. These cross-national skills were not necessarily rare in Asian America, but those who possessed them were severely underrepresented in the medical profession during the 1960s and 1970s. The lack of support for students of color in US medical schools, as well as the dearth of awareness that cultural skills are important components of medical practice, contributed to the underrepresentation.[27] When Asian American physicians returned to their community, then, they faced a range of problems rooted in social inequality, and they were equipped to see the lack of health care for US *hibakusha* as one of these problems that required a change from the ground up.

US survivors' activism related to issues of health, illness, and medicine, until the mid-1970s, was filled with uncertainty. The difficulty of proving radiation illness, as well as the multifaceted – physical and psychosocial – nature of the illness, made it a moving target. It was unclear if any examinations conducted in this era would bring much-needed treatment. Neither was it clear if treatment was defined as a matter of civil rights, as most of the supporters of medical legislation under consideration claimed, or as a matter of human rights, as Doub's comment about "humanitarian responsibility" and Dymally's statement about humanitarianism (Chapter 5) suggested. Gradually, though, community medicine began to fill the gap. While the medicine endorsed by the national institutions waited for scientific proof of illness, Asian American community medicine took off with US *hibakusha*'s many concerns as patients as its priority.

The Rise of Asian American Community Care

Community medicine's ability to respond to US *hibakusha*'s needs had its origin in the understanding of health disparity as an emblematic symptom of structural racism. Eventually, this critical view worked as a conceptual bridge between the medical examinations conducted by government-employed scientists in 1972–1974 and a trans-Pacific medicine based on community needs that began in 1977. Here, a brief look into the history of Asian American critiques of health disparity is informative. The difference between the research conducted by the national institutions and the practice organized by local physicians was not simply a result of a division between the research and clinical arms of medicine. Rather, it was a disagreement over where to allocate resources – whether to establish medically and statistically significant causal relationships or to attend to health disparities that had social roots outside the science laboratory.

The broader Asian American community of the early 1970s was determined to shift the balance toward community care. *Getting Together*, a Chinese American newspaper issued by the civil rights group I Wor Kuen (IWK) in New York City, published an article in 1971 with the provocative headline "Stop Killing Us!" As the article claimed, "our health problems are closely related to the social oppressions surrounding us." Because of overcrowded, unsanitary living conditions and the lack of affordable therapeutic and preventive care, "common diseases in ghettos like TB, anemia, lead poisoning, . . . venereal diseases" and "asthma, pneumonia, allergies" are difficult to stem. Under the banners of "health care is a right, not a privilege" and "medicine must serve the people," IWK in 1970 established a free health clinic on Henry Street in Chinatown, staffed by bilingual Chinese American doctors and offering free medical advice, prescriptions, and exams such as pap smears, VD, and TB tests. The group also lobbied hard in 1971 and 1972 for the neighborhood's Gouverneur Hospital to "hire more Chinese-speaking workers." The IWK members formed an ad-hoc committee with "students, working people, and elderly residents of Chinatown," and information about the committee was issued both in English and Chinese. The IWK's effort to establish bilingual medicine, underpinned by intergenerational collaboration, assisted older and younger immigrants alike by aligning medicine closely with the needs of the community. Reiterating the value of the endeavor, *Getting Together* proudly published a thank you letter, originally written in Chinese and translated into English, by a recent immigrant from Hong Kong who was able to treat her neurosis free of cost.[28]

Similarly, community-based health care initiatives sprang up across the West Coast, often with an explicit linkage to a critique of America's wars against Asia. In June 1972, about 200 health workers in the Bay Area were joined by Asian Americans concerned about the lack of health care in their communities in a demonstration organized in response to the American Medical Association's conference in San Francisco. In the protesters' view, the "AMA ... works in conjunction with imperialist forces in this country, such as drug companies," whose products do not reach Asian America. Instead of investing in linguistically and culturally fluent medicine, the AMA encouraged "the development of research to further the biological and chemical warfare against our Asian brothers and sisters in Vietnam."[29] This statement mirrored the Asian Americans' increasing propensity to link cases of health disparity and state violence in Asia and Asian America. In August, an antiwar group called the Bay Area Asian Coalition Against the War held a rally to commemorate the twenty-seventh anniversary of the Hiroshima and Nagasaki atomic bombings at the Presidio Army Base in San Francisco, "because a biological and chemical warfare research center – the 'Western Medical Institute of Research' – is currently being constructed there" for winning the Vietnam War.[30] Here again, communal remembering shaped a markedly interethnic Asian American activism, bringing together the Pacific War and the Vietnam War around the issues of the misuse of science against Asians.

In some activists' view, health disparity was so severe in the Asian American community that it could be used as a means for men to defer military service in protest of the Vietnam War. One draft-counseling agency stated if men had "medical conditions" common among Asian Americans, these conditions "may get [the men] out of the army" on a medical deferment.[31] There were incidents that made the use of health disparity as a means of draft deferment the best option. In August 1970, in Homer, Georgia, two Japanese students were attacked by two veterans, shouting "We just got back from fighting you communists in Vietnam." Instead of being taken to a hospital to have their injuries treated, the victims spent a night in jail.[32] The number of Asian American soldiers multiplied who reported being referred to as "gook," "Chink," or "Jap" in the army or being used as educational materials in training sessions to teach GIs what the enemy looked like. Women, too, were dehumanized. "In Marine Corps boot-camp," one Asian American soldier recalled, "every instructor would tell a joke before he began class.

It would always be a dirty joke usually having to do with prostitutes they had seen in Japan or in other parts of Asia ... [The view] of the Asian women being a doll, a useful toy or something to play with usually came out in these jokes, and how they were not quite as human as white women."[33] These incidents likely prompted some Asian American men to consider using an existing health problem intentionally in order to be exempt from the military service. For them, the military sent too many signals that it was not safe for Asian Americans. In their community's understanding of the military, racism, and illness as a continuum, there was little room to endorse the idea that scientific research supporting the war must come before medical treatment benefitting the community.

This blend of community engagement, critique of racial injustice, and antiwar sentiment shaped the career of Geri Handa, one of the FOH founders.[34] Trained as a social worker at UCLA in the early 1970s, Handa was one of the earliest generations of Asian Americans to form a career inspired by the Asian American civil rights movement. Long before FOH formally came into existence in 1982, Handa's work as a community organizer had been underway. Even before attending college, she already had been working with a group called Asians for Community Action, created by students of the Asian American Studies Program at San Jose State University. A product of the Asian American movement that demanded that universities create academic programs relevant to their culture heritage, these students were particularly concerned about the absence of senior services. Soon after Handa left for school in Los Angeles, their group successfully established Yu-Ai Kai, the first Japanese American senior center in San Jose. Once at UCLA, Handa found herself surrounded by other like-minded students. As she recalled, the School of Social Welfare she had attended "recruited actually more ethnic students, and so the ethnic students were in the majority and the white students were in the minority." In this environment emblematic of ethnic studies programs in the early 1970s, her interests in senior services deepened. Among other things, Handa created an ethnic meal service program at senior centers in San Jose, including one that catered to the first generation Chinese, Filipino, Korean, and Japanese immigrants.

At first, Handa was nervous, "because [she] thought [that] a lot of these people probably remember the war and their common enemy was Japan.'" As Sansei, she was not sure if she would be accepted or if the seniors would interact with each other. Then, a remarkable incident happened:

And one time when we were meeting, oh, they were arguing . . . because of all the feelings they had because of the war. One senior citizen spoke up and he said – and he was Filipino – he says ". . . in the past . . . we might have been enemies. But we are here in America, and we have to learn to work together because we have something in common: we are all seniors here in America, and there are certain things that we face . . . sometimes we do not get the services we need, and we all must work together to, to find some common goal." And after that, everybody . . . understood that.[35]

Although the war under discussion here is the Asia–Pacific War, this episode resonated profoundly with Asian Americans' broader effort to transcend differences in nationality, race, gender, and generation in the face of the Vietnam War. Without the effort, there would be no push-back against the discrimination against Asians in America.

In the Asian America that nurtured Handa, the lack of health care attentive to cultural diversity was critically gendered.[36] Traditionally, caretaking was considered women's responsibility in Asian America; among US *hibakusha*, too, stories of care delivered by women in Hiroshima and Nagasaki remained part of their collective identity. In the 1970s and 1980s, Asian American women, both survivors and non-survivors, continued to play caretaking roles, but in a growing alliance with community medicine conscious of gender inequality. For instance, the Resthaven Psychiatric Hospital and Community Mental Health Center, the oldest nonprofit mental hospital near Chinatown in Los Angeles, became a leader in the mid-1970s in offering culturally and linguistically attuned mental health care services to Asian Americans after repeated demands by community members. Their staff members, including psychiatrists, psychologists, and social workers, offered services in up to eight Asian languages. This was particularly helpful for monolingual patients, many older but some younger because of the influx of Asian immigrants after the 1965 immigration reform. Moreover, the facility specialized in the care of female patients until 1962, offering treatment for conditions such as insomnia, anxiety, and depression more common among women. After the center opened its doors to male patients, these experiences in gender-conscious medical care continued to benefit immigrant communities.[37]

It is not surprising, then, that Resthaven representatives met with CABS members including Kazue Suyeishi early in 1971 and offered to provide "psychiatric support" and opportunities to meet with "group leaders to conduct monthly group meetings ... to coordinate this joint effort." The facility promised to accept Medicare and Medi-Cal, and the fees for the initial appointment and treatment would be "on a 'sliding scale' and according to what the family can afford."[38] This kind of accommodation based on awareness of social inequality, as well as an attention to gendered aspects of illness in Asian America, was precisely what US survivors needed. As seen in Chapter 4, some US *hibakusha* who were particularly marginalized – women and Korean Americans – recognized discrimination against racially minoritized immigrants and came to value interracial alliances. As we will see, a similar pattern became salient as some US survivors by the end of the century expressed empathy for sexual minorities. These incidents did not happen in a vacuum; in fact, the Asian American community in the 1970s and 1980s deemed health disparity shaped by sexism as one of the community's major problems.

Gidra, the Asian American newspaper, offers a glimpse into the community's increasing awareness of the many forms of women's marginalization and the urgent need to eradicate it in health care. In its issue on women's liberation in 1971, an article, "The Warbride" by Carolyn Saka, featured "Asian women ... [who are] married to [American] servicemen," who endured a triple rejection, from their families back home, the ethnic community in America, and "unsympathetic White society." Additionally, a high rate of divorce struck these "most disadvantaged groups of women." These Asian divorcees often became dependent on meager public assistance or "limited employment as barmaids, waitresses, or [at] low-salaried clubs" because of language barriers, child care responsibility, and ill-health due to reasons ranging from psychological breakdown to sexually transmitted disease. This contributed to a further stigmatization of the women in the Asian American community where many held punitive views of welfare recipients and women in the service industry. Saka argued that these women deserved empathic care instead of rejection, pity, and patronization. Indeed, one of the communal responsibilities would be to establish a community health center that operated on a principle similar to Resthaven's or IWK Health Clinic's. Childcare centers, too, would be necessary, to assist single mothers.[39]

US *hibakusha* were a predominantly female and, increasingly, older population, including a substantial number of military brides. Many were monolingual or felt more comfortable with Japanese than English, especially when they discussed health problems that required familiarity with technical terms. In this light, it is important that Asian Americans in the 1970s articulated medical care that directly spoke to their concerns. In effect, they argued, not only physical ailments but also psychosocial ills must be cared for; otherwise, no illness would be cured.⁴⁰ Thanks to this awareness, US survivors found assistance from medical professionals such as Umekubo and Sakurai, or social workers such as Handa. The emerging consensus was that caring for the marginalized is a communal responsibility, which in turn helps eradicate sexism. At Resthaven, for instance, the patient population included a large percentage of "chronically ill and mostly severely psychotic patients who [had] been kept at home and taken care of by their families."⁴¹ A clear intention here was to lessen the burden on caretakers, chiefly women in Asian America in the 1970s and 1980s.⁴² Handa's career, too, pointed to benefits generated by the community's engagement with women. One of the happy byproducts of the program she helped create in San Jose was that it offered services not only for seniors but also for caretakers. Most of these were young mothers, so they needed childcare while they volunteered. Handa had the program's kitchen double as a childcare center, and to her delight, this arrangement helped some mothers think, as she put it, "Well, maybe [I] can go back to work or go back to school or, you know, do something else." In Handa's remembering, gratification she found in this kind of development shone: "I found that within each ethnic group, the women are always very strong. Yeah. And once you establish trust and work together, especially with the women, and they confer, in terms of 'yes, we agree that these certain things need to be done.'" Given these experiences, it seemed only reasonable to Handa that she assist the predominantly female US *hibakusha*'s group, which also relied on intergenerational coming together within the Asian American community.⁴³

Kathy Yamaguchi, a Sansei physician who helped create FOH and began to volunteer for the biannual checkups in the early 1980s, could easily have been one of the beneficiaries of Handa's earlier program. Similar to Handa's, Yamaguchi's career was shaped by desires to advance civil rights, community care, and gender equality. And yet, Yamaguchi differed from Handa because medicine was predominantly populated by white men and required persistence in a setting not particularly supportive of female students of color. After experiencing a youthful involvement "on the fringe" of the Third World Strike at Berkeley in 1969, she became keenly aware of what it meant to be one of the first Asian American women attending medical school at University of California, San Francisco, in the early 1970s. During her years there, Yamaguchi struggled to become "verbal" in order to succeed. Having grown up in an extremely "non-verbal" Asian American family, and surrounded by outspoken, mostly white male, classmates, she felt that her inability to speak originated from both her gender and her race. In 1971, her first year in medical school, the percentage of female students went up from 15 to 25 percent. "Women's liberation has started, and then right after that, it [the ratio of female students] just started going up," said Yamaguchi. Nevertheless, "being where I was, there weren't very many women role models":

> I actually cried my way through medical school and residency. . . . I think it was harder because I don't come from a professional family. My father's a gardener and my mother never worked outside the home until I was out of college. So, I didn't have preparation, I didn't see this kind of profession – I didn't see this around me, and the whole idea of making, making decisions, being responsible for other people was very difficult for me. I was a girl. I think I was supposed to just get married.[44]

Despite the increase in the number of female students, then, Yamaguchi's medical training was shaped by a struggle to break boundaries on many different levels.

Yamaguchi realized that it was important to her that US survivors were "quiet" Americans for whom it was a "huge struggle" to speak up. It also struck a special chord that US *hibakusha*'s activism was sustained by women's work: "I think if you look at most organizations . . . [and ask] who's doing all the work? It's the women!" said Yamaguchi. Their attempt to overcome silence, and to assert their identity as survivors by pushing gender boundaries, thus resonated with her effort to become a physician. That Yamaguchi's difficulty in speaking up had nothing to do with her language skills (she is a native English speaker) did not stop her from feeling empathetic to another group of silenced women. Psychosocial barriers, not a particular ability or lack thereof, constituted inequality.

This conviction only became stronger as she began to work at institutions similar to IWK Health Clinic and Resthaven. After graduation, she took a position in a public health clinic in the East Bay where she advocated for a single-payer health insurance, and soon, another position in a similar clinic near San Francisco's Japantown where many of her patients were "young women who have babies . . . single mothers or they have American fathers who aren't really there." It is unmistakable that the care and compassion for the "war brides" that Carolyn Saka discussed, and more broadly, Asian women left behind in America, infused Yamaguchi's work. Around the same time, she joined an informal study group, the East Bay Socialist Doctors Group, which tried to ensure that poor patients exercised their rights to health care. Yamaguchi also became a member of the Physicians for Social Responsibility, a well-known antinuclear group of medical doctors. Ultimately, it was her participation in these groups that brought US *hibakusha* to her attention. One of the participants in the socialist doctors' group was working at City View Hospital, where the initial biannual examinations took place. When the hospital closed, the group took it upon themselves to find another location. St. Mary's Hospital came forward, and it was here that Yamaguchi began to work with Umekubo for US survivors. For someone who always felt challenged about her decision to be a physician, it seemed like "a treat" to see US *hibakusha* because they were "kind and generous, grateful" for what she had to offer. That they reciprocated her care with theirs was an important reason for Yamaguchi to keep on.[45]

As Yamaguchi's and others' career trajectories show, Japanese American professionals came to support US survivors for a range of reasons, all of which were shaped by transformations of race and gender awareness in Asian America. Again, unlike the medical exams led by research institutes such as Oak Ridge, these community-based professionals did not grapple with the tension between test and treatment. Their careers were shaped by structural inequality and health disparity, leading them to give priority to clinics instead of laboratories. These physicians were not primarily concerned about whether America took "humanitarian responsibility" or guaranteed human rights; rather, they practiced medicine to protect civil rights that they felt were not readily accessible to their community. In these physicians' minds, concern for human rights would be moot without securing civil rights, suggesting how local specificity was not reducible to the abstraction of a larger philosophy. As discussed in Chapter 5, US survivors by the late 1970s showed an identity as survivors that strikingly differed from that of the "Hiroshima Maidens." US *hibakusha*'s identity was substantiated by their community, allowing them to define illness, care, and treatment apart from the individualistic approach all too common in modern medicine. Tellingly, whenever surveys were conducted among US survivors, few expressed a desire for more research to be conducted about radiation illness. Desire for the treatment of existing illness and for health care allowances that offered a safety net always topped the survey results.[46] This consensus indicates how US *hibakusha* considered community-specific inequality foundational to their experiences of illness.

Spurred by this belief, US survivors actively sought and disseminated information about existing resources for care and treatment. After the initial arrangement was made between CABS and Resthaven, someone in CABS, most likely Kazue Suyeishi judging from the handwriting, translated the mental health services available at the hospital (see Figure 6.1). A Nisei who had grown up in Japan, Suyeishi was bilingual but more fluent in Japanese than in English. Seeing Suyeishi struggle with the language barrier, Julie Kumi Fukuda, a Nisei survivor whose English was

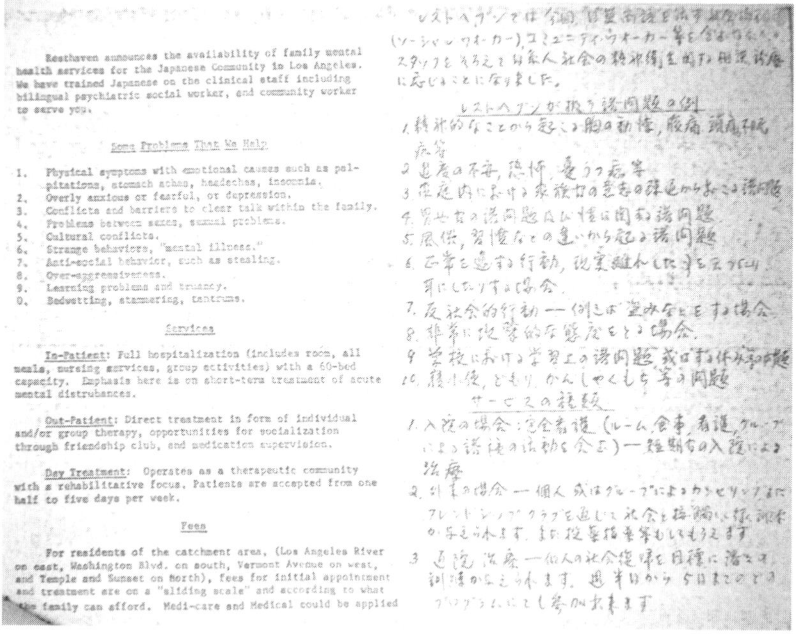

Resthaven announces the availability of family mental health services for the Japanese Community in Los Angeles. We have trained Japanese on the clinical staff including bilingual psychiatric social worker, and community worker to serve you.

Some Problems That We Help

1. Physical symptoms with emotional causes such as palpitations, stomach aches, headaches, insomnia.
2. Overly anxious or fearful, or depression.
3. Conflicts and barriers to clear talk within the family.
4. Problems between sexes, sexual problems.
5. Cultural conflicts.
6. Strange behaviors, "mental illness."
7. Anti-social behavior, such as stealing.
8. Over-aggressiveness.
9. Learning problems and truancy.
0. Bedwetting, stammering, tantrums.

Services

In-Patient: Full hospitalization (includes room, all meals, nursing services, group activities) with a 60-bed capacity. Emphasis here is on short-term treatment of acute mental distrubances.

Out-Patient: Direct treatment in form of individual and/or group therapy, opportunities for socialization through friendship club, and medication supervision.

Day Treatment: Operates as a therapeutic community with a rehabilitative focus. Patients are accepted from one half to five days per week.

Fees

For residents of the catchment area, (Los Angeles River on east, Washington Blvd. on south, Vermont Avenue on west, and Temple and Sunset on North), fees for initial appointment and treatment are on a "sliding scale" and according to what the family can afford. Medi-care and Medical could be applied

レストヘブンでは今回[illegible]
(ソーシャルワーカー)、コミュニティーワーカー等を含む[illegible]
スタッフをそろえて日系人社会の精神衛生[illegible]
に応じることになりました。

レストヘブンが扱う諸問題の例

1. 精神的なことから起こる胸の動悸、腹痛、頭痛、不眠症等
2. 過度の不安、恐怖、憂うつ症等
3. 家庭内における家族間の意志の疎通からおこる諸問題
4. 男女間の諸問題及び性に関する諸問題
5. 風俗、習慣などの違いから起る諸問題
6. 正常を逸する行動、[illegible]耳にしたりする場合
7. 反社会的行動 — 例えば盗みなどをする場合
8. 非常に攻撃的な態度をとる場合
9. 学校における学習上の諸問題或はずる休み等の問題
10. 寝小便、どもり、かんしゃくもち等の問題

サービスの種類

1. 入院の場合：完全看護（ルーム、食事、看護、グループによる諸種の活動を含む）— 短期間の入院による治療
2. 外来の場合 — 個人或はグループによるカウンセリングまたフレンドシップクラブを通じて社会と接触し[illegible]が与えられます。また投薬指導等もしてもらえます
3. 通院治療 — 個人の社会復帰を目標に[illegible]訓練がなされます。週半日から5日までのどれ[illegible]プログラムに参加出来ます

Figure 6.1 A document dated January 31, 1975, explaining in both English and Japanese the medical services that may be available to US *hibakusha* at the Resthaven Psychiatric Hospital and Community Mental Health Center in Los Angeles. Frank F. Chuman papers, Japanese American Research Project Collection, Young Research Library, University of California, Los Angeles, Box 551, Folder 10.

stronger than her Japanese, decided to assist Suyeishi in translating and typing. Soon, Fukuda recalled, she realized that "hibakusha ... would [not] even be recognized if it were not for her [Suyeishi]." Fukuda went on to say a few things about Suyeishi during her interview in 1976, when there still was hope for the passage of the congressional bill:

> She ... spends all day long at this, every day. ... But she gets TOO involved in it and it makes her sick, too ... and she's not a very well person. So she really should not be doing all this work, but if anything, if anything at all comes of the legislation in Congress, from Congressman Roybal's office, it'll be because she's worked so hard. ... I think some of the men [in CABS] don't like, you know, in the group, think she's too much, and all that. But nobody's going to do that [which Suyeishi does].[47]

Similar to how Yamaguchi fought back the expectation for her to "just get married," Suyeishi fought across many boundaries to open up a path for US *hibakusha* to find their identity as survivors. We do not know for certain if the bilingual document about Resthaven was created by Fukuda and Suyeishi; it is unsigned. Nevertheless, it illuminates the tireless work of US survivors to gain access to the care they needed. To attend to psychosocial, as well as physical, ailments was important. Communicating information in a welcoming way, too, was crucial. After decades of silence, shaped by the questioning of their national loyalty and discrimination based on racism, ableism, and sexism, treatment of patients today felt more urgent than research of illness tomorrow. By asserting these priorities, US *hibakusha* raised a question about the research being conducted by the national institutions: Why, and for whom, is it necessary? Certainly, the research could fuel treatment, but it had not. Studies of radiation illness might be inconclusive, but this did not stop the Japanese government from caring for survivors. So, US *hibakusha* asked: What about the American government?

Despite repeated demands for care and treatment for US survivors, the research-driven exams in 1972–1974 ultimately did not offer any impetus for the medical legislation to pass. Sidney Marks, who had spoken about social stigma attached to survivors, offered his testimony during the 1974 hearing for the California bill. Yet he made it clear that he was "speaking not as an official of the Atomic Energy Commission, but as an individual whose work in the AEC falls within the areas this hearing is concerned with." He went on to point out how "it is impossible to characterize the specific case as being a radiation-induced case ... that is, if these things are seen only in a statistical sense there has been an increased incidence of leukemia linked [to radiation]; but the individual case of leukemia cannot be characterized specifically for radiation as opposed to the naturally occurring leukemia."[48] Such reasoning sharply cut against the main line of argument supporting the bill's passage – that, indeed, US survivors suffered from radiation illness and needed medical care and treatment. In the 1978 hearing for the congressional bill, a representative from Oak Ridge, John Auxier, presented an array of slides meant to demonstrate how the risk for most "exposed person[s]" to become ill is smaller than the risk "associated with ... driving an automobile." Such scientific testimony, purely focused on physical manifestations of illness, flew in the face of US survivors' efforts. Surely, the congresspersons supporting the bill noticed how medical research became a hindrance to patient care. George E. Danielson, the chair of the hearing committee and the bill's supporter, responded to Auxier's slides by bluntly stating: "They are interesting pictures, but I didn't understand a darn one of them." He would include the scientific information in the hearing's record if "it tells a story" relevant to US *hibakusha*. Norman Mineta, after ascertaining that the report was about "the physical part" of radiation effect, pointed out: "Of course, the main complaints [of US survivors] was the preoccupation with the fear of illness."[49]

Both Danielson and Mineta addressed how the accuracy of the scientific data was only part of what caused the conflict. More urgently of concern was how scientists were doing what scientists did best: studying medically and statistically tangible evidence, passing over what they deemed to be less tangible factors – psychosocial factors, for instance. As discussed in Chapter 3, this approach was fundamental to the ABCC from its beginning. If there was an increased risk of illness but no proof of its relationship to individuals, radiation illness simply disappeared in scientific discourse. The burden of proof, then, fell on patients. In this light, it is particularly problematic that the 1972–1974 "medical examinations" that were supposed to "reassure" survivors did not publicize any test results. The only exception to this concerned the thirteen patients who were told to seek immediate medical attention after the initial tests in 1972.[50] The radiation exposure dosages among US *hibakusha* that Yamada Hiroaki reported to the AEC were published by Oak Ridge, but these were not communicated to individual survivors who "assist[ed] in the survey."[51] The burden of proof placed on US survivors was augmented by the nondisclosure of scientific information. In the face of the uncertainty created by this nondisclosure and by the failure to pass the medical legislation, US survivors continued to rely on the resource they held close: trans-Pacific ties assisted by Asian and Asian American communities. Their hope was that some parts of the medical legislation, namely, the certification of survivorhood and the medical care offered by physicians familiar with radiation illness, would be accomplished. In 1977, the hope seemed to materialize in the refurbished medical examinations conducted by Hiroshima doctors.[52]

Illness and Identity as Survivors in America, Japan, and Korea

When a team of Hiroshima doctors came to Los Angeles and San Francisco in 1977 for the first of the biannual medical examinations, US survivors were surprised, excited, and anxious. Before then, only a small number of them had seen an "atomic bomb specialist." Many did not have *techō*, a certificate of survivorhood issued by the Japanese government, because of their residency, and in many cases, citizenship in the United States.[53] Other than CABS meetings, they had not had many opportunities to express their survivorhood related to radiation illness. But now, specialists were here, and they would examine *hibakusha* more thoroughly than ever before. *Should I take up this opportunity, and what would it mean for me?* asked many. To be sure, these questions were not necessarily unique to US survivors. When the 1957 and 1968 laws to assist Japanese survivors were passed in Japan, some felt as if this legislation was an insult to their ability to self-support and live with dignity.[54] Still, for US *hibakusha* left out of these laws, the coming of Hiroshima doctors was a special kind of opportunity, generating a range of reactions. CABS president Kanji Kuramoto could not hide his excitement. In an interview with *Hokubei Mainichi* in March 1977, Kuramoto told how the upcoming visit "feels as if a spring has come after thirty-two years" of waiting.[55] Tsuruko Nakamura at first could not believe that doctors were coming. She thought the doctors were only for Japanese survivors. She talked to a friend, a Kibei Nisei, who reassured her that, indeed, the exams at this time were for US survivors. *It was in a newspaper.* After she began to attend the checkups regularly, Nakamura "became more aware" of her identity as a survivor. Seeing doctors specialized in radiation illness, and being treated as a survivor, became an essential part of her self-perception.[56] For Tokie Akihara, the reason for having the exam was to discuss her worries about the hair loss that she had endured shortly after the bomb. She was struck by how immediately the doctors recommended that she apply for *techō*. *Could someone in America have it?* she wondered. As it turned out, the answer was yes; soon, she became eligible for free medical care and treatment if she were to stay in Japan.[57]

For some survivors, the reason for attending the examination was concern about their children's health. Mitsuko Okimoto's oldest child was "delicate" and prone to sickness. She wondered if this was because she had been exposed to radiation.[58] There was no scientific research that confirmed radiation's effect on the second generation.[59] Nevertheless, many survivors had children who were weak and easily fell ill. Sayoko Utagawa recalled how she had not thought of herself as a survivor for a long time. When her oldest son was diagnosed with leukemia and passed away at age twenty-one, though, she wondered if his death might have been related to her irradiation. She decided to go to the checkup, and was satisfied on a few counts. First, she liked that it was open to both first and second generation survivors. She made it a routine to take her surviving children with her. Utagawa also felt that the doctors were "kind." One of the internists took her blood pressure, which turned out to be high. Seeing that Utagawa was anxious because the exam took place only once every other year, the internist said, "Let's do it again a little later." Her blood pressure was down to normal the second time around. It also made a difference that all the conversations could take place in Japanese, even in Hiroshima dialect.[60] In fact, many, if not most, physicians were second generation survivors. Setsuko Kohara found the thoroughness of the exam reassuring. With her family doctor, "a checkup would be only about a certain set of things." In contrast, "these bomb doctors checked everything," a feeling augmented by the fact that they explained everything in Japanese, Kohara's strongest language. She and her husband Tadachi, also a Nisei survivor, had worried if their children would be able to "grow up to become independent." Like Utagawa, the Koharas made it a habit to bring the whole family to the checkups.[61]

Not all survivors were able to attend the medical examinations even if they wanted to, because of the tenacious stigma of being *hibakusha.* As late as 1981, four years after the initial examinations took place on the West Coast, *Nichi Bei Times* reported that a number of survivors did not come to the checkups because they "were afraid to let others know their plight [as survivors]." In one case, "a husband [of a survivor] threatened to divorce his wife if she came to San Francisco to be examined" by Japanese physicians.[62] In light of these cases, the experience of a San Jose survivor who fell ill with pneumonia right before the medical visit was of particular import. He wrote about his problem to Kuramoto, CABS president, who then discussed the matter with one of the visiting physicians, Yamakido Michiko. She agreed to accompany Kuramoto from San Francisco to San Jose on Sunday to see the man.[63] If there were no extraordinary gesture like this, the man would have remained unseen. This shows how it was not only the thoroughness and flexibility of the exam, mentioned by Utagawa and Kohara, that made it appealing to US survivors, it was also the caregiving. Stripped of the facility and equipment, it is not likely that Yamakido was able to conduct a full examination for this San Jose survivor. Nonetheless, the trip resulted in effective care because of other reasons, including social and psychological ones. Although the biannual checkups did not include medical treatment, they differed sharply from the 1972–1974 tests in two major ways. First, these checkups did not place the burden of proof on patients; doctors took patients' worries seriously. Second, the checkups by Hiroshima physicians offered a direct route to acquiring *techō* and free medical treatment in Japan. These benefits, of course, did not erase the distance between Japanese facilities and American patients. Still, US survivors had not enjoyed anything like this before.

How did these biannual medical checkups come into existence? In many ways, it was the fruit of the relationship across the Pacific that US survivors had built tirelessly with Japanese and Japanese American community members, medical professionals, and government officials. Similar to the short-lived 1972–1974 medical examinations sponsored by the ABCC, AEC, and Oak Ridge, this trans-Pacific relationship that took shape in the latter half of the 1970s started locally, then expanded nationally and internationally. But the scopes of the 1972–1974 and the 1977 examinations differed sharply. The former reflected US research interests, while the latter embodied not only US–Japan relations but also ties created between Japan and South Korea. In December 1976, the mayors of Hiroshima and Nagasaki, Araki Takeshi and Morotani

Yoshitake, came to meet US *hibakusha* in Los Angeles and San Francisco. The meetings were cosponsored by CABS and the Hiroshima and Nagasaki Kenjinkai in Northern and Southern California.[64] The mayors then requested Mayor Thomas Bradley of Los Angeles to help arrange medical examinations at a municipal hospital, to which Bradley responded by "pledg[ing] to give full cooperation." The mayors of the Japanese cities, accompanied by the president of the Hiroshima-ken Ishikai (Hiroshima Prefectural Medical Association, or HPMA), also met with "five Japanese American doctors" at a luncheon hosted by the Los Angeles County Medical Association.[65]

These medical associations' collaboration was absolutely necessary for the program, because Hiroshima doctors would not be able to practice medicine in Los Angeles unless they were designated as "medical interns" working under "supervisors," physicians licensed to practice in America. The county and the prefectural medical associations "established a sistership tie-up" at the luncheon, which made the framework of internship possible.[66] This was an important step, especially given the fact that the American Medical Association had been slow to come out in support of the congressional medical bill under consideration.[67] The "sistership" relationship, then, was more a result of the affiliations that US survivors had established with community-based physicians than it was a reflection of overall support from the national organization of US physicians. In the winter of 1976–1977, the Japanese government negotiated terms of collaboration with its American counterpart. Ultimately, it was determined that the checkups would be cosponsored by HPMA and the Nihon Kōshūeisei Kyōkai (Japan Public Health Association, or JPHA), another nonprofit, nongovernmental organization.[68] Beginning in 1983, the Hiroshima Atomic Bomb Casualty Council (a nonprofit organization that is a separate entity from the ABCC), the city and the prefecture of Hiroshima, and the Hiroshima RERF (formerly the Hiroshima ABCC, reorganized and cofunded by the Japanese and American governments) began to cosponsor the program.[69] Initially, though, it was HPMA–JPHA that sponsored the program, meaning that it was not publicly funded. The US AEC and the MHW in Japan signed off on the program, but did not pay for it. Similar to US *hibakusha*'s attempt to obtain medical care in Asian America, their cross-national effort was largely grassroots and nongovernmental.

Equally as important as US survivors' persistent efforts to sustain trans-Pacific ties for the making of the medical checkup system was the collaboration between South Korean survivors and their Japanese supporters that began around the same time. Indeed, if there had been no convergence of the activism in America, Japan, and Korea, with the resultant redefinition of 1957 and 1968 Japanese laws from narrowly defined civil rights legislation to broadly applicable principles of human rights, there might have been no biannual checkups for US *hibakusha* until decades later. In fact, as late as July 1976, the Japanese government's approach to US survivors was unambiguously obstructive. At this time, Kazue Suyeishi met with Tanaka Masami of the MHW, who stated how "the Japanese laws are meant to offer social security for survivors residing in Japan only." Moreover, the minister went on to say, "we do not have a budget to send Japanese radiation illness specialists to the United States. Besides, the United States is the country that dropped the bomb." If Japan interfered with the treatment of US survivors, "we might rub the US government in a wrong way."[70] This was a little more than a year after US survivors were told during the senate hearing in California that they had been "our enemies" during the war, underscoring the challenge that US survivors' cross-nationality faced on both shores of the Pacific. And yet, several months after making these statements, Tanaka agreed to support the medical checkup program in San Francisco and Los Angeles. Such an abrupt change was linked to the rising activism of Korean survivors in Korea, with backing by their Japanese supporters, chiefly in Hiroshima, Nagasaki, and Osaka. Unlike 7,000 Korean survivors who had stayed in Japan after the war, 23,000 Korean survivors who had gone back to South Korea before the enactment of the 1957 and 1968 laws were not covered. This exclusion came to haunt the Japanese government, as Korean survivors began to voice their discontent in the mid-1960s.

South Korean survivors' history in the 1970s and 1980s is complex, and I will not detail it fully in my analysis here.[71] Nonetheless, it is useful to highlight key moments in the history, moments when the large number of Korean survivors and the strong pressure they exercised as victims of Japanese colonialism became relevant to US *hibakusha*'s history. By bringing attention to non-Japanese survivors outside Japan, Korean survivors and their Japanese supporters helped US survivors create a medico-legal system that allowed for

294 / American Survivors

a cross-national definition of survivorhood on the one hand and a psychosocial definition of radiation illness on the other.

A group of survivors in Korea was established in 1967 under the leadership of Sin Yŏng-su, just two years after American survivors held their first meeting in Los Angeles. Similar to their American counterparts, Korean survivors' history had been colored by silence and stigmatization, making it difficult for them to find each other. Some of the reasons were similar to those of US survivors, but others were unique because of Korean *hibakusha*'s entanglement with legacies of Japanese colonialism and the Korean War. The brutality of Japanese colonial rule helped create a national consensus in South Korea that the destruction of Hiroshima and Nagasaki was a necessary step toward ending the war. This understanding of the bomb was enhanced by Cold War ideology that fueled nuclear proliferation and the idea of a nuclear umbrella extended by the American military for the protection of Asia. In this political climate, Korean survivors were considered by their fellow Koreans unfortunate but necessary casualties of the war. To further complicate the matter, the history of the forced migration of people from the Korean Peninsula to Japan in the 1930s and 1940s was swept under the rug by the urgent need for the countries to become Cold War allies, culminating in the 1965 Treaty of Basic Relations between Japan and South Korea. Among other things, the treaty lacked any basis for individual compensation for Korean forced laborers, bomb survivors, or sex slaves euphemistically called "comfort women." Meanwhile, the division of Korea at the thirty-eighth parallel gave birth to North Korea, where an estimated 2,000 survivors returned after the Pacific War and remained nonresponsive to inquiries from either South Korea or Japan about their medical and social conditions.[72]

This stagnant situation started to change when several Korean survivors came to Japan in the late 1960s and early 1970s. They demanded that they be certified as survivors with *techō* in order to receive treatment for their radiation illness free of cost at the A-bomb Hospitals in Japan, and to become eligible for health care benefits including monetary allowances. In particular, the case of Son Chin-du, who entered Japan illegally in 1968 to have his illness treated, became a cause for celebration for Korean survivors and their supporters in both Japan and Korea. Son's determination to gain recognition inspired Japanese citizens to come together as a support group called Kankoku no Genbaku Higaisha o Kyūensuru Shimin no Kai (Shimin no Kai), or the Citizens' Group to Assist Korean Survivors, in 1971, led by strong female figures such as Matsui Yoshiko, Kuroki Ai, and later, Ichiba Junko. In the same year, four doctors from a Japanese antinuclear group, in collaboration with Shimin no Kai, went to Seoul, Busan, and Hapch'ŏn, examining 920 Korean survivors.[73] Some Korean grassroots organizations, too, began to offer assistance, the most notable of which, the National Church Women's Association (NCWA), succeeded in setting up beds at the Gospel Hospital in Busan and Severance Hospital in Seoul designated for the treatment of Korean survivors. The women's association also conducted a national survey to confirm the number of Korean survivors in South Korea, serving as an important representative agency when no governmental assistance from either Korea or Japan was forthcoming.[74] These grassroots efforts laid a foundation for the Japanese government-sponsored medical treatment of Korean survivors in Japan, which continued for six years between 1980 and 1986, benefitting 349 Korean survivors.[75]

Son's persistence also led to a series of lawsuits in Japan beginning in 1972, which revolved around the Japanese government's refusal to apply the 1957 and 1968 laws to non-Japanese survivors overseas. By 1974, a district court in Fukuoka handed him a victory. Prompted by this breakthrough, the prefecture of Tokyo issued the first *techō* to a Korean applicant, Sin Yŏng-su, in an act of defiance against the Japanese government which, until 1975, did not allow local governments to issue *techō* to non-Japanese applicants even if they had entered Japan legally.[76] Four years later, in 1978, Japan's Supreme Court confirmed Son's victory with a clear recognition that the laws are not "social security" legislation applicable only to Japanese citizens and residents. Instead, the laws are "national compensation" meant to serve "humanitarian purposes," applicable to all survivors regardless of citizenship or residency. Moreover, it was determined that Son's illegal entry into Japan did not deprive him of his rights as a survivor.[77] Although in practice the Japanese government refused to recognize the compensatory character of the laws and took steps to limit their applicability to those physically present in Japan (meaning that if certified Korean survivors left Japan they were not entitled to the monetary allowances),[78] Son successfully gained the right to treatment at Japanese hospitals at no cost. The news of this courtroom victory traveled across the Pacific quickly because of its obvious implication for US *hibakusha*. When the first Korean survivor was issued *techō*,

Nichi Bei Times featured it with a comment by Kuramoto: "This is good news for American survivors."[79] *We could have* techō, *too.*

The growing activism of Korean *hibakusha* and their supporters, which led to the possibility for non-Japanese survivors to receive medical treatment in Japan, literally created a flow of US survivors to Japan. In this context, the biannual medical checkup that began only three years after Son received *techō* became the primary channel through which US survivors applied for *techō* across the Pacific. At the checkup, they received CABS members' support to apply for *techō* – instructions for the application form, the documents that needed to be attached, and the requirements for the two necessary "witnesses" (individuals who could attest that the applicant was in either one of the Japanese cities in August 1945). Japanese physicians conducting the checkup, too, assisted the application process, by issuing diagnoses accompanied by explanations that indicated a link between the survivors' medical conditions now and their exposure to radiation then. These physicians' endorsement carried not only medical clout but also sociopolitical import. Junji Sarashina recalled:

> Some of the people [survivors], they came [to the checkup] without techō. And, you know, they couldn't do anything. So the Japanese doctor's office said [to the government]: "What's wrong with you guys, can't you tell that this person is suffering?" One month later she's got a techō. .... So, it's important, you know, that you connect with those doctors.[80]

Equipped with medical authority and well versed in the politics of diagnosis, these physicians could turn what seemed impossible into a tangible possibility. Despite the Japanese government's reluctance to issue *techō* to non-Japanese survivors, the program endorsed by the government but staffed by local, more sympathetic personnel, began to generate a number of Japanese *techō*-certified American survivors.

Still, obtaining *techō* was not easy, and the process often proved daunting for many. First, applicants had to be physically present when they submitted their applications. They had to receive *techō* in person, too. At the time of application, applicants were not told when *techō* would be issued, making it necessary for them to wait in Japan for weeks or months. For those without families in Hiroshima or Nagasaki, finding two witnesses to prove the applicants' presence in either city in 1945 posed a challenge. This was particularly true for Korean and Korean

American survivors, because many of their acquaintances had returned to Korea and also because many did not have a lot of Japanese acquaintances during wartime. Especially for the monolingual Korean immigrants confined to newer Korean neighborhoods discussed in Chapter 1, interacting with the Japanese was neither easy nor desirable particularly after the forced migration and mobilization policies began in the late 1930s. Shimin no Kai offered significant support for non-Japanese survivors in this difficult situation. Toyonaga Keizaburō, an early member of the group, recalled how he found witnesses for Sin Yŏng-su, the president of the group of Korean survivors and the first among Koreans to obtain *techō*, while he was in Japan to treat his keloids:

> He was in Tokyo [for surgery], so I searched for his witnesses. He kept a very good record [of the wartime], so relying on it I went to Kōchi prefecture to look for his former supervisor. He agreed to be a witness. The other witness was supposed to be in the City of Hatsukaichi near Hiroshima. Sin remembered that he had received a treatment for his burns from a beautiful female physician there. I thought, well, there could not have been too many female physicians at that time. Sure enough, I found one. . . . But the physician said that she did not remember Sin. So I asked the first witness to come with me, and he explained to the physician how Sin must have smelled bad because of the burns on his face. At that point, the physician said: "Yeah, maybe. There might have been such a case," so I thought "Yes!" and asked her to write it down. So that's how I got two witnesses' statements and sent them to Tokyo.[81]

The success of Sin's application led to the next successful case, that of Ch'oe Yŏng-sun. Like Sin, Ch'oe came to Japan for treatment of radiation illness. But Ch'oe had been farther away from the hypocenter than Sin, making it easier for Toyonaga to find witnesses; there were many more who were still alive. It also worked to Ch'oe's advantage that she stayed in the Kawamura Byōin (Kawamura Hospital) in Hiroshima, where the director was highly sympathetic to Korean survivors. Like the physicians conducting medical checkups in Los Angeles and San Francisco, physicians at this hospital knew how to write a medical diagnosis in a way that assisted *techō* applications. In Ch'oe's case, it proved crucial that her medical record stated that she needed to be treated at the hospital over a period of several months. The City of

Hiroshima, which was initially highly reluctant to issue *techō* because "it would take three months" for them to review the application, ran out of excuses.[82]

Toyonaga's stories point to the grassroots activism that brought together medical professionals and nonprofessionals, something that paralleled the effort of doctors and social workers in the United States. The Japanese network of support assisted not only Korean survivors but also survivors from America. During his interview with me in 2013, Aoki Katsuaki, a Hiroshima physician at the Hiroshima Kyōritsu Byōin (Hiroshima Kyōritsu Hospital) who was sympathetic to Korean survivors, showed me a roster of non-Japanese survivors who had been accepted to the hospital, which included *hibakusha* from America.[83] To be sure, this list did not erase the difference in nationality, as Korean survivors occupied a special place for many of their Japanese supporters. As the triple victim of Japanese colonialism, America's use of the bomb, and Korean neglect after the war, Korean survivors were an important focus of the Japanese grassroots effort to offer apology and reparation. And yet, the activism had a broad impact on how all non-Japanese survivors overseas were perceived by their Japanese supporters. These neglected survivors, Koreans or otherwise, embodied the Japanese government's failure to recognize the cross-national, indiscriminate effect of the nuclear destruction, by refusing to see it as something that required a "humanitarian" response.[84] No wonder, these supporters thought, the nation had accepted the protection of the US nuclear umbrella, first by adopting the Treaty of Mutual Cooperation and Security between the United States and Japan (originally signed in 1950 and renewed in 1960), then by coming close to agreeing to let the United States keep nuclear missiles in Okinawa beyond its reversion in 1972. Without someone keeping tabs, the government would easily slide into supporting nuclear policies nationally and internationally, whereby it would happily continue to brush aside the counter-memory of the bomb.[85]

Just as a number of physicians who came to America to conduct medical checkups were second generation survivors, doctors who assisted non-Japanese survivors in Hiroshima and Nagasaki had significant ties to the war and the bomb. These connections offered compelling reasons for them to join the grassroots activism in support of anti-nuclear causes, fuller and flexible approaches to radiation illness, and a cross-national definition of *hibakusha*. Kawamura Toratarō, the director of Kawamura Byōin, was born in 1914 in Korea. A graduate of the School of Medicine at Keijō Imperial University, Seoul, Kawamura felt that his affinity with Korean culture, as well as his remorse over the fact that he had been one of the Japanese "colonialists born in Korea," was the source of his decision to treat Koreans as equals to the Japanese.[86] Aoki of Kyōritsu Byōin was a second generation survivor, something that propelled him to become an organizer of a grassroots program that began to invite Korean survivors to Japanese hospitals for treatment after the Japanese government terminated its publicly funded visiting treatment program for Korean survivors in 1986. Aoki also helped create a Japanese survivors' co-op within Kyōritsu Byōin, which formed a sister affiliation with a Korean survivors' self-support group in Hapch'ŏn, where the largest number of survivors in Korea resided. No doubt, this affiliation facilitated Korean survivors' trips to Japan by giving them a reassurance that they would be admitted to a hospital accepting of Korean *hibakusha*. These engagements later prompted Aoki to join the Physicians Against Nuclear War, an anti-nuclear group consisting of medical doctors in Japan.[87]

Toyonaga Keizaburō, himself a survivor, felt that his work for Korean survivors gave him a chance to discover his own identity as a survivor. As a schoolteacher in postwar Hiroshima, he was struck by how Korean students continued to be marginalized as if nothing had changed since the war's end. He was particularly troubled by the continuing use of Japanese names by virtually all Korean students. Now that they were free of Japanese rule, which had demanded Koreans adopt Japanese names legally, Koreans in Japan should be able to "come out" as Koreans by proudly proclaiming Korean names. This was not the case, however, because of the likelihood that Korean name-holders would be discriminated against in education, employment, and marriage. Toyonaga began to teach about the history of Japanese discrimination against Koreans, and soon, the subject led him to invite both Japanese and Korean *hibakusha* to his classroom to share their remembering of the nuclear destruction with his students. This was the early 1980s, when it was still uncommon for survivors in Japan to give public testimonials. When Toyonaga could not enlist sufficient numbers of survivors for his classes, he decided to enlist himself. This decision, along with his tireless legwork for Korean survivors, eventually made him think: *Am I not a survivor, too?*[88]

In some ways, the medico-legal support system for Korean survivors that emerged across Korea and Japan in the 1970s and 1980s carried striking similarities to its counterpart in America. In all three countries, people began to come together inspired by many histories of immigrants punctuated remarkably by the war and the bomb. The marginalization of their remembering in the history of the bomb, furthered by many forms of discrimination based on their nationality, race, and gender, became forceful ties connecting them. The earlier history of the neglected *hibakusha*, shaped on both shores of the Pacific, became a driving force for different generations to gather through collective remembering. *Hayaku engo o!*, Shimin no Kai's newsletter, featured countless recollections of the bomb by Korean survivors, serving as one of the first publications where Japanese readers could see the bomb's cross-nationality. Similar to Asian American community newspapers that criticized the Vietnam War and the Pacific War in a single breath, communities of survivors and their supporters in Korea and Japan discovered in their collective remembering ways to engage the cross-national past by building ties that brought tensions out of silence. A consensus emerged that a judgment based on presumptions of national loyalty, belonging, and citizenship always work to discriminate against *hibakusha*.

In Japan and Korea, too, gender importantly shaped survivors' activism. Women played essential roles in building the grassroots networks of care and treatment, despite their small number in the medical profession and the persistent expectation that they stay at home or play supporting roles. In Japan and Korea, where the participation of female professionals was not as pronounced as it was in America, ordinary female citizen-activists offered essential services through organizations such as Shimin no Kai and NCWA. It is also notable that Sin Yŏng-su played a similar role to that of Kazuo Tosaka or Kuniko Jenkins, by defiantly showing his scarred face in public. Sin's keloid was severe, a sign of his survivorhood that went beyond the reserve expected of *hibakusha* in the earlier decades. Just as Jenkins presented herself on the witness stand with an oxygen tank in tow or Tosaka exhibited his emotional hurt openly in public, Sin walked up to podiums many times across Japan to claim – and show – his need for care. US *hibakusha* inspired female professionals such as Geri Handa and Kathy Yamaguchi in the Asian American community, while Korean survivors like Sin instigated the grassroots activism in both Korea and Japan by challenging gender boundaries and breaking silence about the bomb's ability to injure indiscriminately. In this sense, female survivors shifted gender dynamism in the Pacific region both by going beyond "womanly" roles and by building women-centered alliances that focused on community care and treatment. Male survivors, too, countered gender expectations by accepting and asserting themselves as patients. Their disability, as well as their illness, did not need to be hidden.

In other ways, however, the collaboration between Korean survivors and Japanese supporters differed sharply from the activism that brought together American survivors and Japanese supporters. Legally, the first pair acquired a solid foundation for care and treatment, funded by the Japanese government. This led to the implementation of not only medical examinations but also treatment plans as seen in the 1980–86 program. Failing to obtain any legal support, in contrast, a publicly funded treatment program remained nonexistent for US survivors, except for those who stayed in Japan with *techō* to treat radiation illness. After the biannual checkups began to be cosponsored by the RERF in 1983, US *hibakusha*'s medical records were forwarded to the RERF, adding to its scientific data collection, particularly data related to radiation-induced cancer and life expectancy. Researchers were intrigued by a possible divergence between American and Japanese survivors, which might exist because of different diets, lifestyles, and sociocultural settings.[89] This is the only part funded by any US institution, demarcating again the distinction between treatment and care offered by Asian community members on the one hand and research conducted by American governmental institutions on the other.[90] This distinction had already manifested itself within the United States by the end of the 1970s, when the national facilities of medical research existed in tension with Asian American community health care. By the early 1980s, the distinction seemed to expand across the Pacific; Japanese people became the chief caretakers of American survivors. Despite early expressions of humanitarian concern and recognition of psychosocial illness by some individual scientists, the US government after the early 1980s steered clear of medical, legal, and moral questions surrounding US *hibakusha*. Throughout this era, survivors claimed the universality of survivorhood by coming together across national borders. Many citizens in America, Japan, and Korea came out in support of this claim. And yet, it found a response from only one government, a reluctant one offered by the Japanese government that began to recognize its responsibility to support humanitarianism and human rights. Nonetheless, the government's treatment of Japanese, Korean, and American survivors continued to differ by nationality, showing that the human rights approach, too, continues to discriminate. Moreover, unlike Japanese American camp inmates, who were beginning to be recognized as victims of civil rights violations in the eyes of the American government in the 1980s, US survivors continued to receive no recognition in the United States. Consequently, the notion of human rights as it was defined by the Japanese government failed to generate any meaningful collaboration with the American government. The US government that had not recognized US *hibakusha*'s civil rights did not help their human rights get recognized, either. No tax money was used to assist the biannual checkup program. In this way, the universality of survivorhood was reduced to uniqueness – something to be recognized by only one government. To be sure, US survivors were no longer "enemies" of the United States; and yet, their quest for treatment still rendered them foreigners, whose rights could only be addressed by a foreign government. In this light, the old conception – if you are a survivor, you must be Japanese – still persisted in the trans-Pacific medico-legal system. Along the way, the United States missed opportunities to answer questions not only about civil rights but also about human rights, both of which were deeply ingrained in radiation illness.

Divergence of Experiences: Survivorhood toward the End of the Century

Many US survivors traveled to Japan after the Son case had concluded in 1978 to obtain *techō*, first at their own cost, then for free as part of a program called Satogaeri Chiryō, or the Treatment Back Home Program. Beginning in 1982, the program sponsored by grassroots groups in Nagasaki and Hiroshima assisted in the flow of patients, care, and treatment across the Pacific. Meanwhile, the Japanese government continued to deny monetary allowances to non-Japanese *hibakusha* well into the early 2000s.[91] Nongovernmental programs such as Satogaeri Chiryō tried to fill the gap. If a survivor was diagnosed with radiation illness during a HPMA–JPHA sponsored biennial checkup,

Satogaeri Chiryō could offer a bridge across the ocean toward care and treatment. Sachiko Matsumoto, a conduit of day-to-day communication in CABS, was among those who took advantage of this program, although she insisted on paying her way. During a three-week stay at the Hiroshima Shimin Byōin (Hiroshima Citizens' Hospital), Matsumoto received and recovered from surgery. Tokiko Stuckey from Utah, too, benefitted from the program. Her chronic back pain subsided after two months of intensive treatment at the Hiroshima A-bomb Hospital. A similar program was implemented in Nagasaki, too, inviting two US survivors every year.[92] The community effort by Asian Americans also mitigated shortcomings arising from the lack of publicly funded treatment in the United States. They offered labor, space, and equipment for the examinations, communication, and record-keeping free of cost. The underpinning principle of the community engagement – that Asians in America deserve better access to culturally attuned medicine – continued to facilitate more US *hibakusha* coming together, including Korean Americans. All of the Korean American survivors discussed in earlier chapters came to the medical checkups at some point. One of them, John Hong, benefitted from *techō* after it was issued in 1990, and he began to visit Japan every other year to receive medical treatment.[93] Most of them were more fluent in Japanese than English because of their long-term residence in Japan. One way to look at their participation in the program, then, is that it offered culturally accessible medicine for Korean American survivors as well.

As important as the fact that the examination was open to and used by Korean Americans, though, was the range of meanings that they found in the biannual checkup program. Hong, as seen in Chapter 1, had grown up in Japan speaking Japanese, and he found the medical checkup conducted in Japanese highly appealing. Seeing Japanese physicians at work and hearing about the assistance that they made available to Korean survivors in Korea in the late 1970s and early 1980s, Hong began to feel critical of America by the early 1990s:

> America dropped the bomb, but America does not seem to feel responsible for it. There is no monetary support for people who were irradiated. All that America does is to make this space for the medical checkup available. And it is a space at a private Catholic hospital [St. Mary's]. ... There is no assistance in the United States. The country does not have a sense of responsibility.[94]

Hye-kyo Lee, another Korean American survivor, had a sharply different response to the checkups. After her alcoholic husband passed away
(Chapter 4), Lee continued to suffer from undiagnosed pain. So, she
came to a medical checkup, with the thought that "maybe the Japanese
doctors can tell me what's wrong." She felt as if "she knows that she is
dying," but her American doctors kept on telling her that there was
nothing wrong with her. After seeing Japanese doctors, however, she
thought, "It's more like they're using me as a guinea pig. That's what it
really is." The physicians told her that they would look at the test results
of her "breasts, . . . legs, joints" to identify the cause of pain, and that it
would take two months. Her response was sarcastic: "I said, 'That's
good. I've been waiting 50 years. I can wait two months.'" That the
physicians could not tell the result sooner brought to the surface
a distrust of state-sponsored medicine.[95] Unlike Japanese American
survivors who recognized in the program a pathway toward care and
treatment, Korean American *hibakusha* might have been more likely to
see the program as similar to the ABCC, especially if they were not
interested in Satogaeri Chiryō. The increased recognition by the
Japanese government of Korean survivors, too, might have marginalized Korean American survivors. Their belonging to Korea was not
immediately obvious because they lived in America, creating a barrier
for them to become beneficiaries in Japan. Because of the small number
of Korean America *hibakusha*, it is difficult to identify a pattern.

Nonetheless, Hong and Lee's stories illuminate how meanings
of radiation illness continued to vary and, by extension, how identities
as survivors continued to flow outside nation-based histories of the
bomb. To be sure, Korean survivors were able to obtain some support
from the Japanese government because of the political, legal, and moral
clout they exercised as Japan's former colonial subjects. This support
benefitted Japanese American and Korean American survivors, too,
making them part of the history of Japan's failure to treat all survivors
equally. And yet, this circumstance did not erase questions about the
bomb's legality and morality that require cross-national considerations.
Many survivors continued to grapple with these questions about the
country that seemed immune to them. Despite the modest success of the
trans-Pacific system of biannual checkups and Satogaeri Chiryō, and
the fact that these programs offered some degree of "reassurance" to
some US *hibakusha*, these accomplishments did not completely erase
their distrust of medical researchers or governmental officials. Although

the medical examinations could lead to treatment, some survivors continued to hold a belief that treatment is done for examinations, not the
other way around. By asserting their identity as survivors through
radiation illness, US *hibakusha* demanded that this priority be challenged. They found allies in both Asian and Asian American communities, generating a newly cross-national counter-memory of the bomb. In
fact, one common ground for the production of this counter-memory
was all the states' failure to accept radiation illness as a crucial aspect of
survivors' identity. While American, Japanese, and Korean governments worked to determine what scientific evidence might exist for
radiation illness across the long fifty years after 1945, US survivors
were left to grapple with the illness and with a society that looked on
them callously. The process itself became part of the counter-memory of
the bomb and a source of identity as survivors for those in America. Just
as their remembering had been a process in tension with national
memories of the bomb, their identity continued to take shape as it
conflicted with state- and science-sanctioned definitions of radiation
illness.

Not surprisingly, then, US survivors in the 1980s and 1990s
began to take a distinctive set of actions that embodied the continuing
processes of remembering and identity formation. For one, the absence
of a US-funded treatment program brought a fresh awareness of the
power of medical and social discrimination to some survivors, leading
them to find alliances with a newly stigmatized group in the early 1980s:
HIV/AIDS patients. This surprising expansion of US survivors' awareness occurred individually rather than collectively, and did not lead to
a large-scale, collaborative patient rights movement. And yet, some of
the US survivors' remembering reveals a poignant place that the continuing neglect by the governments led them to occupy, and how standing in that place urged them to consider other marginalized groups as
part of the same problem.

For Seiko Fujimoto, a fresh understanding of social stigma came
in 1981, when her son was diagnosed with leukemia at the age of six. At
that time, her son's school was fearful of any children deemed likely to
be HIV-positive. Soon, teachers began to refuse students who had
recently received a blood transfusion, including Fujimoto's son, then
undergoing the procedure to treat leukemia. To make matters worse,
Fujimoto's husband did not respond well to this development. Learning
for the first time that Fujimoto was a survivor, her husband worried that

her radiation exposure, and her son's illness that might have been caused by it, could compromise his business reputation. They could be seen as infectors. Fujimoto decided to divorce him rather than "hurting children." Be it leukemia patients or people with HIV/AIDS, she felt as if "she understood" them as a neglected population and decided not to be part of "this simplistic way" of stigmatization.[96]

US *hibakusha*'s expanded awareness of social and medical discrimination held the potential for making a broad impact. As discussed earlier, Kyohei Sakata, a minister, became a member of FOH in 1979. Shortly thereafter, one of the members of his church in San Francisco attempted suicide after confessing to his fiancée that he was gay. Disheartened by this incident, Sakata began to reflect on silence. Just as survivors suffered silently, sexual minorities endured the lack of acceptance by remaining in the closet. Sakata took this line of thinking further when he moved to a church in Sacramento, which counted a handful of HIV-positive individuals among its members. One of them had become infected after he came out to his family, only to be accused of his "shameful" sexuality and expelled from home. He sought multiple sexual partners to ease his isolation and financially support himself. It seemed obvious to Sakata that this person had to choose between two unacceptable options: to remain silent or to be infected by a deadly disease. To create another option, there had to be social acceptance. Thus, Sakata unhesitatingly accepted an invitation from his friend, a minister at another Sacramento church, to perform a marriage for a lesbian couple. As many as ninety-six ministers joined the ceremony so as to preempt potential church discipline, a strategy that worked. In Sakata's narrative, it is clear that his activism for *hibakusha* and sexual minorities worked to shape each other. He continued to volunteer for the medical checkups for US survivors and, simultaneously, he agreed to serve as a minister of another church where members were predominantly gay men and lesbians.[97] Being openly recognized and treated with respect was the key for both facets of Sakata's activism.

Such small acts were what shaped the grassroots activism of US *hibakusha* from its inception in the mid-1960s, and they continued to be as the end of the century approached. Such acts were rarely overarching, but taken together they were building blocks for survivors' identities. The ambiguousness of radiation illness and the resultant lack of formal recognition of it compelled US survivors to rely on each other. The persistent social and medical neglect sometimes brought about unexpected alliances, whether with Korean survivors, their Japanese supporters, or sexual minorities who are HIV-positive. This breadth of alliances suggests important, if under-recognized, roles that US *hibakusha* played in the Asian American community in the 1980s and 1990s. Building on their cross-nationality, many, if not all, US survivors, both personally and collectively, created spaces where different identities of race, gender, generation, and nationality came together. In the Asian American community, traditionally not known for acceptance of sexual diversity, this coming together spurred an expansion of the notion of social and medical justice to include LGBT individuals. Karl G. Yoneda, a non-survivor whose remembering of the bomb was discussed in Chapter 5, showed one example of this expansion in 1986, when he gave a speech at the Stonewall Gay Democratic Club in San Francisco in opposition to Proposition 64, an anti-AIDS patients California ballot initiative. Recalling how swiftly "'Jap Hunting' posters appeared here in San Francisco the second week of December 1941," Yoneda asked: "Who can guarantee that 'AIDS Hunting' posters will not appear if Prop 64 became California law?" To Yoneda, then, the proposition was "not a health issue. It is a civil rights issue."[98] This resoundingly echoed his reason for supporting US survivors and their demand to be cared for.

In fact, it would be even more accurate to say that US *hibakusha* continued to claim that radiation illness was at once a health and a civil rights issue. This claim had been made through both legislative and legal routes; the former reached a dead end, while the latter led US survivors to spur the Japanese government to recognize their illness based on the logic of human rights sanctioned by the Japanese highest court's ruling. Here, civil rights seemed to be replaced by human rights, defined not by legislative but by judicial terms. This shift appeared to return US survivors to relative invisibility in the 1980s in the United States, however, even as the Redress Movement on behalf of former inmates of Japanese American concentration camps, as well as the antinuclear movement, picked up momentum. In 1981, for instance, Yoneda was testifying before the Commission on Wartime Relocation and Internment of Civilians, a nine-member commission empowered by the Congress to investigate Executive Order 9066 that had placed Japanese Americans on the West Coast in incarceration in 1942. This was one of the milestones on the road to redress, squarely based on a claim of a civil rights violation. The antinuclear cause, too, seemed to reach one of its high points around the same time. In 1980, a public hearing was held in Washington, DC, to consider a bill introduced by Senator Edward Kennedy. The purpose of the bill was at once broadly antinuclear and specifically compensatory for radiation victims in the United States, including Native Americans irradiated in uranium mines, soldiers who unknowingly became "atomic veterans," workers irradiated at nuclear power plants or medical clinics, and "downwinders" – residents of Nevada and the Marshall Islands. According to the bill's supporters, these individuals' civil rights had been gravely neglected. This claim was gradually accepted by the US government, making it possible for these *hibakusha* to be compensated in various ways by the early 1990s.[99]

But the list of beneficiaries did not include US survivors of Hiroshima and Nagasaki, prompting CABS president Kuramoto to protest: "For some reason, we are not included in the list. Because we had not been visible enough, American society appeared to have decided to ignore us."[100] By then, the 1978 bill had failed in Congress, and the Department of Defense had expressed its opposition to any similar bill that may be written in the future.[101] The assumed legitimacy of the bomb as the nation's necessary war-tool overrode the civil rights neglect and the endlessness of radiation illness. Kennedy likely wanted to avoid putting the bill's passage at risk by including an already-dismissed group. To be sure, he invited four US survivors to the witness stand, including one of the "Hiroshima Maidens," Shigeko Sasamori, and Francis Mitsuo Tomosawa, who was to become the president of a group of US survivors. But these witnesses' mission was to help "end the use of nuclear weapons" by telling the horror of ground zero. Their stories had nothing to do with US *hibakusha*, their identity, and their remembering, an erasure disturbingly similar to the experience of Jack Motoo Dairiki with the California Civil Defense in the early 1950s. Just as Dairiki had been made to seem a Hiroshima survivor with no history of connection to America, no major newspapers cited Tomosawa's US citizenship by birth.[102] Obscured by this incomplete telling, too, was Tomosawa as a Hawaiian boy in Hiroshima in 1945, riding on his American bicycle until shortly before the bomb's explosion.

As an estimated one million antinuclear demonstrators filled the streets of New York City in 1982, US survivors seemed to be exiled to a historical oblivion in the United States. The irony was not missed by some observers. For instance, Susan Lambert, a FOH member and a physician who assisted the medical checkup by Hiroshima doctors at the University of California Medical Center in San Francisco in 1987, called for "US financial aid to American survivors." In a press conference, she made it clear that the "United States has not really taken care of its own."[103] These critiques of the civil rights neglect notwithstanding, most US survivors' efforts after the mid-1980s followed the only path left, one across the Pacific, which relied on human rights narrowly defined by the Japanese government. For example, *techō* was effective only during one's stay in Japan. US *hibakusha*'s frustration over such restrictions grew particularly after the Japanese government began to offer limited funds for the biannual checkups through the Hiroshima RERF.[104] Now that both the laws for Japanese survivors and the programs for non-Japanese survivors were sponsored by the government, their difference – how much the latter fell short of the former – became abundantly clear. As Japan emerged as an economic giant in the 1980s and 1990s, the unequal treatment of US survivors carried an even sharper edge. This was the era when Japantown in both Los Angeles and San Francisco transformed into a hub for the booming Japanese economy. In the discriminatory process of "urban renewal," Japanese American businesses and community centers began to disappear from the districts. Japanese corporations flooded in, catering to Japanese businessmen and tourists.[105] Earlier, in the 1960s and 1970s, corporate America and its appetite for purging ethnic communities was the force to fight against for Asian America. Now, in the last decades of the century, the competition seemed to come chiefly from across the Pacific. In this context, the discriminatory treatment of survivors based on their nationality or residence felt problematic to US survivors. Particularly, the lack of monetary allowances for any survivors outside Japan remained a sore concern.

The increasing awareness among American survivors of the unequal treatment by the Japanese government gave rise to a conspicuous strain in the biannual medical examinations. Unlike the overwhelmingly cordial relationship between generous Japanese doctors and grateful American survivors in the late 1970s and early 1980s, the relationship in the later years became undeniably tense. Francis Mitsuo Tomosawa, for one, recalled how Itō Chikako, one of the Japanese physicians who led the biannual program during much of the 1980s and early 1990s, was taken aback by US *hibakusha*'s concerns about the discriminatory treatment by the Japanese government. "You are American survivors, who are getting benefits out of the (Japanese) program. ... You should be thankful for that and demand nothing more,"[106] she told him bluntly. Masako Kawasaki was told by a physician during a checkup: "You can always come see us in Hiroshima." When she fell ill and asked if she could come to Hiroshima, however, her request was flatly denied. Kawasaki was "shocked."[107] It felt as if the Japanese government, as well as the American, refused her identity as a survivor. As this kind of tension arose, it was hardly missed by US survivors that Japanese physicians flew to America in business class. When US survivors flew to Japan for treatment as part of Satogaeri Chiryō, they were paid to fly in economy class.[108] Because the program by definition required that a sick person travel internationally, with travel times often extending to more than thirty hours, it was unclear if Satogaeri Chiryō was the best way to attend to sickness. To further complicate the matter, the program's participants were not necessarily survivors who were actually sick. In Toshiro Kubota's observation, the program was run rather "randomly." "I didn't have any health problem," Kubota remembered. "But there was no one who wanted to go [to Japan] at that time. So I was asked to go ... it would look bad if all slots [for treatment] were not taken."[109] Given how the program invited five survivors per year only, Kubota's experience in the mid-1990s indicated a declining interest in Satogaeri Chiryō among US survivors.

As these concerns became part of hallway talk during the medical examinations, there emerged different opinions among US survivors about how to approach their unequal treatment by the Japanese government. Some thought that they should ignore the difference, or, to put it more precisely, that they should not see the difference as inequality. According to this view, US survivors came or returned to the United States of their own will, and thus they had no business claiming any benefits from a foreign government. National belonging, then, set the basic boundary, separating survivors into distinctive categories of the deserving and undeserving.[110] Other survivors were less concerned about this boundary and continued to see value in the biannual checkup and Satogaeri Chiryō programs. Interestingly, Kazue Suyeishi, who had taken leadership roles in US survivors' efforts in Los Angeles to pass the medical legislation throughout the 1970s, was one of the most outspoken survivors who took this position in the 1980s and 1990s. In her view, "it was important not to say that the Japanese government was being unkind to us." According to her, the aim of her many meetings with Japanese politicians and physicians was to serve as "a messenger" of US survivors, and to express "gratitude" for the existing programs. These meetings were not for demanding "payment for us or to treat us equally as Japanese survivors." Even her appearance seemed to conform to her conciliatory message, as Suyeishi recalled:

> They thought that this woman from America must look like one of these scary Japanese middle-aged women, who ... wear a sash [with a political message on it] across the chest. Then, this woman [Suyeishi] walked in, looking casual, and said "Hello, everyone!"[111]

Clearly, Suyeishi was not as "scary" as politically active women. Her approach was that of a friendly, physically unassuming, and apolitical woman, who would not make any unconventional demands. In this way, Suyeishi performed a gender role that best suited her purposes. She took pride in the role; she recalled fondly that people called her *Mama-san*, a term that evokes a maternal, gentle, capable, and facilitating figure. This differed from the Suyeishi who emerged in Julie Kumi Fukuda's remembering, the one who was "too much" for some male US survivors. Perhaps, Suyeishi brought out different gender expressions depending on which country she was in. My impression during talking to the later Suyeishi was that she was conscious of the need to be flexible. After experiencing the Cold War conformity in the 1940s and 1950s and the civil rights movement in the 1960s and 1970s, US survivors reached a point in the last decades of the century where they might play a variety of gender roles without losing a sense of identity. This was one way in which they kept the "strength of weak ties."

Meanwhile, US survivors in the San Francisco group, such as Kanji Kuramoto, Mitsuko Okimoto, and Ayako Elliott, began to make precisely the kind of direct demands from which Suyeishi refrained. Frustrated by the existing programs, they took a step to press the Japanese MHW that they directly pay US survivors (as they do Japanese survivors) medical expenses incurred in the treatment of radiation illnesses. As Elliott saw it, it was "of course more logical for US survivors to get help from the US government." And yet, it was also necessary for the Japanese government to recognize *hibakusha* "regardless of where they are, who they are."[112] Unlike those who believed that survivors should be divided into distinct groups based on the uniqueness of their national belonging, then, she considered a universal definition of survivorhood essential. Okimoto agreed, although she understood that some might see the group's demands as greedy. But for her, her labor was not something that could be compensated by money. "Sometimes, I felt as if I didn't know why I was doing it," explained Okimoto:

> Once, I assisted someone from Nagasaki who was invited to participate in Satogaeri Chiryō. She did not have a passport, because her parents had died of the bomb and she escaped from her aunts and uncles who had taken her in and abused her as a child laborer. She married a black soldier she met at the US military base. . . . Her relatives then deleted her from their family record. I called up the Consulate General of Japan [to put her back in the family record]. . . . Then, her uncle started to complain to me: "Who are you to tell us that we must change our way?"[113]

To Okimoto, then, the problem was the unequal distances that survivors must travel to find equal treatment. Not everyone benefitted from the existing program; citizenship could be arbitrary, national belonging layered. Racism and sexism remained potent, shaping US *hibakusha*'s identity continuingly influenced by illness. The best way to remedy the unevenness was direct coverage for medical costs. Equally important, when asked why she decided to "spend so much time" on cases like this Nagasakian, Okimoto responded: "Because [as a woman] I don't think of logic. I want to fix problems at hand. I don't think you can take actions if you think of logic too much. People call me luck-pusher, but it is true that I get strengths from immediate problems."[114] Notable here is that she used the term "logic" not as the antonym of "illogic," a descriptor often associated with women. Instead, "logic" is something that gets in the way of taking action. Rather than a facilitator like Suyeishi, then, a person unafraid of conflicts is what Okimoto's gender identity propelled her to become. Both of these gender expressions proved crucial in keeping, and simultaneously, changing, the Japanese treatment of US survivors. Eventually, not only those in San Francisco but also members of the Los Angeles group became beneficiaries of the monetary support implemented by the Japanese government in the early 2000s.

EPILOGUE

I think it's very important to tell. People should not forget. And it's just like … the concentration camps … [for] the Niseis … So you should always tell about that, too, because some people don't know about it.
          —May Yamaoka, Interview with Yamaoka, STC

When I go to a gathering at a veterans' club … I tell them that I am an atomic bomb survivor. They express sympathy in a good way – not just to be nice, but to tell me that they experienced the war, too. … So it is not as though everybody hates us.
          —Miyuki Broadwater, Interview with Broadwater, STC

They all get together on the atomic bomb memorial day, to show that they oppose nuclear weapons. They ask me how I feel. But I cannot tell them how I truly feel.
          —Fumie Schutt, Interview with Schutt, STC

If one thing remains constant in the history of US survivors, it is that their remembering comprises silence as much as speech. No doubt Yamaoka, Broadwater, and Schutt want to remember. They participate in occasions reminding them of the bomb, and they agree to be interviewed. And yet, they also struggle with silence. Yamaoka begins to talk about the bomb, only to find herself discussing the camp. Broadwater surprises us with her courageous act of speaking to WWII veterans. Then, we are surprised again by how her bravery stands side by side with her bleakness; some Americans might hate her if she revealed her survivorhood. Schutt goes to a bomb memorial, but she finds her reasons to attend it at odds with others'. Others' remembering comes to the fore, while immigrants' remembering recedes into the background. US survivors are still speaking, but the bomb somehow finds a way to disappear.

The coexistence of speech and silence might be found in any remembering of the past, especially of an event of extraordinary magnitude. But for US *hibakusha*, the coexistence is pronounced because of the still-absent recognition. After failing to obtain US government recognition, their only source of support has been from the Japanese government. But the disparity between Japanese and non-Japanese survivors has persisted. Japanese survivors could bring the costs to close to nothing by being recognized by *techō*, while American survivors enjoyed no support if they received medical services in the United States. The biannual examinations by Japanese physicians might be free, but all else had to be paid personally. Satogaeri Chiryō might pay for sick survivors to travel across the Pacific, but only a handful per year could be the program's beneficiaries. When aging US survivors faced a myriad of illnesses, expenses they incurred in America began to pile up.

As US survivors tried to close this gap, one of the aspirations that originally had brought them together – to gain access to Hiroshima and Nagasaki physicians – began to divide them. As seen in Chapter 6, some US *hibakusha* continued to see great worth in the biannual checkups, while others began to see them as a cover for unequal treatment in the name of humanitarianism. The former stressed both physical and psychosocial benefits of the exams. The latter group, in contrast, considered the checkup that occurs only once every two years therapeutically obsolete and politically disingenuous. The disagreement made CABS untenable as a single umbrella for all US survivors. In 1992, they split into two groups, one in San Francisco and the other in Los Angeles and Hawai'i. In 2004, the Los Angeles group split, again because of members' disagreement over the biannual checkups.[1] Around the same time, *hibakusha* in Washington and Vancouver established their own organization, becoming the fourth group of survivors in North America.[2]

US *hibakusha*'s supporters, too, felt that the Japanese programs led to mixed results. Many of these supporters continued to appreciate cross-national opportunities that ties across the Pacific afforded US survivors. Asian American supporters – medical professionals, community and family members – continued to find unique worth in assisting US *hibakusha*. In a way, to care for US survivors was to keep alive the legacy of the Asian American movement, which had originated in the community's aspiration in the 1970s to "serve the people." And yet, even after US *hibakusha* obtained in 2003 the right to Japanese government-issued monetary allowances comparable to those given to Japanese survivors, there arose new reasons for concern, most notably the activism that centered on litigation instead of legislation. Some supporters of US *hibakusha* were disappointed that the litigation-based approach, which developed since the turn of the century vis-à-vis the Japanese government, offered no possibility of civil and human rights recognition by the US government. It was also important that court cases concerning American survivors largely followed precedents set by Korean survivors. Consequently, Japan's history of colonialism became highlighted in the bomb's history, continuing to obscure the cross-national impact and import of nuclear weaponry. As their communities became expansive and more deeply connected to Asian and American countries including not only Korea but also Brazil, Peru, and Mexico, US survivors' cross-national history once again raised unsettling questions; they are questions about national belonging, race, and gender identity, all of which are uniquely Asian American and, at the same time, universally critical to the history of nuclear weaponry.

Gender, Race, and National Belonging across the Pacific: A Snapshot

US survivors by the end of the twentieth century, thus, had substantial disagreements over the biannual checkups, Satogaeri Chiryō, and monetary allowances. The biannual exams, for instance, posed particular challenges for the increasingly older, predominantly female, *hibakusha*. Aging US survivors were growing less mobile. And yet, there were only four sites for the checkups – Honolulu, Seattle, San Francisco, and Los Angeles. The full examination could take half a day or longer, so anyone living outside the nearby areas had to come a day or two early.[3] Moreover, as one survivor attested, CABS members "must host members of the doctors' team, cook their meals" at their homes. Their volunteer work also included "driving and preparing snacks" for the physicians, often paid for by *hibakusha* themselves.[4] Cross-national collaboration was not easy, and the task of filling gaps fell disproportionately on female survivors.

It was not only survivors themselves who noticed gaps in the Japanese programs. Asian American medical professionals and community members, too, recognized that something was amiss. Speaking about Japanese physicians who came to America biannually, Kathy Yamaguchi, a Japanese American physician who regularly assisted the checkups, observed:

> I've seen them [Japanese physicians] ... have a very good time. They ... have a good time with each other, and they have some good meals. I've gone out, I've been invited along with them, to these celebratory, end of the exam, dinners, and, without the survivors. Not with the survivors. ... I had a great dinner ... at a fancy hotel. They're getting drunk, they're hilarious! Because they were done, they were finished; they had worked really hard.[5]

Yamaguchi did not overtly criticize the physicians. She recognized that they had immense responsibilities: their travel extended to a month, including stops at four locations. They examined more than 200 survivors over a course of a few days.[6]

And yet, Yamaguchi's description of the physicians, whom she also noted "get to go shopping" during their stay, contained an unmistakable irony. Their visits were made possible not solely by their own efforts. They were well compensated by the Japanese government, which began to pay for most of the program in 2003.[7] On the US side, where there was no governmental support, Asian American community members made arrangements mostly uncompensated. As Ayaka Sakurai, married to Japanese American physician Fred Yutaka Sakurai, discussed in Chapter 6, attested, the support work "took up time":

> It went far beyond the realm of volunteer. It felt as if we were donating in addition to volunteering. ... [American] doctors and nurses [who conducted exams] were paid by the [Japanese] Ministry of Health and Welfare. But I know that they spent much, much more time than hours covered by the payment.[8]

Although Sakurai took pride and pleasure in her work, she also did not fail to note that all the communication with the Japanese side fell on her, not the hosting facility as it should have. This was because "the Hiroshima side found it ... difficult to communicate in English. So they ended up sending everything in Japanese to me."[9] Again, the problem of cross-cultural communication was to be fixed by the Asian American community, with no assistance from the state. The lack of support that had set into motion the community medicine in the 1970s persisted. Asian Americans worked as hard as their Japanese counterparts; but the ways in which their efforts were recognized were uneven.

The difference in recognition was accentuated by gender roles that varied across the Pacific. Female US *hibakusha* seemed to play the most unrecognized roles as cooks and caretakers. For Sakurai, too, her role as a cross-cultural mediator reaffirmed, rather than dismantled, gender expectations. "My husband did not communicate [with the Japanese side] because it was not his profession," recalled Sakurai. "So, in the end, I had to be the one to get in touch with [Japanese participants]." On the day of my interviews with the Sakurais, the gendered dynamism was salient. Sakurai insisted that I interview her first, then her husband. This was to ensure that I hear from her a general history of his accomplishments. In this way, he would be able to focus on more important specifics. It was not easy for me to get her to tell her story. Born in Japan and coming to America as a professional woman, Sakurai seemed to feel both a pressure to play supporting roles and a frustration with being confined in them. Yamaguchi, born and raised in the United States, by contrast, found her work "immensely rewarding" because she felt accepted "as one of the guys." Her feeling had roots in her initial concern that Japanese physicians, mostly men, would not accept her as an equal. "I didn't have a visible boyfriend, I didn't have a family," said Yamaguchi. "I thought they [Japanese physicians] ... were going to see me ... [as] a lesbian communist." Although her comment was lighthearted, it is clear that she was relieved when Japanese physicians treated her with respect. She was a third generation Asian American woman who pursued a medical career before it was even on the horizon for most in her community. She did not follow a traditional path of marriage and reproduction. Now, her desire to be accepted as a woman and a professional became a reality as she worked with her male colleagues from across the ocean.[10]

Yamaguchi, a monolingual speaker of English, gained recognition as a modern female professional, while the bilingual Sakurai played assisting roles that kept her labor unrecognized. If Yamaguchi fit the image of the "model minority" of the twenty first-century United States, Sakurai seemed to recede into the image of "perpetual foreigner" because of her cross-cultural ability. In the 1950s and 1960s, these racial images were particularly potent in the United States; in the 2000s, they were replicated in the gendered interactions between Japanese and American professionals. This signaled an expansion of American racial and gender dynamisms across the Pacific, shaped by an international hierarchy set after the war. In Japanese perception, someone who made it solely in the United States was deemed more successful than a person who possessed cross-national abilities. The former was an American, the latter dubiously a Japanese American. As American hegemony and its asymmetrical alliance with Japan matured in the Pacific region in the early twenty-first century, this perception continued to marginalize US *hibakusha*. Nearly a quarter century after the US Congress rejected US survivors as being *too Japanese*, their ancestral land seemed to turn its back to their layered national belonging deemed *too American*. They had been in the United States for a long time; they should be doing just fine. That they have not uniformly done so, something made clear by their demand for assistance from Japan, rendered them failed Americans – Japanese Americans – in the eyes of some Japanese.[11] In response, US *hibakusha*'s trans-Pacific activism in the 2000s aimed to reverse the process of disavowal by the Japanese government.

Cross-National Coalitions: Their Korean Origins and Growth in the Americas

"We owe our [monetary] allowances to Korean people," said Joyce Ikuko Moriwaki confidently. "First, it was Korean 'comfort women' who got them" from the Japanese government, followed by Korean survivors of Hiroshima and Nagasaki. Then, finally, money came to US *hibakusha*.[12] Sachiko Matsumoto seemed to agree: "Korean people started a movement so that they could receive money in their country, where they lived. Thanks to their effort, we all receive the assistance now."[13] Kazue Kawasaki called the process *binjō*, to explain her view that US survivors "jumped on the bandwagon" of their Korean counterparts. "Korean people made a fuss" about the lack of monetary allowances at first; then, "in another country, Brazil, survivors actively sought" the compensations.[14] Like Moriwaki,

Kawasaki believed that US survivors were the last to obtain the assistance because they were the least assertive. This kind of remembering that situates Korean survivors at the center of the trans-Pacific coalition reflects US *hibakusha*'s unique history of seeking assistance cross-nationally. Unlike Korean and Brazilian survivors, who focused almost singularly on getting assistance from the Japanese government, US survivors demanded American support in addition to assistance from Japan. This difference in tactics had its origin in the Treaty of Basic Relations Between Japan and the Republic of Korea signed in 1965, which was aimed at settling the human costs of Japanese colonialism in South Korea. As discussed in Chapter 6, no individual compensations were to be paid to Korean persons by the Japanese government; instead, the Japanese government paid the Korean government. The same principle of no individual compensations had been already established by the San Francisco Treaty of Peace, which normalized the relationship between Japan and the United States in 1952.

And yet, because of the political dynamism that continued to separate the former Allied and Axis Powers, the principle gradually fell apart for the 1965 treaty. As Japanese colonial violence became more loudly criticized by Koreans in the 1990s, it became difficult for the Japanese government to contain the discontent. Moriwaki's reference to "comfort women" pointed to the reason why. These Korean women, forced into sexual slavery by the Japanese military during the Asia–Pacific War, had not come forward publicly by 1965, allowing them to argue by the early 1990s that the 1965 treaty was grossly inadequate. Several of the women lodged a lawsuit against the Japanese government, demanding a public apology and individual compensations paid by the state.[15] This effort gained considerable traction among civilian casualties of the Axis Powers; successful claims for compensation had been already made by the Jewish Holocaust survivors against the government of West Germany since the early 1950s. After an increasing number of Holocaust survivors began to openly speak about their experiences, in the late 1970s and early 1980s, public support for individual compensations for the "crimes against humanity" soared.[16] Soon, Korean *hibakusha* adopted a similar strategy. Their nuclear holocaust was one of the Japanese government's "crimes against humanity," and its aftermaths the government's responsibility.[17] This was a kind of argument missing from US *hibakusha*'s activism. After their demands were turned down by the US government, they were left without anything like the "comfort women" issue that brought the forces of gender, race, and nationality together against the Japanese government. Equally important, there were no treaties for US survivors to condemn as discriminatory. No wonder, they reasoned, they had not been as effective as Korean *hibakusha*.

Reasonable as it is, the account that features the centrality of Korean activism obscures American survivors' continuing efforts to obtain recognition from the Japanese government through cross-national alliances. This is not to suggest that Korean survivors did not play critical roles; they did. But remembering such as Matsumoto's downplays how US *hibakusha*, including Matsumoto herself, played roles as petitioners, donors, and plaintiffs. They might not have been active in the same way as they had been in the 1970s, but to describe them as opportunistic riders on the Korean "bandwagon" is misleading. Such a description might have more to do with US survivors' desire not to "make a fuss" with Japan, where many of their families and friends lived, than it does with an actual absence of political engagement. In a way similar to how Suyeishi adopted a facilitating leadership style, many US *hibakusha* wished to be part of the trans-Pacific activism without being confrontational. Their experiences as immigrants had taught them that a nation-bound argument does not always generate healing, care, and reconciliation. They did not think that the bomb was a necessary military action; they also thought it limiting to call it Japan's crime against humanity. It struck them as ineffective to confront the Japanese government by claiming that it was uniquely responsible for the bombs' universal casualties. Instead, they chose to pursue the argument that the Japanese government apply the existing "humanitarian" Japanese laws to all non-Japanese survivors.[18] When combined with the Korean survivors' claim that the Japanese government is uniquely responsible for compensation, US *hibakusha*'s cross-national activism successfully brought most of what they wanted: the monetary allowances, including both the monthly stipend and the annual reimbursement of the costs incurred by the treatment of radiation illness.

Although Korean *hibakusha* implemented a program similar to Satogaeri Chiryō, between 1980 and 1986, the lack of monetary allowances and free medical care in Korea remained a concern. In 1989, free medical treatment for Korean survivors in Korean hospitals became a temporary reality, as the Japanese and Korean governments agreed to share the cost for a year. In 1990, however, the Japanese government announced that it would pay for medical care up to the total of 400 million yen, fueling the resentment among Korean survivors that this one-time payment fell far short of full compensation.[19] As they continued to press their demands through diplomatic channels, other Korean plaintiffs from the WWII era gained important courtroom victories in Japan. Most notably, Kim Sun-gil, who had been in Nagasaki in August 1945 working for Mitsubishi Heavy Industries, filed a lawsuit in 1992 against the government and the company to pay for both the forced labor and the injury caused by the bomb. By 1995, another lawsuit against the same defendants was brought to the Hiroshima district court by a group of wartime Mitsubishi employees from Korea. These key legal cases addressed the damage caused by the bombs as part of the legacy of the Japanese colonial policies, giving the plaintiffs moral, as well as legal, clout.[20]

In 1998 and 1999, while the earlier cases were still ongoing, two more lawsuits were filed by Korean survivors, this time with a sole focus on compensation for the bomb illness and injury. Because these cases were built on the earlier discourse about Japan's wartime atrocity and compensatory responsibility, they gained strong support from Japan's liberal quarters.[21] Shimin no Kai, for instance, stood in steadfast support of Korean survivors throughout the 1990s. Shortly after the Japanese government announced the plan to make a one-time payment to Korean *hibakusha*, Shimin no Kai's newsletter *Hayaku engo o!* featured sick survivors living in six cities in South Korea. These survivors would be left out of the benefit promised by the Japanese government. "Most of the funds will be allocated for [hospital] buildings" in Seoul, while many survivors in rural areas "will not be able to go to a hospital in Seoul" because they were too sick to travel.

US survivors pressed for equal treatment by the Japanese government throughout the 1990s and early 2000s as well, but their tactics differed greatly from Korean *hibakusha*'s. While *Hayaku engo o!* often adopted a highly critical tone against Japanese governmental officials, the *CABS Newsletter* in this era frequently featured newspaper articles about Japanese politicians and physicians sympathetic to the expansion of the medical assistance to non-Japanese survivors.[22] Too, the newsletter included much media coverage of non-Japanese survivors, including those in Korea, Brazil, Peru, and Mexico, featuring all of them as allies.[23] Not only newspaper articles published in Japan and America, but also issues of *Hayaku engo o!* featuring Korean and Brazilian survivors, were included.²⁴ If this was an expansion of their cross-national approach that began in the 1960s, US *hibakusha* in the 1990s also featured the inequality between Japanese and non-Japanese survivors more explicitly than they had earlier. In a 1996 issue of the *CABS Newsletter*, the organization's president Kanji Kuramoto emphasized how, "as we [US survivors] age, more of us fall ill and poor." Citing a Medi-Cal recipient, Kuramoto went on to argue: "Any survivors could become ill and use up their savings." Still, the words expressing their needs indicated that they were "asking assistance," not necessarily "making demands."²⁵ Although the *CABS Newsletter* was similar to *Hayaku engo o!* in featuring illness and financial difficulties, their tones could not be more different.

In contrast to Korean survivors who claimed illegality and immorality of the Japanese government's contemporary practice, American survivors relied more on the conciliatory rhetoric they adopted at their individual meetings with Japanese politicians. In fact, it was these meetings that allowed US *hibakusha* to meet survivors from Korea and Brazil. During the 1970s, it was chiefly Japanese supporters of Korean survivors who assisted US survivors' quest for *techō*. In the 1990s, in contrast, US survivors stood at the forefront of the appeals to the Japanese government, along with Korean and Brazilian survivors. In 1995, during the ceremony for the fiftieth-anniversary of the Hiroshima bombing, Kuramoto met with representatives of *hibakusha* groups in Korea and Brazil, reaching an agreement on the common goal of making Japanese laws applicable to non-Japanese survivors. In 1997, the Korean, Brazilian, and American groups met again, this time with Japanese left-leaning politicians. When some of them came to San Francisco a few months later, CABS leaders including Kuramoto, Francis Mitsuo Tomosawa, and Mitsuko Okimoto, met them again to make a plea jointly.²⁶

CABS's collaboration with Korean and Brazilian *hibakusha* indicated that the latter groups were willing to use the tactics favored by their US counterpart: meeting, imploring, and petitioning. CABS members reciprocated by becoming more open to the approach taken by Koreans and Brazilians: lawsuits. This blend of conciliatory and confrontational tactics became evident by the end of the 1990s, after US *hibakusha* had spent nearly a decade changing its self-representation from grateful recipients of Japanese assistance to resolute, if polite, petitioners of fairer treatment. In 1999, both Kuramoto and Takashi

Morita, the president of the Brazilian *hibakusha* group, took the witness stand for the aforementioned trial concerning a Korean survivor. For a petition to support the plaintiff, Kwak Ki-hun, American, Korean, and Brazilian groups, along with Shimin no Kai, collected 11,000 signatures and submitted them to the MHW.[27] In 2002, when Morita himself became a plaintiff in another, nearly identical trial against the Japanese government, CABS quickly gathered sixty donations.[28] Around the same time, a group of Japanese antinuclear lawyers, which had assisted in the 1999 case, formed a support group for the Brazilian plaintiffs. This group's leaders, Adachi Shūichi and Tamura Kazuyuki, came to San Francisco later in 2002, urging US survivors to join the cause.[29] This encouragement by Japanese legal experts likely made an impact on those who still felt reluctant. In comparison with US *hibakusha*'s activism that expanded from America to Japan in the 1970s, their activism in the 1990s spread from Korea and Japan, bringing together North and South Americas.[30]

The mid-2000s marked a turning point when US survivors for the first time became plaintiffs in a lawsuit. After the Kwak and Morita cases reached decisive victories in 2002 and 2003, respectively, monetary allowances – both the monthly payment and the annual reimbursement – became available to non-Japanese survivors living outside of Japan. And yet, the problem remained; they had to go to Japan to apply for the benefits. Given the fact that many applicants were ill, financially struggling, or both, this requirement drastically limited *techō* issuance. In response, US survivors Teruko Morimoto and Chisato Kuramoto, both women, came forward to file a formal complaint in early 2004. Throughout, US *hibakusha* presented themselves as distinctively American. They were in need of support not because they were poor but because the US health insurance system was costly. American physicians were not inferior to Japanese doctors, either. "There are many excellent physicians in America, so why can't we ask them" to treat US *hibakusha*, asked Kanji Kuramoto.[31] These arguments were likely made to push back against the image of Japanese Americans as failed Americans.[32] As discussed earlier, the idea of Nikkei as "perpetual foreigners" had crossed the Pacific westward and shaped the intraracial bias against bicultural Nikkei as less than successful Americans in the minds of some Japanese.[33] To counter the bias, US *hibakusha* highlighted their belonging to America and an image of the country as a global leader in the promotion of human rights. Moreover, in 2004, a Nikkei community newsletter reported that the biannual checkups were falling short of American women's needs. A Japanese woman who assisted in the checkup, an employee of the Hiroshima city government, explained how the exams had made her aware of the gender inequality in Japan; only a few female physicians were among the ranks participating in the program highly reputed in Japan. The nearly-all-male team of Japanese physicians made some American female survivors feel uncomfortable. The clear message was that US *hibakusha* expected gender equality, and rightly so.[34] The Japanese should take this to heart and make the program better for Americans.

The coming forward of CABS members, combined with the support they received from Korean, Japanese, and Brazilian groups, propelled US survivors to adopt increasingly confrontational tactics. By March 2004, fifty-seven CABS members had donated a total of US$2,780 for the Morimoto–Kuramoto trial. Three months later, the donation rose to US$14,830, coming from eighty-five people. Not only well-to-do *hibakusha*, but also those who struggled to make ends meet, contributed, leading to a courtroom victory. Meanwhile, Tomosawa, who had been a CABS leader, created a new group in Southern California called North American A-Bomb Survivors' Association (NAABSA), and began to discuss the possibility of a coordinated boycott with Korean and Brazilian survivors.[35] The Brazilian group was dissatisfied with the biannual medical examinations by Nagasaki physicians, which had started in South America in 1985; for many, the medical examinations were simply too distant to attend. Although Americans did not reach a consensus about boycott, most of the NAABSA members stopped going to the checkups after 2005. This was an ultimate "no" to the Japanese program, backed by the sense of American fairness, equality, and justice.[36]

The Counter-Memory of the Nuclear Holocaust

What happened to the counter-memory of the bomb? Is it speaking to us, or has it fallen silent? Tomosawa spoke with concern about forgetting: "I worry about how we forget that the bomb happened, that the holocaust happened,"[37] he said during his interview in 2012. His sentiment echoed the reason why Kyohei Sakata continued to participate in antinuclear rallies at the nuclear laboratory in Livermore. "I want to tell people that weapons made there could kill hundreds of thousand people again. For me to be there – being a person who survived the holocaust – makes our message powerful."[38] Both Tomosawa and Sakata call the 1945 destruction "the holocaust." They believed that it is wrong to keep their remembering on the historical periphery by using a term with less gravity. To call the bomb the nuclear holocaust is also a way to call into question the bomb's legality and morality, and to affix responsibility for it. They both remained convinced that the response must be cross-national, involving not only Asians but also Americans.

Where is the US government in all of the discussions of the nuclear holocaust? This is the question that remains. It came up frequently in US *hibakusha*'s oral histories. "I really think that it is more reasonable for the United States to offer us an assistance," said Aiko Tokito.[39] For Tokie Akihara, the lack of US assistance "is a contradiction that cannot be resolved." She went on to say: "For, the United States is the maker of nuclear — . A lot of it. So they cannot care for survivors as an American policy. Besides, it is the country that dropped the bomb; and the country justifies it. So we are an afterthought; we are a collateral damage."[40] Some, such as Alfred Kaneo Dote, glided over the lack of recognition for US *hibakusha* by making it part of a pattern of neglect applicable to all minorities. "There has been no compensation for American soldiers who were irradiated," insisted Dote.[41] But in 1983, with the passage of the Veterans' Dioxin and Radiation Exposure Compensation Standards Act, US military personnel exposed to radiation as a result of entering Hiroshima or Nagasaki after the 1945 bombings became eligible for compensation. In Dote's mind, Native Americans who had been unknowingly irradiated at uranium mines in the Cold War era were not compensated, either, although in fact these *hibakusha* miners had been compensated since the passage of the Radiation Exposure Compensation Act of 1990. Nonetheless, it is striking that this is the story that Dote tells. *Otherwise, it does not make sense.*

Just as American survivors' activism at the turn of the twenty-first century has been shaped cross-nationally, their critical sentiment about the United States has been shared by Korean survivors of Hiroshima and Nagasaki. Pak Namjoo, a Korean survivor in Japan, recalled that the lack of US support came up occasionally when she participated in Korean *hibakusha*'s gatherings. "We feel sorry for the Japanese government," said Pak. "It was America that dropped the bomb, so it would be good if the country pitch in even a little. . . . Some of us initially thought that that was what the United States was doing."[42] During a gathering hosted by Shimin no Kai, one participant raised a hand and asked why the group did not demand that the US government pay.[43] These critiques of the US policy of nonengagement, however, have been difficult to bring forward legally. In theory, Korean survivors could demand at least partial compensation from the United States, using the logic that chipped away at the principle of no individual compensations advanced by the 1965 Korea–Japan treaty. "The problem, though, is that it is difficult to find American prosecutors" to collaborate in such a lawsuit, said Shimin no Kai's leader Toyonaga.[44] The prospect of dismantling the 1952 US–Japan treaty by the force of Korean activism seemed extremely dim.[45]

Survivors across the Pacific have expressed a shared desire to engage the United States in their remembering the bomb. Their remembering has been a source of resilience, sometimes paradoxically. Although they did not reach all of their goals, *hibakusha*'s shifting remembering has moved them to embrace new approaches and identities. Paradoxical, too, is how the biannual medical checkups continue to be one of the most active sites of remembering, despite the fact that the program has caused much discordance. John Hong, for example, planned to take part in a transportation program for older Korean Americans, inspired by the communal remembering made possible by the biannual exams. "Korean and Japanese are both Asians, and in the United States, [they] are all ... discriminated against. So first of all, I think it would be very nice to have a group of Japanese and Korean old people getting together, and become friends," said Hong.[46]

In other ways, too, the spirit of community embodied by US survivors since the mid-1960s has not disappeared. Ray Chew, a medical technician volunteering for the biannual exams, thought that they are not "just exams." These occasions are for him "to meet with people ... eating cookies or something with them, in the hallway, and they are talking to you. Then you see what happened to them, in the film or something, you see the horror, horrible things that happened. And yet, they are so resilient, they are so happy; [this] give[s] you a hope."[47] For Shannon Cheng, also a long-term volunteer, the exam has been a "family tradition." "It's beyond just being there," she said. "Not only my family, but also people become kind of like a family, friends. You see them every time. The connection I make, like recent time, I talked to people, and they told me about what happened to them.... And that gives me a sense of why this person is here."[48] In Chew's case, his interactions with US *hibakusha* did not include specific remembering of the bomb; in Chang's case, her conversations clearly involved what had happened in 1945. Regardless, they both reflected on the bomb and its consequences; both silence and speech communicated.

On the other side of the Pacific, a similar sense of care and commitment persists. Ch'oe Ha-un, who came from Korea to Japan in 1990, joined Shimin no Kai because she "is an immigrant, too." When she worked at a senior center in Hiroshima, she realized how everyone she met there was Korean *hibakusha*. More than anything else, their presence impressed on her the link between nuclear weaponry and immigration. Too, survivors' cross-nationality has inspired a desire among their supporters to continue remembering and recording. Ichiba Junko, a leader of Shimin no Kai, published in 2005 the first known collection of oral history interviews with Korean survivors in Korea, learning the Korean language along the way.[49]

When US survivors touch on US responsibility for the bomb in their remembering, they are not simply questioning the legality or morality of the US decision to use the weapons. They are also questioning the lack of US engagement with the bomb's human consequences in the many decades following the war. If their experiences as immigrants made them unique, their cross-national history that connects eras before, during, and after 1945 has pushed them to address a need to see nuclear weaponry as universally abhorrent. Their counter-memory continues to show it is not enough to define the bomb as a result of one country's misguided policy or another's colonial aggression. Differences in nationality, race, and gender have certainly generated different modes of activism; and yet, survivors' coming together at key moments in history has always been a move toward universality. Diverse as they are, survivors have stayed in close touch with how they suffer together. Their counter-memory has also rejected the belief that radiation illness is a necessary price to pay to win a nuclear war. This is not only because the illness may be medically endless, being passed on to the next generation. The illness incurred by the war has become psychosocial and political as well, joining it to a history of discrimination by race, gender, and nationality, shaping many generations to come.

Nuclear weapons' indiscriminate power to destroy has illuminated nation states' power to discriminate among the sick, dying, and dead. As we have reached three quarters of a century after 1945, there is no doubt that US survivors' history has attested to key moments when opportunities for trans-Pacific justice surfaced. And yet, it also is the case that US survivors' history has been largely absorbed into the history of Japanese war culpability and the search for Japanese justice, without critical reflection about an American justice that refuses to recognize histories that disrupt it. If we are to spare the world a nuclear holocaust, we must first recognize its cross-nationality; our response to it, too, must be cross-national, to counter the authority of nation states. There are abundant examples of cross-national responses suggested by US survivors, as they have communicated to us many times in both silence and speech. It is perhaps too easy to say that their history is a cautionary tale for a nuclear holocaust that may happen again in the future. More difficult is to see that we have been coolly inattentive to their history. In response to the first nuclear holocaust that has generated trans-Pacific memories, we have shown a remarkable capacity to forget, blinded by the nation-specific images that war-makers affix to sufferers. That nuclear weapons far exceeded our imagination of Hiroshima and Nagasaki can no longer be left out of our history.

NOTES

Introduction

1. Maruki Iri and Maruki Toshi, *Pika-don* [Pika don] (Tokyo: Roba no mimi, 1979 [original publication in 1950]), no page number.
2. There is one book-length scholarly study of US survivors, by Sodei Rinjirō, first published in Japanese as a series of articles in 1977 and 1978, then translated into English in 1998. In addition, there are Kamisaka Fuyuko's journalistic account, a memoir written by US survivor Kanji Kuramoto, a report issued by the Hiroshima-ken Ishikai (Hiroshima Prefectural Medical Association) about the medical check-ups that Japanese physicians conducted for American *hibakusha*, and a book written by a Japanese physician, Itō Chikako, who conducted the medical checkups many times. There are also a few articles about psychosocial challenges that US survivors face, by Ikeno Satoshi and Nakao Kayoko. See Sodei, *Were We the Enemy?*; Kamisaka, *Ikinokotta hitobito*; Kuramoto, *Zaibei gojūnen*; Hiroshima-ken Ishikai, *Hiroshima-ken Ishikai*; Itō, *Hazama ni ikite*; Ikeno and Nakao, "Kōreika suru zaibei hibakusha"; —, "Zai Amerika hibakusha"; —, "Zaibei hibakusha kyōkai."
3. Gar Alperovitz, *The Decision to Use the Atomic Bomb and the Architecture of an American Myth* (New York: Vintage, 1996); Barton J. Bernstein, "Truman and the A-Bomb: Targeting Noncombatants, Using the Bomb, and His Defending the 'Decision,'" *Journal of Military History* 62 (July 1998): 547–70; Michael Gordin, *Five Days in August: How World War II Became a Nuclear War* (Princeton, NJ: Princeton University Press, 2007); Barton C. Hacker, *The Dragon's Tail: Radiation Safety in the Manhattan Project, 1942–1946* (Berkeley: University of California Press, 1987); Sean L. Malloy, "'A Very Pleasant Way to Die': Radiation Effects and the Decision to Use the Atomic Bomb against Japan," *Diplomatic History* 36.3 (June 2012): 515–45; Rotter, *Hiroshima: The World's Bomb*; Sherwin, *World Destroyed*; J. Samuel Walker, "The Decision to Use the Bomb: A Historiographical Update," in Hogan, ed., *Hiroshima in History*, 11–37.
4. Boyer, *By the Bomb's Early Light*; Broderick, *Hibakusha Cinema*; Hein and Selden, *Living with the Bomb*; Jacobs, *Dragon's Tail*; Miyamoto, *Beyond the Mushroom Cloud*; Orr, *Victim as Hero*; Zwigenberg, *Hiroshima: The Origin*.

5. My discussion of the counter-memory of the bomb is informed by Herman, *Trauma and Recovery*; Langer, *Versions of Survival*; Lifton, *Death in Life*; R. Tachibana, *Narrative as Counter-memory*; Treat, *Writing Ground Zero*; Wieviorka, *Era of the Witness*, all of which explore the near impossibility of telling things that lay beyond the common understanding of the civilly and humanly adequate.

6. Chandra Mohanty, "Under Western Eyes; Feminist Scholarship and Colonial Discourse," in *Third World Women and the Politics of Feminism*, edited by Chandra Mohanty, Ann Russo, and Lourdes Torres (Bloomington: Indiana University Press, 1991): 51–80 (see 73–4).

7. Jacques Derrida in 1984 wrote that "a nuclear war [had] not taken place" by defining Hiroshima and Nagasaki as the end of a "conventional war ... [that] did not set off a nuclear war." Jacques Derrida, "No Apocalypse, Not Now," *Diacritics* 14.2 (1984): 20–31 (see 23). The power of the nuclear fear that the 1945 bombings provoked has been delineated productively by studies of science and society in Cold War America. See, for example, Paul Erickson, "Saving the Planet from Nuclear Weapons and the Human Mind," in *How Reason Almost Lost Its Mind: The Strange Career of Cold War Rationality*, by Paul Erickson, Judy L. Klein, Lorraine Daston, Rebecca Lemov, Thomas Sturm, and Michael D. Gordin (Chicago: University of Chicago Press, 2013): 81–106; Joseph Masco, "Engineering the Future as Nuclear Ruin," in *Imperial Debris: On Ruins and Ruination*, edited by Ann Laura Stoler (Durham, NC: Duke University Press, 2013): 252–86; David Walker, "The Early Nuclear Age and Visions of Future War," in *The Atomic Bomb and American Society: New Perspectives*, edited by Rosemary B. Mariner and G. Kurt Piehler (Knoxville: University of Tennessee Press, 2009): 285–306.

8. Hans J. Morgenthau, "Death in the Nuclear Age," *Commentary* (September 1961), commentarymagazine.com, accessed on August 27, 2014.

9. Biswas, *Nuclear Desire*; Hagopian, *American Immunity*; Jones, *After Hiroshima*; Nakamura, *Asia kei America*; Yoneyama, *Cold War Ruins*.

10. Yuji Ichioka, "Introduction," in Yoneda, *Ganbatte*, xi–xvii (see xii); Jin, "Transnational Generation," 185, 194; Robert G. Lee, "Introduction," in Tomita, *Dear Miye*, 1–22 (see 18–19). Iida Kōjirō shows that the number of Japanese Americans in Japan in 1938 was as large as 40,000. In this light, 20,000 in 1941 might be a conservative estimate. See Iida Kōjirō, "1930-nendai ni okeru Hiroshima shinai no Nikkei Nisei no bunpu to Issei to no kankei" [The second generation Nikkei in the city of Hiroshima in the 1930s and their relationship to the first generation], *Discover Nikkei*, May 4, 2010.

11. *Ibid.*; Nakano, *Japanese American Women*, 182; Sodei, *Were We the Enemy?*, 11–18. Iida notes that the number of Japanese Americans in Hiroshima prefecture was 11,300, including 5,500 within the city of Hiroshima, in 1932, while Sodei estimates that their number in Hiroshima city was about 3,200 in 1941. Nakano argues that "close to 700 Japanese Americans survived the atomic holocausts of August, 1945" and that "the majority of them returned to the US eventually," but with no citation.

12. Hiroshima-ken Ishikai, *Hiroshima-ken Ishikai*, 69, 96. The number 1,000 is based on 966 certificates of survivorhood issued to US survivors by the Japanese government by 2007. See also Hirano, *Umi no mukō*, 10.

13. This is based on my analysis of the oral histories included in the bibliography. The full demographic information about US survivors is unavailable, and the estimated numbers of US survivors born in either Japan or America have changed over time. *KM*, January 20, 1975, reported that US survivors included "800 American citizens

who were in Japan during the war and who were unable to leave for its duration" in addition to "Japanese who married American citizens, and a small number of war orphans adopted by American couples," without citing the latter's number. *Oakland Tribune East Bay Today*, July 20, 1982, on the other hand, reported that about "65 percent [of US survivors] were born here [in the United States] and about 20 to 25 percent married US servicemen after the war." CABS lacked the organizational capacity to gather its members' complete demographic information, a situation made worse by the reluctance of many to share the information. When CABS conducted membership surveys in the 1970s, only a small percentage, ranging from 27 to 30 percent of those who were asked, responded. See *CABSN*, January 4, 1979; "Hibakusha in America," Bill files, 2; "National Survey of Japanese American Atomic Bomb Survivors Residing in the U.S.A.," February 1974, Dymally papers, Series 1, Box 123, "Material – Atomic Bomb Survivors 5/4/74."

14. Throughout, I use "South Korea" and "Korea" to refer to the Republic of Korea after the Korean Peninsula was divided into the Republic of Korea and the People's Democratic Republic of Korea (North Korea) in 1948. When I discuss the pre-1948 "Korea," I use the term to refer to the region including both of the areas that are currently North Korea and South Korea. "Korean survivors" include people originally hailing from anywhere in Korea. There are no known "Korean American survivors" from North Korea.

15. There is a rich body of journalistic and academic studies about Korean survivors written in Japanese. "Zaikan hibakusha ni sensō wa imada owatte inai" [The war is not over for Korean survivors in Korea], June 29, 2013, Ch'oe Ha-un papers; Chŏng, *Kankoku genbaku*; Hiraoka, *Muen no kaikyō*; Ichiba, *Hiroshima o mochikaetta*; Orii Seigo, *Kankoku no Hiroshima mura, Hapuchon: Wasure enu hibaku kankokujin no tomo e* [Hapch'ŏn, a Hiroshima village in Korea: To an unforgettable friend and a Korean A-bomb survivor] (Tokyo: Shakai Hyōronsha, 2004); Shin Hyung-keun and Kawano Noriyuki, "Kankokujin genbaku shōgaisha kenkyū no katei to sono kadai" [The development of research on Korean survivors and the problems to be solved]," *Hiroshima heiwa kenkyū* 34 (2012): 161–87; Tamura K., "Zaigai hibakusha engo"; —, "Zaigai hibakusha no." Studies available in English include David Palmer, "The Straits of Dead Souls: One Man's Investigation into the Disappearance of Mitsubishi Hiroshima's Korean Forced Labourers," *Japanese Studies* 26.3 (2006): 335–51; Eric Ropers, "Contested Spaces of Ethnicity: *Zainichi* Korean Accounts of the Atomic Bombings," *Critical Military Studies* 1.2 (2015): 145–59; Yoneyama, *Hiroshima Traces*, chapter 5.

16. On military brides, see Glenn, *Issei, Nisei, War Bride*; Shukert and Scibetta, *War Brides of World War II*; Michael Thornton, "The Quiet Immigration: Foreign Spouses of US Citizens, 1945–1985," in *Racially Mixed People in America*, edited by Maria P. P. Root (Newbury Park, CA: Sage Publications, 1992): 64–76; Teresa Kay Williams, "Marriage between Japanese Women and US Servicemen since World War II," *Amerasia Journal* 17.1 (1991): 135–54; Yuh, *Beyond the Shadow*; Zeiger, *Entangling Alliances*.

17. Peggy Pascoe suggests that about a quarter of the marriages between American soldiers and Japanese civilians during the Cold War involved Japanese American men. See Pascoe, *What Comes Naturally*, 199.

18. Barker, *Bravo for the Marshallese*; Peter Eichstaedt, *If You Poison Us: Uranium and Native Americans* (Santa Fe, NM: Red Crane Books, 1994); Voyles, *Wastelanding*; Jonathan M. Weisgall, *Operation Crossroads: The Atomic Tests at Bikini Atoll* (Annapolis, MD: Naval Institute Press, 1994).

19. On the shifting image of Asian Americans in the mid-twentieth-century United States, see Brooks, *Alien Neighbors*; Cheng, *Citizens of Asian America*; Hsu, *Good Immigrants*; Klein, *Cold War Orientalism*; Phu, *Picturing Model Citizens*; E. Wu, *Color of Success*. The persistence of Asian Americans seen as "perpetual foreigners" has been excellently shown by Simpson, *Absent Presence*.

20. The notion of the "strength of weak ties" was first introduced by Granovetter, "Strength of Weak Ties," and it was further developed by Fugita and O'Brien, *Japanese American Ethnicity*.

21. Autobiographical accounts by Kibei include Kiyota, *Beyond Loyalty*; Tomita, *Dear Miye*; Nobuko Yamane, "A Nisei Woman in Rural Japan," *Amerasia Journal* 23.3 (1997): 183–96; Yamashiro, *Kibei Nisei*; Yoneda, *Ganbatte*. There are article-length studies about Kibei, including Jin, "Transnational Generation"; Eliko Kosaka, "Caught in between Okinawa and Hawai'i: 'Kibei' Diaspora in Masao Yamashiro's *The Kibei Nisei*," *Amerasia Journal* 41.1 (2015): 23–36; Yoshimi Kaoru, "Aru Nikkei Amerikajin Kibei Nisei gaka no kōjutsu seikatsushi: Senjika ni ikita Lewis Suzuki no hansen shisō o chūshin ni (Oral History of a Japanese American *Kibei* Nisei Artist: Focusing on the Pacifism Developed by Lewis Suzuki during the War-era)," *Nagoya gaikokugo daigaku gendai kokusai gakubu kiyō* 5 (2009): 393–425. See also Azuma, *In Search of Our Frontier* and Yoshida, *Amerika nihonjin imin*, which consider Kibei experiences in trans-Pacific contexts.

22. Boyer, *By the Bomb's Early Light*, 198–9; Dower, *War without Mercy*, 36–41; Gregg Herken, *The Winning Weapon: The Atomic Bomb in the Cold War, 1945–1950* (New York: Knopf, 1980), 13; Rotter, *Hiroshima: The World's Bomb*, 166–8; Sherwin, *World Destroyed*, 194–9; Walker, *Prompt and Utter Destruction*, 20–23, 44, and 96.

23. Barker, *Bravo for the Marshallese*; Benjamin P. Greene, *Eisenhower, Science Advice, and the Nuclear Test-Ban Debate, 1945–1963* (Stanford, CA: Stanford University Press, 2006); Vincent J. Intondi, *African Americans against the Bomb: Nuclear Weapons, Colonialism, and the Black Freedom Movement* (Stanford, CA: Stanford University Press, 2015); Jones, *After Hiroshima*; Nina Tannenwald, *The Nuclear Taboo: The United States and the Non-use of Nuclear Weapons since 1945* (Cambridge: Cambridge University Press, 2007).

24. Similar to US survivors' birthplaces, their gender breakdown is difficult to specify. According to the medical researchers who conducted a study of 300 US survivors in 1973–1975, the female-to-male ratio among US survivors who were naturalized citizens or permanent residents was "four to one," while it was "two to one" among all US survivors including US-born citizens. CABS also reported in 2001 that the gender breakdown among 384 respondents of a survey conducted in 2000 was about 65 percent female, 35 percent male. See Kerr, Yamada, and Marks, "Survey of Radiation Doses"; *CABSN*, March 5, 2001.

25. Lindee, *Suffering Made Real*; Sasaki-Uemura, *Organizing the Spontaneous*; Ubuki Satoru, "Nihon ni okeru gensuibaku kinshi undō no shuppatsu: 1954 nen no shomei undō o chūshin ni" [The beginning of the antinuclear movement in Japan: The 1954 petition movement], *Hiroshima heiwa kagaku* 5 (1982): 199–223; Kathleen S. Uno, "The Death of 'Good Wife, Wise Mother'?," in *Postwar Japan as History*, edited by Andrew Gordon (Berkeley: University of California Press, 1993): 307–12; Naoko Wake, "Atomic Bomb Survivors, Medical Experts, and Endlessness of Radiation Illness," in *Inevitably Toxic? Historical Perspectives on Contamination, Exposure, and Expertise*, edited by Janet Brodie, Vivien Hamilton, and Brinda Sarathy (Pittsburgh, PA: University of Pittsburgh Press, 2018): 235–58;

Mari Yamamoto, *Grassroots Pacifism in Post-War Japan: The Rebirth of a Nation* (London and New York: RoutledgeCurzon, 2004).

26. Jacqueline Castledine, *Cold War Progressives: Women's Interracial Organizing for Peace and Freedom* (Urbana: University of Illinois Press, 2012); Marian Mollin, *Radical Pacifism in Modern America: Egalitarianism and Protest* (Philadelphia: University of Pennsylvania Press, 2006); Amy Swerdlow, *Women Strike for Peace: Traditional Motherhood and Radical Politics in the 1960s* (Chicago: University of Chicago Press, 1993); Lawrence S. Wittner, "Gender Roles and Nuclear Disarmament Activism, 1954–1965," *Gender and History* 12.1 (April 2000): 197–222; Lisa Yaszek, "Stories 'That Only a Mother' Could Write: Midcentury Peace Activism, Maternalist Politics, and Judith Merril's Early Fiction," *NWSA Journal* 16.2 (Summer 2004): 70–97.

27. Studies that highlight these gender dynamisms in Asian America include Creef, *Imaging Japanese America*; Fujitani, *Race for Empire*; Glenn, *Unequal Freedom*; Hune and Nomura, *Asian/Pacific Islander*; S. J. Lim, *Feeling of Belonging*; Matsumoto, *Farming the Home Place*.

28. See the bibliography for a full list of the oral histories.

29. Interview with Yamaoka, NWC; Interview with Okuno, NWC.

30. See, for example, the use of "transnational" in Grewal, *Transnational America*, and Ong, *Flexible Citizenship*. My characterization of "transnational" here is not universally applicable. For instance, Shirley Geok-lin Lim and Wimal Dissanayake have argued how, in "surprising ways … transnational culture intersects with … local rhetorics," and how "globalization has led to a strengthening of local ties, allegiances, and identity politics." Lisa Yoneyama has defined "transnationality" as comprising "insurgent memories, counterknowledges, and inauthentic identities that have been regimented by the discourse and institutions centering on nation-states." See S. G. Lim, Smith, and Dissanayake, *Transnational Asia Pacific*, 4; Yoneyama, *Cold War Ruins*, 7.

31. Recent scholarship has criticized an association between cross-national justice and human rights by proposing transnational justice that, unlike cross-national justice, does not necessarily rely on nation states' authentications. See, for example, Pheng Cheah, "Posit(ion)ing Human Rights in the Current Global Conjecture," in S. G. Lim, Smith, and Dissanayake, eds., *Transnational Asia Pacific*, 11–42; Barbara Rose Johnston, ed., *Life and Death Matters: Human Rights and the Environment at the End of the Millennium* (Walnut Creek, CA: AltaMira Press, 1997); Barbara J. Keys, *Reclaiming American Virtue: The Human Rights Revolution of the 1970s* (Cambridge, MA: Harvard University Press, 2014); Moyn, *Last Utopia*; Schlund-Vials and Gill, *Disability, Human Rights*; Yoneyama, *Cold War Ruins*.

32. Jon Petrie, "The Secular Word HOLOCAUST: Scholarly Myths, History, and 20th Century Meanings," *Journal of Genocide Research* 2.1 (2000): 31–63. See also Richard H. Minear, "Atomic Holocaust, Nazi Holocaust," *Diplomatic History* 19.2 (Spring 1995): 347–65; Peter Schwenger, *Letter Bomb: Nuclear Holocaust and the Exploding Word* (Baltimore, MD: Johns Hopkins University Press, 1992); Mark Selden, "A Forgotten Holocaust: US Bombings of Hiroshima and Nagasaki Justified?," in *Bombing Civilians: A Twentieth-Century History*, edited by Yuki Tanaka and Marilyn B. Young (New York: The New Press, 2009): 77–96, about the use of the term "holocaust" for the 1945 bombings.

33. Jacob S. Eder, *Holocaust Angst: The Federal Republic of Germany and American Holocaust Memory since the 1970s* (Oxford: Oxford University Press, 2016); Arlene Stein, *Reluctant Witnesses: Survivors, Their Children, and the Rise of*

Holocaust Consciousness (Oxford: Oxford University Press, 2014); Wieviorka, *Era of the Witness.*

34. Hannah Arendt, *Eichmann in Jerusalem: A Report on the Banality of Evil* (New York: Viking Press, 1963), 22–3, 46–8, and 253–6; A. C. Grayling, *Among the Dead Cities: Was the Allied Bombing of Civilians in WWII a Necessity or a Crime?* (London: Bloomsbury, 2006), 154–6, 233, and 271–7; Treat, *Writing Ground Zero,* 14–16.

Cities of Immigrants

1. One measure of the map's prevalence in our understanding of the bomb is the frequency and certainty with which survivors discuss their distance from the hypocenter at the time of the explosion. The map has been used by scientists to locate survivors in relationship to the bomb, and to measure the extent of their radiation exposure. The Japanese government, too, has used survivors' distance from the hypocenter to determine how much medical and monetary assistance they should receive. Interestingly, the outermost distance for survivors to receive government assistance has continued to increase between the initial use of the measure in 1960 to the present, as if to follow the trajectory of radiation itself.

2. On US suppression of the information about the bomb after the war, see Braw, *Atomic Bomb Suppressed*; Lifton and Mitchell, *Hiroshima in America*; Takahashi Hiroko, *Fūin sareta Hiroshima Nagasaki: Beikoku kaku jikken to minkan bōei keikaku* [Hiroshima Nagasaki suppressed: US nuclear tests and civil defense] (Tokyo: Gaifūsha, 2008). Paul S. Boyer, "Exotic Resonances: Hiroshima in American Memory," and John W. Dower, "The Bombed: Hiroshimas and Nagasakis in Japanese Memory," in *Diplomatic History* 19.2 (Spring 1995): 297–318 and 275–95, respectively, and Hogan, *Hiroshima in History*, illuminate conflicting views of the bomb held by American and Japanese people fifty years after the bomb. Hein and Selden, *Living with the Bomb*, and Yui, *Naze sensoukan wa*, explore the cultural and political conflicts that continue to surround the bomb in both the United States and Japan.

3. On Korean laborers and military conscripts mobilized to serve in the Japanese empire during World War II, see, for example, Fujitani, *Race for Empire*; Kang Duk-sang, *Chōsenjin gakuto shutsujin: Mouhitotsu no wadatsumi no koe* [Another voice of the sea: Korean student conscripts depart for the front] (Tokyo: Iwanami Shoten, 1997); Miyata, *Chōsen minshū*; Palmer, *Fighting for the Enemy*; Tonomura, *Chōsenjin kyōsei renkō*.

4. Chŏng, *Kankoku genbaku*; Hiraoka, *Muen no kaikyō*. The 1970s and 1980s witnessed soaring grassroots activism in Japan to assist Korean survivors not only in Korea but also in Japan, which explains the publication of a series of studies about Korean survivors. See, for instance, Nagasaki Zainichi Chōsenjin, *Chōsenjin hibakusha*; Zaikan Hibakusha Mondai, *Zaikan hibakusha*.

5. Gary Y. Okihiro recounted his reaction to the abundance of studies about Japanese American incarceration in the preface to his book on the subject: "I must confess that I resisted the idea of this [book] ... When first asked ... to write yet another history of the wartime experience of Japanese Americans, I refused the suggestion. Not another book on a much-discussed subject, I thought to myself." Okihiro, *Storied Lives*, ix. Cherstin Lyon argued how Japanese Americans who did not fit into the dominant image as sufferers of injustice who nonetheless remained loyal to the United States – those who pursued draft resistance, renounced US citizenship, or requested a return to Japan – continued to escape the public's attention until the

successful conclusion of the Redress Movement in the early 1990s. See Lyon, *Prisons and Patriots*, 179–87. Recent studies about the camp include Allan W. Austin, *From Concentration Camp to Campus: Japanese American Students and World War II* (Urbana: University of Illinois Press, 2004); Brian Masaru Hayashi, *Democratizing the Enemy: The Japanese American Internment* (Princeton, NJ: Princeton University Press, 2004); Howard, *Concentration Camps*.

6. Collins, *Native American Aliens*, 70–3; R. G. Lee, "Introduction," in Tomita, *Dear Miye*, 1–4; Palmer, *Fighting for the Enemy*, 6–11; Utsumi Aiko, *Chōsenjin "kōgun" heishitachi no sensō* [The Korean "imperial army" soldiers' war] (Tokyo: Iwanami Shoten, 1991), 4–6, 39–42. Studies about experiences of Nikkei in Japan during wartime include Azuma, "Lure of Military Imperialism"; Kelli Nakamura, "'They Are Our Human Secret Weapons': The Military Intelligence Service and the Role of Japanese-Americans in the Pacific War and in the Occupation of Japan," *Historian* 70.1 (2008): 54–74.

7. Studies that employ Japanese colonial settler expansionism as the chief analytical concept to examine the history of Japanese overseas immigration include Azuma, *In Search of Our Frontier*; Andrea Geiger, *Subverting Exclusion: Transpacific Encounters with Race, Caste, and Borders, 1885–1928* (New Haven, CT: Yale University Press, 2011); Sidney Xu Lu, *The Making of Japanese Settler Colonialism: Malthusianism and Trans-Pacific Migration, 1868–1961* (Cambridge and New York: Cambridge University Press, 2019); Louise Young, *Japan's Total Empire: Manchuria and the Culture of Wartime Imperialism* (Berkeley: University of California Press, 1998).

8. Scholars have also explored experiences of Chinese and Japanese immigrants in turn-of-the-century America mainly as histories of emerging Asian American minorities. See, for example, Chan, *Asian Americans*; Fugita and O'Brien, *Japanese American Ethnicity*; Lee, *Making of Asian America*; Mae Ngai, *Impossible Subjects: Illegal Aliens and the Making of Modern America* (Princeton, NJ: Princeton University Press, 2005); Eileen T. Tamura, *Americanization, Acculturation, and Ethnic Identity: The Nisei Generation in Hawaii* (Urbana: University of Illinois Press, 1994).

9. See, for example, Fujitani, *Race for Empire*; Kang, *Chōsenjin*; Miyata, *Chōsen minshū*; Palmer, *Fighting for the Enemy*; Tonomura, *Chōsenjin kyōsei renkō*.

10. Some of the most compelling analyses of these colonial contradictions are found in Azuma, *Between Two Empires*, 3–14; Palmer, *Fighting for the Enemy*, 3–14; Gi-Wook Shin and Michael Robinson, "Introduction: Rethinking Colonial Korea," in G.-W. Shin and Robinson, *Colonial Modernity in Korea*, 1–18.

11. Glenn, *Issei, Nisei, War Bride*, 25; Hiroshima-ken, *Hiroshima kenjin*, 1–3; Hiroshima-ken Henshū Iinkai, *Hiroshima-ken ijūshi*, 8–9.

12. Kobayashi, *Nikkei imin*, 17.

13. Ibid., 23–36; Kodama, *Nihon iminshi*, 413–30, 435–63, 474–7, and 520–51; Nanka Hiroshima Kenjinkai ed., *Nanka Hiroshima kenjinkai sōritsu 75-shūnen* [The seventy-fifth anniversary of the Hiroshima Kenjinkai of Southern California] (Los Angeles, CA: Nanka Hiroshima Kenjinkai, 1985), 13–21.

14. Azuma, *In Search of Our Frontier*, 34–7, 83–5, and 220–2.

15. Kobayashi, *Nikkei imin*, 17. Kodama, *Nihon iminshi*, 473, shows somewhat different numbers for overseas immigrants from Hiroshima (43,940) and Nagasaki (6,345). Still, Hiroshima ranked first among all Japanese prefectures, while Nagasaki ranked ninth as of 1910.

16. Hiroshima-ken, *Hiroshima kenjin*, 13; Hiroshima-ken Henshū Iinkai, *Hiroshima-ken ijūshi*, 51–6, 67–70, and 106–10.

17. See, for example, Interview with Hishinuma, NWC; Interview with Okano, NWC; Interview with Oshima, FOHC.
18. Azuma, *Between Two Empires*, 135–8; Takahashi, *Nisei/Sansei*, 75–6; Yoo, *Growing Up Nisei*, 33–5.
19. See, for example, Interview with Dote, NWC; Interview with Masako Kawasaki, NWC; Interview with Sachiko Matsumoto, NWC. These memories of acceptance by the Japanese, held by some Nikkei, differ sharply from others' experiences of being treated poorly in Japan. For instance, Hawaiian-born Nisei Miya Sannomiya, who worked in Japan during the mid-1930s, recalled how some Japanese people deemed Nisei "children of low class" who could speak only in "horrible, low class, boorish, country style" Japanese (Yoo, *Growing Up Nisei*, 35). Some survivors, too, recalled difficulty in being accepted by their Japanese classmates in the 1930s. See, for example, Interview with Hamada, NWC; Interview with Ohori, STC. These experiences suggest a range of relationships that took shape between Japanese Americans and the Japanese in prewar Japan, a subject that calls for a fuller inquiry taking into consideration geographical and generational differences.
20. Interview with Nakagawa, NWC.
21. Interview with Saiki, NWC.
22. See, for example, Interview with the Kubotas, NWC.
23. Interview with Sarashina, NWC.
24. Interview with Okuno, NWC.
25. Interview with Kazuko Aoki, NWC.
26. Interview with Hirano, NWC; Interview with Suyeishi, NWC.
27. See Interview with Fujioka, NWC; Interview with Saiki, NWC; Interview with Yanagawa, FOHC. True as it may have been for some, the story of successful returnees was a myth rather than a reality for many of those who returned from the United States to Japan in the 1920s and 1930s. See Azuma, *Between Two Empires*, 79–80; Masako Suzuki, "Success Story? Japanese Immigrant Economic Achievement and Return Migration, 1920–1930," *Journal of Economic History* 55 (December 1995): 889–901 (see 895–6). In the mid-1910s, the amount of money sent by Japanese immigrants in America to their family members in Japan was largest among those who were in financial crisis – tenant farmers and growers who relied on the production of increasingly devalued rice and wheat. In 1925, in Gozen-chō, Hiroshima, a resident observed how the wealth brought by returnees from America was used to recover from the economic hardship that struck the village decades earlier. This suggests how the "success" of return immigrants must be measured in the context of economic depression that had prompted overseas immigration in the first place. See Hiroshima-ken Henshū Iinkai, *Hiroshima-ken ijūshi*, 167–9, 245–6.
28. Hamasaki Kunio, *Nagasaki ijingai shi* [A bulletin of Nagasaki foreigners' district] (Fukuoka, Japan: Ashi Shobō, 1978), 90–8, 158–74, 181–2, and 234–8; Seno Seiichiro, Saeki Kōji, Gonoi Takashi, Shinkawa Tokio, Komiya Kiyora, eds., *Nagasaki-ken no rekishi* [The history of Nagasaki prefecture] (Tokyo: Yamakawa Shuppansha, 1998), 130–9, 228–30, and 281–2.
29. "Tenth Anniversary: The Museum of Hawaiian Immigrants in Nihoshima-mura," *AS*, December 19, 2007. The article is based on an interview with the director of the immigration museum located in Nihoshima. On the large number of immigrants who migrated from Nihoshima to the United States, see Kodama, *Nihon iminshi*, 488–9.

30. "American Village" was a nickname given to Jigozen-mura, Hiroshima, another village that sent a large number of immigrants to America. See Kodama, *Nihon iminshi*, 488.
31. Interview with Yanagawa, FOHC.
32. Interview with Takahashi, FOHC.
33. Interview with Fukino, NWC.
34. Interview with Saiki, NWC. For similar stories about Japanese bathrooms, see Interview with Nagano, NWC; Interview with Suyeishi, NWC.
35. Interview with Kazuko Aoki, NWC.
36. Interview with Okimoto, NWC.
37. Interview with Jeong, NWC.
38. Interview with Kazue Kawasaki, NWC.
39. Interview with Hirano, NWC.
40. Interview with Pak, NWC.
41. Interview with Hirano, NWC.
42. Interview with Fujioka, NWC.
43. Interview with Fujimoto, NWC.
44. Interview with Dote, NWC.
45. Fugita and O'Brien, *Japanese American Ethnicity*, 85–9; Nakano, *Japanese American Women*, 55–7; Yoo, *Growing Up Nisei*, 28–30. See also Interview with Gaudette, FOHC.
46. Interview with Sarashina, NWC.
47. Interview with Tomosawa, NWC. For similar stories about racial relationships at school, see Interview with Furubayashi, NWC; Interview with Saiki, NWC.
48. This perceived lack of racial hostility does not suggest that, indeed, there were no racial or ethnonational tensions in Hawai'i. See Noriko Asato, "Mandating Americanization: Japanese Language Schools and the Federal Survey of Education in Hawai'i, 1916–1920," *History of Education Quarterly* 43.1 (Spring 2003): 10–38; Glenn, *Unequal Freedom*, chapter 6; Hiroshima-ken Henshū Iinkai, *Hiroshima-ken ijūshi*, 277–81; Gary Y. Okihiro, *Cane Fires: The Anti-Japanese Movement in Hawaii, 1865–1945* (Philadelphia, PA: Temple University Press, 2010), 107–8, 116–18.
49. Interview with Nagano, NWC.
50. Interview with Fukino, NWC.
51. Interview with Aida, NWC.
52. Interview with Imai, NWC.
53. Interview with Aida, NWC.
54. Interview with Saiki, NWC.
55. Interview with Takahashi, FOHC.
56. Interview with Saiki, NWC.
57. Interview with Dairiki, NWC.
58. Interview with Yamaoka, NWC.
59. Hing, *Making and Remaking*, 33; Erika Lee, "Immigrants and Immigration Law: A State of the Field Assessment," *Journal of American Ethnic History* 18.4 (Summer 1999): 85–114 (see 90).
60. Interview with Takahashi, FOHC. A similar concern about Nisei's future shaped many Peruvian Japanese parents' decision to send their children to Japan for language education before World War II. See Interview with Uematsu, STC.
61. Interview with Kurihara, FOHC; Interview with Sarashina, NWC.
62. Komai Hiroshi, *Nihon no gaikokujin imin* [Foreign immigrants in Japan] (Tokyo: Akashi Shoten, 1999), 24–25; Miyako Inoue, "The Listening Subject of Japanese

Modernity and His Auditory Double: Citing, Sighting, and Siting the Modern Japanese Woman," *Cultural Anthropology* 18.2 (May 2003): 156–93 (see 161). This assumption about foreigners as Westerners persisted although there were many Koreans in Japan. See Matsuda, *Senzenki*, 39–40; Miyata, *Chōsen minshū*, 119.

63. US survivors recalled how songs, too, were signs of difference when they first arrived. Often, they found that Japanese schoolchildren knew Japanese children's songs they had not learned at their Japanese language schools in the United States. See, for example, Interview with Dote, NWC; Interview with Saiki, NWC.

64. Interview with Sarashina, NWC.

65. *Ibid.*

66. Interview with Hirano, NWC.

67. Interview with Saiki, NWC.

68. Interview with Kurihara, FOHC.

69. Interview with Gaudette, FOHC. See also Interview with Utagawa, NWC, for a similar memory of how Nikkei's English pronunciation stood out in Japan.

70. On intersectionality between race, ethnonationality, and immigration regulation, see Lowe, *Immigrant Acts*; Anna Pegler-Gordon, David Roediger, Allison Varzally, Eiichiro Azuma, and Mark Overmyer-Velázquez, "Forum on the Racial Turn in Immigration and Ethnic History," *Journal of American Ethnic History* 36.2 (Winter 2017): 40–93; Mae Ngai, "The Architecture of Race in American Immigration Law," *Journal of American History* 86.1 (June 1999): 67–92.

71. Soon-Won Park, "Colonial Industrial Growth and the Emergence of the Korean Working Class," in G.-W. Shin and Robinson, *Colonial Modernity in Korea*, 128–60; Theodore Jun Yoo, *The Politics of Gender in Colonial Korea: Education, Labor, and Health, 1910–1945* (Berkeley: University of California Press, 2008), chapter 3.

72. Chapman, *Zainichi Korean*, 16–17; Duus, *Abacus and the Sword*, 364–96.

73. My discussion of Koreans in Japan proper here is based on Morris-Suzuki, *Borderline Japan*, 33–41. On Korean survivors, see Ichiba, *Hiroshima o mochikaetta*, 158–63, 264–6, and 284–6; Nagasaki Zainichi Chōsenjin, *Genbaku to Chōsenjin*, 3–17.

74. Mark E. Caprio and Yu Jia, "Occupations of Korea and Japan and the Origins of the Korean Diaspora in Japan," in Ryang and Lie, *Diaspora without Homeland*, 21–38 (see 26–7).

75. Tonomura, *Zainichi Chōsenjin*, 96–8.

76. *Ibid.*, 261–8.

77. Interview with Yi, NWC.

78. *Ibid.*

79. Wan-yao Chou, "The *Kōminka* Movement in Taiwan and Korea: Comparisons and Interpretations," in Duus, Myers, and Peattie, *Japanese Wartime Empire*, 40–68 (see 52–4); Higuchi Yūichi, *Senjika Chōsen no minshū to chōhei* [People and conscription in wartime Korea] (Tokyo: Sōwasha, 2001), 154; Miyata, *Chōsen minshū*, 114–18; Palmer, *Fighting for the Enemy*, 26–8.

80. The majority of Korean language schools in Japan were established in the 1930s and 1940s at workplaces to teach Korean adults basic reading and writing skills in Han'gŭl. At the end of the Pacific War, 22 percent of people in South Korea were literate in Korean. In Japan proper, the percentage was likely smaller, because of the increased proportion of second generation Koreans who were Japanese monolinguals. See Tonomura, *Chōsenjin kyōsei renkō*, 24; —, *Zainichi Chōsenjin*, 228–9.

81. Ichiba, *Hiroshima o mochikaetta*, 309–10. See also Hiromitsu Inokuchi, "Korean Ethnic Schools in Occupied Japan, 1945–52," in *Koreans in Japan: Critical Voices from the Margin*, edited by Sonia Ryang (London and New York: Routledge, 2000): 140–56 (see 143), and Tonomura, *Zainichi Chōsenjin*, 230.

82. Carter J. Eckert, "Total War, Industrialization, and Social Change in Late Colonial Korea," in Duus, Myers, and Peattie, *Japanese Wartime Empire*, 4–39 (see 29); Matsuda, *Senzenki*, 35–9; Tonomura, *Zainichi Chōsenjin*, 84–9.

83. Tonomura, *Zainichi Chōsenjin*, 89–91.

84. Interview with Matsumoto Kisō, NWC.

85. *Ibid.*

86. Ichiba, *Hiroshima o mochikaetta*, 298; Nagasaki Zainichi Chōsenjin, *Genbaku to Chōsenjin*, 175.

87. Mark E. Caprio, *Japanese Assimilation Policies in Colonial Korea, 1910–1945* (Seattle: University of Washington Press, 2009), 116; Duus, *Abacus and the Sword*, 419–23; Eckert, "Total War," 16, 33. On the complexity of racial classification by the Japanese empire, see also Mariko Asano Tamanoi, "Knowledge, Power, and Racial Classifications: The 'Japanese' in 'Manchuria,'" *Journal of Asian Studies* 59 (2000): 248–76.

88. Interview with Pak, NWC.

89. *Ibid.*

90. Interview with Yi, NWC.

91. *Ibid.*

92. Interview with Pak, NWC.

93. *Ibid.*

94. Interview with Matsumoto Kisō, NWC.

95. *Ibid.*

96. Interview with Hong, NWC.

97. *Ibid.*

98. *Ibid.*

99. Interview with Jeong, NWC.

100. Barbara J. Brooks, "Japanese Colonialism, Gender, and Household Registration: Legal Reconstruction of Boundaries," in *Gender and Law in the Japanese Imperium*, edited by Susan L. Burns and Barbara J. Brooks (Honolulu: University of Hawai'i Press, 2014): 219–39; Chikako Kashiwazaki, "The Foreigner Category for Koreans in Japan: Opportunities and Constraints," in Ryang and Lie, *Diaspora without Homeland*, 121–46; Michael Kim, "Sub-nationality in the Japanese Empire: A Social History of the *Koseki* in Colonial Korea 1910–45," in *Japan's Household Registration System and Citizenship: Koseki, Identification and Documentation*, edited by David Chapman and Kirk Krogness (London: Routledge, 2014): 111–26.

101. Interview with Jeong, NWC.

102. Hong's military schoolteacher, who was "very nice," was a rare exception.

103. Interview with Yi, NWC.

104. *Ibid.*

105. Matsuda, *Senzenki*, 59.

106. On the complex meaning for Koreans in wartime Japan to wear *chŏgori*, see Tonomura, *Zainichi Chōsenjin*, 178.

107. Matsuda, *Senzenki*, 81–7, 117–18.

108. Interview with Sumida, STC.

109. *Ibid.*

110. Chan, *Asian Americans*, 130–1; Fujitani, *Race for Empire*, 166–82.

111. Cherstin Lyon, "Denaturalization Act of 1944/Public Law 78–405" and "Segregation," *Densho Encyclopedia*, encyclopedia.densho.org, accessed on December 25, 2017. See also Lyon, *Prisons and Patriots*, 181.

112. Edward N. Barnhart notes that in 1942 and 1943, "those who applied for repatriation, most of them aliens and their minor American citizen children, believed that they would be sent to Japan. Two shiploads did go, but Japan refused to accept any others and the Department of State announced that no more exchanges of persons would be made." According to Jacob TenBroek, Edward N. Barnhard, and Floyd W. Matson, the numbers of the people on the ship (*S. S. Gripsholm*) were 54 in 1942, 314 in 1943. See Edward N. Barnhart, "The Individual Exclusion of Japanese Americans in World War II," *Pacific Historical Review* 29.2 (May 1960): 111–30 (see 127); TenBroek, Barnhart, and Matson, *Prejudice, War, and the Constitution*, 175.

113. Interview with Fukuda, FOHC.

114. *Ibid.*

115. Interview with the Koharas, NWC.

116. Interview with Yamaoka, STC.

117. Interview with Saiki, NWC.

118. Interview with Nakamoto, FOHC. Joe Ohori, a Japanese Canadian *hibakusha*, recalled how he was spared of bullying because of his Canadian citizenship, suggesting how American citizenship carried a specific stigma in wartime Japan. See Interview with Ohori, STC.

119. Interview with Masako Kasawaki, NWC.

120. Interview with Saiki, NWC.

121. Interview with Tomosawa, FOHC; Interview with Tomosawa, NWC.

122. Interview with the Koharas, NWC.

123. Interview with Yamashita, NWC.

124. Interview with Kazuko Aoki, NWC.

125. Interview with Hirano, NWC. For a similar story see also Interview with Aida, NWC. This kind of imperial indoctrination targeting Nisei was not uncommon in Tokyo, where the Japanese government made a systematic effort to educate "foreign-born compatriots about the essential elements of Japanese spirit." In most cases, the Nikkei students who attended this nationalistic schooling were older (secondary school- or college-age) than the soon-to-be *hibakusha* children discussed here, indicating generational as well as geographical divergence among Nikkei youths in Japan during the 1930s. See Azuma, *In Search of Our Frontier*, chapter 8 (quote from 249).

126. Interview with the Kubotas, NWC.

127. Interview with Ogawa, FOHC.

128. Interview with Igarashi, NWC.

129. Interview with Nakamoto, FOHC.

130. *Ibid.*

131. See also Ichiba, *Hiroshima o mochikaetta*, 179, 306; Chŏng, *Kankoku genbaku*, 84, 102, and 334–5.

132. Chŏng, *Kankoku genbaku*, 102–8.

133. Ichiba, *Hiroshima o mochikaetta*, 298; Nagasaki Zainichi Chōsenjin, *Genbaku to Chōsenjin*, 175.

134. Chŏng, *Kankoku genbaku*, 279–80.

135. Interview with Tomosawa, FOHC; Interview with Tomosawa, NWC.

136. Chŏng, *Kankoku genbaku*, 280.

137. *Ibid.*, 108.

138. Interview with Pak, NWC.
139. *Ibid.*
140. *Ibid.*
141. Interview with Ichiba, NWC.
142. Interview with Hong, NWC.

Remembering the Nuclear Holocaust

1. On the strong desire among survivors of mass-killings to tell intimate details of their families' deaths, see Clendinnen, *Reading the Holocaust*, 29, 32–4; Hayslip with Wurts, *When Heaven and Earth*, 15–17; Nguyen, *Nothing Ever Dies*, 27, 44, and 229; Treat, *Writing Ground Zero*, 49–50.
2. On the changing, often gendered, relationship between speech and silence in oral and written testimonies about events of extraordinary magnitude, see Susan Stanford Friedman, "The Return of the Repressed in Women's Narratives," *Journal of Narrative Technique* 19.1 (1989): 141–56; Henry Greenspan, "Collaborative Interpretation of Survivors' Accounts: A Radical Challenge to Conventional Practice," *Holocaust Studies: A Journal of Culture and History*, 17.1 (Spring 2011): 85–100; Lifton, *Death in Life*, 23–31; Ôfer and Weitzman, *Women in the Holocaust*, chapters 18–21; Rittner and Roth, *Different Voices*, chapters 14 and 26; Brian Schiff, "Telling It in Time: Interpreting Consistency and Change in the Life Stories of Holocaust Survivors," *International Journal of Aging and Human Development* 60.3 (2005): 189–212; Treat, *Writing Ground Zero*, 25–30, 203–4.
3. Studies published well after the existence of Korean survivors became widely publicized in the late 1970s and early 1980s, which nonetheless employed the Japan–US dualism almost exclusively in their consideration of those affected by the bomb, include Lifton and Mitchell, *Hiroshima in America*; Richard B. Frank, *Downfall: The End of the Imperial Japanese Empire* (New York: Random House, 1999); Walker, *Prompt and Utter Destruction*.
4. An important exception to this is Yoneyama, *Hiroshima Traces*, which highlights a range of responses to bomb commemorations by Korean survivors in Japan. See also Kawaguchi Takayuki, "Chōsenjin hibakusha o meguru gensetsu no shosō: 1970 nen zengo no kōkei" [The multilayered discourse surrounding Korean A-bomb survivors: Before and after 1970], *Proburematikku: Bungaku kyōiku* 4 (July 2003), home.hiroshima-u.ac.jp/bngkkn/hlm-society/Kawaguchi5.html, accessed on November 22, 2015.
5. One of the most conspicuous displays of the US memory of the B-29s was the famous controversy surrounding the Smithsonian Museum's 1995 exhibit on the Enola Gay. See Tom Engelhardt and Edward T. Linenthal, eds., *History Wars: The Enola Gay and Other Battles for the American Past* (New York: Metropolitan Books, 1996); Michael Hogan, "The Enola Gay Controversy: History, Memory, and the Politics of Presentation," in Hogan, *Hiroshima in History*, 200–32; Yoneyama, *Cold War Ruins*, chapter 5. A still-powerful Japanese representation of the faceless bombers can be found in the animated film by Mori Masaki, *Barefoot Gen* (1983).
6. Interview with Nagano, NWC.
7. Interview with Yanagawa, FOHC.
8. Interview with Fukino, NWC.
9. Interview with Suyeishi, NWC.
10. Interview with Kashihara, NWC.

11. Interview with Suyeishi, NWC.
12. See, for instance, Interview with Dairiki, NWC.
13. Oral histories that referred to the blackness of the landscape in the bomb's aftermath include Interview with Hishinuma, NWC; Interview with Nagano, NWC; Interview with Okimoto, NWC; Interview with Tanemori, NWC.
14. US survivors frequently discussed "black rain," thick, highly radioactive rain containing dirt and dust, which fell shortly after the bomb's explosion and became famous after the publication of Ibuse Masuji's novel of the same title in 1965. See, for example, Interview with Masako Kawasaki, NWC; Interview with Matsumoto Kisō, NWC; Interview with Sakai, NWC.
15. Interview with Fukuda, FOHC.
16. Interview with Saiki, NWC.
17. Interview with Yanagawa, FOHC.
18. Interview with Fukino, NWC.
19. Interview with Hamada, NWC.
20. Interview with Jeong, NWC. All the subsequent quotes in the following paragraphs are from this interview.
21. As of 2010, Jeong still had not applied for a certificate of survivorhood.
22. On the rise of fear of nuclear weaponry during the Cold War, see Jacobs, *Dragon's Tail*; Laura McEnaney, *Civil Defense Begins at Home: Militarization Meets Everyday Life in the Fifties* (Princeton, NJ: Princeton University Press, 2000); Kenneth D. Rose, *One Nation Underground: The Fallout Shelter in American Culture* (New York: New York University Press, 2001); Winkler, *Life under a Cloud*. Studies that conceptualized Hiroshima and Nagasaki chiefly as a trigger of a fear that a nuclear holocaust might happen sometime in the future include Schell, *Fate of the Earth*; Sharpe, *Savage Perils*.
23. Interview with Hong, NWC.
24. Interview with Hirano, NWC.
25. Interview with Moriwaki, NWC.
26. Interview with Frank, FOHC; Interview with Imai, NWC.
27. Interview with Kazue Kasawaki, NWC.
28. Interview with Kazuko Aoki, NWC.
29. Interview with Sumida, STC.
30. Interview with Yamashita, NWC.
31. Interview with Kazue Kawasaki, NWC.
32. Interview with Hirano, NWC.
33. Interview with Nagaishi, STC.
34. See, for example, the *hibakusha* author Ōta Yōko's description of how most survivors she saw were "naked to the waist." Although her story in fact includes a range of torn clothes that survivors wore, nakedness became strongly associated with the bomb's aftermath. When Ōta's work was translated into English, it was accompanied by select images from "The Hiroshima Murals," the famous series of paintings by Maruki Iri and Maruki Toshi, which featured naked men and women. See Minear, *Hiroshima: Three Witnesses* (quote from 188). Some US survivors, too, contributed to the image of prevalent nakedness on the post-nuclear ground. See, for example, "Hiroshima Atom Bomb Victim Finds Home in San Francisco," *HM*, August 9, 1972, in which a US survivor discusses how "many were without clothes, and many were suffering." Andrew Rotter offers an insightful critique of these depictions. See Rotter, *Hiroshima: The World's Bomb*, 202–3.
35. See, for example, Interview with Kazue Kawasaki, STC.
36. Interview with La Mica, NWC.

37. Interview with Ogawa, FOHC.
38. Interview with Nagano, NWC. All the subsequent quotes in this paragraph are also from this interview.
39. Interview with Okuno, NWC.
40. Interview with Yamaoka, NWC; —, STC; "An Empty Urn," March 29, 2006, May Yamaoka papers.
41. See, for example, Interview with Furubayashi, NWC.
42. Interview with Pak, NWC.
43. Interview with Tanemori, NWC.
44. Interview with Frank, FOHC.
45. Interview with Yi, NWC.
46. Interview with Pak, NWC.
47. Interview with Suyeishi, NWC.
48. Yanagida Jutsurō, "The 18th Medical Examination of Atomic Bomb Survivor Residents in North America" (presentation given during the eighteenth biannual medical checkup in San Francisco), July 15, 2011.
49. On Sasaki, see Hersey, "Hiroshima," chapter 5. Concerning Nagai, see Miyamoto, *Beyond the Mushroom Cloud*, chapter 4; Nagai Takashi, *Nagasaki no kane* [The bells of Nagasaki] (Tokyo: Hibiya Shuppansha, 1949).
50. On the ABCC and its findings, see Lindee, *Suffering Made Real*; William Schull, *Effects of Atomic Radiation: A Half-Century of Studies from Hiroshima and Nagasaki* (New York: Wiley-Liss, 1995). On the "Hiroshima Maidens" project, see Rodney Baker, *The Hiroshima Maidens* (New York: Viking, 1985); Phu, *Picturing Model Citizens*, chapter 3; Serlin, *Replaceable You*, chapter 2; Shibusawa, *America's Geisha Ally*, chapter 6; Simpson, *Absent Presence*, chapter 4; Michael J. Yavenditti, "The Hiroshima Maidens and American Benevolence in the 1950s," *Mid-America: A Historical Review* 64.2 (1982): 21–39.
51. Interview with Sarashina, NWC. Many US survivors attest to the lack of medical care for hours, days, and weeks after the bomb. See, for example, Interview with Fujioka, NWC; Interview with Thurlow, STC.
52. Interview with Yi, NWC.
53. Interview with the Kubotas, NWC.
54. Interview with Dote, NWC.
55. Interview with Fujioka, NWC.
56. Interview with Oshima, FOHC.
57. Interview with Okimoto, NWC. For similar stories about the use of human bones, see Interview with Kashihara, NWC; Interview with Nambu, NWC. Some survivors used the membrane from the inside of eggshells for the same purpose of covering exposed injuries. See Interview with Kitamura, FOHC.
58. Interview with Nambu, NWC.
59. Interview with Carpenter, STC.
60. Interview with Benevedes, NWC; "A Speech by Michiko B.: A Recollection of Her Experiences During and Following the Atomic Bombing of Nagasaki," 1995, Michiko Benevedes papers.
61. Although human bones were not used for therapeutic purposes in ordinary times, Japanese people have long eaten fish bones as part of their diet and used them as a fertilizer. It was, and still is, common to keep bones of deceased family members at home for a long time after cremation. In the ceremony of cremation itself, family members themselves pick bones from the coffin and place them in an urn. Thus, it is plausible that people's familiarity with bones' benefits and their common presence in daily life, combined with the lack of other resources at ground zero, prompted the

therapeutic use of human bones in 1945. For similar reasons, many survivors felt it crucial that they identified deceased family members' bones. This was a difficult task because of a number of mass cremations that occurred in the days after the bomb. See, for example, Interview with Furubayashi, NWC; Interview with Matsumoto, STC.

62. Interview with Sumida, STC.

63. Interview with Pak, NWC.

64. *Ibid.*

65. See, for example, Interview with Kazuko Aoki, NWC; Interview with Nakamura, NWC; Interview with Sarashina, NWC.

66. Interview with Fujioka, NWC.

67. Interview with Yoshida, NWC.

68. Rotter, *Hiroshima: The World's Bomb*, 18–22.

69. Interview with Saiki, NWC. This is one of the few references made in the oral histories to "modern medicines" offered on the ground immediately after the bomb. Other examples can be found in Interview with Hong, NWC; Interview with Yi, NWC. Hong was treated at a military hospital – he received stitches and bandages for his cuts – because he was a student at the Imperial Army Weapons School. Yi received merbromin solution at a branch of the hospital dedicated to treatment of employees of the railroad company he worked for. These examples suggest how survivors' access to "modern medicine" relied on their social status.

70. Interview with Saiki, NWC.

71. Interview with Pak, NWC.

72. Viet Thanh Nguyen calls this coexistence of victimhood and perpetratorhood the "disturbing universality of shared inhumanity," arguing that expressions of inhumanity, as much as those of humanity, are fundamental to war's history. See Nguyen, *Nothing Ever Dies*, 86–9, 216–17.

73. Interview with Sarashina, NWC.

74. Interview with Okimoto, NWC.

75. Interview with Sumioka, NWC.

76. Interview with Watanabe, NWC.

77. Interview with Tokito, NWC.

78. Interview with Yanagawa, FOHC.

79. Chicken *sukiyaki* was one of the dishes that Japanese Americans often mentioned as memorable from the prewar era. See, for example, Interview with Furubayashi, NWC.

80. Interview with Yanagawa, FOHC.

81. *Ibid.*

82. By highlighting individual attitudes or approaches to life in our explanation of why some, but not all, have survived a holocaust or genocide, we risk blaming victims. See Clendinnen, *Reading the Holocaust*, 45–8; Langer, *Versions of Survival*, 9–10, 30–5, 46–7, 65, and 142–4.

83. Interview with Jeong, NWC.

84. *Ibid.*; Interview with Hong, NWC.

85. Interview with Yi, NWC.

86. Interview with Imai, NWC.

87. "May's Recollection of Lodi's Japan Town," July 14, 2009, May Yamaoka papers.

88. Interview with Yamaoka, NWC; —, STC.

89. "An Empty Urn," March 29, 2006, May Yamaoka papers.

Reconnecting Families

1. As discussed in the Introduction, studies that take a cultural history approach to the bomb are rich and many. Jacqueline Foertsch, *Reckoning Day: Race, Place, and the Atom Bomb in Postwar America* (Nashville, TN: Vanderbilt University Press, 2013); Robert A. Jacobs, ed., *Filling the Hole in the Nuclear Future: Art and Popular Culture Respond to the Bomb* (Lanham, MD: Lexington Books, 2010); Hiroko Okuda, *Genbaku no kioku: Hiroshima/Nagasaki no shisō* [Memories of the A-bomb: Toward a philosophy of Hiroshima/Nagasaki] (Tokyo: Keiōgijuku Daigaku Shuppankai, 2010) are notable recent examples. Eckart Conze, Martin Klimke, and Jeremy Varon, eds., *Nuclear Threats, Nuclear Fear, and the Cold War of the 1980s* (New York: Cambridge University Press, 2016) and Lawrence S. Wittner, *Toward Nuclear Abolition: A History of the World Nuclear Disarmament Movement, 1971–Present* (Stanford, CA: Stanford University Press, 2003), are excellent studies of the antinuclear movement.
2. On the initial animosity between American occupiers and Japanese civilians, see Hachiya Michihiko, *Hiroshima Diary: The Journal of a Japanese Physician, August 6–September 30, 1945* (Chapel Hill: University of North Carolina Press, 1995), 16; Hiroshima-shi, *Hiroshima shinshi: Rekishihen* (A new history of Hiroshima: History volume) (Hiroshima: Hiroshima-shi, 1984), 16–17.
3. See Mark E. Caprio, "Resident Aliens: Forging the Political Status of Koreans in Occupied Japan," in Caprio and Sugita, *Democracy in Occupied Japan*, 178–99 (see 183–4); Kim T., *Sengo Nihon seiji*, 220–59; Morris-Suzuki, *Borderline Japan*, 59–62.
4. On the pre-*Virginia v. Loving* (1967) era regulation of marriages between American men (including servicemen) and Asian women, see Glenn, *Issei, Nisei, War Bride*, 8, 36; Lee, *Making of Asian America*, 264–8; Zeiger, *Entangling Alliances*, 166–7, 179–82.
5. On US military men's fraternization with Korean and Japanese women, see Kovner, *Occupying Power*; Katharine H. S. Moon, *Sex Among Allies: Military Prostitution in U.S.–Korea Relations* (New York: Columbia University Press, 1997); Yuki Tanaka, *Japan's Comfort Women: Sexual Slavery and Prostitution during World War II and the US Occupation* (London: Routledge, 2002); Yuh, *Beyond the Shadow*.
6. Interview with Sakata, NWC.
7. Interview with Fujimoto, NWC.
8. Interview with Fujita, NWC.
9. Interview with Sakata, NWC.
10. Interview with Kurihara, FOHC.
11. Interview with Nakamura, NWC; Interview with Shin, NWC.
12. Interview with Sakai, NWC.
13. Interview with Gaudette, FOHC; Interview with Smith, FOHC. On discrimination against survivors, see also Miyamoto, *Beyond the Mushroom Cloud*, 31, 171–2; Ōe, *Hiroshima nōto*, 4–7; Zwigenberg, *Hiroshima, The Origin*, 68–9.
14. Interview with Shinmoto, NWC.
15. Interview with Hirano, NWC.
16. *Ibid.*
17. Interview with Hishinuma, NWC.
18. Interview with Oshima, FOHC.
19. On American censorship of Japanese literature about the bomb, see Kamei Chiaki, "Shōwa nijūgonen-ban *Shikabane no machi* no bunmyaku: Ōta Yōko ga

mikiwameta hibaku gonengo" [The historical context of the 1950 version of *City of Corpses*: Ōta Yōko's observation of the five years after the bomb], *Genbaku bungaku kenkyū* 4 (2005): 113–119; Jay Rubin, "From Wholesomeness to Decadence: The Censorship of Literature under the Allied Occupation," *Journal of Japanese Studies* 11.1 (Winter 1985): 71–103.

20. Interview with Fujimoto, NWC. See also Interview with Kashihara, NWC.
21. Interview with Hamada, NWC.
22. Interview with Akihara, NWC.
23. *Ibid.*; Interview with Peters, STC.
24. Interview with Shin, NWC.
25. Interview with Imai, NWC. Here, what Imai means by "small leakage" is the small amounts of radiation detected at locations far from the plant. She is not referring to the absolute amount of leakage at the Fukushima facility, which was considerable.
26. Interview with Okimoto, NWC.
27. Interview with Gendernalik, NWC; Interview with McCrea, NWC; Interview with Monberg, NWC.
28. Interview with Okimoto, NWC.
29. Interview with Shin, NWC.
30. Interview with Pak, NWC.
31. Ibuse, *Kuroi ame*, 232–8; *Kuroi ame*, directed by Imamura Shōhei, performed by Tanaka Yoshiko, Kitamura Kazuo, and Ichihara Etsuko, Tokyo: Toei Co., Ltd., 1989, film.
32. John W. Dower, *Embracing Defeat: Japan in the Wake of World War II* (New York: W. W. Norton, 1999), 75–82; Steven J. Fuchs, "Feeding the Japanese: Food Policy, Land Reform, and Japan's Economic Recovery," in Caprio and Sugita, *Democracy in Occupied Japan*, 26–47 (see 29, 33–4); Takemae Eiji, *Inside GHQ: The Allied Occupation of Japan and its Legacy*, translated by Robert Ricketts and Sebastian Swann (New York: Continuum, 2002), 339–46.
33. Interview with Blakes, STC.
34. Interview with Fukuda, FOHC.
35. Interview with Saiki, NWC.
36. Interview with Sakai, NWC.
37. Interview with Nakagawa, NWC.
38. Interview with McCrea, NWC.
39. Interview with Fujimoto, NWC.
40. Interview with Nakagawa, NWC.
41. Interview with Hirano, NWC.
42. Interview with Furubayashi, NWC.
43. Interview with Oshima, FOHC.
44. On iconic images of joyous Americans on VJ-Day and how they embodied the beginning of the US global hegemony, see Roberts, *What Soldiers Do*, 258.
45. Interview with Hong, FOHC.
46. Shibusawa, *America's Geisha Ally*, 19–20, 51. On the American occupation forces' policies concerning Japanese women's rights, see Nishi, *Senryōka no Nihon fujin*.
47. Shibusawa, *America's Geisha Ally*, 13–15.
48. Azuma, "Brokering Race, Culture, and Citizenship," 2–5.
49. Interview with Furubayashi, NWC.
50. Interview with the Kubotas, NWC.
51. Kibei Nisei Masao Yamashiro recalled how it had taken a year for the Red Cross to deliver a letter across the Pacific in the years after the war. See Yamashiro, *Kibei Nisei*, 54.

52. Interview with Utagawa, NWC.
53. Interview with Fukino, NWC.
54. Interview with Yanagawa, FOHC.
55. Collins, *Native American Aliens*, 69–73; TenBroek, Barnhart, and Matson, *Prejudice, War, and the Constitution*, 174–8.
56. Interview with Yamaoka, STC.
57. Interview with Yanagawa, FOHC.
58. Dower, *War without Mercy*, 52–5; Beverly Ann Deepe Keever, *News Zero: The New York Times and the Bomb* (Monroe, ME: Common Courage Press, 2004), 68–71.
59. Interview with Kazue Kawasaki, NWC.
60. Interview with Dazai, FOHC; Interview with Moriwaki, NWC; Interview with Sakai, NWC.
61. Interview with Fukuda, FOHC; Interview with Igarashi, NWC; Interview with Tomosawa, NWC.
62. Interview with Frank, FOHC.
63. Interview with Kazuko Aoki, NWC.
64. Interview with Okimoto, NWC.
65. Interview with Yanagawa, FOHC.
66. Illuminating examinations of Japanese people's response to American policies and programs of Cold War alliance-making can be found in Koikari, *Pedagogy of Democracy*; Yukiko Koshiro, *Trans-Pacific Racism and the US Occupation of Japan* (New York: Columbia University Press, 1999); Sasamoto Yukuo, *Beikoku senryō-ka no genbaku chōsa: Genbaku kagaikoku ni natta Nihon* [A study of the A-bomb under US occupation: Japan as a perpetrator] (Tokyo: Shinkansha, 1995).
67. Simpson, *Absent Presence*, 125–8, 133–6.
68. Lindee, *Suffering Made Real*, 151, 154–5; Vassiliki Betty Somocovitis, "Genetics behind Barbed Wire: Masuo Kodani, Émigré Geneticists, and Wartime Genetics Research at Manzanar Relocation Center," *Genetics* 187 (February 2011): 357–66 (see 364).
69. Zeiger, *Entangling Alliances*, 182–3.
70. Lindee, *Suffering Made Real*, 4–5, 110–14; James N. Yamazaki and Louis B. Fleming, *Children of the Atomic Bomb: An American Physician's Memoir of Nagasaki, Hiroshima, and the Marshall Islands* (Durham, NC: Duke University Press, 1995), 46–8.
71. Interview with McCrea, NWC.
72. Interview with Monberg, NWC.
73. Interview with Oshima, FOHC.
74. Interview with Pak, NWC.
75. Interview with Fujita, NWC.
76. Miriam Gebhardt, *Crimes Unspoken: The Rape of German Women at the End of the Second World War* (Cambridge, UK, and Malden, MA: Polity, 2017); Kovner, *Occupying Power*; Roberts, *What Soldiers Do*; Yuh, *Beyond the Shadow*.
77. For example, Matsumoto Kisō and Yi Jougkeun, both Korean survivors interviewed in Japan in 2013, expressed a strong animosity toward the ABCC, as they felt that the institution interfered with survivors' silence about the bomb while offering no treatment for them. See Interview with Matsumoto Kosō, NWC; Interview with Yi, NWC.
78. Interview with Ohori, STC.
79. *Ibid.*
80. Interview with Fukuda, FOHC.

81. Interview with Oshima, FOHC.
82. Interview with Hirano, NWC.
83. Interview with Ogawa, FOHC.
84. The same restriction based on political participation applied to men, too. See, for example, Interview with the Kubotas, NWC.
85. Interview with McCrea, NWC; Interview with Nagano, NWC; Interview with Oshima, FOHC.
86. Interview with Dote, NWC; Interview with Okimoto, NWC; Interview with Saiki, NWC.
87. Interview with Nagano, NWC.
88. Interview with Yi, NWC.
89. Interview with Jeong, NWC.
90. Interview with La Mica, NWC.
91. Interview with Fujioka, NWC.
92. Interview with Elliott, NWC.
93. Interview with Moriwaki, NWC.
94. Interview with Nakamura, NWC. On racial segregations that military brides experienced, see also a series of articles entitled "War Brides in the USA" published by CS in 1989 in the Tsuruko Nakamura papers.
95. Interview with Sachiko Matsumoto, NWC.
96. Interview with Nakamura, NWC.
97. Interview with Sachiko Matsumoto, NWC.
98. Interview with Fujioka, NWC.
99. Interview with La Mica, NWC.
100. Interview with Kazue Kawasaki, NWC.
101. Pascoe, *What Comes Naturally*, 231–8; Shukert and Scibetta, *War Brides of World War II*, 208–18; Simpson, *Absent Presence*, 167–71.
102. Interview with Hong, NWC.
103. Interview with Ch'oe, NWC. See also Chŏng, *Kankoku genbaku*, 309–10, 330; Zaikan Hibakusha Mondai, *Zaikan hibakusha*, 23–4, 97–8.
104. Interview with Lee, FOHC.
105. Interview with Pak, NWC.

War and Work Across the Pacific

1. Mark E. Caprio and Yu Jia, "Occupations of Korea and Japan and the Origins of the Korean Diaspora in Japan," in Ryang and Lie, *Diaspora without Homeland*, 21–38; Morris-Suzuki, *Borderline Japan*, 52–70.
2. Hing, *Making and Remaking*, 37; Hsu, *Good Immigrants*, 126–7; Lowe, *Immigrant Acts*, 9–10, 19–20.
3. Cumings, *Korea's Place in the Sun*, and Masuda, *Cold War Crucible*, offer useful analyses of the Korean War as a conflict driven by sociopolitical and ideological divides. Su-kyoung Hwang, *Korea's Grievous War* (Philadelphia: University of Pennsylvania Press, 2016) is a compelling examination of the Korean War's casualties especially among civilians.
4. Matsumoto, *Farming the Home Place*, 156–8; Robinson, *After Camp*, 51–3, 57–8, and 61–5; Takahashi, *Nisei/Sansei*, 113–16; L. Tamura, *Nisei Soldiers*, chapters 10, 11, and 12.
5. See Glenn, *Issei, Nisei, War Bride*, 137–40, 241–2; Koshy, *Sexual Naturalization*, 10–12; Yuh, *Beyond the Shadow*, 1–4, 162–4. Although no US survivors in my oral history collections said that they had married African Americans, an analysis of such

marriages can be found in Michael Cullen Green, *Black Yanks in the Pacific: Race in the Making of the American Military Empire after World War II* (Ithaca, NY: Cornell University Press, 2010).

6. On the politics of US racial minorities' participation in the Cold War that played on the logics of both inclusion and exclusion, see Azuma, "Brokering Race, Culture, and Citizenship"; —, "Lure of Military Imperialism"; Cheng, *Citizens of Asian America*, 155–6.

7. Brooks, *Alien Neighbors*, 4, 184–6, 196–8, and 222–4; Cheng, *Citizens of Asian America*, chapters 2 and 4 in particular.

8. Orr, *Victim as Hero*, 50–68; Sasaki-Uemura, *Organizing the Spontaneous*, 120–3; Winkler, *Life under a Cloud*, 94–104.

9. On the complex nature of Japanese Americans' silence about the camp in this era, see Cheung, *Articulate Silences*, chapter 4; Creef, *Imaging Japanese America*, 168–9; Duncan, *Tell This Silence*, chapter 3; Inouye, *Long Afterlife*, 1–3; Murray, *Historical Memories*, 108–10, 121–8, and 194–6; Yamamoto, *Masking Selves*, 164, 187–97.

10. Dorothy Swaine Thomas and Richard S. Nishimoto, *The Spoilage (Japanese American Evacuation and Resettlement)* (Berkeley: University of California Press, 1946), 39, claimed that women inmates appeared to take pleasure in a life without household duties (Cited by Gary Okihiro, *The Columbia Guide to Asian American History* [New York: Columbia University Press, 2001], 166). On positive depictions of the camp, see also Howard, *Concentration Camps*, 99–107; Lon Kurashige, *Japanese American Celebration and Conflict: A History of Ethnic Identity and Festival in Los Angeles, 1934–1990* (Berkeley: University of California Press, 2002), 95–8; Nakano, *Japanese American Women*, 145–7.

11. On the "model minority" myth, see Hsu, *Good Immigrants*, 236–49; Phu, *Picturing Model Citizens*, 8–15; E. Wu, *Color of Success*, chapters 5 and 6 in particular.

12. Interview with Nagano, NWC.

13. Interview with Shinmoto, NWC.

14. Interview with Nagano, NWC.

15. Interview with Shinmoto, NWC.

16. Interview with Hirano, NWC.

17. Interview with Yoshida, NWC.

18. These stereotypes were articulated most notably by William Petterson, "Success Story, Japanese-American Style," *NYT*, January 9, 1966.

19. See, for example, Interview with Monberg, NWC; Interview with Nambu, NWC; Interview with Okimoto, NWC.

20. Cheung, *Articulate Silences*, 2–10, 17–20; Duncan, *Tell This Silence*, Introduction; Yamamoto, *Masking Selves*, 160–5.

21. Fugita and O'Brien, *Japanese American Ethnicity*, 148–52; Murray, *Historical Memories*, 197–200; Robinson, *After Camp*, chapters 4 and 5; Takahashi, *Nisei/Sansei*, 125–31, 152–4.

22. See Natsumi Aida's experiences discussed later in this section. For similar examples, see also Interview with Igarashi, NWC; Interview with Utagawa, NWC; Interview with Yamashita, NWC.

23. The following discussion about Okano is based on Interview with Okano, NWC.

24. The following discussion about Aida is derived from Interview with Aida, NWC.

25. Interview with Okano, NWC.

26. Interview with Suyeishi, NWC.

27. Interview with Saiki, NWC.

28. Interview with Yamaoka, STC.

29. Interview with Kurihara, FOHC.
30. Interview with Fukino, NWC.
31. Interview with Dote, NWC.
32. Interview with Ogawa, FOHC.
33. Interview with Okimoto, NWC. See also Interview with Igarashi, FOHC, for a similar depiction of Nikkei's relationship to Caucasians.
34. Interview with Nakamoto, FOHC.
35. Interview with Saiki, NWC.
36. *Ibid.*
37. Interview with Dote, NWC.
38. See Dempster, *Making Home,* 7–9, 39–41; Glenn, *Issei, Nisei, War Bride,* 107–8, 112–16, and 124–8. In the "schoolgirl" and "schoolboy" system, Asian children offered household labor to white families in exchange for room and, sometimes, board.
39. Interview with Aida, NWC.
40. Interview with Kazuko Aoki, NWC.
41. *Ibid.*
42. Interview with Nakamura, NWC.
43. On health effects of the camps, see James Kyung-Jin Lee, "Elegies of Social Life: The Wounded Asian American," *Journal of Race, Ethnicity and Religion* 3.2.7 (January 2012): 1–21; Dana K. Nagata, Jackie H. J. Kim, and Teresa U. Nguyen, "Processing Cultural Trauma: Intergenerational Effects of the Japanese American Incarceration," *Journal of Social Issues* 71.2 (2015): 356–70.
44. Interview with Nakamoto, FOHC.
45. *Ibid.*
46. Interview with Broadwater, STC.
47. Interview with Gendernalik, NWC.
48. Klein, *Cold War Orientalism,* 148–52; Koikari, *Pedagogy of Democracy,* 10–17, 38–41, 57–60, and 134–6; Phu, *Picturing Model Citizens,* 97–105; Shibusawa, *America's Geisha Ally,* 232–9, 245–9; Simpson, *Absent Presence,* 119–25.
49. Interview with McCrea, NWC.
50. Interview with McClary, NWC.
51. *Ibid.*
52. *Ibid.*
53. Interview with Thurlow, STC.
54. Interview with Lee, FOHC.
55. Interview with Kurihara, FOHC.
56. Interview with Kazue Kawasaki, NWC.
57. Interview with Gaudette, FOHC.
58. Interview with the Kubotas, NWC. See also Interview with Fujiyama, FOHC.
59. Interview with Yoshida, NWC.
60. For the definition of the "bomb illness" in social contexts, see, for instance, Interview with Fujimoto, NWC; Interview with Kazue Kawasaki, NWC.
61. Interview with Yamaoka, STC.
62. *Ibid.*
63. Interview with the Koharas, NWC. See also Interview with Saiki, NWC; Interview with Tanemori, NWC; —, STC, all of which suggest that American doctors held an unfounded concern that survivors' bodies were "poisonous," still contagious decades after exposure.
64. Interview with Tanemori, NWC.
65. *Ibid.*

66. Interview with Shinmoto, NWC.
67. Interview with Saiki, NWC.
68. Interview with Sumida, STC.
69. Interview with Dote, NWC.
70. Interview with Dairiki, NWC; Sodei, *Were We the Enemy?*, 66–9. For similar stories of the repression of US survivors' memories during this time period, see Interview with Gaudette, FOHC; Interview with Schutt, STC.
71. Interview with Dairiki, NWC
72. Interview with Nakagawa, NWC.
73. *Ibid.*
74. *Ibid.*
75. Interview with Sarashina, NWC.
76. Scholars have richly explored similar, conflicted feelings of belonging and non-belonging to America among refugees from Vietnam. See, for example, Mimi Thi Nguyen, *The Gift of Freedom: War, Debt, and Other Refugee Passages* (Durham, NC: Duke University Press, 2012); Phuong Tran Nguyen, *Becoming Refugee American: The Politics of Rescue in Little Saigon* (Urbana: University of Illinois Press, 2017).
77. Sasaki-Uemura, *Organizing the Spontaneous*, 30–1, 113, and 122.
78. Holly M. Barker, "From Analysis to Action: Efforts to Address the Nuclear Legacy in the Marshall Islands," in Johnston, *Half-Lives & Half-Truths*, 213–47; Miyamoto, *Beyond the Mushroom Cloud*, 35–6.
79. Interview with Shin, NWC.
80. I did not find any evidence of US survivors' participation in the pacifist organizations that flourished in the 1940s and 1950s in the United States, including Women's International League for Peace and Freedom, Women Strike for Peace, and Non-Violent Actions Against Nuclear Weapons. These predominantly white organizations failed to build sustained interracial coalitions, suggesting how the absence of US survivors in the work of peace activism might be partially explained by racial barriers. On Japanese survivors' participation in peace activism, see S. Tachibana, "Quest for a Peace Culture."
81. Shibusawa, *America's Geisha Ally*, 235–8; Serlin, *Replaceable You*, 79.
82. Interview with Fujiyama, FOHC.
83. Simpson, *Absent Presence*, 117.
84. Interview with Benevedes, NWC; Interview with Elliott, NWC; Interview with Oshima, NWC.
85. For instance, Aiko Tokito compared her status to her mother's, highlighting the new normal in Japan: "My mother had never worked. But after the war, it was assumed that women work after finishing (high) school. This really was true. I don't think that there was any friend of mine who did not go to work." See Interview with Tokito, NWC. On the changing status of women as labor force after the war, see Koikari, *Pedagogy of Democracy*, 128–34, 136–40; Nishi, *Senryōka no Nihon fujin*, 46–52, 153–7, and 160–4. Lisa Yoneyama, "Hihanteki feminizumu no keifu kara miru Nihon senryō," *Shisō* 955 (2003): 60–84, offers a critical examination of US representation of Japanese women's "advancement" during the occupation. Yuki Miyamoto points out how the number of women employed in postwar Hiroshima was larger than the national average, likely because of the lower marriage rate among female survivors. See Miyamoto, *Beyond the Mushroom Cloud*, 150.
86. Elaine Tyler May, *Homeward Bound: American Families in the Cold War Era* (New York: Basic Books, 1999 [original publication 1988]). On diversity of American women's experience in the postwar era, see Joanne Meyerowitz, *Not*

June Cleaver: Women and Gender in Postwar America, 1945–1960 (Philadelphia, PA: Temple University Press, 1994).

87. Interview with Moriwaki, NWC.

88. Betty Friedan, *The Feminine Mystique* (New York: W. W. Norton, 1963); Kirsten Fermaglich and Lisa Fine, eds., *The Feminine Mystique; Annotated Text, Contexts, Scholarship* (New York: W. W. Norton, 2013).

89. Interview with Yanagawa, FOHC.

90. Interview with Imai, NWC.

91. Interview with Shinmoto, NWC.

92. Interview with Fukuda, FOHC.

93. Interview with Okano, NWC.

94. *Ibid.*

95. Interview with Imai, NWC.

96. On the femininity associated with Asian Americans in the mid-century, see Judy Tzu-Chun Wu, *Doctor Mom Chung of the Fair-Haired Bastards: The Life of a Wartime Celebrity* (Berkeley: University of California Press, 2005); Chiou-Ling Yeh, "A Saga of Democracy: Toy Len Goon, American Mother of the Year, and the Cultural Cold War," *Pacific Historical Review* 81.3 (August 2012): 432–61.

97. Interview with Jeong, NWC.

Finding Survivorhood

1. *PC*, April 7, 1978; *Payments hearing*, 86–90, 97–8. The quote is taken from CABS president Kanji Kuramoto's interview with *PC*.

2. *NYT*, August 4, 1974.

3. *HM*, February 28, 1978.

4. There is a rich body of literature about the Asian American civil rights movement and related sociocultural changes. In this chapter, I rely on Ho et al., *Legacy to Liberation*; Maeda, *Rethinking the Asian American Movement*; Pulido, *Black, Brown, Yellow*; Linda Trinh Võ, *Mobilizing an Asian American Community* (Philadelphia, PA: Temple University Press, 2004); Wei, *Asian American Movement*; J. T.-C. Wu, *Radicals on the Road*; Young, *Soul Power*.

5. "Health hearing," 24–5.

6. Interview with Suyeishi, NWC.

7. Interview with Hishinuma, NWC.

8. Interview with Sachiko Matsumoto, NWC.

9. Interview with Elliott, NWC.

10. *PCr*, Summer 1986, Yoneda papers, Box 42, Folder 2. See also Interview with Sachiko Matsumoto, NWC.

11. Interview with Aida, NWC.

12. See, for instance, Interview with the Kubotas, NWC; Interview with Utagawa, NWC.

13. See, for example, Interview with Dote, NWC. See also *HM*, August 3, 1971; *NBT*, July 4, 1969; *RS*, July 29, 1969, which indicated that the Hiroshima and Nagasaki bombings were commemorated by the Hiroshima Nikkeijinkai, the Hiroshima Kenjinkai, and the Nanka Hiroshima Kenjinkai, respectively. Reflecting a smaller number of immigrants from Nagasaki, no similar notice appeared in these Japanese American newspapers in the late 1960s and early 1970s about a Nagasaki Kenjinkai hosting a bomb commemoration in America.

14. Interview with Sachiko Matsumoto, NWC.

15. *CABSN*, July 5, 1977; Interview with Masako Kawasaki, NWC.
16. Interview with Suyeishi, NWC.
17. *HM*, December 2, 1971; *NBT*, October 28, 1971. During the California Senate hearing in 1974, Tomoe Okai, the first president of CABS's Los Angeles branch, stated that the branch had about twenty people in 1965, and in 1967, sixty. These numbers are somewhat larger than the number that US survivors mentioned in their oral histories, which was slightly more than a handful, indicating how the exact number of US survivors before 1971 was anyone's guess. See "Health hearing," 6–7.
18. Interview with Hishinuma, NWC.
19. Ayako Elliott was one of the main participants of the "Personal History Project," organized by the Friends of Hibakusha in 1988, which collected eighteen oral history interviews with American survivors between 1989 and 1996 (mostly in 1989 and 1991 in San Francisco). Thanks to the effort by Elliott and several others, we have at least one oral history collection that dates back to the 1980s. The collection also includes one oral history conducted in 1976 by Sodei, the author of *Were We the Enemy?* This interview was integrated into the FOHC at one point after the "Personal History Project" began.
20. Interview with Fujita, NWC.
21. *Ibid.*
22. *Evening Tribune*, June 21, 1974; *HM*, August 9, 1972; *NE*, August 27, 1972; *NBT*, August 4, 1974; —, May 27, 1976.
23. "Beikoku genbaku hibakusha kyōkai no ayumi" [The history of CABS] (no date), Toshiro Kubota papers.
24. Interview with Suyeishi, NWC.
25. Interview with Elliott, NWC.
26. This was not a view held by Okai herself, nor was she shy about asserting her leadership in public. See, for instance, her testimony during the 1974 hearing for the California Senate Committee, in which she introduced herself as "President/ Founder of the Committee of the Atomic Bomb Survivors." See "Health hearing," 5.
27. Interview with Suyeishi, NWC.
28. Esther Ngan-Ling Chow, "The Feminist Movement: Where Are All the Asian American Women?," in *Making Waves: An Anthology of Writings by and about Asian American Women*, edited by Asian American United of California (Boston, MA: Beacon Press, 1989): 362–77; Susie Ling, "The Mountain Movers: Asian American Women's Movement in Los Angeles," *Amerasia Journal* 15.1 (1989): 51–67; Pulido, *Black, Brown, Yellow*, 204–14; Karen Brodkin Sacks, "Gender and Grassroots Leadership," in *Women and the Politics of Empowerment*, edited by Ann Bookman and Sandra Morgen (Philadelphia, PA: Temple University Press, 1988): 77–94.
29. Noguchi is perhaps best known for officiating in the deaths of Marilyn Monroe in 1962 and Robert F. Kennedy in 1968.
30. See, for instance, *Gidra*, I.7, October 1969, which featured Noguchi as a keynote speaker of an event celebrating the 100th year of the Japanese arrival in America, attended by "hundreds of people of all generations." "Judging from the reaction of the crowd," the article maintained, Noguchi had become "a hero to the local Japanese community."
31. "Resolution to the Board of Supervisors County of Los Angeles," January 28, 1970, JACLH collection, Series I, Box 12. On Noguchi's dismissal, see also Daniel Okimoto, "The Intolerance of Success," in *Roots: An Asian American*

Reader, edited by Amy Tachiki and University of California, Los Angeles, Asian American Studies Center (Los Angeles: Continental Graphics, 1971): 14–19.

32. Quote from Gidra, I.3, June 1969. See also Gidra, I.1, April 1969; —, II.1, January 1970.

33. Gidra, I.2, May 1969.

34. Gidra, I.4, July 1969.

35. "J.U.S.T.: Japanese United in Search of Truth, Noguchi Defense Fund Committee – Chicago," July 18, 1969, JACLH collection, Series I, Box 12.

36. Ibid. On J.U.S.T., see also Gidra, I.5, August 1969; —, I.6, September 1969; RS, July 14, 1969.

37. Gidra, I.1, April 1969.

38. Gidra, II.1, January 1970.

39. Habal, San Francisco's International Hotel, chapters 5, 6, and 7; Maeda, Rethinking the Asian American Movement, 58–64; Wei, Asian American Movement, 23–4.

40. "Interviews of Tenants," The Worker (supplement), February 6, 1977, Louie collection, Series 1, Box 1, Folder 48.

41. Quotes from "J.U.S.T.: Japanese United in Search of Truth."

42. Gidra, II.1, January 1970.

43. Similar to Kuramoto's, Noguchi's English was "his second language" and, thus, "he may sometimes select words which have an inappropriate connotation." Among Asian American youths, this sign of difference helped, rather than hindered, their support for Noguchi. Quotes from Gidra, II.1, January 1970.

44. There were important exceptions to this characterization. Concerning individuals who legally challenged the Japanese American incarceration, see, for example, Gordon Hirabayashi, James A. Hirabayashi, and Lane Ryo Hirabayashi, A Principled Stand: The Story of Hirabayashi v. United States (Seattle: University of Washington Press, 2013). On Japanese American draft resisters who also expressed a critical mode of citizenship early on, see Lyon, Prisons and Patriots; Muller, Free to Die for Their Country.

45. In 1969, Jeffrey Matsui, an officer in JACL's Southern California Regional Office, expressed his appreciation of Noguchi and his frustration about how the support for Noguchi among JACL officials was not uniform: "Throughout the entire ordeal he [Noguchi] stood tall and proud like a dragon. He didn't display dignity, the doctor had dignity.... Dr. Noguchi didn't appear too concerned about himself but about the Japanese [American] community. He didn't want the community to be shamed.... And very, very few people really appreciate the guts it took to carry on the fight." Partly because of a desire for uniting community, JACL officers in late 1969 considered whether the organization should prosecute those who wrongfully accused Noguchi. See "Letter from Jeffrey Matsui to Jerry Enomoto," September 23, 1969, JACLH collection, Series 1, Box 12.

46. Daian C. Fujino, Samurai Among Panthers: Richard Aoki on Race, Resistance, and a Paradoxical Life (Minneapolis: University of Minnesota Press, 2012), 164.

47. HM, August 4 and 10, 1971. See also Akahata, December 4, 1975, Yoneda papers, Box 42, Folder 2.

48. Interview with Noguchi, NWC.

49. Payments hearing, 26.

50. Concerning the breaking of silence around Japanese American incarceration, see William M. Hohri, Repairing America: An Account of the Movement for Japanese American Redress (Pullman: Washington State University Press, 1988); Yasuko

I. Takezawa, *Breaking Silence: Redress and Japanese American Ethnicity* (Ithaca, NY: Cornell University Press, 1995).

51. Interview with Suyeishi, NWC.
52. Interview with Oshima, NWC.
53. *Ibid.*
54. "Los Angeles Hearing on August 5, 1981, and San Francisco Hearing on August 11–12, 1981," Yoneda papers, Box 28, Folder 8. While Yoneda was incarcerated in Manzanar, he became critical of Nikkei whom he perceived to be pro-Japan. This complicated his role as a supporter of reparations in the 1980s. See Murray, *Historical Memories*, 291, 344–5, and 363; Glenn Omatsu, "Karl Yoneda," *Densho Encyclopedia*, encyclopedia.densho.org, accessed October 20, 2017.
55. "Meaning of Hiroshima and Nagasaki," August 6, 1971, Yoneda papers, Box 26, Folder 8; "No More Hiroshimas and Nagasakis," August 8, 1970, Yoneda papers, Box 42, Folder 3. Yoneda contributed a similar story to the *San Francisco Chronicle* on August 2, 1985, and he received an angry letter from a reader who charged him with not caring about "perhaps up to a million Caucasian men [who] would have died invading Japan." Yoneda papers, Box 42, Folder 3.
56. Yoneda papers, Box 42, Folder 2, contains both *CABSN* and newspaper articles featuring Nikkei survivors. On January 5, 1983, Yoneda received a thank you note from CABS president Kanji Kuramoto for his "constant support."
57. *Gidra*, II.7, August 1970.
58. Ichioka in the early 1970s considered the dropping of the bomb a result of "American 'overkill' psychology," which cannot be separated from "the long racist treatment of the Japanese here in America." See "Hiroshima–Nagasaki, Twenty-Six Years Ago," 1971, Ichioka papers, Box 144, Folder 3.
59. "25 Years Ago ... Hiroshima–Nagasaki," August 6–9, 1970, Louie collection, Series 2, Box 5, Folder 5.
60. "Articles and By-Laws of the Committee of Atomic Bomb Survivors of the United States of America Inc., November 1971," Bill files.
61. *HM*, December 2, 1971.
62. *HM*, March 30, 1972.
63. *NBT*, May 30, 1972.
64. *HM*, August 6, 1974; "Presentation at JACL Northern California – Western Nevada District Council by Kanji Kuramoto, February 9, 1975," Bill files.
65. *NYT*, August 4, 1974; *Wall Street Journal*, August 15, 1974.
66. Interview with Gendernalik, NWC.
67. That Matsumoto has been playing these crucial roles first became clear to me because many other US survivors mentioned her. In addition to Lisa Gendernalik, Sayoko Utagawa, a survivor in Fresno, explained how she had obtained a certificate of survivorhood because of Matsumoto's urging: "Ms. Sachiko Matsumoto in San Francisco told me that I should get a certificate, and I started to think that well, maybe I will get it the next time I visit Japan. So it is thanks to her [that I have a certificate]." Comments like this came without prompting. See Interview with Utagawa, NWC. The membership directories in the Sachiko Matsumoto papers contain numerous handwritten updates by Matsumoto, confirming the key roles that she played in communication.
68. Interview with Kanji Kuramoto's spouse, who requested anonymity, NWC.
69. Interview with Suyeishi, NWC.

70. See, for instance, "KTVU Channel 2," March 12, 1974, Dymally papers, Series 1, Box 123, "Material – Atomic Bomb Survivors 5/4/74," which is an outline of a TV program featuring Kuramoto.
71. *NBT*, January 23, 1975.
72. *HM*, August 9, 1972.
73. *NBT*, August 6, 1974. Journalists in Asian American communities played key roles in featuring US survivors in a sympathetic light. See, for example, Sumiko Tatematsu's story featured in *RS*, July 11, 1972.
74. *CABSN*, November (no date), 1976; —, January 4, 1979.
75. *HM*, August 22, 1974. FOH was not formally established until 1982, but supporters of US survivors began to come together on a voluntary basis in the mid-1970s.
76. Interview with Handa, NWC; Interview with Tamaki, NWC. Tamaki was a member of Asian Law Caucus.
77. Quote from Interview with Noguchi, NWC. Concerning Sansai lawyers' work, see Interview with Handa, NWC. Handa has been one of the most active members of FOH.
78. *PC*, August 18, 1972; —, August 16, 1974.
79. *PC*, September 20 and October 11, 1974.
80. Increased support for US survivors in Asian American communities likely played a role, too. One of the 1974 issues of *PC*, for instance, published a letter from a reader who criticized the JACL's lukewarm attitude toward US survivors. "Don't you believe that problem of the survivors ... is the type of issue with which JACL should involve itself?" asked the reader sarcastically. See *PC*, August 30, 1974.
81. "Hibakusha in America," Bill files, 6; *HM*, September 12, 1974; *NBT*, September 12, 1974.
82. On JACL's changing relationship with CABS, see *CABSN*, October 10, 1982; "Letter from Shigeki J. Sugiyama, the National President of JACL, to Kanji Kuramoto, CABS president," January 9, 1975, Bill files; *PCr*, Winter 1991.
83. JACL reported its membership in 1974 as 30,000 across ninety-five chapters nationwide. See *PC*, August 16, 1974.
84. Japan's three nonnuclear principles of not possessing, not manufacturing, and not introducing nuclear weapons into Japan were officially adopted in 1971, when the Japanese House of Representatives voted on the return of Okinawa. The historical root of the nonnuclear principles can be found in a much earlier era, the mid-1950s, when Prime Minister Hatoyama Ichiro rejected the introduction of nuclear warheads to US military bases in Japan. See Tsuneo Akaha, "Japan's Nonnuclear Policy," *Asian Survey* 24.8 (August 1984): 852–77 (see 852–3); Peter J. Katzenstein, *Cultural Norms and National Security: Police and Military in Postwar Japan* (Ithaca, NY: Cornell University Press, 1998), 128–9.
85. *Asian-Americans for Action Newsletter*, November 1969, Ichioka papers, Box 144, Folder 6; *Asian American Political Alliance Newspaper*, 1.5 (September 1969), Louie collection, Series I, Box I, Folder 9; *NBT*, May 24, 1971; *RS*, July 14, 1972.
86. "Letter from Jane Uyesaka to Mas Satow," May 8, 1970; "Letter from Bob Suzuki to Mas Satow," May 9, 1970; "Letter from Fowler JACL to Mas Sato," May 25, 1970, JACLH collection, Series I, Box 10.
87. Sodei, *Were We the Enemy?*, 236–7.
88. Interview with Sakata, NWC.
89. Sodei, *Were We the Enemy?*, 186–9.
90. "Health hearing," 2.

91. Law Concerning Medical Care for Atomic Bomb Survivors, No. 41, 1957; Law Concerning Special Measures for Atomic Bomb Survivors, No. 53, 1968, House of Representatives, Japan.
92. "Health hearing," 20; "Letter from Mervyn M. Dymally to Concerned Citizens," June 5, 1974, Bill files.
93. "News from Senate Subcommittee on Medical Education and Health Needs," May 23, 1974, Dymally papers, Series 1, Box 123, "Material – Atomic Bomb Survivors 5/4/74."
94. "'Hearing on Atomic Bomb Survivors' Set by Senator Dymally," April 3, 1974, Dymally papers, Series 1, Box 123, "Hearing Request – Atomic Bomb Survivors 5/4/74"; "Hibakusha in America," Bill files, 12.
95. American-born citizens were Arai (first name not recorded in the proceeding), Kanji Kuramoto, Kazue Suyeishi, and Kazuo Tosaka. The Japan-born US permanent resident was Shigeko Morimoto. Arai's first name is most likely Satoru, given the newspaper article that featured "members of the Atomic Bomb Survivors organization" on *KM*, May 6, 1974, and "Potential Witness Hearing on Atomic Bomb Survivors," May 4, 1974, Dymally papers, Series 1, Box 123, "Agenda – Atomic Bomb Survivors 5/4/74," both of which cited "Satoru." "Health hearing" recorded Tosaka's first name as "Kazno" and his last name either "Tasaka" or "Tsaka," while "Potential Witness" recorded his name as "Kazuo Tosaka." I use "Kazuo Tosaka" because the latter document shows a recorder's effort to correct misspelling (letters were crossed out and corrected), while "Health hearing" shows no such attempt. This inconsistency in spelling is evidence for how, as discussed in Chapter 3, some US *hibakusha*'s US citizenship was difficult to prove because of incorrect documentation created beyond their control.
96. "Health hearing," 24.
97. *Ibid.*, 36–8.
98. *Ibid.*, 68–9.
99. *Ibid.*, 71.
100. "Hibakusha in America," Bill files, 5.
101. Interview with Elliott, NWC.
102. *NBT*, May 17, 1975.
103. As indicated by note 65, 1974 was when CABS drew major attention from media outside of Asian American communities. Prior to 1974, US survivors drew sporadic attention from newspapers not geared to Asian American readership. See, for example, *Los Angeles Herald Examiner*, April 17, 1972; *NE*, August 27, 1972; *Newsweek*, April 10, 1972. See also "Letter from Paul T. Bannai (Assemblyman, California Legislature) to Kazue Suyeishi," January 30, 1975, Chuman papers, Box 551, Folder 10, which reassured CABS of both Lt. Governor Dymally and local JACL groups' support for the bill.
104. *HM*, June 10, 1975; Sodei, *Were We the Enemies?*, 119.
105. Kuramoto, *Zaibei gojūnen*, 47–9; Sodei, *Were We the Enemy?*, 114–16.
106. *Los Angeles Times*, December 3, 2002.
107. Randy Shilts, *The Mayor of Castro Street: The Life and Times of Harvey Milk* (New York: St. Martin's Press, 1982), 106. See also the American Civil Liberties Union's publication, aclu.org/getting-rid-sodomy-laws-history-and-strategy-led-lawrence-decision, accessed June 19, 2018.
108. See, for example, "Letter from Edward Roybal to Robert C. Weaver," November 30, 1965, Roybal papers, Box 614, Folders 18–21; "Letter from Edward Roybal to Vincent P. Barabba," October 8, 1975, Roybal papers, Box 615, Folder 16. On Mink's antinuclear activism that carefully attended to the

tension between US military and indigenous populations, see Judy Tzu-Chun Wu, "The Dead, the Living, and the Sacred: Patsy Mink, Antimilitarism, and Reimagining the Pacific World," *Meridians: Feminism, Race, Transnationalism* 18.2 (October 2019): 304–31.

109. On Wayne Horiuchi, see Mitchell T. Maki, Harry H. L. Kitano, and S. Megan Berthold, *Achieving the Impossible Dream: How Japanese Americans Obtained Redress* (Urbana-Champaign: University of Illinois Press, 1999), 74, 252n; *Salt Lake Tribune,* July 12, 2005.

110. *NBT,* April 6, 1976.

111. "Letter from Wayne K. Horiuchi to Barbara Jordan," August 26, 1975, Roybal papers, Box 615, Folder 15; *NBT,* February 13, 1976.

112. "Japanese American Citizens League Northern California–Western Nevada District Council, February 9, 1975," Bill files, is accompanied by a note that says: "passed unanimously 2/9/75 Southern California Dist. also passed similar resolution."

113. *NBT,* August 4, 1976.

114. *NBT,* April 26, 1978; *PC,* October 7, 1977; —, March 17, 1978.

115. *PC,* August 22, 1975.

116. *PC,* February 10, 1978.

117. Roybal initially introduced the bill in 1977 as HR-1994. Since then, the bill was revised and assigned the following numbers: HR-5150, HR-8440, HR-8893, HR-10283, HR-10502. During the hearings in 1978, all these bills were discussed together. See *Payments hearing,* 1–19.

118. For typical opposition to the bill, see, for example, "Letter from the California Manufacturers Association to Senator Alfred H. Song," January 21, 1975, Bill files, in which Robert T. Monagan, the president of the association, states that "some of our members, who are involved in industrial applications of nuclear energy, have serious concerns about . . . [the bill's] provisions . . . on accidents, and exposure to radiation on the job." The association posited that because the existing employer-paid insurances should cover the cost of treatment of irradiated employees, its inclusion in the legislation was unnecessary and damaging to the industry's public relations.

119. *Payments hearing,* 3, 6, 9, 12, 15, and 18.

120. *Payments hearing,* 43.

121. *NBT,* April 9, 1978.

122. In 1982, historian Peter Irons discovered a document showing that Japanese American incarceration during the Pacific War had been based on false evidence: John L. Dewitt's *Final Report: Japanese Evacuation from the West Coast, 1942.* In this 1942 report, DeWitt claimed that the camps were a "military necessity" because Japanese Americans had engaged in espionage activities. The document Irons found in 1982 made it clear that, by 1942, the evidence for these activities had been soundly refuted by the Federal Bureau of Investigation. See Shiho Imai, "Korematsu v. United States," *Densho Encyclopedia,* encyclopedia.densho.org, accessed on August 2, 2017.

123. Edwin A. Martini, *Agent Orange: History, Science, and the Politics of Uncertainty* (Amherst: University of Massachusetts Press, 2012), 159–62. See also US Department of Veterans Affairs, "Agent Orange Settlement Fund," benefits.va.gov/COMPENSATION/claims-postservice-agent_orange-settlement-settlementFund.asp, accessed on October 22, 2017.

124. *NBT,* March 4, 1978; *PC,* March 17, 1978.

125. *PCr,* Spring 1985.

126. Interview with Oda, NWC.

Endlessness of Radiation Illness

1. These benefits for Japanese survivors were guaranteed by the Law Concerning Medical Care for Atomic Bomb Survivors, No. 41, 1957; Law Concerning Special Measures for Atomic Bomb Survivors, No. 53, 1968, House of Representatives, Japan.

2. See, for example, Interview with Broadwater, STC; Interview with the Carpenters, STC; Interview with Peters, STC.

3. Interview with Suyeishi, NWC.

4. Interview with Kazuko Aoki, NWC.

5. Interview with the Carpenters, STC. Other US survivors experienced similar difficulties with their physicians. See, for example, Interview with Gomez, FOHC; Interview with Kashihara, NWC; Interview with Yoshimi, NWC.

6. Currently, scientific evidence exists that traces twenty-one cancers to radiation exposure. Although it is debatable if coronary and liver diseases such as myocardinal infarction, chronic hepatitis, and cirrhosis are traceable to irradiation, the Japanese government defines these conditions as possibly related to radiation exposure and thus one of the radiation illnesses qualified for coverage under law. On the changing definition of radiation illness, see Stuart C. Finch, "Occurrence of Cancer in Atomic Bomb Survivors," in *The Final Epidemic: Physicians and Scientists on Nuclear War*, edited by Ruth Adams and Susan Cullen (Chicago: University of Chicago Press, 1981): 151–65; Klervi Leuraud, David B. Richardson, Elisabeth Cardis, Robert D. Daniels, Michael Gillies, Jacqueline A. O'Hagan, Ghassan B. Hamra, Richard Haylock, Dominique Laurier, Monika Moissonnier, Mary K. Schubauer-Berigan, Isabelle Thierry-Chef, and Ausrele Kesminiene, "Ionising Radiation and Risk of Death from Leukaemia and Lymphoma in Radiation-Monitored Workers (INWORKS): An International Cohort Study," *Lancet Haematol* 2.7 (July 2015): 276–81; Lifton, *Death in Life*, chapter 4.

7. *HM*, June 9, 1971; *NBT*, June 9, 1971.

8. *NBT*, July 18, 25, and 30, 1972.

9. *NBT*, August 6, 1972; Sodei, *Were We the Enemy?*, 103.

10. *NBT*, July 4, October 28 and 31, 1971; —, July 7, 25, and 30, 1972; *RS*, July 8, 17, 26, and August 1, 1972.

11. Sodei, *Were We the Enemy?*, 105.

12. *RS*, August 11, 1972.

13. *NBT*, August 10, 1972.

14. *NBT*, February 27 and March 27, 1974.

15. *NBT*, September 22 and 28, 1974.

16. *HM*, August 20, September 12 and 28, 1974; *PC*, October 11, 1974; Sodei, *Were We the Enemy?*, 122–32.

17. *RS*, July 11, 1972.

18. *HM*, August 5, 1974.

19. *Ibid.*

20. Interview with Elliott, NWC. Reynolds became a dedicated CABS supporter. See "Beikoku genbaku hibakusha kyōkai no ayumi" [A history of CABS] (no date), Toshiro Kubota papers.

21. *HM*, April 7, 1972; Sodei, *Were We the Enemy?*, 92.

22. Interview with Suyeishi, NWC.

23. Interview with Sarashina, NWC.

24. "Dr. Fred Yutaka Sakurai's Brief Autobiography" (circa 2010), Fred Yutaka Sakurai papers; Interview with Fred Yutaka Sakurai, NWC.

25. The author's conversation with John Umekubo, July 17, 2011; Interview with Yamaguchi, NWC.

26. Chan, *Asian Americans*, 147–8; Laura Uba, "Supply of Health Care Professionals," in *Confronting Critical Health Issues of Asian and Pacific Islander Americans*, edited by Nolan W. S. Zane, David T. Takeuchi, and Kathleen N. J. Young (Thousand Oaks, CA: Sage Publications, 1994): 376–96 (see 381–8).

27. US Department of Health and Human Services, *Minorities and Women in the Health Fields* (Washington, DC: Government Printing Office, 1975), 6–9, 11, and 13.

28. *GT*, 1.1, February 1970; —, 1.3, July 1970; —, 2.5, June 1971; —, 2.6, July–August 1971; —, 3.3, March 1972, Louie collection, Series 1, Box 2.

29. *GT*, 3.10, June–July 1972, Louie collection, Series 1, Box 2.

30. *GT*, 3.14, August–September 1972, Louie collection, Series 1, Box 2.

31. *GT*, 1.1, February 1970, Louie collection, Series 1, Box 2.

32. *NBT*, August 30, 1970.

33. *Gidra*, III.1, January 1971; *NBT*, April 27, 1971. See also J. T.-C. Wu, *Radicals on the Road*, 257–8, for the important role that the degradation of women played in the racial education of US soldiers.

34. All the following discussion about Handa is based on Interview with Handa, NWC.

35. *Ibid.*

36. Maeda, *Rethinking the Asian American Movement*, 128; Nakano, *Japanese American Women*, 112–15.

37. "The Champions of Resthaven," 1968, RAR, Box 1, Folder 2.

38. "Letter from Joseph L. Krofcheck to Atomic Bomb Survivors' Committee," January 31, 1975, Chuman papers, Box 551, Folder 10.

39. *Gidra*, III.1, January 1971.

40. See, for instance, Interview with Iwano, FOHC, for an emphasis on psychosocial aspects of radiation illness.

41. Joe Yamamoto, "Beginning An Asian/Pacific Mental Health Clinic," in *Uprooting and Surviving: Adaptation and Resettlement of Migrant Families and Children*, edited by Richard C. Nann (Dordrecht, Holland: Springer, 1982): 41–7.

42. Katherine Gould-Martin and Chorswang Ngin, "Chinese Americans," in *Ethnicity and Medical Care*, edited by Alan Harwood (Cambridge, MA: Harvard University Press, 1981): 130–71 (see 152); Karen L. Ito and Alvin So, *Asian American Field Survey: Re-analysis of Health Data* (Paper presented at National Association for Interdisciplinary Studies Annual Conference) (Los Angeles: Asian American Studies Center, University of California, Los Angeles, 1982), 1.

43. Interview with Handa, NWC.

44. Interview with Yamaguchi, NWC.

45. *Ibid.*

46. *CABSN*, March 20, 1977; —, September (no date), 1986; —, November 1, 1998; —, September 16, 2002.

47. Interview with Fukuda, FOHC. A similar relationship involving a woman giving another female survivor inspiration to join the activism can be seen in Interview with Okimoto, NWC.

48. "Health hearing," 17.

49. *Payments hearing*, 76–80.

50. *RS*, August 11, 1972; Sodei, *Were We the Enemy?*, 128–9.

51. Kerr, Yamada, and Marks, "Survey of Radiation Doses."

52. Hiroshima medical professionals came to the United States, while Nagasaki physicians went to South America to conduct medical checkups for survivors. This is because of the large number of people in North America hailing from Hiroshima, and of immigrants in South America who originally came from Nagasaki.

53. *CABSN*, January 4, 1979, indicated that 65 out of 106 CABS members who responded to an inquiry did not have *techō*.

54. See, for example, Interview with Kazuko Aoki, NWC; Interview with Fujimoto, NWC; Interview with Fujita, NWC.

55. *HM*, March 16, 1977.

56. Interview with Nakamura, NWC. See also Interview with Yamashita, NWC, which expressed an appreciation of Hiroshima doctors' familiarity with radiation illness.

57. Interview with Akihara, NWC.

58. Interview with Okimoto, NWC.

59. Although the Radiation Effects Research Foundation (the successor of the ABCC) continues to study the radiation effect on the children of survivors, no evidence has been revealed for a higher rate of illness in this population. Regardless, the Japanese government issues the second generation a *techō* certificate, which grants the beneficiaries an annual medical examination free of cost.

60. Interview with Utagawa, NWC. See also Interview with Hirano, NWC; Interview with Igarashi, NWC.

61. Interview with the Koharas, NWC.

62. *NBT*, May 14, 1981.

63. *Ibid.*

64. *CABSN*, November (no date), 1976.

65. *HM*, December 9, 1976.

66. *Ibid.*

67. *CABSN*, July 5, 1977; *NBT*, July 2, 1977.

68. *CS*, March 9, 1977.

69. Hiroshima-ken Ishikai, *Hiroshima-ken Ishikai*, 226.

70. *HM*, July 9 and 15, 1976.

71. On Korean survivors, see Duró, "Confronting Colonial Legacies"; H. Shin, "Kankoku genbaku higaisha."

72. Hirano, *Umi no mukō*, 11; Ichiba, *Hiroshima o mochikaetta*, 30.

73. In 1972, Japanese physicians also conducted the first medical examinations in Okinawa, indicating that the biannual checkup program in America was shaped by a broader expansion in the 1970s of the system of medical tests, treatment, and care implemented by the 1957 and 1968 laws. See *CS*, March 16, 2015.

74. *HE*, November 30, 1974; —, July 31, 1975; —, January 20, 1976. On Korean women's effort to assist Korean survivors, see Duró, "Confronting Colonial Legacies," 16–17.

75. H. Shin, "Kankoku genbaku higaisha," Appendix 18–20; Zaikan Hibakusha Mondai, *Zaikan hibakusha*, 66–71.

76. *HE*, July 31 and October 5, 1975.

77. *HE*, October 10, 1978; Zaikan Hibakusha Mondai, *Zaikan hibakusha*, 62–4.

78. Japan's Ministry of Health and Welfare issued a directive (called Directive Number 402) in 1974 to all Japanese prefectures and the cities of Hiroshima and Nagasaki, indicating that, when survivors relocate, their certificates must be cancelled and new certificates must be issued by the prefecture in which they currently live. Because only prefectural and Hiroshima and Nagasaki city governments had authority to issue the certificate, survivors living outside Japan automatically lost

all benefits when they returned to their residence. The directive was found to be illegal in 2003.

79. *NBT*, August 9, 1974.

80. Interview with Kashihara, NWC. Sarashina made this comment when he briefly joined the interview.

81. Interview with Toyonaga, NWC.

82. *Ibid.*

83. Interview with Aoki Katsuaki, NWC; "Korean Enlistee in Hiroshima after the Bomb" (no date), Aoki Katsuaki papers.

84. Zaikan Hibakusha Mondai, *Zaikan hibakusha*, 64, 171, and 192–3.

85. *Akahata*, May 24, 1982; "Nihon gensuikyō dai-125-kai jōnin rijikai shiryō" [A resource for the 125th executive board meeting of the Japan Council against Atomic and Hydrogen Bombs], 1978, both of which are in Yoneda papers, Box 49, Folder 7. See also Sasaki-Uemura, *Organizing the Spontaneous*, 170–1.

86. *MS*, June 22, 2015.

87. Interview with Aoki Katsuaki, NWC.

88. Interview with Toyonaga, NWC. See also Yoneyama, *Hiroshima Traces*, 92.

89. See Ikeno and Nakao, "Kōreika suru zaibei hibakusha"; —, "Zai Amerika hibakusha."

90. See Interview with Shin, NWC, which raised a doubt about the checkup being conducted primarily for research, not for treatment.

91. *CABSN*, December 25, 2000; —, March 5, 2001; —, May 1, 2002; —, January 25, 2003; Tamura K., "Zaigai hibakusha no," 585–6.

92. *CS*, February 13, 1986; *CABSN*, March (no date), 1986.

93. *CS*, July 18, 2002.

94. Interview with Hong, NWC.

95. Interview with Lee, FOHC.

96. Interview with Fujimoto, NWC.

97. Interview with Sakata, NWC.

98. "Proposition 64 – Stonewall Gay Democratic Club, S.F.," October 6, 1986, Yoneda papers, Box 26, Folder 8.

99. With the passage of the Veterans' Dioxin and Radiation Exposure Compensation Standards Act in 1983, US veterans exposed to radiation during the American occupation of Hiroshima and Nagasaki in 1945 and 1946 became eligible for compensation. With the Radiation Exposure Compensation Act of 1990, not only "atomic veterans" and "downwinders" irradiated near nuclear test sites in Utah, Nevada, and Arizona, but also employees in the uranium mining industry essential for nuclear weaponry development in the Cold War, became eligible for disability compensation. See Veterans' Dioxin and Radiation Exposure Compensation Standards Act, HR 1961, 98th Congress, 1983–1984 and Radiation Exposure Compensation Act, HR 2372, 101st Congress, 1989–1990.

100. *CABSN*, January 21, 1980.

101. *NBT*, May 19 and July 3, 1981.

102. Paul S. Boyer, *Fallout: A Historian Reflects on America's Half-Century Encounter with Nuclear Weapons* (Columbus: Ohio State University Press, 1998), 238; Interview with Tomosawa, NWC.

103. *RS*, June 22, 1987.

104. Hiroshima-ken Ishikai, *Hiroshima-ken Ishikai*, 226–7.

105. Tomoji Ishi, "Adjusting to the Rim: Japanese Corporate Social Responsibility in the United States," in *What is in a Rim? Critical Perspectives on the Pacific Region Idea*, edited by Arif Dirlik (Boulder, CO: Westview Press, 1993): 121–34. On the

changing economic dynamism between the United States and Asia at the end of the twentieth century, see Grewal, *Transnational America*; Ong, *Flexible Citizenship*.

106. Interview with Tomosawa, NWC.
107. Interview with Masako Kasawaki, NWC.
108. Interview with Morita Hiromi, NWC.
109. Interview with the Kubotas, NWC.
110. Interview with Fujimoto, NWC; Interview with Fujita, NWC. Some US survivors did not apply for *techō* until recently because of a similar reservation. See, for instance, Interview with Furubayashi, NWC.
111. Interview with Suyeishi, NWC.
112. Interview with Elliott, NWC.
113. Interview with Okimoto, NWC.
114. *Ibid.*

Epilogue

1. "A.S.A. American Society of Hiroshima–Nagasaki A-Bomb Survivors (Nonprofit)," May 24, 2012, Junji Sarashina papers.
2. *CABSN*, January 12, 1993; Ikeno and Nakao, "Zaibei hibakusha kyōkai"; Kuramoto, *Zaibei gojūnen*, 74–85.
3. *CABSN*, August 25, 2001; *NBT*, July 19, 2001; Interview with Gendernalik, NWC; Interview with Yoshimi, NWC.
4. *Association of Nikkei & Japanese Abroad (ANJA) Seasonal*, March 10, 2004 (included in *CABSN*, March 15, 2004).
5. Interview with Yamaguchi, NWC.
6. Hiroshima-ken Ishikai, *Hiroshima-ken Ishikai*, 226–31. In recent years, two teams of Japanese physicians have come to America; one goes to Honolulu and Los Angeles, the other goes to San Francisco and Seattle. See *Hiroshima-ken Ishikai sokuhō* (Hiroshima Prefectural Medical Association breaking news) 2125 (July 15, 2011): 4–14.
7. Hiroshima-ken Ishikai, *Hiroshima-ken Ishikai*, 230. As of 2003, the Japanese government began to pay about 90 percent of the total cost. The remaining cost was paid by Hiroshima-ken Ishikai. In 2007, the government started to pay the full cost of the program.
8. Interview with Ayaka Sakurai, NWC.
9. *Ibid.*
10. Interview with Yamaguchi, NWC.
11. Interview with Tomosawa, NWC.
12. Interview with Moriwaki, NWC.
13. Interview with Sachiko Matsumoto, NWC.
14. Interview with Kazue Kawasaki, NWC. See also Interview with the Kubotas, NWC; Interview with Shin, NWC.
15. Soh, *Comfort Women*, 41–4; S. Tachibana, "Quest for a Peace Culture."
16. Alyson Cole, *The Cult of True Victimhood: From the War on Welfare to the War on Terror* (Stanford, CA: Stanford University Press, 2007), 15–16, 44; Conference on Jewish Material Claims Against Germany, "History," claimscon.org/about/history, accessed June 28, 2018; Wieviorka, *Era of the Witness*, chapter 3.
17. *HE*, October 31, 1987; —, March 27, 1990; —, August 2, 1992; Shimin no Kai, ed., *Zaikan hibakusha no sengo hoshō* [Postwar compensation for Korean survivors] (Toyonaka, Japan: Shimin no Kai, 2011), 4–8, 10–14.
18. *CABSN*, June 2, 1990; —, January 12, 1993.

19. *HE*, September 10, 1989; —, July 25 and December 5, 1990; —, March 15, 1992; Zaikan Hibakusha Mondai, *Zaikan hibakusha*, 66–72, 91–5.
20. *HE*, June 3, 1995; —, January 10, 1996; Mitsubishi Hiroshima and Moto Chōyōkō Hibakusha Saiban o Shiensuru Kai (Shiensuru Kai), ed., *Mitsubishi Hiroshima and moto chōyōkō hibakusha saiban kousai hanketsu o megutte* [On the former Korean employees of Mitsubushi in Hiroshima, their trial, and the ruling by the Supreme Court] (Hiroshima: Shiensuru Kai, 2005).
21. Shimin no Kai, ed., *Hibakusha ga hibakusha de nakusareru toki* [When survivors are denied survivorhood] (Toyonaka, Japan: Shimin no Kai, 2000), 2, 66–71; Tamura K., "Zaigai hibakusha engo."
22. *CABSN*, March 5, 1990; —, March 30, 1998; —, July 15, 2000; —, August 25, 2001.
23. *CABSN*, January 1, 1990; —, April 19 and December 18, 1996.
24. *CABSN*, August 1, 1998.
25. *CABSN*, July 20, 1996.
26. *NBT*, October 30, 1997.
27. *HE*, December 7, 1999.
28. *CABSN*, May 1, 2002.
29. *CABSN*, February 20, 2002; *HM*, April 11, 2002.
30. *CABSN*, August 1, 1998; —, July 15, 2000; —, August 25, 2001.
31. The quote is from *CABSN*, March 15, 2004. See also *NBT*, April 9, 2002; *ZBZAH*, December 2004; —, June 2005.
32. Indeed, some US survivors' families in Japan expressed the concern that US survivors' demands for support from the Japanese government would be seen as proof of their poverty, thus it would do damage to their families' reputation in Japan. See Interview with Morita Hiromi, NWC.
33. See, for instance, Interview with Moriwaki, NWC, in which Moriwaki expressed a strong distaste for Japanese tourists in Hawai'i who expressed a bias against Japanese Americans.
34. *ANJA Seasonal*, March 10, 2004.
35. Interview with Tomosawa, NWC.
36. *Ibid.*; *ZBZAH*, February and July 2006.
37. Interview with Tomosawa, NWC.
38. Interview with Sakata, NWC.
39. Interview with Tokito, NWC.
40. Interview with Akihara, NWC.
41. Interview with Dote, NWC.
42. Interview with Pak, NWC. See also Interview with Wes Aoki, NWC, in which Aoki suggested the idea of the United States and Japan each paying 50 percent to care for US survivors.
43. Interview with Shibata, NWC.
44. Interview with Toyonaga, NWC.
45. Interview with Adachi and Tamura, NWC.
46. Interview with Hong, NWC.
47. Interview with Chew, NWC.
48. Interview with Cheng, NWC.
49. Ichiba, *Hiroshima o mochikaetta.*

GLOSSARY

hibakusha When spelled 被爆者, *hibakusha* means survivors of the Hiroshima and Nagasaki atomic bombings in 1945. When spelled 被曝者, *hibakusha* means people irradiated in other circumstances such as nuclear power plant accidents

Issei The first generation immigrants from Japan. Before 1952, they were ineligible for US citizenship

Kibei American citizens of Japanese ancestry who grew up in Japan then returned to the United States

Nikkei People of Japanese ancestry. Nikkei includes Issei, Nisei, Sansei, and any other generation

Nisei The children of the first generation immigrants from Japan. Nisei are US citizens by birth

Sansei The children of Nisei. Like Nisei, Sansei are US citizens by birth

Satogaeri Chiryō The program established in 1982 by Japanese nongovernmental organizations in order to medically treat American survivors at hospitals in Japan

Shin Issei The first generation immigrants from Japan who came to the United States after 1945

techō (*hibakusha techō*) A passport-size booklet that denotes a person as a survivor of the Hiroshima or Nagasaki atomic bombing. *Techō* allows survivors to receive medical treatment, monetary allowances, and other benefits from the Japanese government

SELECT BIBLIOGRAPHY

Oral Histories

Friends of Hibakusha Collection of US Survivors' Oral Histories, Regional Oral History Office, Bancroft Library, University of California, Berkeley

Interview with Norio Dazai (pseudonym), July 11, 1991.
Interview with Chisa Frank (pseudonym), June 18, 1989.
Interview with Satoshi Fujiyama (pseudonym), June 23, 1989.
Interview with Julie Kumi Fukuda (pseudonym), June 18, 1976.
Interview with Asako Gaudette (pseudonym), December 12, 1989.
Interview with John Hong (pseudonym), May 19, 1991.
Interview with Miyoko Igarashi (pseudonym), June 23, 1991.
Interview with Sister Sara Shakucho Iwano (pseudonym), June 22, 1991.
Interview with Yasuko Kimura (pseudonym), June 17, 1989.
Interview with Fusae Kurihara (pseudonym), June 18, 1989.
Interview with Hye-kyo Lee (pseudonym), June 22, 1991.
Interview with Tim Nakamoto (pseudonym), June 23, 1991.
Interview with Yasuko Ogawa (pseudonym), April 12, 1996.
Interview with Jeremy Oshima (pseudonym), March 10 & 27, 1989.
Interview with Noriko Smith (pseudonym), June 22, 1991.
Interview with Kenji Takahashi (pseudonym), June 22, 1991.
Interview with Francis Mitsuo Tomosawa, April 29, 1989.
Interview with Katie Yanagawa (pseudonym), May 12, 1989.

Shinpei Takeda Collection of Oral Histories of North and South American Survivors, G. Robert Vincent Voice Library, Michigan State University, East Lansing

Interview with Kazuko Aoki, February 19, 2008.
Interview with Chizuko Blakes, January 5, 2007.
Interview with Miyuki Broadwater, March 26, 2009.
Interview with Hideko Campana, March 25, 2009.
Interview with Lonnie Carpenter and Sue Carpenter, April 27, 2005.
Interview with Sue Carpenter, January 5, 2007.
Interview with Izumi Hirano, February 17, 2008.
Interview with Junko Inoue, April 1, 2009.
Interview with Kazue Kawasaki, March 29, 2009.
Interview with Yuriko Kelly, January 5, 2007.
Interview with Masako Konen, January 5, 2007.
Interview with Atsuko La Mica, March 29, 2009.
Interview with David Laskey, March 23, 2009.
Interview with Miyoko Manalisay, April 1, 2009.
Interview with Sachiko Matsumoto, April 2, 2009.
Interview with Magohei Nagaishi, July 20, 2008.
Interview with Kiyoko Oda, March 29, 2009.
Interview with Joe Ohori, April 2, 2010.
Interview with Takeko Okano, March 29, 2009.
Interview with Michiko Peters, January 5, 2007.
Interview with Fumie Schutt, January 5, 2007.
Interview with Mizuho Stevens, March 29, 2009.
Interview with Minoru Sumida, February 19, 2008.
Interview with Takashi Thomas Tanemori, June 18, 2009.
Interview with Setsuko Thurlow, April 2, 2010.
Interview with Tōru Uematsu, January 5, 2007.
Interview with May Yamaoka, April 1, 2009.
Interview with Takeo Yamashiro, March 23, 2009.

Naoko Wake Collection of Oral Histories of US Survivors, Families, and Supporters, in possession of the author, East Lansing, Michigan

Interview with Adachi Shūichi and Tamura Kazuyuki, July 3, 2013.
Interview with Natsumi Aida (pseudonym), June 25, 2012.
Interview with Tokie Akihara (pseudonym), July 25, 2011.

Interview with Aoki Katsuaki, July 2, 2013.

Interview with Kazuko Aoki, June 19, 2013.

Interview with Wes Aoki, July 22, 2011.

Interview with Arita Takeo, August 5, 2015.

Interview with Michiko Benevedes, July 21, 2011.

Interview with Shannon Cheng (pseudonym), June 12, 2012.

Interview with Ray Chew, June 12, 2012.

Interview with Ch'oe Ha-un (pseudonym), July 2, 2013.

Interview with Jack Motoo Dairiki, July 13, 2010.

Interview with Alfred Kaneo Dote, June 25, 2012.

Interview with Akira Edagawa (pseudonym), July 16, 2011.

Interview with Ayako Elliott (pseudonym), June 11, 2012.

Interview with Deborah Fehn, June 5, 2012.

Interview with Seiko Fujimoto, July 19, 2011.

Interview with Nobuko Fujioka, June 14, 2012.

Interview with Yasuo Grant Fujita, June 19, 2012.

Interview with Hayami Fukino, June 6, 2012.

Interview with Yuriko Furubayashi, June 21, 2013.

Interview with Lisa Gendernalik (pseudonym), July 17, 2011.

Interview with Masako B. Hamada, June 3, 2012.

Interview with Geri Handa, July 20, 2011.

Interview with Yuko Haneishi, June 15, 2012.

Interview with Izumi Hirano, June 17, 2013.

Interview with Toshiko Hishinuma (pseudonym), June 2, 2012.

Interview with John Hong (pseudonym), July 16, 2010.

Interview with Ichiba Junko, May 19, 2017.

Interview with Miyoko Igarashi (pseudonym), June 22, 2012.

Interview with Fumiko Imai, June 21, 2012.

Interview with James Jeong (pseudonym), July 15, 2010.

Interview with Atsuro Kahara (pseudonym), June 3, 2012.

Interview with Yasuko Kashihara (pseudonym), June 2, 2012.

Interview with Kazue Kawasaki, June 18, 2012.

Interview with Masako Kawasaki, June 20, 2012.

Interview with Setsuko Kohara and Tadachi Kohara, June 5, 2012.

Interview with Sumie Kubota and Toshiro Kubota (pseudonyms), June 23, 2012.

Interview with Kanji Kuramoto's spouse, July 25, 2011.

Interview with Atsuko La Mica, July 6, 2012.

Interview with Matsumoto Kisō, July 5, 2013.

Interview with Sachiko Matsumoto, July 23, 2011.

Interview with Kim McClary, June 12, 2012.

Interview with Kazue McCrea (pseudonym), June 12, 2012.

Interview with Jennifer Miller (pseudonym), July 17, 2010.
Interview with Yasue Monberg (pseudonym), June 12, 2012.
Interview with Morita Hiromi, July 2, 2013.
Interview with Takashi Morita, January 16, 2013.
Interview with Joyce Ikuko Moriwaki, June 20, 2013.
Interview with Stephen Morrison and Rachel Harrison (pseudonyms), July 17, 2011.
Interview with Haakai Nagano (pseudonym), June 11, 2012.
Interview with Mike Kiyoshi Nakagawa, June 27, 2012.
Interview with Tsuruko Nakamura, July 19, 2011.
Interview with Tokiko Nambu, June 19, 2012.
Interview with Thomas Noguchi, March 27, 2014.
Interview with Mae Oda, June 23, 2013.
Interview with Takeko Okano, June 18, 2012.
Interview with Mitsuko Okimoto, June 9, 2012.
Interview with Tae Alison Okuno (pseudonym), June 15, 2012.
Interview with Jeanna Oshima (pseudonym), July 22, 2011.
Interview with Pak Namjoo, July 1, 2013.
Interview with George Kazuto Saiki, June 24, 2013.
Interview with Tokie Sakai, June 21, 2012.
Interview with Kae Sakamoto (pseudonym), August 6, 2015.
Interview with Kyohei Sakata (pseudonym), July 14, 2011.
Interview with Ayaka Sakurai, June 5, 2012.
Interview with Fred Yutaka Sakurai, June 6, 2012.
Interview with Junji Sarashina, June 6, 2012.
Interview with Paul Satoh, August 23, 2015.
Interview with Shibata Toshio, July 1, 2013.
Interview with Isamu Shin (pseudonym), June 20, 2013.
Interview with Keiko Shinmoto, July 25, 2011.
Interview with Tomiko Shoji, Minoru Shoji, and Isao Shoji, July 14, 2015.
Interview with Kazue Suyeishi, June 4, 2012.
Interview with Donald Tamaki, September 27, 2015.
Interview with Takashi Thomas Tanemori, July 18, 2011.
Interview with Aiko Tokito, June 19, 2013.
Interview with Francis Mitsuo Tomosawa, June 7, 2012.
Interview with Toyonaga Keizaburō, July 3, 2013.
Interview with Ueda Yasuo, July 30, 2015.
Interview with Sayoko Utagawa (pseudonym), June 13, 2012.
Interview with Akiko Watanabe (pseudonym), June 18, 2013.
Interview with Kathy Yamaguchi (pseudonym), July 15, 2011.
Interview with May Yamaoka, July 17, 2010.
Interview with Toshiaki Yamashita (pseudonym), June 20, 2012.

Interview with Yi Jougkeun, July 3, 2013.
Interview with Sumiko Yoshida, June 14, 2012.
Interview with Bon Yoshimi, July 21, 2011.

Personal Papers

Natsumi Aida papers, Sacramento, California
Tokie Akihara papers, Alameda, California
Aoki Katsuaki papers, Hiroshima, Hiroshima
Kazuko Aoki papers, Honolulu, Hawai'i
Michiko Benevedes papers, Pacifica, California
Ch'oe Ha-un papers, Hiroshima, Hiroshima
Jack Motoo Dairiki papers, San Francisco, California
Alfred Kaneo Dote papers, Sacramento, California
Yuriko Furubayashi papers, Kailua, Hawai'i
Toshiko Hishinuma papers, Los Angeles, California
John Hong papers, Sacramento, California
Fumiko Imai papers, Pacific Grove, California
Masako Kawasaki papers, Sunnyvale, California
Toshiro Kubota papers, Sacramento, California
Sachiko Matsumoto papers, San Francisco, California
Kazue McCrea papers, Vacaville, California
Jennifer Miller papers, Berkeley, California
Haakai Nagano papers, El Cerrito, California
Kiyoshi Mike Nakagawa papers, Sacramento, California
Tsuruko Nakamura papers, San Francisco, California
Mae Oda papers, Hilo, Hawai'i
Takeko Okano papers, San Jose, California
George Kazuto Saiki papers, Honolulu, Hawai'i
Fred Yutaka Sakurai papers, Torrance, California
Junji Sarashina papers, Buena Park, California
Keiko Shinmoto papers, Stockton, California
Kazue Suyeishi papers, Anaheim, California
Tamura Kazuyuki papers, Hiroshima, Hiroshima
Takashi Thomas Tanemori papers, Berkeley, California
Aiko Tokito papers, Honolulu, Hawai'i
May Yamaoka papers, El Cerrito, California
Sumiko Yoshida papers, Atherton, California

Published Sources

Azuma, Eiichiro. *Between Two Empires*. New York: Oxford University Press, 2005.

"Brokering Race, Culture, and Citizenship: Japanese Americans in Occupied Japan and Postwar National Inclusion." *Journal of American-East Asian Relations* 16, no. 3 (Fall 2009): 187–94.

In Search of Our Frontier: Japanese America and Settler Colonialism in the Construction of Japan's Borderless Empire. Berkeley: University of California Press, 2019.

"The Lure of Military Imperialism: Race, Martial Citizenship, and Minority American Transnationalism during the Cold War." *Journal of American Ethnic History* 36, no. 2 (Winter 2017): 72–82.

Barker, Holly M. *Bravo for the Marshallese: Regaining Control in a Post-Nuclear, Post-Colonial World*. Toronto: Wadsworth, 2004.

Biswas, Shampa. *Nuclear Desire: Power and the Postcolonial Nuclear Order*. Minneapolis: University of Minnesota Press, 2014.

Boyer, Paul S. *By the Bomb's Early Light: American Thought and Culture at the Dawn of the Atomic Age*. Chapel Hill: University of North Carolina Press, 1994 (original publication in 1985).

Braw, Monica. *The Atomic Bomb Suppressed*. Armonk, NY: M. E. Sharpe, 1991.

Broderick, Mick, ed. *Hibakusha Cinema: Hiroshima, Nagasaki and the Nuclear Image in Japanese Film*. London and New York: Kegan Paul International, 1996.

Brooks, Charlotte. *Alien Neighbors, Foreign Friends: Asian Americans, Housing, and the Transformation of California*. Chicago: University of Chicago Press, 2009.

Caprio, Mark E., and Yoneyuki Sugita, ed. *Democracy in Occupied Japan: The US Occupation and Japanese Politics and Society*. London: Routledge, 2007.

Chan, Sucheng. *Asian Americans: An Interpretive History*. Boston, MA: Twayne, 1991.

Chapman, David. *Zainichi Korean Identity and Ethnicity*. London and New York: Routledge, 2008.

Cheng, Cindy I-Fen. *Citizens of Asian America: Democracy and Race during the Cold War*. New York: New York University Press, 2013.

Cheung, King-Kok. *Articulate Silences: Hisaye Yamamoto, Maxine Hong Kingston, Joy Kogawa*. Ithaca, NY: Cornell University Press, 1993.

Chŏng Kŭn-sik, ed. *Kankoku genbaku higaisha kutsū no rekishi* [A painful history of Korean A-bomb survivors]. Translated from Korean to Japanese by Ichiba Junko. Tokyo: Akashi Shoten, 2008.

Clendinnen, Inga. *Reading the Holocaust*. Cambridge and New York: Cambridge University Press, 1999.

Collins, Donald E. *Native American Aliens: Disloyalty and the Renunciation of Citizenship by Japanese Americans during World War II.* Westport, CT: Greenwood Press, 1985.

Creef, Elena Tajima. *Imaging Japanese America: The Visual Construction of Citizenship, Nation, and the Body.* New York: New York University Press, 2004.

Cumings, Bruce. *Korea's Place in the Sun: A Modern History.* New York: W. W. Norton, 1997.

Dempster, Brian Komei, ed. *Making Home from War: Stories of Japanese American Exile and Resettlement.* Berkeley, CA: Heyday, 2010.

Dower, John W. *War without Mercy: Race and Power in the Pacific War.* New York: Pantheon, 1986.

Duncan, Patti. *Tell This Silence: Asian American Women Writers and the Politics of Speech.* Iowa City: University of Iowa Press, 2004.

Duró, Ágota. "Confronting Colonial Legacies: The Historical Significance of Japanese Grassroots Cooperation for the Support of Korean Atomic Bomb Survivors." PhD diss., Hiroshima City University, 2017.

Duus, Peter. *The Abacus and the Sword: The Japanese Penetration of Korea, 1895–1910.* Berkeley: University of California Press, 1998.

Duus, Peter, Ramon H. Myers, and Mark R. Peattie, eds. *The Japanese Wartime Empire, 1931–1945.* Princeton, NJ: Princeton University Press, 1996.

Fassin, Didier, and Richard Rechtman. *The Empire of Trauma: An Inquiry into the Condition of Victimhood.* Princeton, NJ: Princeton University Press, 2009

Fugita, Stephan S., and David J. O'Brien. *Japanese American Ethnicity: The Persistence of Community.* Seattle: University of Washington Press, 1991.

Fujitani, Takashi. *Race for Empire: Koreans as Japanese and Japanese as Americans during World War II.* Berkeley: University of California Press, 2011.

Fujitani, Takashi, Geoffrey M. White, and Lisa Yoneyama, eds. *Perilous Memories, The Asia-Pacific War(s).* Durham, NC: Duke University Press, 2001.

Glenn, Evelyn Nakano. *Issei, Nisei, War Bride: Three Generations of Japanese American Women in Domestic Service.* Philadelphia, PA: Temple University Press, 1986.

Unequal Freedom: How Race and Gender Shaped American Citizenship. Cambridge, MA: Harvard University Press, 2002.

Granovetter, Mark S. "The Strength of Weak Ties." *American Journal of Sociology* 78, no. 6 (May 1973): 1360–80.

Grewal, Inderpal. *Transnational America: Feminisms, Diasporas, Neoliberalisms.* Durham, NC: Duke University Press, 2005.

Grewal, Inderpal, and Caren Kaplan, eds. *Scattered Hegemonies: Postmodernity and Transnational Feminist Practices*. Minneapolis: University of Minnesota Press, 1994.

Habal, Estella. *San Francisco's International Hotel: Mobilizing the Filipino American Community in the Anti-Eviction Movement*. Philadelphia, PA: Temple University Press, 2007.

Hagopian, Patrick. *American Immunity: War Crimes and the Limits of International Law*. Amherst: University of Massachusetts Press, 2013.

Hama Hideo, Arisue Ken, and Takemura Hideki, eds. *Hibakusha chōsa o yomu: Hiroshima/Nagasaki no keishō* [Reading surveys of survivors: Passing on Hiroshima/Nagasaki]. Tokyo: Keiōgijuku Daigaku Shuppankai, 2013.

Hayslip, Le Ly, with Jay Wurts. *When Heaven and Earth Changed Places: A Vietnam Woman's Journey from War to Peace*. New York: Doubleday, 1989.

Hein, Laura, and Mark Selden, eds. *Living with the Bomb: American and Japanese Cultural Conflicts in the Nuclear Age*. Armonk, NY: M. E. Sharpe, 1997.

Herman, Judith Lewis. *Trauma and Recovery*. New York: Basic Books, 1992.

Hersey, John. "Hiroshima." *The New Yorker*. August 31, 1946.

Hing, Bill Ong. *Making and Remaking Asian America through Immigration Policy, 1850–1990*. Stanford, CA: Stanford University Press, 1993.

Hirano Nobuto. *Umi no mukō no hibakusha tachi: Zaigai hibakusha mondai no rikai no tameni* [Survivors across the ocean: Toward a better understanding of *hibakusha* outside Japan]. Tokyo: Hachigatsu Shokan, 2009.

Hiraoka Takashi. *Muen no kaikyō: Hiroshima no koe, hibaku Chōsenjin no koe* [The straits of no crossing: Voices of Hiroshima, voices of Korean survivors]. Tokyo: Kage Shobō, 1983.

Hiroshima-ken, ed. *Hiroshima kenjin kaigai hattenshi nenpyō* [The timetable of Hiroshimans' development overseas]. Hiroshima: Hiroshima-ken, 1964.

Hiroshima-ken Chōsenjin Hibakusha Kyōgikai, ed. *Shiroi chogori no hibakusha* [*Hibakusha* in white *chŏgori*]. Tokyo: Rōdōjunpōsha, 1979.

Hiroshima-ken Henshū Iinkai, ed. *Hiroshima-ken ijūshi: Tsūshi hen* [The history of migration from Hiroshima prefecture]. Hiroshima: Hiroshima-ken, 1993.

Hiroshima-ken Ishikai, ed. *Hiroshima-ken Ishikai zaibei genbaku hibakusha kenshin jigyō suishin sanjusshūnen kinenshi* [Thirty years of health examinations for American survivors]. Hiroshima: Hiroshima-ken Ishikai, 2007.

Ho, Fred, Carolyn Antonio, Diane Fujino, and Steve Yip, eds. *Legacy to Liberation: Politics and Culture of Revolutionary Asian Pacific America*. San Francisco: AK Press, 2000.

Hogan, Michael J., ed. *Hiroshima in History and Memory*. New York: Cambridge University Press, 1996.

Howard, John. *Concentration Camps on the Home Front: Japanese Americans in the House of Jim Crow.* Chicago: University of Chicago Press, 2008.

Hsu, Madeline Y. *The Good Immigrants: How the Yellow Peril Became the Model Minority.* Princeton, NJ: Princeton University Press, 2015.

Hune, Shirley, and Gail M. Nomura, eds. *Asian/Pacific Islander American Women: A Historical Anthology.* New York: New York University Press, 2003.

Ibuse Mazuji. *Kuroi ame* [Black rain]. Tokyo: Shinchōsha, 1966.

Ichiba Junko. *Hiroshima o mochikaetta hitobito: "Kankoku no Hiroshima" wa naze umareta no ka* [Bringing back Hiroshima: The birth of "Hiroshima in Korea"]. Tokyo: Gaifūsha, 2005.

Ikeno Satoshi, and Nakao Kayoko. "Kōreika suru zaibei hibakusha no jittai chōsa: Hibaku ni yoru shintaiteki shinriteki shakaiteki eikyō no hōkatsuteki rikai to seisaku oyobi kenkyū kadai" [A study of aging US survivors: A comprehensive understanding of physical, psychological, and social influences and challenges in policy and research]. *Ningen fukushi-gaku kenkyū* 2, no. 1 (2009): 73–86.

"Zai Amerika hibakusha no engo to kenkyū kadai: Shinri shakaiteki shiza kara no apurōchi" [Practical and research implications for the support of survivors in the United States: From a psychosocial perspective]. *Kansai gakuin daigaku kiyō* 102 (March 2007): 85–100.

"Zaibei hibakusha kyōkai bunretsu no yōin bunseki to kongo no enjo no kadai" [An analysis of the reason for CABS' split and challenges for future support]. *Ningen fukushigaku kenkyū* 6, no. 1 (2013): 47–68.

Inouye, Karen M. *The Long Afterlife of Nikkei Wartime Incarceration.* Stanford, CA: Stanford University Press, 2016.

Itō Chikako. *Hazama ni ikite gojūnen: Zaibei hibakusha no ayumi* [Living in-between for fifty years: The history of survivors in the United States]. Walnut, CA: Committee of Atomic Bomb Survivors in the United States of America, 1996.

Jacobs, Robert A. *The Dragon's Tail: Americans Face the Atomic Age.* Amherst: University of Massachusetts Press, 2010.

Jin, Michael. "A Transnational Generation: Japanese Americans in the Pacific before World War II." *Ritsumeikan gengo bunka kenkyū* 21, no. 4 (2010): 185–96.

Johnston, Barbara Rose, ed. *Half-Lives & Half-Truths: Confronting the Radioactive Legacies of the Cold War.* Santa Fe, NM: School for Advanced Research Press, 2007.

Jones, Matthew. *After Hiroshima: The United States, Race and Nuclear Weapons in Asia: 1945–1965.* Cambridge: Cambridge University Press, 2010.

Kamisaka Fuyuko. *Ikinokotta hitobito* [Those who survived]. Tokyo: Bungei Shunjū, 1989.

Kaufman, Joyce P., and Kristen P. Williams. *Women, the State, and War: A Comparative Perspective on Citizenship and Nationalism.* Lanham, MD: Lexington Books, 2007.

Kerr, George D., Hiroaki Yamada, and Sidney Marks. "A Survey of Radiation Doses Received by Atomic Bomb Survivors Residing in the United States." *Health Physics* 31 (October 1976): 305–13.

Kim, Jodi. *Ends of Empire: Asian American Critique and the Cold War.* Minneapolis: University of Minnesota Press, 2010.

Kim T'ae-gi. *Sengo Nihon seiji to zainichi Chōsenjin mondai: SCAP no taizainichi Chōsenjin seisaku 1945–1952* [A political history of postwar Japan and the problem of Koreans in Japan: SCAP's policies concerning Koreans in Japan 1945–1952]. Tokyo: Keisō Shobō, 1997.

Kiyota, Minoru. *Beyond Loyalty: The Story of a Kibei.* Translated by Linda Klepinger Keenan. Honolulu: University of Hawai'i Press, 1997.

Klein, Christina. *Cold War Orientalism: Asia in the Middlebrow Imagination, 1945–1961.* Berkeley: University of California Press, 2003.

Kobayashi Masanori. *Nikkei imin, kaigai ijū, ibunka kōryū no konjaku* [Nikkei immigrants, overseas migration, and cultural exchange in the past and the present]. Hiroshima: Konbenshon Kurieito, 2004.

Kodama Masaaki. *Nihon iminshi kenkyū josetsu* [Introduction to the study of Japanese immigration history]. Hiroshima: Keisuisha, 1992.

Koikari, Mire. *Pedagogy of Democracy: Feminism and the Cold War in the US Occupation of Japan.* Philadelphia, PA: Temple University Press, 2008.

Koshy, Susan. *Sexual Naturalization: Asian Americans and Miscegenation.* Stanford, CA: Stanford University Press, 2004.

Kovner, Sarah. *Occupying Power: Sex Workers and Servicemen in Postwar Japan.* Stanford, CA: Stanford University Press, 2012.

Kuramoto Kanji. *Zaibei gojūnen: Watashi to America no hibakusha* [Living in the United States for fifty years: US survivors and me]. Tokyo: Nihon Tosho Kankōkai, 1999.

Kwon, Nayoung Aimee. *Intimate Empire: Collaboration and Colonial Modernity in Korea and Japan.* Durham, NC: Duke University Press, 2015.

Langer, Lawrence L. *Versions of Survival: The Holocaust and Human Spirit.* Albany: State University of New York Press, 1982.

Lee, Erika. *The Making of Asian America: A History.* New York: Simon & Schuster, 2015.

Lifton, Robert Jay. *Death in Life: Survivors of Hiroshima.* New York: Simon & Schuster, 1967.

Lifton, Robert Jay, and Greg Mitchell. *Hiroshima in America: Fifty Years of Denial.* New York: Putman's Sons, 1995.

Lim, Shirley Geok-lin, Larry E. Smith, and Wimal Dissanayake, eds. *Transnational Asia Pacific: Gender, Culture, and the Public Sphere*. Urbana: University of Illinois Press, 1999.

Lim, Shirley Jennifer. *A Feeling of Belonging: Asian American Women's Public Culture, 1930–1960*. New York: New York University Press, 2006.

Lindee, M. Susan. *Suffering Made Real: American Science and the Survivors at Hiroshima*. Chicago: University of Chicago Press, 1994.

Lowe, Lisa. *Immigrant Acts: On Asian American Cultural Politics*. Durham, NC: Duke University Press, 1996.

Lyon, Cherstin. *Prisons and Patriots: Japanese American Wartime Citizenship, Civil Disobedience, and Historical Memory*. Philadelphia, PA: Temple University Press, 2011.

Maeda, Daryl J. *Rethinking the Asian American Movement*. New York: Routledge, 2011.

Masuda Hajimu. *Cold War Crucible: The Korean Conflict and the Postwar World*. Cambridge, MA: Harvard University Press, 2015.

Matsuda Toshihiko. *Senzenki no zainichi Chōsenjin to sanseiken* [Koreans and suffrage in Japan before the war]. Tokyo: Akashi Shoten, 1995.

Matsumoto, Valerie. *Farming the Home Place: A Japanese American Community in California, 1919–1982*. Ithaca, NY: Cornell University Press, 1993.

Minear, Richard H., ed. and trans. *Hiroshima: Three Witnesses*. Princeton, NJ: Princeton University Press, 1990.

Miyamoto, Yuki. *Beyond the Mushroom Cloud: Commemoration, Religion, and Responsibility after Hiroshima*. New York: Fordham University Press, 2011.

Miyata Setsuko. *Chōsen minshū to "kōminka" seisaku* [Korean people and the "imperialization" policy]. Tokyo: Miraisha, 1985.

Morris-Suzuki, Tessa. *Borderline Japan: Foreigners and Frontier Controls in the Postwar Era*. Cambridge and New York: Cambridge University Press, 2010.

Moyn, Samuel. *The Last Utopia: Human Rights in History*. Cambridge, MA: Belknap Press, 2012.

Muller, Eric L. *Free to Die for Their Country: The Story of the Japanese American Draft Resisters in World War II*. Chicago: University of Chicago Press, 2001.

Murray, Alice Yang. *Historical Memories of the Japanese American Internment and the Struggle for Redress*. Stanford, CA: Stanford University Press, 2007.

Nagasaki Zainichi Chōsenjin no Jinken o Mamoru Kai, ed. *Chōsenjin hibakusha: Nagasaki kara no shōgen* [Korean *hibakusha*: Testimonies from Nagasaki]. Tokyo: Shakai Hyōronsha, 1989.

Genbaku to Chōsenjin: Nagasaki Chōsenjin hibakusha jittai chōsa hōkokusho, dai-isshū [The atomic bombs and Koreans: A report on research into the situation of Korean *hibakusha* in Nagasaki, Vol. 1]. Nagasaki: Nagasaki Zainichi Chōsenjin no Jinken o Mamoru Kai, 1982.

Nakamura Rika. *Asia kei America to sensō kioku: Genbaku, "ianfu," kyōsei shūyō* [Asian America and war memories: The atomic bombs, "comfort women," incarceration]. Tokyo: Seikūsha, 2017.

Nakano, Mei. *Japanese American Women: Three Generations, 1890–1990.* Berkeley, CA: Mina Press Publishing; San Francisco, CA: National Japanese American Historical Society, 1990.

Narayan, Uma. *Dislocating Cultures: Identities, Traditions, and Third World Feminism.* New York: Routledge, 1997.

Nguyen, Viet Thanh. *Nothing Ever Dies: Vietnam and the Memory of War.* Cambridge, MA: Harvard University Press, 2016.

Nishi Kiyoko. *Senryōka no Nihon fujin seisaku: Sono rekishi to shōgen* [Policies concerning Japanese women during the occupation: A history and witnesses]. Tokyo: Domesu Shuppan, 1985.

Ōe Kenzaburō. *Hiroshima nōto* [Hiroshima note]. Tokyo: Iwanami Shinsho, 1965.

Ōfer, Dāliyyā, and Lenore J. Weitzman, eds. *Women in the Holocaust.* New Haven, CT: Yale University Press, 1998.

Okihiro, Gary Y. *Storied Lives: Japanese American Students and World War II.* Seattle: University of Washington Press, 1999.

Ong, Aihwa. *Flexible Citizenship: The Cultural Logics of Transnationality.* Durham, NC: Duke University Press, 1999.

Orr, James J. *The Victim as Hero: Ideologies of Peace and National Identity in Postwar Japan.* Honolulu: University of Hawai'i Press, 2001.

Palmer, Brandon. *Fighting for the Enemy: Koreans in Japan's War, 1937–1945.* Seattle: University of Washington Press, 2013.

Pascoe, Peggy. *What Comes Naturally: Miscegenation Law and the Making of Race in America.* Oxford and New York: Oxford University Press, 2009.

Phu, Thy. *Picturing Model Citizens: Civility in Asian American Visual Culture.* Philadelphia, PA: Temple University Press, 2011.

Pulido, Laura. *Black, Brown, Yellow, and Left: Radical Activism in Los Angeles.* Berkeley: University of California Press, 2006.

Rittner, Carol, and John K. Roth, eds. *Different Voices: Women and the Holocaust.* New York: Paragon House, 1993.

Roberts, Mary Louise. *What Soldiers Do: Sex and American GIs in World War II France.* Chicago: University of Chicago Press, 2014.

Robinson, Greg. *After Camp: Portraits in Midcentury Japanese American Life and Politics.* Berkeley: University of California Press, 2012.

Rotter, Andrew. *Hiroshima: The World's Bomb*. Oxford: Oxford University Press, 2008.

Ryang, Sonia, and John Lie, eds. *Diaspora without Homeland: Being Korean in Japan*. Berkeley: University of California Press, 2009.

Sasaki-Uemura, Wesley Makoto. *Organizing the Spontaneous: Citizen Protest in Postwar Japan*. Honolulu: University of Hawai'i Press, 2001.

Schell, Jonathan. *The Fate of the Earth*, New York: Knopf, 1982.

Schlund-Vials, Cathy J., and Michael Gill, eds. *Disability, Human Rights and the Limits of Humanitarianism*. Farnham, UK: Ashgate, 2014.

Selden, Kyoko, and Mark Selden, eds. *The Atomic Bomb: Voices from Hiroshima and Nagasaki*. Armonk, NY: M. E. Sharpe, 1989.

Serlin, David. *Replaceable You: Engineering the Body in Postwar America*. Chicago: University of Chicago Press, 2004.

Sharpe, Patrick B. *Savage Perils: Racial Frontiers and Nuclear Apocalypse in American Culture*. Norman: University of Oklahoma Press, 2007.

Sherwin, Martin J. *A World Destroyed: Hiroshima and Its Legacies*. Stanford, CA: Stanford University Press, 2003 (original publication in 1975).

Shibusawa, Naoko. *America's Geisha Ally: Reimagining the Japanese Enemy*. Cambridge, MA: Harvard University Press, 2006.

Shigematsu, Setsu, and Keith Camacho. *Militarized Currents: Toward a Decolonized Future in Asia and the Pacific*. Minneapolis: University of Minnesota Press, 2010.

Shin, Gi-Wook, and Michael Robinson, eds. *Colonial Modernity in Korea*. Cambridge, MA: Harvard University Asia Center, 1999.

Shin, Hyung-keun. "Kankoku genbaku higaisha mondai no jittai to igi ni tuite no kenkyū: Toku ni kannichikan kusanone kyōryoku ni chūmoku shite" [A study of Korean survivors: The grassroots collaboration between Korea and Japan]. PhD diss. Hiroshima City University, 2014.

Shukert, Elfrieda Berthiaume, and Barbara Smith Scibetta. *War Brides of World War II*. New York: Penguin Books, 1989.

Simpson, Caroline Chung. *An Absent Presence: Japanese Americans in Postwar American Cultures, 1945–1960*. Durham, NC: Duke University Press, 2001.

Sodei, Rinjiro. *Were We the Enemy? American Survivors of Hiroshima*. Boulder, CO: Westview, 1998.

Soh, C. Sarah. *The Comfort Women: Sexual Violence and Postcolonial Memory in Korea and Japan*. Chicago: University of Chicago Press, 2008.

Stein, Arlene. *Reluctant Witnesses: Survivors, Their Children, and the Rise of Holocaust Consciousness*. Oxford: Oxford University Press, 2014.

Tachibana, Reiko. *Narrative as Counter-memory: A Half-Century of Postwar Writing in Germany and Japan*. Albany, NY: State University of New York Press, 1998.

Tachibana, Seiitsu. "The Quest for a Peace Culture: The A-bomb Survivors' Long Struggle and the New Development for Redressing Foreign Victims of Japan's War." *Diplomatic History* 19, no. 2 (Spring 1995): 329–46.

Takahashi, Jere. *Nisei/Sansei: Shifting Japanese American Identities and Politics.* Philadelphia, PA: Temple University Press, 1997.

Tamura Kazuyuki. "Zaigai hibakusha engo no genjō to kadai: Yonjū nen no rekishiteki kōsatu o tōshite" [The current status of the support for survivors overseas and the challenges they face: Through a consideration of the forty-year history]. *Chingin to shakai hoshō* 1390 (2005): 4–21.

"Zaigai hibakusha no konnichi teki kadai" [The challenges that survivors overseas face today]. In *Shakai hoshō hō, fukushi to rōdō hō no shintenkai* [New developments in social security, social welfare, and labor laws], edited by Araki Seiji and Kuwahara Yōko, 585–98. Tokyo: Shinzansha, 2010.

Tamura, Linda. *Nisei Soldiers Break Their Silence: Coming Home to Hood River.* Seattle: University of Washington Press, 2012.

TenBroek, Jacobus, Edward N. Barnhart, and Floyd W. Matson. *Prejudice, War, and the Constitution.* Berkeley: University of California Press, 1954.

Tomita, Mary Kimoto. *Dear Miye: Letter Home from Japan, 1939–1946.* Stanford, CA: Stanford University Press, 1995.

Tonomura Satoru. *Chōsenjin kyōsei renkō* [Korean forced labor]. Tokyo: Iwanami Shoten, 2012.

Zainichi Chōsenjin shakai no rekishigaku teki kenkyū: Keisei, kōzō, henyō [A historical study of Korean society in Japan: Formation, structure, and change]. Tokyo: Ryokuin Shobō, 2009.

Treat, John Whittier. *Writing Ground Zero: Japanese Literature and the Atomic Bomb.* Chicago: University of Chicago Press, 1995.

Voyles, Traci Brynne. *Wastelanding: Legacies of Uranium Mining in Navajo Country.* Minneapolis: University of Minnesota Press, 2015.

Walker, J. Samuel. *Prompt and Utter Destruction: Truman and the Use of Atomic Bombs against Japan.* Chapel Hill: University of North Carolina Press, 1997.

Wei, William. *The Asian American Movement.* Philadelphia, PA: Temple University Press, 1993.

Wieviorka, Annette. *The Era of the Witness.* Ithaca, NY: Cornell University Press, 2006.

Winkler, Allen M. *Life under a Cloud: American Anxiety about the Atom.* Urbana: University of Illinois Press, 1999.

Wu, Ellen. *The Color of Success: Asian Americans and the Origins of the Model Minority.* Princeton, NJ: Princeton University Press, 2013.

Wu, Judy Tzu-Chun. *Radicals on the Road: Internationalism, Orientalism, and Feminism during the Vietnam Era*. Ithaca, NY: Cornell University Press, 2013.

Yamamoto, Traise. *Masking Selves, Making Subjects: Japanese American Women, Identity and the Body*. Berkeley: University of California Press, 1998.

Yamashiro Masao. *Kibei Nisei: Kaitai shite iku "Nihonjin"* [The Kibei Nisei: A deconstruction of the Japanese]. Tokyo: Satsuki Shobō, 1995.

Yoneda, Karl G. *Ganbatte: Sixty-year Struggle of a Kibei Worker*. Los Angeles: Asian American Studies Center, University of California, 1983.

Yoneyama, Lisa. *Cold War Ruins: Transpacific Critique of American Justice and Japanese War Crime*. Durham, NC: Duke University Press, 2016.

  Hiroshima Traces: Time Space, and the Dialectics of Memory. Berkeley: University of California Press, 1999.

Yoo, David K. *Growing Up Nisei: Race, Generation, and Culture among Japanese Americans of California, 1924–1949*. Urbana: University of Illinois Press, 2000.

Yoshida Ryō, ed. *Amerika Nihonjin imin no ekkyō kyōikushi* [A history of transnational education of the Japanese immigrants in the United States]. Tokyo: Nihon Tosho Sentā, 2005.

Young, Cynthia A. *Soul Power: Culture, Radicalism, and the Making of a US Third World Left*. Durham, NC: Duke University Press, 2006.

Yuh, Ji-Yeon. *Beyond the Shadow of Camptown: Korean Military Brides in America*. New York: New York University Press, 2002.

Yui Daizaburo. *Naze sensoukan wa tsuitotsu suruka: Nihon to America* [Why views of the war collide: Japan and America]. Tokyo: Iwanami Shoten, 2007.

Zaikan Hibakusha Mondai Shimin Kaigi, ed. *Zaikan hibakusha mondai o kangaeru* [An examination of the problem of A-bomb survivors in Korea]. Tokyo: Gaifūsha, 1988.

Zeiger, Susan. *Entangling Alliances: Foreign War Brides and American Soldiers in the Twentieth Century*. New York: New York University Press, 2010.

Zwigenberg, Ran. *Hiroshima: The Origin of Global Memory Culture*. Cambridge: Cambridge University Press, 2014.

INDEX